Civic Republicanism

'A timely and genuine contribution to the discussion of republicanism ... distinctive.'

Richard Dagger, Arizona State University

'Combining a lucid and accessible style with considerable sophistication of thought, *Civic Republicanism* will be both helpful to students and stimulating to scholars.'

John Horton, University of Keele

Civic republicanism has emerged as a leading alternative to liberalism in dealing with the political challenges presented by the diversity and increasing interdependence of contemporary societies. It recognises that realising freedom requires strong political structures supported by active, public-spirited citizens.

Iseult Honohan here presents a critical interpretation of its central themes – civic virtue, freedom, participation and recognition – and of the different ways in which these have been understood and combined in different strands of civic republicanism.

In Part I she traces its development from classical antecedents such as Aristotle and Cicero to its flowering with Machiavelli and Harrington, and to the diverse responses to modernity advanced by Rousseau, Wollstonecraft and Madison. She highlights the roots of the contemporary revival in the work of Hannah Arendt and Charles Taylor.

In Part II Honohan engages with current debates surrounding civic republicanism as an attractive way forward in a world of cultural diversity, global interdependence, inequality and environmental risk. What is the nature of the common good? What does it mean to put public before private interests? What does political freedom mean, and what are the implications for the political institutions and practices of a republic?

Civic Republicanism is an ideal text for students of politics and philosophy, and also valuable for those studying this important topic in related disciplines such as history and law.

Iseult Honohan teaches Political Theory in the Department of Politics, University College Dublin.

The Problems of Philosophy

Editors: Tim Crane and Jonathan Wolff, *University College London*

This series addresses the central problems of philosophy. Each book gives a fresh account of a particular philosophical theme by offering two perspectives on the subject: the historical context and the author's own distinctive and original contribution. The books are written to be accessible to students of philosophy and related disciplines, while taking the debate to a new level.

Recently published

TIME
Philip Turetzky

VAGUENESS
Timothy Williamson

FREE SPEECH
Alan Haworth

THE MORAL SELF
Pauline Chazan

SOCIAL REALITY
Finn Collin

OTHER MINDS
Anita Avramides

PERCEPTION
Howard Robinson

THE NATURE OF GOD
Gerard Hughes

SUBSTANCE
Justin Hoffman and Gary Rosenkrantz

DEMOCRACY
Ross Harrison

THE MIND AND ITS WORLD
Gregory McCulloch

POSSIBLE WORLDS
John Divers

Civic Republicanism

Iseult Honohan

Routledge
Taylor & Francis Group
LONDON AND NEW YORK

First published 2002
by Routledge
11 New Fetter Lane, London EC4P 4EE

Simultaneously published in the USA and Canada
by Routledge
29 West 35th Street, New York, NY 10001

Routledge is an imprint of the Taylor & Francis Group

© 2002 Iseult Honohan

Typeset in Times by Taylor & Francis Books Ltd
Printed and bound in Great Britain by TJ International Ltd, Padstow, Cornwall

All rights reserved. No part of this book may be reprinted or reproduced or utilised in any form or by any electronic, mechanical, or other means, now known or hereafter invented, including photocopying and recording, or in any information storage or retrieval system, without permission in writing from the publishers.

British Library Cataloguing in Publication Data
A catalogue record for this book is available from the British Library

Library of Congress Cataloging-in-Publication Data
A catalog record for this book has been requested

ISBN 0–415–21210–3 (hbk)
ISBN 0–415–21211–1 (pbk)

Contents

Acknowledgements		vii
Introduction		1

Part I
The Historical Evolution of Republican Thought — 13

I	The Primacy of Virtue: Aristotle and Cicero	15
II	Freedom in Classical Republicanism: Machiavelli and Harrington	42
III	Participation and Inclusion in the Extensive Republic: Rousseau, Wollstonecraft and Madison	77
IV	Roots of the Republican Revival: Arendt and Taylor	111

Part II
Contemporary Debates — 145

V	Common Goods and Public Virtue	147
VI	Freedom: Non-domination and Republican Political Autonomy	180
VII	Participation and Deliberation	214
VIII	Recognition and Inclusion in a Pluralist World	250

Notes	290
Bibliography	302
Index	321

Acknowledgements

The process of writing this book has brought home to me more clearly than before the many dimensions of interdependence.

I owe a particular debt of thanks to Fergal O'Connor for his teaching and encouragement over many years. Others who deserve special thanks for supporting me in this project are Attracta Ingram, Maria Baghramian and Maeve Cooke.

Among many others to whom I owe thanks, I am grateful to my colleagues in the Department of Politics at University College Dublin, especially to John Baker and Niamh Hardiman, who have always been ready with advice and help. Tom Garvin has offered encouragement and support at every stage. Valerie Bresnihan and Joe Dunne were good enough to read several chapters and offered helpful comments. I benefited greatly from discussions with and advice from Vittorio Bufacchi, Aileen Kavanagh and Bríd O'Rourke. Ailsa McCarthy provided research assistance in the early stages. Students in the MA class and tutors of my second year course cheerfully endured and contributed to my process of clarifying these ideas.

I received extensive helpful comments on an earlier draft from Richard Dagger and an anonymous referee. As new strands of republican thought proliferated, Jonathan Wolff waited patiently for the manuscript; Muna Khogali at Routledge was unfailingly helpful.

I should like to acknowledge the receipt of a President's Award at University College Dublin; in the time this gave me, the fundamental conception and argument of the book was initially developed.

Finally, my deepest thanks are due to my family, especially my mother, and to Patrick and Theo.

Iseult Honohan, February 2002

Introduction

Civic republicanism addresses the problem of freedom among human beings who are necessarily interdependent. As a response it proposes that freedom, political and personal, may be realised through membership of a political community in which those who are mutually vulnerable and share a common fate may jointly be able to exercise some collective direction over their lives. This response, older than liberalism, has been expressed and developed by a variety of thinkers through the history of Western politics, and constitutes a more or less continuous and coherent republican tradition. In this approach, freedom is related to participation in self-government and concern for the common good. (The political theory of republicanism is only loosely related to the issue of the presence or absence of a monarchy, which is the common use of the term republicanism.)

Republican politics is concerned with enabling interdependent citizens to deliberate on, and realise, the common goods of an historically evolving political community, at least as much as promoting individual interests or protecting individual rights. Emphasising responsibility for common goods sets republicanism apart from libertarian theories centred on individual rights. Emphasising that these common goods are politically realised sets republicanism apart from neutralist liberal theories which exclude substantive questions of values and the good life from politics. Finally, emphasising the political construction of the political community distinguishes republicans from those communitarians who see politics as expressing the pre-political shared values of a community.

Influential in modern Europe and America until the late eighteenth century, civic republicanism was, until recently, rather overshadowed by the debates between liberalism and socialism. But it has become once more a focus of interest and discussion since the apparently sweeping victory of liberal democracy over socialism. Despite that victory, it is not the case that 'we are all liberals now'. A new line of criticism has been developed by communitarian philosophers who stress the dependence of individuals on communal contexts, in reaction to what they see as the excessive liberal stress on individual independence. Simultaneously, liberal democratic practice has been criticised by political actors who call for the restoration of community, citizenship and moral purpose to politics. Contemporary citizenship is increasingly seen to lack depth and meaning for people who feel alienated from politics and disconnected from the society beyond their personal relationships. So there are theoretical and practical movements to reaffirm community. But moral and cultural diversity are increasingly salient in our society. If a politics of individual freedom carries the risk of fragmentation, a politics of shared values threatens to be oppressive or exclusive.

Communitarian arguments attach too much authority to existing social relationships and identities in defining common goods. In most modern societies, people adhere to diverse sets of ends and values; existing social roles and relationships are often unequal, so to assume a common good between members of society oppresses those who are different. So liberals rightly emphasise that people can reflect critically on their social roles, but they distinguish public, political concerns too rigidly from private, personal concerns, and underestimate the significance and vulnerability of common goods.

In this book I argue that civic republicanism offers the prospect of an alternative to the extremes of the so-called liberal–communitarian debate, with a notion of political community richer than that of mainstream liberalism, and less homogenising and exclusive than nationalism and other forms of communitarianism. This represents an attempt to trace a way in which citizens might realise freedom more effectively than is currently achieved.

The value of historical theory

Why should we look at the historical tradition, rather than addressing immediately the contemporary philosophical issues and arguments? There are a number of reasons, some applying to political theory in general, and some more specifically to civic republicanism, which has been particularly historical in its approach, even though its precise historical roots are strongly contested.

If we can think of history (as E.H. Carr suggested) less as a straight line which makes our ancestors increasingly remote from us, and more as a winding procession, where our circumstances may bring us closer to some parts of the past than others, there are good reasons to consider the thought of earlier times. From a critical point of view, it may warn us against reinventing the wheel, or embarking on what appear to be radical programmes of social change while 'trotting out the identical ideas that had been put forward at an earlier period, without any references to the encounter they had already with reality, an encounter that is seldom wholly satisfactory' (Hirschman, 1977: 133). The study of the history of ideas may not resolve issues but it can raise the level of the debate.

In order to understand a theory it is necessary to understand the question to which it claims to be an answer. In different political, social and economic contexts theorists are concerned with very different questions. So it will be misleading to compare directly arguments on, for example, property or marriage in ancient Greece and nineteenth-century England. Yet, while contexts change, there are aspects of issues, such as the nature of freedom, the scope of government, or the rights and duties of citizenship, that are sufficiently general for arguments to be intelligible across time and place, even if they also have more specific applications.

Political theory tends to be more active in periods of social and political upheaval, when certain thinkers seem to have an especially acute apprehension of issues which do not arise so starkly in more peaceful times. Considering theories developed in other historical contexts makes us aware of the variety of answers possible to the central questions that concern us. Accordingly, looking at other answers to current questions may at least make us realise how specific our ideas are, and shake up our assumptions about what is permanent and what is subject to change in social and political life.

In addition, political theorists have often seen themselves as responding to their predecessors in a conversation across time. In picking up historical threads, modern philosophical interpreters need to be more sensitive to historical hermeneutics, both of context and of reference, than some of their predecessors. But historical theories may be worth reconsidering, particularly if they

Introduction

were cut short because they lost the political battle rather than the normative argument. If economic, social and cultural circumstances rendered them irrelevant and favoured other theories, arguments that seemed to be superseded may be worth revisiting when circumstances change again. Republicanism went into abeyance with the development of the sovereign nation-state, which accommodated the growth of commerce and of populations. If factors such as economic globalisation and environmental risk now reduce the appropriateness of the nation-state, alternative ways of approaching politics may need to be considered.

A civic republican tradition?

Specific problems arise in dealing with civic republican historical thought. Critics have cast doubt on the very existence and continuity of a republican tradition. And matters are not helped by the fact that current exponents identify with different constellations of ancestors.

Centuries and civilisations separate Aristotle from Machiavelli, Cicero from Madison, and our world from theirs. Not surprisingly, given the range of historical societies involved, these theorists address different immediate questions. But they approach politics with similar concerns arising from the human predicament of interdependence; and their responses are structured in terms of the same cluster of ideas. Moreover, of all political theorists, civic republicans are perhaps the most self-consciously historical and classicising, in seeing themselves as the inheritors of the authors and political practices of Greece and Rome. Machiavelli, Harrington, Madison and Rousseau all expressed admiration for, drew on, and modified the ideas of their ancient and more recent predecessors in the tradition. Each indeed decisively redefined certain key concepts and their balance, in ways that shaped the path of subsequent arguments. But, as will become clear, there was significant continuity as well as change.

Even those who agree that there is a distinctive republican tradition differ on the range of ideas and thinkers which should be included. While all recognise Machiavelli as central, some trace the tradition from Aristotle through Rousseau; others see the thread as linking Cicero to Locke and then Madison, thus overlapping with the stars of the liberal firmament. I have tried to conceive of the

Introduction

tradition as inclusively as possible, while offering my own more specific interpretation of the strands which it may be valuable to reappropriate today. I argue that there is an identifiable tradition with Greek and Roman roots, which crystallised in the late middle ages and flourished well into the eighteenth century in Europe and America. In the nineteenth century this was eclipsed by the more prominent movements of liberalism, socialism and nationalism, each of which absorbed some of its themes. Since the mid-twentieth century the tradition has re-emerged. But this tradition is constituted not of a single thread but of multiple interwoven strands. While certain strands persist throughout, some are present in the early phases and become thinner with time; others are introduced at certain points and come to take increasing weight. In any case traditions are always constituted or reconstituted in retrospect, and are as much a matter of affiliation as of genetic descent.

Elements of the classical account

A broad ideal summary of classical republicanism as it had evolved up to the eighteenth century would contain the following elements.

Citizens of a state are free if they are independent of external rule and internal tyranny, and so are in some sense self-governing. Republics do not come into being naturally, and without a political structure there is no basis on which people can form an agreement to live together; so they need a founder or law-giver to establish their basic institutions. In place of a single sovereign, there is 'mixed' government, in which social forces or institutions of government are balanced against one another, to prevent the domination of the state by particular interests and thus to realise the common goods of citizens. Freedom is guaranteed by, and compatible with, the rule of established laws in place of the will of a ruler. Citizens must be active, accepting duties and performing public service both military and political. In this, they need to recognise the value of what they share with other citizens. Thus they must cultivate civic virtue, or a commitment to the common good.

Since humans have private interests as well as those they share with other citizens, from the republican perspective the primary political problem is *corruption*. This is understood quite broadly. All political solutions are fragile and require continuous injections of energy to sustain them. People will always tend to be torn between

Introduction

their private interests and the common good. Institutions too will tend to drift from their original purposes. Therefore the problem of creating public-spirited citizens may be addressed in a number of ways – through laws, training in a citizen militia, civic education and a civic religion. While social approval, or honour, is the reward for civic virtue, more forceful treatment also may be needed to constitute or restore a republic.

A successful republic demands certain material preconditions. Active citizens need to be independent. Thus they need to have property, but excessive wealth and economic inequality undermine political equality. Accordingly there may be measures to limit the accumulation of, or even to redistribute wealth. The republic is a specific community of citizens related by substantial ties and a sense of loyalty more like fraternity or friendship than agreement on institutions or procedures. Political obligation is not wholly voluntarily assumed, but rooted in the citizens' membership of the republic. Given its intensity, as well as more practical difficulties, the scope of the republic must generally be limited in terms of size, numbers and diversity.

So classical republicanism was suited to small states where it was possible to envisage active participation by a significant proportion of the population. The conditions of citizenship were very demanding in terms of public and military service, and included the formation, or moral education, of the citizens by the state. To varying degrees it excluded the lower echelons of the population, women and those outside the narrowly drawn limits of the republic. It emphasised masculine and warrior virtues and was often devoted to military expansion.

The emphasis on common goods and civic virtue, and the ways in which these were formulated in the tradition, have led to charges that civic republicanism is inherently oppressive, moralistic, exclusive, militarist and masculinist. Any contemporary articulation of the theory has to avoid these objections. And it has to show further that it is not hopelessly idealistic or nostalgic in a modern world of extensive states and global economic and social relationships.

The civic republican revival

Civic republican ideas have arisen in a number of closely connected forms in the past twenty-five years: in historical, legal and normative political theory. The diverse strands of the historical tradition reflect a dispute about what republicanism means today and what it has to offer. There is, in effect, a battle for the soul of republicanism, in which alternative historical strands have been marshalled to support the credentials of contemporary expressions.

Its exponents agree in reconnecting freedom with the common good of citizenship, but beyond this they differ on the central elements and their interpretation. In addition, in comparison with classical liberal theory, civic republican theorists tend to locate themselves explicitly in a specific local context both theoretical and practical. Many of these arguments have developed within debates about the nature and future of politics in, for example, the United States, Britain or France. This reflects an emphasis in republican thought on the need to develop political solutions appropriate to particular contexts. It is as if all liberal states resemble each other, but each republican state is republican in its own way.

We can identify three principal strands:

History of political thought   Civic republicanism was put on the theoretical map again through historical scholarship which excavated and re-identified it as a coherent tradition. Two scholars have played a particularly important role in this rediscovery. Drawing on themes from Arendt, J.G.A. Pocock has outlined a continuing thread, from Athens and Aristotle, through Machiavelli and Harrington, to the American revolution. He emphasises the ideas of political participation, civic virtue and corruption, and the historical specificity and fragility of republican politics. His work challenges a conventional view that the American revolution was guided solely by Lockean natural-right principles. Quentin Skinner traces a position with Roman roots, that crystallised in Renaissance humanism, was given its classic formulation by Machiavelli, and was further specified in the English seventeenth-century movement that included Harrington and Sidney. This has at its centre a 'neo-Roman' conception of freedom, as the status of independence guaranteed by legal limitations on a ruler's arbitrary domination.

Constitutional legal theory   In the United States, civic republican ideas have been invoked in a debate on the interpretation of the constitution and the functions of its various parts. This challenges a prevailing understanding of the constitution as primarily a set of

Introduction

rules to limit power, regulate competing interest groups and protect individual rights. Legal scholars, including Cass Sunstein and Frank Michelman, have highlighted the way in which the constitution has a historical and continuing role as a framework for collective self-government, based less on private interests than on deliberation on common goods. This implies a stronger role for the judiciary, and a more active and deliberative role for all branches of government, than a neutralist liberal model supports.

Normative political theory Finally, there is a wide spectrum of expression of republican ideas in normative political thought. Different thinkers evaluate and prioritise the dimensions of republicanism differently. Some are closer to liberalism, some to communitarianism. Some emphasise virtue and the shared values of a political community (Sandel, Oldfield). Others focus on a distinctive account of freedom as central to republicanism (Pettit, Dagger). For others, participation is the key point of a fuller democracy (Barber, Pitkin). Finally, recognition has emerged in debates in which Taylor has taken the initiative.

It should be said that not all the thinkers I discuss describe themselves as republicans. Terminology can be very ambiguous in this area, and labels have often been applied quite broadly. So some clarification of how I understand these terms is in order here. If we can define liberalism very broadly as attaching particular importance to respecting individual freedom, communitarianism may be understood as emphasising the value of belonging to a community. Both of these definitions leave much room for different interpretation as to what constitutes freedom or community, and the implications these may have for politics. Republicanism is a specific variant of communitarianism, which values citizenship: membership of a political community, as distinct from other kinds of community based on pre-political commonality, of, for example, race, religion or culture.

Republican theories approach the problems of interdependence, and integrate the values of freedom, civic virtue, participation and recognition, in a number of ways. But today there are two dominant republican approaches which have attracted particular attention. In what follows, I will refer to these two approaches as 'instrumental' and 'strong' republicanism respectively. *Instrumental republicans* see citizenship as a means of preserving individual freedom, rather than as an activity or relationship which has significant intrinsic value. *Strong republicans* emphasise the inherent value of participating in self-government and realising certain common goods among citizens.

After the liberal–communitarian debate

These republican expressions have emerged in the wake of the so-called 'liberal–communitarian debate'. This debate originated largely in critical reactions to John Rawls's magisterial interpretation of liberalism in *A Theory of Justice* (Rawls, 1971). He attempted to derive a set of liberal principles of justice on which people who held very diverse positions could agree. This could establish certain principles of freedom and equality. But he held that, in a world where reasonable people can differ in their views of the good life, politics should not favour one particular way of life or moral perspective. Individual rights, independently derived and justified, limit the purposes or goods which can be pursued through politics. The state should aim to guarantee fair procedures within which individuals can pursue, and modify, their own conceptions of the good life, but not aim to promote any more substantive goals.

But, communitarian critics argued, it is not possible to distinguish just procedures from substantive goals as conclusively as some liberals have suggested; liberal arguments for a politics of fair procedures rely on a specific conception of the human good, whether this is expressed in the fundamental value of autonomy or in a more complex account of justice.

These critics queried the conception of independent individuals that they saw as the basis of this theory. In their view, individuals are embedded in social roles and projects, central to their purposes, identity and conceptions of the good life. Either they cannot meaningfully detach themselves from these relationships, or they do so only with self-destructive consequences (Sandel, 1982; Walzer 1985; MacIntyre, 1984). These arguments shared some of the points advanced by Taylor on the preconditions of liberal autonomy that we see in Chapter IV – and indeed Taylor himself has been described as a communitarian.

In the course of this debate many issues were clarified, causing theorists on both sides to modify their arguments significantly –

though differences still remain. Liberals have taken on some communitarian points, often holding that they never denied these. But they still resist the idea that there can be a substantial common good shared among members of modern plural societies.

Thus Rawls advanced an idea of 'political liberalism', based not on a particular account of freedom, or conception of the individual, but on the need for tolerance in diverse societies (Rawls, 1993). People with very different views of the good life may be able to agree on political principles and institutions, which are not now seen as independent of, but as having a base in their overlapping 'comprehensive doctrines' or fundamental beliefs. This is not a 'comprehensive liberalism', based on the primacy of the values of freedom, and it recognises the depth of the affiliations that people may claim. But it still relies on a clear distinction between the public and the private. The point of politics is to make possible the pursuit of individual projects. It claims that, in a liberal state where citizens hold many different beliefs, people may bring to political debates only arguments based in public reasons that all can understand and engage with (and not arguments from their own comprehensive doctrines).

Although communitarian arguments imply that politics should be more concerned with substantive goods and with supporting the social relationships essential to individual goals, the exact nature of community and the political implications of these arguments are unclear and contested, and for many it has remained primarily a critical position. But some developed more explicitly political applications. Walzer, for example, has advanced an account of politics as articulating existing shared understandings among members of a political community (Walzer, 1985). Sandel, on the other hand, has outlined an historical interpretation of US politics as originally (and residually) a republican politics of freedom and civic virtue directed to common goods, in contrast to the politics of individual interests and rights which has gradually superseded it (Sandel, 1996). Other communitarians have refused to draw conclusions allocating any significant role to governments in promoting common goods (MacIntyre, 1999).

It is in this context that republican ideas of a politically defined common good among self-determining citizens have come once more to be of interest. (Prior to this, arguments for more participatory politics were advanced without being presented as specifically republican (Pateman, 1970; Barber, 1984)).

Introduction

The foundation of republican theory is the understanding of human interdependence. Now that many liberals recognise the dependence of individuals on social relations and communal practices, an awareness of interdependence as such does not radically distinguish republicans from liberals today. In particular, republicans have much in common with liberals such as Raz who see autonomy as the central political value, often referred to as 'perfectionist liberals' (to distinguish them from neutralist liberals who do not see liberalism as promoting any specific political value). Where the disagreement between republicans and liberals lies is in the political implications. Raz emphasises the social bases of autonomy, but identifies too many risks in promoting it through potentially divisive and oppressive political means (Raz, 1986: 427–8). As Kymlicka puts it, these viewpoints 'disagree not over the social thesis, but over the proper role of the state, not over the individual's dependence on society, but over society's dependence on the state' (Kymlicka, 1990: 230).

Rawls claims that his revised liberal account is compatible with one version of civic republicanism, in which political life is instrumentally valuable in protecting the rights and liberties of citizens who individually pursue diverse ends (Rawls, 1993: 205–6). But he distinguishes this from the comprehensive doctrine of *civic humanism*, which views participation as the fullest realisation or ultimate end of human life.[1]

But there are more complex issues at stake than this distinction between instrumental value and ultimate value conveys. The civic republican arguments I will be considering in the second part of the book aim to go beyond these positions to address the issue of realising politically defined common goods, including the goods of citizenship, in a republican community of equals. Political activity can be intrinsically valuable without being the sole, or ultimate value in human life. A concern for common goods does not fundamentally and of itself conflict with freedom. There are also many questions about the nature and interrelations of freedom, civic virtue and recognition whose answers are not determined by Rawls's distinction. Thus there are now many different expressions of republicanism, and a broader approach to the topic needs to be adopted.

As with many other theories, including liberalism and socialism, there are many interpretations of the central concepts and arguments and aims of civic republicanism. We shall see that the

Introduction

definition of its central values is currently contested. But its exponents agree that republicanism and liberalism cannot be contrasted simply as theories espousing civic virtue and freedom respectively. Instead, it offers an alternative approach to understanding and realising freedom. This account of freedom (itself internally contested) may be seen as one of a cluster of core ideas that includes civic virtue, participation and recognition, each of which has been the central focus at different periods in the light of the central questions of the time.[2] Part I thus outlines the historical development of the central themes of the civic republican tradition. Part II considers the contemporary philosophical arguments advanced on its behalf today under these same headings – the need for civic virtue; the political character of freedom; the expansion of participation; and the deepening of political life entailed in recognition. It outlines the contemporary attraction of civic republican ideas and examines the problems and criticisms they encounter.

PART I

The Historical Evolution of Republican Thought

Introduction to Part I

How the cluster of core republican ideas evolved historically is the subject of the chapters in Part I. The approach is essentially chronological, but in each chapter one of the key ideas – civic virtue, freedom, participation and recognition – comes to the fore.

Chapter I

In ancient Athens and Rome, the key question is how justice is related to politics. The answer of the theorists of those times, who are the precursors of this tradition, is broadly that political life is concerned with the full development of citizens' character; that through politics citizens come to exercise *virtue*, to which political freedom is secondary.

Chapter II

In the fifteenth to the seventeenth centuries the key question considered is the possibility of citizen self-rule as a viable alternative to sovereign power. For Machiavelli and Harrington the primary value of the republic is *freedom*, and virtue is understood in narrower, or more instrumental, terms. But the obverse of virtue, corruption, is understood as the primary threat within the republic.

Chapter III

In the eighteenth century the question is how far free government can be expanded to include larger numbers of equal citizens in vast territorial states and commercial societies. Here the republican response to centralised despotism or elitism is more fragmented, and *participation* is understood in a variety of ways. For example, for Madison it is achieved by representative government with federation and separation of powers. For Rousseau only a radically participatory unitary republic is compatible with freedom, and this is threatened by large numbers and substantial inequalities.

Chapter IV

In the contemporary world the key question that political theorists have come to address is whether morally and culturally diverse citizens can be connected more substantially with each other than is envisaged through the institutions and systems of rights in liberal democracy. Here, *recognition* has emerged as the focal concept of civic republicanism in the work of Arendt and Taylor.

CHAPTER I

The Primacy of Virtue

Aristotle and Cicero

Introduction

Civic republicanism is a modern tradition with roots that extend deeply into the classical past. The exponents of the early modern tradition hark back to ancient theoretical and practical antecedents in Greece and Rome. Machiavelli, Harrington, Madison and Rousseau wrote in very different worlds, but all thought of themselves as building on ancient foundations: the institutions of Athens, Sparta and Rome, the examples of their political heroes, and the ideas of ancient writers, particularly Aristotle and Cicero.

Aristotle and Cicero prefigure many elements of the recurring themes in later republican thinking. They emphasise the value of membership of a political community, and of freedom, contrasted to slavery, as a fragile political achievement, guaranteed by the rule of law and 'mixed' government. They connect this with political participation and active citizenship. They stress that the character, or 'virtues', of citizens are as important as laws in sustaining a civilised society. They see the role of law in shaping character in a way that is compatible with freedom. Finally they identify the state as a bounded community of citizens who share common goods, clearly distinct in form from the family and other associations.

In later chapters we shall see how the tradition has accumulated dimensions and reordered key elements as it has developed historically from the ancient context. *Virtue* is the focus of Aristotle's and Cicero's political theories, and *freedom*, while important, plays a secondary role in the service of virtue. Both take for granted that *participation* in politics will be restricted to a fairly narrow citizen elite. Some issues which are central today are not explicitly addressed by these earlier thinkers. They assume that the state will be relatively homogeneous in important respects, so that citizens gain mutual *recognition* through public action within a bounded political community.

As well as common themes, we shall see that there are also significant differences between the ideas of Aristotle and Cicero; and different expressions of republicanism can be traced back to one or the other. One strand emphasises political participation, and the other the rule of law as the basis of republican freedom. In recent interpretations of the republican tradition, the link to Cicero and Rome has been given greater prominence, but significant elements of modern republicanism can be traced back to Aristotle's account of political life.

These political theorists expressed, refined and challenged more widely held contemporary beliefs about political life. In Greece of the sixth century BC, independent city-states of free, self-governing citizens had emerged from kingdoms and tribal groupings. A sense of pride in the achievement of new forms of government, and of the novelty of such political arrangements, elevated the founding acts of men like Solon at Athens and Lycurgus at Sparta, and the deeds of the great men who sustained them. But the democratic polity of Athens and the militarily disciplined state of Sparta represented two rival versions of the city-state that aroused the admiration of later republicans.

Athens – a city-state of peasant citizens, based on agricultural small-holdings and supported by slaves – pioneered the practice of a self-ruling citizenry. All citizens – native-born, adult males, irrespective of wealth – formed a self-governing body, participated extensively in the assembly, on juries and in public offices, and defended their state in arms. In contrast to slaves or the subjects of a monarch (both subject to the will of another), self-ruling citizens were free. Freedom was exemplified in their equality before the law, and their equal rights to speak in the assembly and to serve in office. While individuals competed for fame and success, in principle matters were settled by discussion and deliberation of the citizens, not by force. Political equality was achieved by appointment to office for short terms on a rotating basis, often by lottery. There was no state apparatus separate from the people. Thus each citizen had a chance and a duty to participate in the decisions and practices that framed their lives. Though citizens held private property and lived in households based on the family, political life was valued more highly than private. As Pericles is reported to have said, 'We do not say that a man who is not interested in politics minds his own business, but that he does not belong here at all' (Thucydides, 1972: 147). Commerce was left to resident foreigners, and foreigners could not easily become citizens. Although Athens was later to be admired as the cradle of democracy and public architecture, none of the major thinkers of the time articulated a normative theory that supported it. Many were notoriously hostile. Above all, Plato saw democracy as the rule of the poor and ignorant, characterised by excessive liberty and leading ultimately to the usurpation of political power by a tyrant.

In the closer community of Sparta, citizens lived from land granted by the state and worked by a subject race of helots. Family life was minimal: at an early age citizens were taken for education in military discipline; as adults they ate communally, and were organised in military bands that were bound partly by homosexual ties. The criterion of good citizenship was martial vigour and devotion to the *polis*; those who could not meet this were subject to shame and social exclusion. The good of the political community was paramount over that of individuals or intermediate communities within it. Foreigners were excluded, and, in theory, the ownership of silver and gold was forbidden. Politics was conducted less publicly and less democratically than in Athens, although every citizen had some input in a popular assembly. Most power was divided between two hereditary kings, a board of five officials called ephors, elected in rotation, and a council of elders, popularly elected for life from a priestly caste.

Where Athens represented democratic freedom and political grandeur, Sparta represented civic devotion and military heroism. Its political system was praised as a system of mixed government by those who distrusted the fuller democracy of Athens.

These states were continuously at war either with external enemies or with one another, so that, even in Athens, the norms of civic commitment were intermixed with the competitive norms of warrior honour. But over time specifically political qualities and devotion to the common interest of the state were increasingly valued. The danger posed to political stability by personal ambition for power and greed for wealth was a key problem, giving rise to the conflict between factions (*stasis*), which undermined the delicate balance of the constitution and led to cyclical upheavals between forms of government.

Ancient thinkers were very conscious that reliably ordered societies that allowed people to live peacefully at a level above mere survival were uncommon and short-lived, and that constructing a political society was a precarious enterprise. Thus it was important to them to establish a connection between politics and virtue rather than force and self-aggrandisement.

In the context of these developments a number of issues arose centrally: What is the purpose of political life? Can power be exercised for the benefit of the citizens, rather than for the good of the rulers alone? What form of politics best realises justice and the good life for citizens? What virtues should citizens have – military or political – and how do the virtues relate to personal success? Is the good life achieved through politics, or independently of it? A separate but related question was whether and how far the mass of the people should have a significant say in politics. Are the common people too ignorant or too self-interested to be given power?

In attributing value to participating in political life according to norms of communal concern, Aristotle and Cicero stand against two other more or less contemporary views. According to one of those views, since only the powerful few can realise themselves, the demands of justice have to be discounted (e.g. the Sophists); according to the other, since justice or virtue are the only ideals worth pursuing, external success may have to be discounted (Plato and the Stoics).

Aristotle

Aristotle (384–322 BC) wrote in the closing years of the Athenian democracy. Not himself a citizen of Athens, he came there from Macedonia to study with Plato and returned as a teacher of philosophy. He observed the vicissitudes of the democracy, had to go into exile when anti-Macedonian feeling arose after the rise of Alexander, and he died shortly afterwards.

Aristotle stands at the head of many modern disciplines. He adopted the same observational approach to politics as in his studies of other fields, ranging from biology to metaphysics. But since human affairs vary with circumstances of time and place, he believed that knowledge of political and moral affairs, unlike the exact sciences, requires specific experience and deliberation. In order to pursue the good in life, people need not just general principles, but practical knowledge. In the *Nicomachean Ethics* and *Politics* Aristotle draws on a range of contemporary opinions, assessing their coherence and viability, so as to elucidate the individual and political dimensions of a worthwhile life. He concludes that politics provides an essential framework for developing and exercising the virtues that are the key to the pursuit of a good life. Thus in politics they must take account of the common good of the political community, of which they are part.

Material and moral interdependence in the polis

For Aristotle human life has natural goals that can be objectively determined and hierarchically ranked on the basis of our knowledge of human nature. Achieving *eudaemonia* – best translated as all-round happiness, or human flourishing – depends on realising the potential present at birth. How far this can be accomplished will depend not only on that initial potential, but also on external conditions such as health, prosperity and friends (external goods). Someone in dire poverty or serious ill-health cannot be described as flourishing even if they are unworldly, calm and resigned to their condition. But, on the other hand, pleasure, wealth or honour are limited and intermediate goals, which are less satisfying in the long run than exercising distinctively human capacities, of which reason stands above all.

Association between families, households, villages and polities rests in part on material interdependence between people whose different and complementary qualities promote their prosperity. But they are morally interdependent too. Because people are naturally undetermined as wholly good or wholly bad, but develop their character through acting, the social and political relationships in which they live are crucial to their possibility of self-realisation. Thus, unlike the instrumental relations of a military alliance or business arrangement, members of a *polis* have an interest in the welfare and character of other citizens, with whom they jointly pursue what is good. 'A state is an association by kinships and villages which aims at a perfect and self-sufficient life....The association which is a state exists not for the purpose of living together but for the sake of noble actions' (*Politics* 1280b29–1281a9).[1]

Aristotle's famous statement that 'man is a political animal' can be unpacked as follows. The political community is the highest, overarching form of association which facilitates development across the whole range of human life in a way that is not possible in the family or smaller social groups. A politics of free and equal citizens is possible because humans are not social just by instinct, but have language and reason (*logos*), through which they communicate with others, think and evaluate: 'the real difference between man and other animals is that humans alone have perception of good and evil, just and unjust; it is sharing these matters in common that make a household and a state' (*Politics* 1253a7) [my translation]. Politics requires not only theoretical reason, but practical reason (*phronesis*) to determine what is best in particular circumstances for a community. In a political community of citizens, joint deliberation on questions of value is possible among equals, whereas relationships between husband and wife, father and child and master and slave are marked by ineradicable inequalities.[2]

This means that anyone who lives outside a political society is lacking something absolutely fundamental to human flourishing. Someone without a *polis* is almost like a wild animal, or an 'isolated piece in a board game' (*Politics* 1253a1). There is a deep, almost organic, interdependence between citizens and the *polis*, just as if you 'separate hand or foot from the whole body, and they will no longer be hand or foot except in name' (*Politics* 1253a18).

Virtue and the good human life

In this context, the key to flourishing is developing and actively exercising a character exhibiting different kinds of virtue (*arete*), through a lifetime shaped by nature, habit and education. This is a broad sense of virtue which includes excellence or superiority of all kinds, as well as ethical goodness (with which virtue is now often identified), and specifically *civic* virtue (concern for the common goods shared by citizens).

Aristotle speaks of 'virtues' in the plural; just as people need a range of external goods, there is also a range of virtues, which fit together in a harmonious life. Some are familiar enough to modern thinking, such as courage, justice, self-control, truthfulness, modesty, self-respect, friendliness, generosity, even-temper; but others seem more incongruous to us, such as pride and magnificence or self-regard. These are not innate qualities; they are dispositions developed through practice, which make those who possess them spontaneously inclined to choose to act in the right way.

'Acting well' is not defined in terms of acting altruistically instead of self-interestedly, but of acting to realise properly conceived personal interests. Thus, if you have to choose between earning more and spending more time with your family, this is not a trade-off between happiness and ethical goodness, but a way to realise both, since external goods are just a means towards time spent with family and friends. So acquiring and exercising virtues constitutes self-realisation, not self-sacrifice, and the good life is one of material and ethical success.

For Aristotle, then, virtue is not a matter of subordinating inclination to duty, but an ingrained disposition to act in a certain way that leads to success in every dimension; it is acquired by 'educating' the desires, and by harmonising them with reason. We need practical reason to act correctly, because what is best in any case has to be identified in deliberation, and cannot simply be deduced from first principles. Aristotle's account of the human good has been well described as being simultaneously 'thick' (based on a very specific idea of what is essential to human nature) and 'vague' (not specified in detail for every instance) (Nussbaum, 1990: 217).

Moreover, simply knowing what is right is not enough, nor is simply possessing the virtues; a worthwhile life needs to be realised in action. Action needs to take place in a social framework, and requires social conditions for its performance. Becoming virtuous requires acculturation, example and education. A good *polis* allows us to realise goods and exercise the virtues. Thus an important part of virtue will be justice in the narrow sense, giving due consideration to the community, and not overemphasising one's own claims.

Institutions

Some kinds of political regime foster the development of citizens better than others. Every *polis* has a guiding principle reflected in the character of its citizens. Democratic citizens are easy-going, citizens in tyrannies fearful, and so on. Political demands and legal constraints can divert people into pursuing power, freedom or wealth instead of the virtues. Only in a good regime is the good man the same as the good citizen (*Politics* 1332b32).

The institutions of politics are thus of great importance. States can be distinguished on two criteria: the number of those who rule, and the interests they pursue. A state may be ruled by one, few or many people, and it may be ruled in the interests of all (monarchy, aristocracy and democracy) or of the ruler alone (tyranny, oligarchy and ochlocracy or mob rule). The best regimes are those that govern in the interests of all; the others are deviant. However, all regimes are unstable, and the inherent flaws of each kind tend to lead to its replacement by deviant forms, resulting in a cyclical succession of forms amid conflict. Under differing conditions, rule by one man, by few, or by many may be appropriate. But in practice there is rarely one person who is so much superior to the rest as to justify his ruling in the interests of all. An aristocracy of the most virtuous citizens might seem the logically ideal regime, but it is difficult to achieve. Besides, virtues and practical wisdom are more widely distributed among the population, thus justifying some participation for those not in the top echelons. But, at the other extreme, in a democracy the sheer weight of numbers tends to swamp all other considerations, and to deflect from rule in the interests of all. In Aristotle's view, the Athenian interpretation of equality of access to political life (*isegoria*) is mistaken, since people are very unequal in talent, wealth and other contributions to society. Political equality should be kept for equals (*Politics* 1283b13). Better regimes give the citizens a say proportional not just to their numbers, but to their contributions in virtue, talent, wisdom and wealth. Number is just one kind of contribution, mistakenly taken by democrats to be the only one that matters (*Politics* 1282b, 1281a2).

In practice, the best regime (termed 'polity' – *politeia*) is a mixture of aristocracy and democracy. It recognises merit and talent as well as numbers, and realises government in the interests of the whole, by some more, and some less, democratic procedures. High offices can be restricted to the virtuous through appointment by election. But the people can have a say in the assembly and juries, can be paid to attend, and many offices can be chosen by lot, with a minimal property qualification. This mixture combines elements of different kinds of regime; it does not imply maintaining a balance (let alone a separation) between institutions, social groups or powers in society, as the term 'mixed government' generally came to convey in later republican thought. It provides a share in self-rule for all classes of citizens; thus this form of government can provide a harmonious arrangement, and keep at bay the ever-present threat of civil war, or of conflict between social groups.

Participation

Just how much value Aristotle attributed to political participation is a contested issue. For some interpreters, Aristotle's notion of the political nature of human beings means that participating in politics is the highest realisation of human nature. However, Aristotle's position is not as clear-cut as this. Even if living in a *polis* is an essential condition for living a good life, it does not necessarily follow that self-realisation depends on actually participating in politics, or that participation constitutes the best kind of life, or is even worthwhile itself.

We might accept that no one can be virtuous unless he lives in a well-ordered *polis*, but still not see actual political participation as important. Indeed Aristotle regards the contemplative life of a philosopher as an alternative way of realising one's highest rational nature (*Politics* 1325b14). This is a higher form of activity (with its own virtues), and one which requires a degree of leisure that political activity does not allow. Despite this emphasis on the claims of philosophy, it is not fully clear whether Aristotle concluded that the ideal of rationality was best achieved in a life of practical reason in the *polis*, or in a life devoted more exclusively to philosophical contemplation. A number of other points are relevant here: Even the wise man must live in a political community, and will suffer from living in a bad regime. Even those capable of philosophy cannot attain it until late in life. And it is still not a complete life, as humans are embodied and social as well as rational beings, and need to act in the world. Thus the pursuit of wisdom does not exclude political participation as part of a worthwhile life, and politics is a significant arena for the development and exercise of the virtues. Political action affords a unique opportunity to exercise practical wisdom and justice, which is available only to a citizen, not to any resident in the *polis*.

So, participation is valuable in itself because it allows the exercise of reasoned deliberation among equals. To be a citizen, by

Aristotle's definition, is to participate actively in deliberation, to serve in office and to defend the *polis*, though the qualification for citizenship is differently defined in different states. Citizens are engaged in collective self-rule among equals, which is distinguished from the rule of a master over slaves and that of a father over family by its temporary and alternating nature. Political rule is 'over men who are free and similar in birth; the good citizen must have the knowledge and the ability both to rule and to be ruled' (*Politics* 1277b7). And playing a role in politics confers honour on those who participate (*Politics* 1281a28): 'rule over free men is nobler than master-like rule and is more connected with virtue' (*Politics* 1333b26).

Participation is valuable in another way, because decisions made by a larger number of people are more likely to be correct. Though suspicious of the extent of political equality in democracy, Aristotle advances two important arguments for allowing wider political participation than the individual distribution of reason would support. First, the people are collectively wiser than any individual. Even those who are not particularly talented or virtuous bring a variety of perspectives that can cast light on political affairs (in the same way, he says, as a pot-luck supper is better than a meal cooked by a single cook) (*Politics* 1281a39). Second, consumers in any area have experience which makes them extremely valuable judges of experts; it is the person who wears the shoe, and not the shoemaker, who knows if it fits (*Politics* 1282a14). Thus people are interdependent in their pursuit of practical wisdom, which is realised in interaction in political communication and deliberation. (Note that this epistemic argument for participation is based on the value of the outcome, not on an innate right to participate.)

None the less, attaching a value to participation does not imply that everyone is capable of participating in this deliberation among equals. Some fail to reach the minimum threshold of reason. This, for Aristotle, is true, to different degrees, of children (who have yet to develop reason) and of women (whose emotions distort their reason).[3] It is also true of some male adults who are incapable of independent reason, and whom he accordingly terms natural slaves. These natural slaves will never be able to achieve full human flourishing. Others, who make their living through manual labour, are not categorically excluded from participation, but lack the time to devote to serious political activity, and are therefore not really capable of active citizenship. Urban dwellers are more volatile and easily influenced than rural ones.

Thus Aristotle combines a belief in the inherent value of political participation with a distrust of the capacity for participation of a wide range of specific groups. Participation is valuable in so far as it allows people to exercise the virtues.

Freedom

In exercising self-rule citizens can become free. In democracy freedom (*eleutheria*) is a central value. But Aristotle's own view is somewhat more guarded. Athenians valued freedom in two senses, both contrasted to slavery, a condition which they despised and feared. In the first place the term 'the free' describes ordinary citizens who are not otherwise distinguished by wealth, talent or position. This freedom is not a natural quality of pre-social individuals; it is the status or privilege of citizens, who are individually free if not subject to a master, and collectively free if not ruled by a tyrant or subject to another state.

Politically speaking, this democratic freedom has two elements (*Politics* 1317a40). First, it means participating in self-rule, which is achieved by alternating in rule: 'ruling and being ruled in turn'. In this way people can be ruled and yet not be subject to a master. Second, freedom is understood as 'living as you like'. This entails personal freedom running in tandem with the former. Democratic citizens expect to be left in peace to run most of their lives themselves. (Though this implies neither any fixed or predetermined limits to government, nor a theoretical claim about the independence of individuals, embodied in any notion of natural rights.)

If Aristotle preferred a mixed 'polity' to pure democracy, what are his views on freedom? As we have seen, despite his anti-democratic scepticism, Aristotle values the diverse perspectives and practical experience that ordinary citizens can bring to bear on politics. So, while he has strong reservations about giving the many too dominant a role, for those who are capable the dimension of freedom constituted by participation in self-government is quite compatible with exercising the virtues in political life.

'Living as one likes', on the other hand, is much more open-ended, including the pursuit not only of valuable ends, but of immediate pleasures. Thus it is closer to 'licence'. 'Freedom to do exactly what one likes cannot do anything to keep in check that element of badness which exists in each and all of us' (*Politics* 1318b27). Since the good life, not purely pleasure, is the ultimate goal for humans, it appears that 'ruling and being ruled in turn' is a more valuable kind of freedom than 'living as you like'. So, while the contrast with slavery includes this sense of freedom, it is subordinate to what is good for citizens. For interdependent members of a *polis*, other people's needs also set limits on how far you can live as you like.

For Aristotle freedom is valuable primarily in so far as it allows the exercise of virtue, realising human excellence. On this basis freedom is compatible with – indeed requires – the extensive rule of law. The *polis* not only allows the exercise of virtues, but can also foster their development, and shape the character of the citizens.

Shaping citizens

Because human character is neither wholly good nor wholly bad, and not fixed at birth, without proper laws and education people are liable to degenerate in various ways, setting the wrong priorities, or failing to develop the right habits.

Law To live a worthwhile life it is necessary to live in a law-governed *polis*. 'For as man is the best of all animals when he has reached his full development, so he is worst of all when divorced from law and justice' (*Politics* 1253a30–4). It is better to be ruled by law than to be dominated by another person, as even the wisest of men can be subject to passions which make him volatile. Law is like wisdom without desire, since passions corrupt the rule of even the best of men (*Politics* 1287a23). As law is the product of reason rather than the arbitrary will of another, its rule is compatible with the sense of freedom as ruling and being ruled in turn, if not with 'living as you like'.

Laws do not just constrain anti-social behaviour; they can and should shape citizens' characters: 'that which is genuinely and not just nominally called a state must concern itself with virtue', and 'all who are anxious to ensure government under good laws make it their business to have an eye on the virtue and vice of the citizens' (*Politics* 1280a34).

Good laws develop the best aspects of human nature, rather than artificially constraining or running counter to human nature.

The greatest power of the laws lies in their educative role, in shaping the desires of citizens with regard to wealth, for example, so that they do not desire more than they need (*Ethics* 1179). This is most important for young people, but even adults need the guidance of law to encourage them in the practice of virtues. On this view law is not excluded in principle from any area of life, though it is general in its provisions, and details that cannot be specified in advance have to be determined by officials in practice (*Politics* 1282a41). Freedom does not imply a right to be immune to law in any area, and indeed Aristotle envisages far-reaching laws on marriage, reproduction and education, among other things, since he believes that it is not oppressive for the law to lay down decent behaviour. If, for Aristotle, 'the state' is the focus of virtue, it should be borne in mind that this means the ensemble of the actions of the citizens, as there is no 'state' in the modern sense of an independently existing authority. Anything that the *polis* does is through the citizens.

Education Because character is initially indeterminate, education in acting well is also very important. Moreover, the educative function of law is paralleled by making education itself a responsibility of the state, an unusual step in contemporary terms. This does not primarily instil communal beliefs or values, but develops the virtues needed by citizens. Education develops their aesthetic and social awareness, and shapes their desires towards the goals of life higher than pleasure, money-making, technical skills and so on. As communication and deliberation are a key part of political activity, these should be encouraged by education: 'each ruler can judge nobly when educated by the laws' (*Politics* 1287b15). Even military training has as its ultimate purpose the enjoyment of peace (*Politics* 1333a37). Education makes the citizens aware of their interdependence and of the importance of supporting the common goods shared in the *polis*: 'no one should think he belongs just to himself; he must regard all citizens as belonging to the *polis*, for each is a part of the *polis*' (*Politics* 1337a11).

Material pre-conditions of political equality

Virtue depends not only on institutions and education, but also on wider social and economic conditions. These include relative prosperity. The extent of economic inequality should be limited, so that even less well-off citizens can be relatively independent of the wealthy. A successful *polis* will have a large middle class. As well as independence, citizens need the resources for leisure to take time for political activity. In a democracy, a ceiling may be set to land ownership, and poorer citizens should be given employment and land to ensure their independence in interacting as genuine political equals with others (*Politics* 1319a4; 1320a35). But, in general, educating desires so that people are generous, rather than grasping, is more effective than equalising property. Thus property may be privately owned, but should be used in the public good, just as the wealthy were expected to fund the Athenian navy and public festivals.

Intensity and scope of the political community

The *polis* is a partnership of those who are politically equal and similar in important respects, distinct from family relationships. There is a strong bond between citizens, who should think of each other as 'friends'. Aristotle advances a specific account of friendship in relationships important to a good life, which is found at three levels – utility, pleasure and good. Some friends are valued because of the advantage they bring, others are enjoyed because they are witty or clever, but at the highest and more enduring level of friendship we value, and are concerned for, friends for themselves, as parents are for their children. This is the kind of friendship citizens share, because they are linked not just by contractual utility or even pleasure in each other's company, but by a concern for each other's welfare, and the common goods they share. Thus 'law-givers seem to make friendship more important than justice' (*Ethics* 1155a24).

Furthermore, in a polity people share certain values. If we recall, 'humans alone have perception of good and evil, just and unjust; it is sharing these matters in common that makes a household and a state' (*Politics* 1253a7). But translations differ, and interpreters disagree on the meaning of this phrase (*de touton koinonia poiei oikian kai polin*). Does it mean sharing common views of justice, or sharing in deliberations about justice? How much diversity among citizens does this allow? Some take it to mean that citizens must share a very extensive range of values or a single view of the good life (MacIntyre, 1984; Mulgan, 1999). Others, interpreting the phrase differently, take it to mean that the polity is a forum for determining matters of just and unjust among those who have many perspectives (Waldron, 1999; Yack, 1993).

For Aristotle, the individual is not wholly submerged in the community. There could be too close a unity between citizens, as he thought was the case in Sparta and in Plato's *Republic*. Aristotle does say that the concord between citizens does not depend on agreement of opinions on every subject, such as, for example, the nature of the universe or astronomy. It concerns practical agreement between citizens. It comes about when they 'agree about their interests, adopt the same policy, and put their common resolves into effect' (*Ethics* 1167a18). This agreement is subject to deliberation, and does not rule out significant differences of perspective between citizens.

Aristotle sees these bonds and responsibilities as specific to each *polis*, the community that makes the fullest degree of self-realisation possible for citizens. Thus the scope of this community is naturally limited. Every kind of friendship has limits beyond which it cannot be extended without distorting its meaning. Citizenship and participation are deep rather than extensive. A state must be limited in territory, population and social diversity. Fewer than ten or more than 100,000 cannot count as a *polis* at all. Citizens must be able to share and communicate among themselves, and have mutual knowledge of the character of other citizens to whom they are entrusting offices and whose performance they will be auditing.

Moreover, the hierarchical division of human nature means that the obligations of citizens to anyone outside the political community are very limited.

Thus Aristotle in practice offers a very elusive ideal. Even if he understands political participation in a free, self-governing community as being important to a life of virtue, he does so within the frame of a teleologically determined account of human nature, and appears to cater for a very limited cross-section of humanity, excluding by definition non-Greeks, slaves and women from any such possibilities. His theory seems to assume that all virtues can be in harmony, that virtue will be accompanied by success, and that the *polis* can be harmonious. Yet Aristotle himself saw the precariousness of all such arrangements, and did not conclusively endorse the value of political life over that of contemplation.

Cicero

> We are not born for ourselves alone, but our country claims for itself one part of our birth, and our friends another.
> (Cicero, 1991: 22, quoting Plato Letter 9 358a)

Three centuries separate Aristotle and Cicero. Even in Aristotle's own time the self-ruling city-state became an anachronism, swept up in the Macedonian empire of Aristotle's one-time pupil, Alexander. Before long Rome dominated the Mediterranean, and extended its rule to a vast territorial empire maintained by its army. Greece, though culturally influential, became a political backwater. The Roman republic was not only more extensive, but also more aristocratic than the Athenian *polis*. There were three major categories of citizen: a land-owning senatorial class, a propertied class of equestrians, and the people or plebs (as well as a large body of slave labour). Each class had its assembly, and in principle the people were sovereign, but in practice a narrow elite exercised power through the senate, which dominated the popular assemblies. Politics was marked by power struggles between the classes and among politicians who championed their different interests. Freedom was still understood in opposition to slavery, but expressed as a status guaranteed by law rather than as equal rights of political participation. A more extensive and impersonal system of law to which property was central covered all citizens, and was applied by professional lawyers and jurists. Important elements of modern republicanism can be traced to Roman sources. The term republic itself derives from the Latin *res publica*, the key term virtue from the Latin *virtus*, and honour (the precursor of recognition) from *honor*, a central Roman value.

Cicero (106–43 BC) articulated ideas supporting a republican government in very different circumstances, both political and intellectual, from Aristotle. He made a career as a lawyer in the last years of the Roman republic. He served in the highest offices as an active politician, but a stormy term as consul later led to his exile from Rome. The immediate context in which Cicero wrote was a period of rival bids for political power waged by successful generals, culminating in Julius Caesar, Anthony and Octavian. These men represented a dangerous departure from the commitment to public service that Cicero believed essential to maintain the republic. *On Duties* (Cicero, 1991) takes the form of a letter to his son, Marcus, studying philosophy in Greece, to impress on him how members of the Roman elite should serve the political community and achieve honour. It is his republican testament, written as a plea for government in the interests of the whole, to stave off the impending collapse of the republic before the power of Octavian who, as Augustus, would make himself emperor. When Cicero returned from exile to make his famous set of speeches excoriating those who were destroying the republic, he was condemned and killed.

When Rome supplanted the Greek city-states, philosophers tended to reduce the role of political activity in the good life. Cicero was greatly influenced by the Stoics, for example, who addressed a new set of issues. They replaced the radically exclusive particularism of the Greeks with a belief in a common human nature and a natural moral law. Their idea of universal justice denied the existence of natural slaves and affirmed moral obligations to all mankind.

They debated the question whether virtue and success in life necessarily go hand in hand, or if virtue entails self-sacrifice. Perhaps because of the political upheavals that they had experienced, they were not optimistic that right behaviour would necessarily lead to external success. They concluded that virtue should be sought for its own sake, and no significance should be attached to personal advantage. In their more exacting account than Aristotle's, virtue is sufficient for happiness. Freedom is a matter of subjective will rather than legal status or participation in rule. No losses can affect the virtuous man. They questioned the idea that virtue requires action, that political activity is intrinsically worthwhile, and that the political community is the highest level of human association.

Cicero, while influenced by the questions posed by the Stoic thinkers, elaborated a more wholehearted defence of the value and obligations of political participation than Aristotle. His writings offer a less systematic philosophical account of human nature and the human good than Aristotle, whose works he may not have read, though he was certainly exposed to his ideas.

Interdependence and politics

For Cicero, human beings are naturally social; they form societies not just to meet material needs, but because they are gregarious.

Individuals are members of a range of associations from the family to humanity at large, each of which has claims on their allegiance, but the political community is the highest form of association. Though a central part of politics is concerned with distinguishing and preserving both private and public property, Cicero insists against early contractualist accounts that, while society is founded in an agreement on laws, it does not exist merely for reciprocal defence or advantage. In a republic citizens share many things central to their lives, from physical objects and spaces like the forum, temples and porticos, to ideas of justice and common benefit. Citizens value common living, and develop bonds based on familiarity and similarity.

The republic should be understood as a partnership of those united in a significant common life by the bond of law. This is destroyed when justice is not observed. Aristotle had seen all forms of political community as natural, with some better at creating the conditions for a good life than others. For Cicero though, the republic is not just one form of government among others, but the only legitimate one. Where a tyrant rules, the state is not so much defective as non-existent. More than the absence of a monarch, or of the presence of any particular institutions, a republic is a state distinguished by the fact that the people constitute the original authority, and power is exercised in their interests even when it is delegated to magistrates. The term *res publica* literally means 'the public thing'. Cicero's briefest definition – '*res publica res populi*': the republic is the people's affair – indicates that the people are both the primary concern of government and the source of authority; so all government should be in their common interest, and they retain rights over the exercise of power. If their authority, like property, can be transferred or usurped, it can also be reclaimed. The citizen body can intervene at crucial moments in political affairs, either directly or through their own magistrates. But this does not mean that the people exercise continuous direct control over their affairs. For Cicero this society is not, as it was to some extent for the Athenians, and Aristotle, a union of equals, but includes different classes and ranks, the poor and the wealthy, plebs and patricians (Cicero, 1991: 22, 23). Government is the responsibility of an aristocratic elite, a political class dedicated to leadership.

The values of Cicero's republic are those of active citizenship. He contrasts virtue with a variety of forms of corruption: avarice, ambition for power, laziness, negligence, despair at the possibilities of politics, or preoccupation with philosophy or learning. The state is undermined if the guardians of the people's power become corrupt, and are driven by the lust for wealth or for glory. The most serious threats to the well-being of the republic come from self-aggrandising militaristic exploits which threaten the internal rule of law.

Virtue

Maintaining freedom depends crucially on the virtue of the political classes, and their pursuing the interests of the whole. We might say that for Cicero it is more that virtue is essential for *participants* than that participation is essential to virtue. The health of the republic is threatened at one extreme by tyrants and at the other by revolts of the mass of the plebs. He lays down an ideal of political virtue for the elite. They must 'fix their gaze so firmly on what is beneficial to citizens' and 'care for the whole body of the republic rather than protect one part and neglect the rest' (Cicero, 1991: 33).

Virtue is a matter of activity rather than right thinking, and is best exemplified in actively contributing to affairs of state. Undertaking public business is a primary duty and an intrinsically valuable activity. Statesmen ensure the freedom and common good of all, and earn the highest honours for themselves. Honour can take many forms, including military glory, political honour and personal respect. Political activity is superior not only to private life, but also to philosophy or the pursuit of learning, which are only justified by enforced absence from politics (Cicero, 1991: 60). 'Those...who have adapted themselves to great achievements in the service of the political community, lead lives more profitable to mankind and more suited to grandeur and fame.' But glory can also be destructive. 'Beware the desire for glory...For it destroys the liberty for which men of great spirit ought to be in competition' (Cicero, 1991: 28).

The virtues are focused more closely on socially necessary qualities than on purely personal ones. They reflect the behaviour appropriate to a social role as well as what we might think of as moral responsibilities. They are also less like ingrained dispositions than consciously assumed duties. Like Plato before him, Cicero sees four principal virtues: wisdom, courage, moderation and – the primary virtue – justice. These came to be known as the cardinal virtues, and were an important reference point in defining the concept of civic virtue as it became central to civic republican thought.

Wisdom (prudentia) is practical reason guiding actors to put justice, or the common good, before personal advantage (Cicero, 1991: 53, 59–60).

Courage (fortitudo) is the ability, essential for a statesman, to transcend material concerns. It is distinguished from soft, 'effeminate' behaviour (Cicero, 1991: 129). This is connected with the derivation of *virtus* from the Latin *vir* (man, as distinct from woman). But it is not best exemplified in military courage. Statesmen provide better examples of courage contributing to the public good. 'The courageous deeds of civilians are not inferior to those of soldiers. Indeed the former should be given even more effort and devotion than the latter' (Cicero, 1991: 31).

Moderation (decorum) includes self-control and self-discipline, but also a range of concerns about acting appropriately in different contexts – to be dignified, and serious in ways that were important to Romans (for example, not singing in the forum) – what later might be termed 'propriety'. What it requires is generally determined by socially defined roles and the needs of specific circumstances. This is less a matter of educating the passions than of adapting to changing conditions.

Justice (justitia) is the most important virtue, since it most directly concerns our dealings with others. It requires us to tell the truth, keep promises, to respect the property of others, and to be fair in exchanges with all. It rules out in particular the use of both force and fraud, suited to the lion and the fox respectively, but not to human beings (Cicero, 1991: 19). The virtuous man will help others when he can do so at no cost to himself, and not harm others unless his survival depends on it. But even then, it may be preferable to die in the cause of justice:

> Any serious courageous citizen...will devote himself entirely to the republic, pursuing neither wealth nor power, and will protect the whole in such a way that the interest of

none is disregarded....He will...so adhere to justice and what is honourable that in preserving them he will endure any reverse, however serious, and face death rather than abandon those things I have mentioned.

(Cicero, 1991: 34; see also 111)

Having defined virtue more narrowly than Aristotle in social terms, Cicero has to deal with the objection that those who act virtuously do not necessarily achieve personal success. Then, as now, it was possible to feel that nice guys finish last. Against the Stoic belief that virtue must be practised even at the cost of individual advantage, Cicero tries to reconcile individual interests and social demands, arguing that we are mistaken if our interests appear to conflict with virtue. Because honour is the most important reward, we are always better off doing the honourable thing. 'We must...be more eager to risk our own than the common welfare, and readier to fight when honour and glory, rather than when other advantages are at stake' (Cicero, 1991: 33). Acting against the interest of society as a whole cannot be, but only seems, advantageous, because we are dependent on the society of which we are part. It would not be entirely unfair to summarise Cicero's approach in the phrase: honesty is the best policy.[4]

Mixed government and participation

For Cicero, as for Aristotle, none of the traditional pure forms of government – democracy, aristocracy or monarchy – is wholly desirable. All are subject to cyclical degeneration. Instead Cicero advocates the form of mixed government he identifies with the golden age of Roman republicanism. This owes less to Aristotle than to Polybius, the second-century BC historian of Rome, whose influential theory identified a balance between the wealthy and the plebs in Rome that allowed it to escape the constant cycles from one regime to the next. This is an equilibrium of *classes*, quite different from Aristotle's mixture of *forms of government*.

In Cicero's account of mixed government the rule of law prevents the dominance of any section of society. All, including the rulers, are subject to law, 'the mind of the state', which reflects reason rather than personal will. That all are subject to the law does not imply exact equality before the law; there are different ranks and degrees of citizens, and there are laws appropriate to each. This is a balance between those who are different, in which the aristocratic few, though accepting responsibilities, should predominate.

This conception of balance limits the popular role in deliberation, and gives a major role to the original legislator or founder, who identifies the laws that the people endorse. Different classes of people can then coexist and respect their common interest under the rule of law. And in periods of decline like his own, another figure may be needed: a dictator or *rector*, who would literally 'correct' the deviations.

But in addition, different ranks of citizens have different rights of participation. So, despite invoking the idea of mixed government, Cicero sees little role for popular involvement in political decisions. The freedom of citizens does not depend on equal participation in politics or in taking turns in ruling.

While Cicero maintains that political activity undertaken for the common good is an eminently honourable life, the audience he addresses is a very narrow Roman elite. His claim is not that political participation is the fullest realisation of human potential, to which all should have access. Rather, he is urging those who rule to do so with the interests of the whole of society at heart.

Freedom

In Rome, citizens were distinguished not by their right to participate but by their *legal status*, or right to claim the protection of law. Freedom (*libertas*) did not mean equality in participation, or automatic freedom of speech, as in Athens.

For Cicero the rule of law not only provides for the common good of all members of society, but guarantees their freedom. Rather than ruling in turns, the citizens are free because they enjoy the legal status of *libertas*. This is not a natural possession of individuals but a status acquired politically with citizenship in a republic where government is carried on in the interests of the whole people. They would not be free in a monarchy or aristocracy, but subject to the will of others.

For the Romans, being subject to a master was incompatible with freedom, but removing the bonds of slavery to a specific master was not sufficient to make someone free; rather, the citizens of Rome gained the status of freedom as the bearers of the legal capacity to possess certain rights and not to be subject to another. It is thus a social relation of members rather than an individual possession, entailing both rights and duties (Wirzsubski, 1968: 8). It is distinct from licence, requiring not only the absence of a personal master, but the active presence of law: 'we obey the law that we may be free' (Cicero, 1927: 379). So Cicero too distinguishes freedom from licence, as when he condemns those who think it means having no needs and living as they like, like a king (Cicero, 1991: 70). Freedom requires restraint or moderation, not all of which is self-imposed; some is imposed by the laws. It is compatible with censorship and sumptuary legislation limiting luxuries. In contrast with a modern account of freedom as the absence, or limits, of law and government authority, here law is the guarantor of freedom.

Law and education

Law was thus central to the whole project. But we should note that, here, law is much more designed to maintain the structure of society than to shape the character of citizens. Overall, the role of the state is less to shape ethical ideals than to preserve property and the distribution of political power. Cicero distinguishes between the public which all citizens share and the private which belongs to individuals. The protection of both kinds of property is central to the common good of society. As well as lacking Aristotle's emphasis on the educative aspect of law, Cicero downplays the political importance of education more generally. For him both universal human qualities and differences of character are given at birth, not developed through habituation, as for Aristotle. Further dimensions of personality are the outcome of individual choice, the requirements of social roles and of chance. Thus shaping characters is not a political imperative. The role of good laws and institutions is rather to channel and constrain (Coleman, 2000a: 263). The goal of human life may be happiness, achievable by practising the virtues. But politics is less concerned with facilitating the virtues than with supporting the rule of law.

Material pre-conditions of political equality

Cicero is critical of extravagance and excessive wealth, seeing the destabilising effects of great inequalities in Rome. He recognises the threat to social solidarity that great inequalities constitute, and argues that poverty should be alleviated. Leaders should ensure that the basic necessities are available to the people.

Yet the function of the state is to preserve property, both private and common, and this is more important than reducing inequality. While citizens must respect each other, then, and should be prepared to put their private goods at the service of the state voluntarily, Cicero is more reluctant than Aristotle to envisage any redistribution from the rich to the poor. The ambitious politicians who propose agrarian laws to redistribute property to the landless cause political turmoil, and effectively destroy the rationale on which the state is based.[5]

Intensity and scope of the republic

The republic is a limited community, but in a smoother continuum of human relationships than in Aristotle's view. There is a fellowship of the entire human race, united by reason, speech and natural law. But there is a particularly strong bond between citizens. We do not owe the same to everyone. We have deeper commitments to certain relations: to friends and family, but above all to fellow citizens.

> Of all fellowships, none is more serious and none dearer than that of each of us with the republic. Parents are dear, and children, relatives and acquaintances are dear, but our country has on its own embraced all the affections of all of us.
>
> (Cicero, 1991: 23)

Thus the strength of commitment does not extend in concentric circles from family to world, but peaks at the point of the republic. While sometimes expressed in contractual terms, based on living under a set of laws, the relationship between citizens is in general a closer bond of feeling that springs from the shared benefits and familiarity that develops between them. Thus, faced with a choice between supporting friend or country, we should always put our country first.

Citizenship is a different kind of relationship from those of race, tribe or language; it can include considerable diversity of wealth and rank, and can extend to larger numbers and a larger territory than Aristotle allows.

Aristotle and Cicero

The two strands of the republican theory prefigured

Aristotle and Cicero both affirm that social and political life are natural to human beings, and allow the attainment of individual and common goods. Power is not its own justification; politics is an arena in which admirable qualities are both required and developed. This is qualitatively different from and more important than family, household or friends. Membership in a state is not just a means to self-defence, but an important focus of moral commitment and obligation that constitutes a 'morally important stopping-place' at least (Annas, 1995: 78).

Virtue is the focal concept. These theories distinguish the virtues required in active citizens from self-aggrandisement, and make them central to political life. In opposition to influential trends, they deny that politics is inevitably concerned with the ruler's self-interest at the expense of the rest of society, and that the motivation of political actors must be power or material advantage. Aristotle focuses on shaping character through law and education, while Cicero highlights the rule of law and the civic and social role of the statesman.[6]

A life devoted to political *participation* is a worthy one. Politics requires the cultivation of citizens committed to the good of the polity. But for both, unrefined democracy is unstable, and should at most be only an element in a more complex political structure. Both Aristotle and Cicero assume only the few will attain the highest levels of virtue, and both draw the bounds of citizenship very narrowly. They do not offer an argument for political participation by all the citizens or for majoritarian democracy. Yet they outline images of a political society in which citizenship entails mutual commitment to common goods. Aristotle in particular asserts the worth of political deliberation among equals as a central part of citizenship. Cicero affirms the value of political action in terms of public service.

For both, *freedom* is politically defined as the status of a citizen of a free *polis* or republic, who is not subject to the rule of a master. This was realised for Aristotle by ruling and being ruled in turn; for Cicero simply by the rule of law. For neither is freedom a pre-political quality of individuals that entails limiting the power of government, as in the modern contractarian tradition. The existence of laws is understood to guarantee rather than to infringe on freedom.

This freedom is in the service of virtue. The value of political freedom derives from the more important goal of the pursuit of the good, or virtue in the largest sense. For Aristotle it is secondary to the pursuit of natural goals which determine the parameters of a worthwhile life. For Cicero freedom is distinct from participation. But the freedom of Cicero's statesmen is constrained by the imperatives of the specifically civic virtues.

While recognising the military contribution of citizens, both Aristotle and Cicero minimise the warrior and heroic virtues and advocate a more persuasive and harmonious politics. Their accounts of politics may more accurately be criticised as masculinist; not only are women excluded from participation, but the virtues required in politics are partly defined by reference to their exclusion.

In the civic republican tradition, the differences between the two thinkers are reflected in differing strands, one emphasising participation in self-government, the other the rule of law as constituting republican freedom.

Initially, Aristotle's influence on the development of civic republicanism was somewhat indirect. His *Politics* was not available in Latin, and not very widely read in the medieval West before the thirteenth century. By contrast, Cicero's *On Duties* was one of the most widely taught texts throughout the medieval and early modern period, and when printing was invented, it was one of the first Latin texts to be printed.[7] When the themes of citizenship were picked up again in the late middle ages, then, it was in the writings of Cicero before those of Aristotle. Yet Aristotle's philosophy set the framework for later thinkers in many areas. His account of virtue conveys an understanding of human motivation which provided not only a vocabulary for civic republicans, but also the idea, often implicit in the idea of civic virtue, of an ingrained orientation towards the good. And Aristotle's richer account of political life was increasingly picked up. Republican thought has strong Greek as well as Roman foundations.

In the sixteenth and seventeenth centuries, early modern republicans looked back as much to Rome and Sparta as to Athens, and to the historical example of heroes from ancient history which they found, for example, in Plutarch's *Lives* of Greek and Roman heroes, and Livy's *History of Rome*, as they did to political theorists.

Aristotle and Cicero

In contrast with the princely and monarchical cult of Julius Caesar and Augustus, the founders of empire, republicans held up different heroes for citizens to emulate. A recurrent example was Junius Brutus, one of the republican founders who expelled the early Tarquin kings from Rome, and who, as consul, insisted on overseeing the execution of his sons who had been conspirators. Another was Marcus Brutus, the friend of Julius Caesar, who, out of loyalty to the republic, joined in the conspiracy to assassinate him, when his ambition threatened its survival.

Aristotle and Cicero lay out significant elements of two threads in the republican tradition, but they should be regarded as antecedents rather than strictly as republican thinkers.

CHAPTER II

Freedom in Classical Republicanism
Machiavelli and Harrington

Introduction

For more than a thousand years after the Roman republic was superseded by the rule of emperors, there was little scope for republican thought or practice. So it was that, when in the thirteenth century the issues of virtue, freedom and self-rule were connected as topics of practical concern and philosophical debate, the participants' debate self-consciously followed Greek and Roman models.

This debate culminated in strikingly original and influential formulations by Machiavelli and Harrington. This chapter analyses the arguments of these thinkers who established the essential themes of classical republicanism and transmitted them into the world of modern states in the sixteenth and seventeenth centuries. They portray a political life of freedom and civic virtue realised in self-governing republics by active citizens who participate in political and military service. Here *freedom* emerges as the focal concept of republicanism. While virtue, along with its obverse, corruption, remains an important theme, its meaning has shifted, and it becomes largely a means towards freedom. Machiavelli extracts republican thought from a determinate and teleological account of human goods; Harrington brings republican argument into the modern world by tackling the issue of establishing a republic in a large territorial state.

Historical context

Self-governing city states gave way in turn to Imperial Rome and then to the dual hierarchy of Pope and Emperor, bishops and kings, clergy and lords. Political life in medieval Europe became remote from most people; power and freedom – as participation in self government – were limited to a few. The view of society and history as cyclical was displaced by a linear progression from Creation and Fall through Incarnation and Last Judgement, in which God's providence and grace shaped events more than chance or human actions. Augustine, one of the most influential voices in medieval Europe, presented politics as a holding operation to channel the pilgrim faithful through this world in order to attain eternal salvation. The interdependence of those who share a political community was less significant than the dependence of all on God and His providence in the eternal order. The value of political activity in human life, and the possibility of humans actively shaping their collective destiny in the secular world, were correspondingly downgraded. Kingship and other forms of hierarchical rule were generally taken to be essential for a peaceable existence for fallen humankind. The cardinal virtues were reworked in a more passive mode as justice, fortitude, temperance and wisdom, and were secondary to the specifically Christian virtues of faith, hope, charity and humility, which relied less on individual character development than on the gift of God's grace.

Cicero, though much read, tended to be interpreted as an advocate of the contemplative life and Christian virtues (Baron, 1938; Tuck, 1990). Aristotle's political writings became more widely influential in the later thirteenth century, after they had been translated into Latin. Aristotle increasingly became the dominant influence in theorising, especially after Thomas Aquinas created a synthesis of Aristotelian and Christian beliefs in which political activity derives from positive human capacities, not from the Fall. But political ends are closely determined more by a theological ranking of human goods than by deliberation among equals. Aquinas too argued that monarchy was the best form of government, and that cities and provinces not ruled by a single person would always be divided and never achieve peace.[1]

From about the eleventh century, especially in Northern and Central Italy, city-states practising a variety of forms of citizen self-rule appeared. As both political experience and practical problems grew, thinkers found resonant political messages in the works of Cicero that they studied originally as part of their literary, grammatical or rhetorical training. The citizens of these city-states became very conscious of the parallels between their concerns and those of Cicero and engaged in debates about the possibility of enduring free republics, the best constitutions, and the ideal citizen: the '*vir virtutis*' or man of virtue, who could combine the Christian and the pagan virtues.

They argued that a republic was the best form of rule because it allowed people to be free in the two senses of independence from outside powers and from internal tyrants. In an era of commercial expansion, literary, artistic and architectural innovation, optimistic thinkers drew on classical support for the idea that humans could shape their own destiny. Political life was revalued: some writers, known as 'civic humanists', came to see participation in civic activity as 'the good life' or the highest realisation of human nature (Pocock, 1975; Skinner, 1978). But they saw republics as naturally short-lived. Indeed by 1500, most of the Italian states – with the exception of Florence and Venice – had fallen under the sway of autocratic rulers or of other states. Accordingly the very possibility of creating and sustaining a free republic became an issue. These thinkers were acutely conscious of the contrast between free political institutions, which are fragile and ephemeral, and the permanence of God's eternity. They understood the cyclical tendency of states to rise and fall as the problem of corruption; the body politic was subject to decay like other organic bodies. They debated a variety of alternative solutions to this: designing complex political institutions, rousing the citizens to more active defence of their cities, or replacing conflict between classes or factions with concord among citizens. Some advanced the aristocratic model of Venice, others the more democratic model of Florence. The most widely favoured solution saw human energy as the key, and exhorted citizens to a life that combined Christian and Roman virtues. By developing the virtues citizens might temper the vicissitudes of fortune. As time went by, however, the ideal of a harmonious self-ruling citizenry seemed more and more unrealistic. Threatened by aristocratic dynasties, and the power of France, the Papacy and the Emperor, some concluded that freedom was incompatible with security and peace, and that citizens would be better off as passive and obedient subjects of monarchs, who should themselves possess all the virtues.

Machiavelli

Nicolo Machiavelli (1469–1527) was a member of a lesser Florentine family, who served the government as a diplomat and secretary during the city's last stages of republican rule after the aristocratic Medici family had been expelled in 1494. But the Medici were restored to power in 1512 when Florence fell to Spanish troops, and Machiavelli was exiled to the countryside near Florence – within sight of its cathedral, but excluded from its politics. He then set to writing his works: *The Prince* (1974), and *The Discourses* (*Discorsi*) (1983) – a commentary on part of Livy's *History of Rome*. Both these works dwell on the unpredictability of politics and the vulnerability of citizens to one another and to fate, and respond critically to the solutions of harmony through all the virtues proposed by his contemporaries. In the *Discorsi* he outlines a republican theory, in which he redefines virtue as what is needed to guarantee freedom, the central value of politics.

Machiavelli's experience in government made him more interested in the example provided by classical politicians than in classical political philosophy. His *Discorsi* explicitly compares the political strategies adopted in the Roman republic with the contemporary difficulties of Florence, and refers back to the Roman historian Sallust as well as to Livy. But he picks up threads of arguments we have seen elaborated in Aristotle and Cicero without explicitly referring to them. Instead of arguing systematically, he adopts a rhetorical and anecdotal style, studding his theory with stories of ancient heroes and villains. Since he does not always define his terms clearly, and often uses them ambiguously, if not inconsistently, we have to reconstruct his argument from the ways in which he uses them. Although we can identify the bones of an argument in this way, it leaves a notoriously wide latitude for interpretation, and inconsistencies and problems of interpretation remain. He has been interpreted as an early political scientist, a fascist collectivist, a proto-liberal, and a cynical realist, as well as a republican theorist of freedom as self-government. Here I confine myself mainly to considering the issues most important for understanding Machiavelli's expression of republican theory.

Interdependence and the problem of corruption

Machiavelli takes for granted that human beings live in society, and that the 'body politic' is a living unit to which they need to belong to reach their fullest realisation. He make no attempt to consider humans outside a political order, or in a 'state of nature', as later contractarians were to do. But creating and maintaining any political order is a difficult task, since '[a]ll human affairs are ever in a state of flux and cannot stand still' (Machiavelli, 1974: 123). Human action takes place within the framework of necessity and chance, the fickle goddess *Fortuna*. Change is inevitable and cyclical. Good fortune tends to be followed by bad, and societies rise and fall.

The problem of change is exemplified in the persistent threat of corruption. In a world dominated by change, corruption or decay is understood not just as a characteristic of short-sightedly selfish or misled individuals, but as a natural hazard affecting the body politic as well as natural organisms. In politics it is associated with cyclical decline from freedom to domination. Every kind of regime tends to deviate from the principles on which it was originally founded and needs restoration on a regular basis. A republic is an historical creation, a fragile and temporary solution to the problem of political order.

Human beings in Machiavelli's view are not definitively good or bad, selfish or altruistic in character. They are unreliable; they are often deceitful, grasping and ungrateful, and in their worse moments can do great damage to the possibilities of peaceful human living. So anyone designing political institutions should not assume that people can be relied upon. It must be 'taken for granted that all men are wicked and that they will always give vent to the malignity that is in their minds when opportunity affords' (Machiavelli, 1974: 112). But there are other inclinations in people which can be called on, and ways in which their characters can be shaped. Human nature is deficient but educable; human beings can develop a 'second nature', the virtue which is the obverse of corruption.

By corruption in individuals Machiavelli means putting particular interests ahead of the common good. This is a much wider sense than most modern usages. Today corruption most commonly means using political power to gain illegal, often financial advantages, or using wealth to get undue political influence (Shumer, 1979). For Machiavelli there are many additional forms which it can take. Citizens are corrupt if they rely on mercenaries to fight for the state instead of defending it themselves. Not only blatant avarice, but any preoccupation with material success and reluctance to take the time or effort to perform public duties counts as corruption. But excessive ambition and the arrogant exercise of power are equally dangerous. Acting deceitfully to gain fame counts as much as lining your pockets from the public purse. Even religious devotion can be a form of corruption. Christianity has encouraged people to focus on their own salvation in the next life rather than maintaining free institutions in this one. It fosters the wrong virtues: humility, charity and honesty, instead of the courage and determination which the republic needs in its citizens:

> Our religion, having taught us the truth and the true way of life, leads us to ascribe less esteem to worldly honour...our religion has glorified humble and contemplative men rather than men of action. It has assigned as man's highest good humility, abnegation and contempt for mundane things, whereas the other identified it with magnanimity, bodily strength and everything else that conduces to make men very bold. And if our religion demands that in you there be strength, what it asks for is strength to suffer rather than strength to do bold things.
>
> (Machiavelli, 1974: 277–8)

As a result evil men can dominate. 'This pattern of life therefore appears to have made the world weak and to have handed it over as a prey to the wicked' (Machiavelli, 1974: 278).[2]

Corruption undermines the freedom that citizens in a well-ordered republic may be able to enjoy. People who put their own particular or sectional interests before the common good cannot remain self-governing and independent of domination by an autocratic ruler or external force.

Citizens are interdependent because freedom and the other benefits of living in an ordered society are shared goods which can only be enjoyed collectively, and require the support of all through a commitment to practise virtue. The freedom of each depends on the virtue of all (Pocock, 1975: 184). Interdependence and the danger of corruption make virtue necessary for free citizens.

To counter, if only for a time, the continuous flux of political life and the threat of corruption, specific political institutions are necessary.

Republican political institutions

> When the populace is in power and is well-ordered, it will be stable, prudent and grateful, in much the same way or a

better way than is a prince however wise he be thought.
(Machiavelli, 1974: 254)

Machiavelli is best known for his advice to politicians on maintaining power in *The Prince*. Yet even in that work Machiavelli expressed his admiration for a republican form of government, and his unvarnished account of the behaviour of princes in political life led Rousseau to describe the book as 'a handbook for republicans' (Rousseau, 1968: 118). The *Discorsi* compares the success of the republic of ancient Rome with the decline of Florence.

Machiavelli denies that a single ruler can resolve the problem of the instability of political life. A republic is better than a monarchy or princedom for two reasons. First, republics are greater and more glorious. They achieve more and provide better for the common good. 'It is only in republics that the common good is looked to properly in that all that promotes it is carried out' (Machiavelli, 1974: 275). This is because the people are inherently more reliable than a single leader, and although not competent to create a political order from scratch, or to draft general laws, are shrewd when it comes to particular judgements of potential leaders. They are less grasping, more stable, less suspicious than princes, and more grateful to other political actors (Machiavelli, 1974: 184, 254). In addition, a republic is more flexible in dealing with adversity, since it can call on a wider range of talents as circumstances demand.

Second, there is more freedom for citizens in a republic: 'Those who have displayed prudence in constituting a republic have looked upon the safeguarding of liberty as one of the most essential things for which they have had to provide' (Machiavelli, 1974: 115). In a republic individuals can hope to benefit from their efforts: 'Every man is ready to have children since he believes that he can rear them and feels sure that his patrimony will not be taken away, and since he knows that, not only will they be born free, instead of into slavery, but that, if they have virtue, they will have a chance of becoming rulers' (Machiavelli, 1974: 280).

In maintaining a 'well-ordered' republic, there is a complex interrelationship between institutions, individual character and wider political practices. Good institutions are ineffective if the people are wholly corrupt, but moderately good citizens are powerless without institutions. Machiavelli's treatment of institutions (*ordini*) does not provide a detailed blueprint for the machinery of government, but a more general account of the structure of society and laws in a republic. These institutions include a mixed government, practices of popular accountability and equal political opportunity, a civic militia and a civic religion.

Such institutions do not arise spontaneously, as the people are a fairly shapeless mass of raw 'material' until political structures or laws are initiated. Thus, like kingdoms, republics need a man of extraordinary ability to set them up. Machiavelli invokes the concept of a founder, or *lawgiver*, to explain how political communities exist at all. He cites the examples of Romulus (Rome), Solon (Athens) and Lycurgus (Sparta) as the quintessential founders and lawgivers (Machiavelli, 1974: 133). But while it takes a single person to form a constitution, it needs popular support to continue. 'If princes are superior to populaces in drawing up laws, codes of civil life, statutes and new institutions, the populace is so superior in sustaining what has been instituted that it indubitably adds to the glory of those who have instituted them' (Machiavelli, 1974: 256).[3]

Mixed government

Mixed government plays a central role in a well-ordered state. Machiavelli dismisses the traditional pure forms of monarchy, aristocracy and democracy as well as their deviant forms: 'the three good ones because their life is so short, the three bad ones because of their inherent malignity' (Machiavelli, 1974: 109). Instead of a single sovereign or a pure democracy, a mixed government provides better security for citizens, because it is stronger and can delay, if not quite avoid, the cycles to which governments are prone.

In fact what Machiavelli recommends is less an Aristotelian mixture of forms or functions of government than a largely informal Polybian balance of social classes or estates, specifically the people and the nobility, in which each restrains the other.

If either class rules alone, the process of decline will be quicker. Aristocrats are ambitious and avaricious, obsessed with extending their wealth and power over others: 'men are inclined to think that they cannot hold securely what they possess unless they get more at others' expense' (Machiavelli, 1974: 118). The ordinary people are less grasping; they want freedom rather than power over others. He distinguishes between the few who seek to be free in order to dominate others and 'the vast bulk of those who demand freedom, who desire but to live in security' (Machiavelli, 1974: 156). The ordinary people are less inclined to put sectional interests before the common good: 'The brutalities of the masses are directed against those whom they suspect of conspiring against the common good; the brutalities of a prince against those whom he suspects of conspiring against his own good' (Machiavelli, 1974: 257). Yet the people too are not wholly reliable; even if they do not want to expropriate the wealthy, they can have an excessive desire for freedom, and can fall for grandiose military adventures that turn out to be disastrous for freedom. Because the people oscillate between resenting power and desiring order, they need leadership.

Thus, against arguments that an aristocratic republic on the lines of Venice will survive longer, Machiavelli gives the republic a much more popular colour than Cicero would have accepted. A republic with mixed government in which power is tilted towards the people will be better at achieving the common good and ensuring freedom and glory than will either a monarchy or an aristocratic republic. (A republic with a more popular tilt will be best suited to expansion; one with a more aristocratic tilt will be better at holding its own.)

Looking for concord between factions is not the solution. On the contrary, factions can provide a constructive tension; in Rome the clashes between the plebs and the Senate produced the best policies. 'In every republic there are two dispositions, that of the populace and that of the upper class, and...all legislation favourable to liberty is brought about by the clash between them' (Machiavelli, 1974: 113). This cannot be harmonious, as even when they intend the common good, each faction interprets it differently, but the struggles between them favour freedom rather than endangering it. Even unruly street protests, the 'tumults' of the people, serve to limit the sense of power of officials and the upper class. Machiavelli abandons the civic humanist emphasis on harmony or *concordia* for a healthy tension in which different classes check one another in a vibrant, jostling republic.

Participation

Despite his belief in the people, Machiavelli is not arguing for a radical direct democracy on Athenian lines. Italian city-states were governed by a number of councils; he does not specify procedures involving the citizens in regular decisions, and seems to go along with the widespread administration of the city's business by a mixture of elected and appointed officials. 'In all states whatever be their form of government, the real rulers do not amount to more than forty or fifty citizens' (Machiavelli, 1974: 156).

It has been suggested that Machiavelli's citizen participates in service rather than decision-making, and in military rather than political service. (His own role in creating a Florentine militia was one of Machiavelli's proudest achievements.) Machiavelli's ordinary citizen is, on one account, 'less a man performing a certain role in a decision-making system than a man trained by civic religion and military discipline to devote himself to the *patria* and carry this spirit over to civic affairs, so that he conforms to the dual model of the Machiavellian innovator displaying *virtù* ...and the Aristotelian citizen attentive to the common good' (Pocock, 1975: 203).

But we should not underestimate the political role of citizens. There is considerable scope for popular involvement. To begin with, there should be equal opportunity: 'if they have virtue they will have a chance of becoming rulers' (Machiavelli, 1974: 280). Positions should be open to all on the basis of talent, without property or age restrictions. The people can propose measures and call leaders to account; they should be able to speak out freely, and to indict those suspected of offences that threaten the freedom of the state (but with severe penalties for false accusations). Citizens will choose magistrates, judge rulers, give opinion on policy issues and serve in the militia. The people can recognise and accept a good policy when it is put before them. The people have the valuable moderating force of experience: 'a wise man will not ignore public opinion in regard to particular matters, such as the distribution of offices and preferments, for here the populace when left to itself does not make mistakes' (Machiavelli, 1974: 228).

Thus in a properly constituted republic the people play a part in political life without ruling directly. In Machiavelli's words, they 'neither arrogantly dominate nor humbly obey' (Machiavelli, 1974: 253; my translation).

But another distinction needs to be made: that between a corrupt people and a virtuous one. The people are still corruptible, if less so than nobles. The clash between classes is only beneficial when each is promoting what they take to be the common good, rather than sectional interests (Machiavelli, 1974: 159). In a corrupt society people will lose sight of the common good. Under those circumstances the republic is threatened: 'a people which has become wholly corrupt cannot even for a moment enjoy its freedom' (Machiavelli, 1974:154). To sustain a free republic there must be virtuous citizens.

Virtue

Although freedom is a more important goal than virtue for Machiavelli, it thus depends crucially on the cultivation of virtue (in Italian, *virtù*), invoked repeatedly in his work. He draws on its established rhetorical power to support his argument that political freedom requires a dynamic approach to politics. Engaging in the debates on the virtues of leaders and citizens, he argues that political success is not necessarily compatible with otherwise admirable characteristics. Thus, while not denying the need for virtue in politics, he redefines it to denote a much narrower range of qualities, those which sustain political power, or, in the *Discorsi*, the institutions of a free republic.

The virtù *of princes* Machiavelli's most extensive and most often cited discussion of virtue appears in *The Prince*. Here it refers to the qualities needed to maintain a political leader's position. This is quite different from both Aristotle's all-round excellence and Cicero's public service. It is a dynamic self-reliance in military and political life displayed in an active character that can grasp opportunities and deal creatively with necessity, chance and unreliable humans. He portrays *Fortuna* as a woman who must be mastered by a successful prince. This highlights the masculine connotations of *virtù*, putting the *vir* back into *virtù*, so to speak. A central part of princely *virtù* is military prowess, courage, decisiveness and a readiness to do whatever it takes to achieve your purposes.

What was perhaps most shocking in this account to contemporaries was the way it relentlessly spelled out how princely *virtù* is incompatible with the Christian virtues. *Virtù* may require the opposite of what is conventionally regarded as good: 'some of the things that appear to be virtues will ruin him, and some of the things that appear to be vices will bring him security and prosperity' (Machiavelli, 1974: 92). Anyone who is conventionally good when others are not is liable to be trampled. Being honest and humble, keeping promises, showing generosity to subjects and compassion to enemies, these are admirable in their way, but lead to political disaster. So a prince must learn how *not* to be virtuous in the conventional sense. Being loved by subjects is less important than overawing them, and developing a reputation for determination and cruelty if necessary. Yet princes will need to pay lip service to the Christian virtues in order to be held in respect. Therefore *virtù* is intrinsically deceptive.

Machiavelli not only dissociates the *virtù* of a leader from the Christian virtues, but also further narrows down the pagan virtues that Cicero believed essential to success. He explicitly reworks Cicero when he says that a politician must at times act like both a lion and a fox, using force and fraud to stay in power (Machiavelli, 1974: 99). Princely courage is primarily understood in military terms; wisdom leans towards cunning; moderation is flexibility in response to circumstances, which sometimes needs drastic action, sometimes a waiting game. And the need for flexibility vis-à-vis *Fortuna* governs the application of the other virtues. It is not possible to plan for every eventuality, so those who can adapt to circumstances are best endowed.

Yet Machiavelli does not adopt a clearly immoralist, or amoral, stance. He does not deny the validity of Christian virtues. He makes it quite clear that these are worthy, and that it would be good if a prince could observe them. 'He should not deviate from what is good, if that is possible, but he should know how to do evil if that is necessary' (Machiavelli, 1974: 101). He condemns the practice of cruelty when it is not essential to maintain princely power. The problem is that you cannot pursue all goods simultaneously. There is a trade-off between the conventional virtues and success.

Thus, while *virtù* sometimes appears as the skill of a leader, it is not simply a morally neutral, technical 'virtuosity'. Success is not its own justification. Nor is it a realistic description of how politicians act in practice. This is an alternative, albeit narrower morality, a set of praiseworthy ideals of life, more reminiscent of heroic pagan warrior norms than either Ciceronian or Christian virtues (Berlin, 1982: 58). A man of *virtù* can be master of himself in an uncertain world; he uses power as a way to freedom (Grant, 1997: 154). But this is at the expense of repressing everything associated with the feminine outside and within himself (Pitkin, 1984).

Citizen virtù *in the* Discorsi   While different strengths are needed by those who set up states and those who maintain them, there is much in common between the qualities needed by princes and those of republican citizens. Founders of republics need exceptional *virtù*. But those turning to the *Discorsi* hoping to find a gentler or more deliberative account of republican politics will be disappointed. Republics too will be short-lived if they do not play tough, grasp fortune, take decisive action and change with the times. Because of the problem of corruption, creating and sustaining a republic is a heroic enterprise. The main guarantee of the security of a republic is the political and military activity of virtuous individuals. While princely *virtù* maintains princely power, citizen *virtù* maintains the republic. Thus it too is in tension with the Christian virtues; it cannot be understood in terms of humility or other-directed charity; it is not possible to be effective politically while being consistently compassionate, pious and honest.

Virtù is the core of an ideal of citizenship which requires people to put their country first, notably by limiting their pursuit of wealth, taking up office when needed, fighting in the militia, paying taxes, and deferring to the better qualified (Machiavelli, 1974: 225). In serving the common good, rather than their own narrow good, great citizens deserve and gain legitimate honour and glory.

Courage is central to this, and so is moderation in the sense of self-restraint and flexibility. But wisdom is mainly a matter of practical prudence, and justice, most strikingly of all, may have to be set aside when it clashes with the interests of the republic. Where Cicero saw justice as the most important virtue, Machiavelli claims that in emergencies the republic may not be able to take account of all individual claims to justice.

> When the safety of one's country wholly depends on the decision to be taken, no attention should be paid either to justice or injustice, to kindness or to cruelty, or to its being praiseworthy or ignominious. On the contrary, every other consideration being set aside, that alternative should be wholeheartedly adopted which will save the life and preserve the freedom of one's country.
>
> (Machiavelli, 1974: 515)

Actions are required in politics which are hard to conscience in ordinary life, ranging from betraying faith to exemplary killings. For Machiavelli, the benefits excuse (rather than justify) such necessary evils.

In this way Machiavelli definitively shifts the sense of *virtù* to a much more specifically *civic* virtue, which is sharply distinct from other senses.

Relating common and individual good

How does this *virtù* relate to the welfare or self-realisation of individuals? If *virtù* means acting to promote the common good, is this compatible with, or at the expense of, the good of individuals? (For Aristotle and Cicero, we saw that virtue was part of self-realisation, and individual and the common good were connected.)

Machiavelli sometimes suggests that in a republic the common good and individual interest coincide: 'in competition one with the other, men look both to their own advantage and to that of the public' (Machiavelli, 1974: 280). But elsewhere he speaks as if this *virtù*, unlike that of the prince, requires the self-sacrifice of individual acting citizens, since it is the survival of the republic that is at stake, not the power of the individual. Yet we should bear in mind that Machiavelli is not thinking in terms of a concept made familiar by Hobbes, an impersonal state with an existence over and above its citizens. For him the state and the citizens were still one and the same. So he is not asking citizens to sacrifice themselves for an entity over and above them (Skinner, 1989: 112).

However, he sometimes seems to identify the common good with the interest of the majority, or an aggregate of costs and benefits to citizens: 'however this or that private person may be the loser on this account, there are so many who benefit thereby that the common good can be realised in spite of those few who suffer in consequence' (Machiavelli, 1974: 275). Thus the interests of one or more citizens may be sacrificed for the good of the majority.

At one level, then, there is a tension between the demands of *virtù* and the particular interests of individuals in, for example, wealth, a quiet family life, comfort or convenience. But at another level the survival of a republic is a precondition for the secure enjoyment of any of these. The immediate costs of *virtù* are outweighed by the eventual benefits. In addition, *virtù* receives (or should receive) the reward of honour and glory. On this view, civic virtue is *logically* prior to other individual benefits; citizens must do their duty in order to achieve the long-term rewards it secures. *Virtù* is at best instrumentally valuable for individuals. Working for the common good is the necessary precondition of individual goods (Skinner, 1990: 304).

On another interpretation, what is involved in *virtù* is not so much foresight in realising self-interest, as a clearer vision of where your real advantage lies – in membership of a self-governing republic more than in individual benefits. Machiavelli's notorious statement that 'I love my country more than my soul' may be understood not as an expression of self-denial, but as an expanded view of what is central to the self – as: 'I see myself more as a citizen of Florence than as an individual Christian soul.' It involves identifying with a different community, as a different self. This interpretation sees a tension within each person between the immediately perceived particular advantage of individuals and the general interest of the citizen as an interdependent member of the polity. *Common goods* are the shared interests of members of a community (Pitkin, 1984: 95).

Here we can see in Machiavelli several of the distinct interpretations of the common good and the requirements of civic virtue which arise as issues for later republican theorists. Whichever of these interpretations we take, we can see that citizens will not always put the common good first, but will often be liable to be corrupt, to put short-term or narrower private interest ahead of *virtù*.

Shaping citizens

So republics must encourage *virtù* and minimise corruption. If people are not automatically civic-spirited, exhorting them to virtue will not be enough to change them. But *virtù* can be inculcated by incentives, in rewarding citizens for exceptional service to the state, and by the connected means of laws, education, military training, example and a civic religion: 'good examples proceed from good education, good education from good laws' (Machiavelli, 1974: 114).

Honour and glory are incentives that the state can employ to encourage citizens to perform their civic duties. So offices should be open to all, irrespective of background, age or wealth. But the legitimate ambition for honour and glory has a corrupt mirror image in false glory: someone like Julius Caesar, who pursues extravagant schemes with no clear aim or limit, may become famous, but does not deserve glory.

So laws play a dual role in the republic. The basic law is given by a lawgiver at the founding of a republic and provides the framework for citizens' freedom (Machiavelli, 1974: 246). Although without laws the people are less bad than a prince, as they are still easily corrupted quite extensive laws are needed to constrain human desires and deter wrongdoers (Machiavelli, 1974: 217). Clearly defined punishments must be imposed without respect for status, position or any previous contribution to the state (Machiavelli, 1974: 173). But laws do not just constrain citizens' behaviour through their sanctions; they also mould their characters: 'Hunger and poverty make men industrious and the laws make them good' (Machiavelli, 1974: 112). The exercise of legal authority is less objectionable than usurped or irregular exercises of power. In contrast with arbitrary power, the enforcement of an extensive system of law – 'such force as is employed by public authority which functions within specified limits' – is compatible with freedom (Machiavelli, 1974: 125). In extreme situations those who are hopelessly corrupt will need to be forced to act virtuously if there is to be any chance of reform.[4]

Citizens can also be educated by exposure to the examples of heroic men of great *virtù* whom they should emulate. But the key form of education is universal military training and continuing participation in the *citizen militia*. Bearing arms is a core duty. Through military discipline citizens learn courage and identify with the republic so they will be more prepared to sacrifice personal interests for the common good. A citizens' militia provides a more committed defence of their state than mercenaries, and their training will make them better citizens.

A *civic religion* like that of ancient Rome is also essential to inculcate *virtù*. This is a social use of religion to support the republic, which has nothing to do with transmitting true doctrines, as is made abundantly clear with respect to the inculcation of martial virtues. The idea of a higher power instils fear or shame in citizens; if they have sworn an oath to the gods, they will be slower to abandon their duty: 'Where there is religion it is easy to teach men to use arms' (Machiavelli, 1974: 140). Ceremonials bring the people together, and the regime gains added legitimacy if it can claim a divine hand in its origin.

Freedom

For Machiavelli, citizen *virtù* is justified in terms above all of freedom. A republic is preferable to other forms of government because it allows freedom from external rule and native aristocrats. Here again, freedom is contrasted to slavery: living in a free republic, citizens are not subject to the will of a tyrant. Citizens of a republic have a free way of life (*vivere libero*), which is a fragile condition that has to be achieved, and is not possessed naturally. Those who are free in this sense are neither wholly self-sufficient nor wholly dependent on a ruler.

Machiavelli, like his contemporaries, believed that humans can choose to shape their destiny to some extent. He explicitly breaks with the Aristotelian tradition in which the general ends of human life are hierarchically predetermined by human nature. In the absence of such a teleological account of human nature, the citizens of the self-governing republic may legitimately pursue a variety of life-goals, such as moderate money-making, military glory or a quiet family life (Machiavelli, 1974: 280). Where, for Aristotle, freedom is subordinate to the virtues determined by objective human goods, in this perspective freedom can become the focal value, because the goods pursued in politics are not predetermined by nature. They are determined by the particular historical people who form the republic.

However, what Machiavelli means by freedom needs further explication. The account of law, military discipline and education shows that even this opportunity to pursue diverse ends does not imply minimal government. It is possible both to be free and to be subject to laws.

Machiavelli's account of freedom can be construed in a number of ways, each of which has grounds in his writings, though none is fully developed:

Self-mastery At one extreme, Machiavelli sometimes aligns freedom with radical independence, self-sufficiency, or the mastery of the man of extraordinary *virtù*. This is the ideal for princes or founders; it is more like power than freedom, and it cannot be a possibility for interacting citizens, as it denies interdependence (Pitkin, 1984: 22, 323–4).

Proto-fascism At the other extreme, it sometimes appears as if the freedom of the republic rather than that of the citizens is at stake. Citizens are seen (at least some of the time) as 'material' being organised by a founder, shaped by laws, drilled in the militia, and

Machiavelli and Harrington

overawed if not indoctrinated by civic religion. They can even be subject intermittently to the arbitrary rule of dictators. Diversity must be limited: 'the aim of a republic is to deprive all other corporations and to weaken them' (Machiavelli, 1974: 280). Does this distort the word beyond reasonable limits, evoking an Orwellian 'freedom is slavery'? This makes participation look more like top-down mobilisation of citizens than their actively determining their destiny. In this case dependence on individuals seems to be replaced by dependence on the republic as a whole. But this position may reflect the measures needed in the most corrupt republics, rather than the ideal realisation of freedom (Pitkin, 1984: 19).

These conceptions are not the only ones that emerge in the *Discorsi*. There are also more substantial ideas of freedom that take account both of social interdependence and of the plurality of goals that humans may pursue in life. These ideas hinge on Machiavelli's description of free citizens who neither arrogantly dominate nor humbly serve.

Non-interference Stating that men can be free in a republic only if they are not corrupt, he may imply that citizenship is the precondition for a life free of the arbitrary impositions and extractions of a tyrant. Thus freedom is a matter of 'the possibility of enjoying what one has, freely and without incurring suspicion...the assurance that one's wife and children will be respected, the absence of fear for oneself' (Machiavelli, 1974: 154). On this basis, it may be suggested that freedom should be understood in negative terms, as the non-interference that citizens enjoy, rather than the political activity that makes it possible (Skinner, 1990: 306). But it should be noted that this does not guarantee any specific area of non-interference, and is not expressed in terms of rights.

Non-domination A variation on this interpretation suggests that freedom is the *security* from the danger of personal domination and dependence that laws and institutions guarantee, rather than the simple fact of non-interference. Only in a republic with strong laws and virtuous citizens can the citizens reliably avoid arbitrary incursions on their persons, family and property. Instead of mastery, here freedom is defined in terms of secure 'non-mastery' (Pettit, 1997a: 71).

Mutual self-rule We have seen that another strand in Machiavelli hints at a more 'participatory republican'. If interdependence is taken seriously, what is involved in neither arrogantly dominating nor humbly serving may need to involve some participation in mutual self-rule, more akin to Aristotle's 'ruling and being ruled in turn', which allows that the people may collectively gain more control of their destiny than as individuals. Whereas an individual may be free in one sense if left to himself, it may be argued that his freedom is extended when he has a say in decisions made collectively. Here, participating in political activity itself becomes an important aspect of freedom (Pitkin, 1984: 324–7).

Machiavelli does not definitively adopt any one of these accounts of freedom; they represent alternative approaches that are reflected in later expressions of republican freedom.

The material preconditions for political equality

Unlike a monarchy, which can successfully accommodate an aristocratic class of landed gentry, a republic needs to be based on relative economic and social equality (Machiavelli, 1974: 248). But Machiavelli does not advance a consistent argument on how the state should deal with wealth and inequalities.

Extravagant wealth and wide economic divisions are dangerous, but a republic is not hostile to all trade and business (Machiavelli, 1974: 247). Greater prosperity, and the chance of passing on an inheritance to one's children, are specific benefits citizens can expect to reap from living in a free republic. But flamboyant wealth and luxury encourage idleness and increase envy. So he recommends austerity: 'well-ordered republics have to keep the public rich but the citizens poor' (Machiavelli, 1974: 201). In part this is a matter of limiting inequalities, and reducing the political effects of wealth. The demand for riches is reduced when people know that poverty is not a bar to office (Machiavelli, 1974: 475). Conversely, ambitious men should not be able to rise to power by doing services for private individuals (Machiavelli, 1974: 482). However, an agrarian law, setting a maximum on land holdings or distributing enemies' land among the citizens, does more harm than good. It destabilised Roman politics, disrupting the constructive tension of classes and ultimately leading to the downfall of the republic. In consequence the republic needs to promote austerity and to limit conspicuous wealth rather than to introduce broad redistributive measures to create greater material equality.

The intensity and scope of the republic

A republic is a particular unit, in which citizens are committed to a place and people, and the way of life that they share in the city-state. This patriotism is more particular than an abstract loyalty to republican institutions in general, or instrumental obedience to a regime which protects their personal security and prosperity. The love of liberty that Machiavelli sees as essential to a republic is an attachment to the *vivero libero*, the specific republican practices that they share and defend together.

Republics do not have to be confined to a small city-state. In fact, expansion is one of the options for continuing to flourish. A more democratically inclined republic will need and be better suited to grow (Machiavelli, 1974: 284). Otherwise it cannot remain self-sufficient or militarily secure: 'It is impossible for a state to remain for ever in the peaceful enjoyment of its liberties and its narrow confines' (Machiavelli, 1974: 335). Even if a republic does not have designs on others' territories, its neighbours will see it as a potential threat. In addition, citizens need the opportunities given by expansion to realise their ambitions. Although he considers the issue tactically rather than ethically, this expansion should come through confederation and alliances with other states and establishing colonies, rather than through imperial conquest. Membership of the republic is potentially extensible to outsiders, though newly incorporated citizens should be taken in on initially less favourable terms. Although always speaking within the Italian context, Machiavelli does not define citizenship in intrinsically cultural or racial terms.[5] But one should not downplay the level of imperialist domination that may be entailed in this expansion.

In conclusion then, Machiavelli advances a theory of republican government in which the freedom of citizens depends on their practising civic virtue.

In this view, political life is not itself necessarily the highest realisation of human nature, but it offers the possibility of achieving glory and freedom (either in itself or as security to realise other ends). Corruption is the primary problem which must be guarded against in individuals, laws and states. Citizens must perform military and political service and be prepared to accept some cost to their personal interests as a precondition of realising wider or more varied interests.

He introduces a notion of citizen *virtù* which assumes at least a potential gap between some private personal interests and the public interest of the political community. Compared with Aristotle or Cicero's accounts, this notion of *virtù* is narrower and more focused on the dynamic and militaristic dimensions of virtue and citizenship. Freedom is still understood primarily in terms of a contrast to slavery, which depends on a strong frame of laws and on the participation of citizens. This is sustained through active citizenship, and depends on the practice of civic *virtù*, in putting the good of the whole before particular goods.

So Machiavelli may be seen as offering just two cheers for participation. Political participation is not necessarily the highest realisation of human nature, though it makes possible other dimensions. And popular involvement is more a matter of public opinion and meritocratic opportunity than of continuing equal voice. But it is compatible with a fairly high level of political conflict, and does not depend on the achievement of harmony.

While civic humanists optimistically believed that conventionally virtuous citizens could live in harmony, Machiavelli's formulation of classical republicanism sees political life as fundamentally divided and tragic. Civic *virtù* requires certain sacrifices and great determination in the face of forces that doom all political solutions to ultimate failure. 'Men may second their fortune, but cannot oppose it;…they may weave its warp, but cannot break it…Since there is hope, they should not despair, no matter what fortune brings or in what travail they find themselves' (Machiavelli, 1974: 372). If the ancients saw political life as a way out of the futility of a life tied to material needs, Machiavelli recognises the momentary nature of political solutions, while still seeing it as an attempt that it is important to make.

Machiavelli laid out the framework of ideas within which subsequent republican thought developed. Corruption, rather than government power, was taken to be the central problem of politics. Virtue in the service of freedom, mixed government, and an active citizenry shaped by laws, became the core features of the resolution proposed by republican thinkers.

In the twilight of Renaissance republicanism, he advanced an uncompromising, heroic and muscular version of republican theory. A 'republican for hard times', he died in exile shortly before the republic was finally extinguished when the Medicis returned and consolidated their power as Grand Dukes of Tuscany (Pitkin, 1984: 19).

This left Venice and Switzerland as the principal remaining examples of a republic in the modern world; one aristocratic, but enduring, the other made up of small, isolated communities.

Harrington

Historical context

In other parts of Europe conflicts about sovereignty gave rise to political debates in which republican thinking took a different form. In seventeenth-century England a power struggle between King and Parliament and bitter conflicts over religious freedom and establishment led to a protracted civil war and the execution of King Charles I. When the king was dead, a republic, or 'commonwealth' (then the standard English translation of *res publica*) came about almost by accident. But while there had been a ferment of debate on the nature and limits of kingly power, and on the scope of citizenship, there had been little systematic thinking on the shape of a republic.

By 1656, when James Harrington (1611–77) wrote *Oceana*, many thinkers had pursued the question how, if at all, freedom and political rule can coexist. Thinkers tended increasingly to represent government as artificial, and as derived from a contract of free and equal rights-bearing individuals in a pre-political state of nature. But they derived very diverse conclusions on the proper form of government. Some advocated surrendering freedom, rights and political voice to a strong sovereign in order to guarantee peace – a view expressed most spectacularly by Hobbes in his *Leviathan*, published in 1651. Others argued for limited government and distinguished the political rights that could be entrusted to government from the inalienable rights of life, liberty and property, most famously in John Locke's *Two Treatises on Government* of the 1680s.

Harrington's solution to the problem was quite different: it was a defence of republican freedom and active citizenship.[6] He advocated a free self-governing republic, in which all are subject to laws which they play a part in making. This would be 'an empire of laws and not of men' (Harrington, 1992: 8). He consciously drew on classical inspiration and praised Machiavelli as 'the onely polititian of later ages', who had followed classical writers to defend 'ancient prudence' – rule for the common good rather than in the interests of the powerful few (Harrington, 1992: 10). For all its classical trappings, Harrington's republican theory addressed the particular circumstances of an England in which the House of Lords had been abolished, the House of Commons reduced to a compliant shadow of its former self, and power was exercised by Oliver Cromwell as Lord Protector, who stopped just short of becoming King. *Oceana* is a plan for the republic that England could be; a republic in a large territorial state of mainly rural landowning citizens; it is dedicated to Oliver Cromwell as much as a warning against arbitrary rule as an invitation to found such a republic.

Harrington's republicanism is a theory of the freedom of citizens under the rule of law and relies as heavily on strong institutions of mixed government as on an active, independent and virtuous citizenry.

Interdependence and dependence

Harrington displays a heightened awareness of the ways in which people are vulnerable to domination by others, so that their freedom is interdependent. Citizens share a common fate, and can collectively shape their destiny. Destructive forms of dependence come about through economic inequality and political domination. Citizens can be free only if they can construct and operate a political society in which these are limited.

Harrington emphasises the relationship between economic and political power. He sees the ownership of property as essential for the capacity for independent citizenship. Only an independent property holder, on however small a scale, can escape being dependent on others. A republic is feasible only if property is widely distributed among citizens; otherwise they are open to the influence of patrons. But this is the case in England since, under previous monarchs, land has come to be more widely distributed. The system of monarchical government was based on feudal landownership and is now anachronistic; the current balance of property favours a republican form of government.

In addition to individual dependence, the people as a whole may become dependent on the goodwill of a ruler who has arbitrary power. People are politically interdependent in their common exposure to the power of rulers. The freedom of each depends on their ability to come together within structures that foreclose on arbitrary power. Human beings can be free only if they live in a state under fixed laws that they have made themselves, and are not subject to the will of any individual.

In order to live together harmoniously, people must be virtuous. Virtue is a matter of recognising and acting according to these common interests. Human actions are not predestined by the will of God, as much religious belief at the time suggested, nor driven by passions, as scientific accounts were beginning to suggest. They are capable of acting well or badly, and circumstances and education play a substantial role in shaping their behaviour. People collectively can creatively shape their destiny. Harrington designs a set of political institutions to elicit virtue, protect independent citizens from the domination of others, and balance the need for efficiency and experience against the need to distribute political power widely.

The possibility of a commonwealth: the major attack on republican thinking

Harrington's first concern is to defend republics against the criticisms levelled at them by Hobbes. Hobbes attacks from a social contract perspective in which naturally free and pre-social humans are motivated by self-interest, and will engage in destructive conflict unless they agree to surrender their rights to a sovereign. Though not all contractarians share Hobbes's assumption of universal self-interest or absolutist conclusions, his criticisms go to the heart of the difference between contractarians and republicans, so they are worth considering in some detail. Hobbes criticises republican political arguments and their underlying assumptions, and is fully aware of their Aristotelian origins.[7] To begin with he denies that humans are naturally social or political. They are not gregarious animals because they compete for honour and dignity as well as for material resources. Second, unlike bees and ants for whom individual and common good are the same, humans are only concerned about their own private good, which depends in part on being better-off than others. Whereas Aristotle rooted political community in the human capacity to have conceptions of good and evil, for Hobbes each person identifies good and evil differently with their own pleasures and pains, so that this cannot be the basis of community. In addition, humans are always critical of their governments, and use language misleadingly to stir up discontent among others (Hobbes, 1968: 225-6). Consequently there will always tend to be conflict. Accordingly he argues that harmonious collective self-government is an unattainable illusion. Those who want peace and prosperity should agree to subject themselves to an absolute sovereign to resolve disputes (Hobbes, 1968: 226). In the interests of peace, the dangerous passion for honour should be subordinated to the desire for material prosperity. Virtue should be seen as nothing more than outward behaviour that allows peaceful co-existence (Hobbes, 1968: 216).

Next Hobbes argues that a republic such as Lucca may be free, but that does not mean its citizens are any freer than subjects of a regime, such as Constantinople, ruled by the sultan (Hobbes, 1968: 266). For he defines freedom in a negative sense, simply as the absence of interference with motion. The freedom which people naturally possess outside states is necessarily reduced by laws within states. So free republics do not guarantee the liberty of particular men. Citizens are no freer than subjects of a monarch; in either case any freedom they enjoy depends on the absence, or the 'silence', of law in any area.

In recommending sovereignty, he rejects the very idea that there are good and bad forms of government, apart from feelings of the observer. Tyranny and oligarchy 'are not the names of other formes of government, but of the same formes misliked' (Hobbes, 1968: 240). Moreover, he rejects the very idea of mixed government (Hobbes, 1968: 372). Any division in power weakens it; a good government is simply one that provides security and a bad government one that allows anarchy.

Republican freedom: the empire of laws and not of men

Harrington responds that individual freedom *is* greater in a free state or republic than in a monarchy because individuals are not subject to the arbitrary will of the ruler. While neither citizens in

Lucca nor subjects in Constantinople are free *from the law*, those in Lucca gain immunity *by the law* from the power of a ruler. By contrast the most privileged subject of a king or sultan retains his life only as long as it suits the ruler: 'the greatest bashaw is but a tenant of his head' in Constantinople, because the law depends only on the ruler's will (Harrington, 1992: 20). A subject's life and possessions are literally at the discretion of the monarch. Being subject to law is *not* the same as being subject to another person. In a republic laws express the common good. 'There is a common right, law of nature or interest of the whole which is more excellent and so acknowledged to be by the agents themselves than the right or interest of the parts only' (Harrington, 1992: 21). The liberty of the commonwealth goes hand-in-hand with the liberty of the citizens, 'the liberty not only of the commonwealth but of every man' (Harrington, 1992: 19).

But the existence of an objective set of laws (or constitutional rights) does not protect citizens from arbitrary rule; they must somehow participate in 'framing' the laws. Citizens are free in so far as they participate in making the laws, in a process that ensures that no individual or political figure can direct the law. Laws are 'framed by every private man under no other end...than to protect the liberty of every private man, which by that means comes to be the liberty of the commonwealth' (Harrington, 1992: 20).

Freedom is incompatible with dependence on another's will, not with interference *per se*. Laws may interfere with someone, but, in contrast to domination by another person, this is not incompatible with freedom. In a republic, all are subject to law; but being subject to law is quite different for those who have a say in making the law from those subject to arbitrary decrees.

Thus there is greater freedom in a republic because it is 'an empire of laws and not of men'. This freedom is not a natural possession of individuals, but is achieved in a well-constructed state. Harrington goes on to design a system in which citizens can participate and law be equitably formed even in a modern territorial state with a large population.

Institutions

Compared with Machiavelli, Harrington places emphasis on the role of institutions more than on the character of citizens in maintaining a free republic, and argues that if a state gets its institutions right, it may last indefinitely. These institutions are designed to encourage the virtuous side of citizens and to allow them to participate in politics without pressure on their independence. Next to the general primacy of law, the key institutions are a system of mixed government, an agrarian law limiting economic inequality, a civil religion and education, and a citizen militia. These institutions are multiply interconnected in that citizens gather together in parish units for purposes of taxation, military drill, and the lottery and election of representatives (Harrington, 1992: 97–8).

Mixed government

First Harrington describes a complex machinery of mixed government to ensure the sharing of power. Here this means distinguishing two institutions according to the functions of debate and decision, rather than balancing social classes. There are two houses of parliament: a senate and a popular assembly. In contrast to parliament at that time, these exist continuously and are subject to frequent elections. The property qualification to be elected to either house is small (for the senate, only half the actual qualification for voting in the 1650s). One-third of the senate is re-elected each year, and there is a compulsory resting period between periods in office. Experience is thus carried over between parliaments, but the same people cannot monopolise power continuously. There is no permanent landed aristocracy because, as we shall see, the amount of property anyone can inherit is restricted by law.

Harrington provides for representation more because in a large state the citizens constitute too large a body to assemble than because some are not capable of participating. He does not explicitly exclude the majority of citizens from participation, or establish a permanent aristocracy or class of the virtuous. Citing Aristotle and Machiavelli on the value of many opinions, Harrington emphasises that participation should be widely open (Harrington, 1992: 166), and that upward mobility should be possible on a meritocratic basis – 'where a man from the lowest cannot rise...the commonwealth is not equal' (Harrington, 1977: 677).

While Harrington provides for formal participation, he does not welcome popular mass interventions in politics outside the normal channels. He does not allow for popular initiatives. He anticipates and advocates a more harmonious picture than Machiavelli, and sees no place for 'tumults' among his rural, landowning citizens. Those who are by definition subject to the will of another, servants, are excluded from citizenship. Women too, in so far as they are dependent on the will of their father or husband, are also excluded by implication.[8]

In a complex series of procedures, representatives are chosen in a multi-stage process, partly by the aristocratic device of election and partly by the democratic device of lot. Harrington takes this process of ballot to be one of the two fundamental laws of the republic. Here Harrington cites the example of Venice extensively. Secrecy of the ballot promotes independence. There is regular rotation, especially among electors, but also in office, as much to provide for widespread participation as to ensure that all interests are represented. Thus citizens are as much like ancient citizens taking turns in office as representatives in the modern sense.

But a kind of natural aristocracy of wisdom and virtue will condense in the senate, as the people will defer to virtue in elections. The two assemblies have different roles: deliberation and decision. The senate deliberates on the issues arising in every matter and proposes measures. The popular assembly then takes policy decisions without further debate. This is not because there is anything inherently unrepublican about deliberation, but because actual decisions need to be insulated from various kinds of illegitimate influence. The whole process is designed to restrict the danger of biased decisions by neutralising divergent interests. It operates in the same way, he says, as the 'you cut and I'll choose' procedure for sharing a cake fairly (Harrington, 1992: 22). On the cake-cutting principle, those who deliberate (senate) and those who choose (popular assembly) should be separate. This form of mixed government reconciles diverse interests, combines wisdom with interest, and provides stability.

The material pre-conditions of political equality: the agrarian law

For Harrington the constitution of the laws according to the common good requires that citizens can act independently of the influence or pressure of others. Anyone who has not got independent means of support must be a servant, subject to another. Only those who have independent means can be free men capable of citizenship.

This means that citizens must be property owners, at least on a modest scale. As well as slavery and political subjection, economic inequality presents a major threat to political independence. He cites Aristotle in support of the belief that people who are super-rich threaten the stability of the republic (Harrington, 1992: 14). Equality undermines monarchy but is the life and soul of a commonwealth.

The second fundamental law in Harrington's republic addresses the problematic effects of economic inequality on the political independence of citizens. To prevent the very wealthy having a destabilising influence requires measures that limit economic inequality, not just the use of economic power. The Roman device of an agrarian law can support a republic of equals. No one may inherit land worth more than £2000 per annum. This prevents anyone accumulating a fortune large enough to distort the balance of political power over generations.

This is not so much a proto-marxist analysis of the economic roots of political power as a normative argument that political power should be distributed to reflect the change in land ownership that made men potentially politically independent. Although Harrington's proposal is couched in historical terms, that economic power has changed the basis of politics, its force is an argument for the wider distribution of property on political grounds in order to guarantee an independent citizenry. For example, he suggests the redistributive effects of an agrarian law on Scotland, where the land is still monopolised by the nobility (Harrington, 1992: 211).

Virtue and corruption

But in addition to institutional provisions, virtue is an important part of the solution, if one less lengthily discussed. Even a republic with highly institutionalised safeguards against bias requires the support of virtuous citizens. Though natural inclinations are neither irredeemably bad nor reliably good, virtue can be elicited relatively easily by the right institutions, and is shaped by circumstances and education: 'good orders make evil men good, and bad orders make good men evil' (Harrington, 1992: 274).[9] It does not require heroic self-sacrifice against the odds. Thus Harrington calls on institutions, not only to balance self-interest but also to inculcate virtue.

Virtue consists essentially in the exercise of reason over the passions. It thus moves further away from Aristotle's notion of habit, or educated passions. There is a natural tension between, on the one hand, particular passions, and on the other, reason and the common good. But it does not require repressing nature, since reason is one part of nature which can be stronger than the passions and can lead men to agree. Virtue is aligned with the real interests identified by reason, and conforms with the common good. Harrington's understanding of virtue is more conventional than Machiavelli's, and shows more continuity with Christian and conventional moral virtues.

But he distrusts the claims of contemporary religious fanatics or 'saints' to represent virtue (Harrington, 1992: 63) and to impose it on others. There cannot be a commonwealth of saints, relying on the infallible virtue of citizens (or at least of the most virtuous). Even apparently good citizens should be subject to law. The experience of Protestant faith had also taught that virtue in the largest sense cannot be produced by coercion. He followed Milton, for whom virtue is only possible in freedom, and focused his attention on providing for this freedom.[10]

As institutions are the key to virtue, they are affected more seriously than citizens by corruption: 'the people never die, nor as a political body are subject unto any other corruption than that which derive from their government' (Harrington, 1992: 218). This is not as intractable a problem as it was for Machiavelli. Interpersonal dependence presents a more serious problem than intrapersonal partial inclinations. A state's corruption is a function of its institutions and rulers: 'the vices of people are from their governors' (Harrington, 1992: 196).

The weaknesses of individual citizens will not be enough to destroy a properly constituted republic: 'for as man is sinful but yet the world is perfect, so may the citizen be sinful and yet the commonwealth be perfect' (Harrington, 1992: 218). Though Harrington refers to corruption in terms of sin, it is less a matter of confirmed and deliberate evil than of human imperfection and unreliability. Citizens who are neither irretrievably evil, nor heroically virtuous, may still enjoy freedom in a republic.

Shaping citizens

Civic religion   Harrington advocates a civic religion to serve several purposes. First, it unites the citizens, and avoids the subversive potential of independent religions. Second, it frees citizens from inherently dominating and authoritarian forms of religion.

This civic religion is more a matter of organisation and structure than doctrinal matters. Harrington is aware of the great variety within Christianity, and he does not wholly condemn its effects on political life. Clerical authority (for which he coined the term 'priestcraft') presents a greater danger than any religious belief. To preclude it, there needs to be a religion which makes no claims to mystical powers, excludes clerics from political power, and does not dismiss worldly concerns. This creates not so much a secular and rational religion as a commonwealth of believers. Like Machiavelli, Harrington distinguishes true and corrupt religion, and looks back – in this case to the early Christian church – for a model of elected ministers or the priesthood of all believers. Rather than replacing Christianity with Roman religion, this combines features of both. The state church is run by the laity and elected ministers, and dovetails with the state framework, as the parish is the basis of taxation, election and military levy. It is established in the universities, but adherents of other, non-subversive religions should enjoy freedom of conscience (Harrington, 1992: 202).

Civic education   As well as being guaranteed by formal procedures, virtue is more deeply instilled by a state education, which shapes individuals into citizens: 'the formation of the citizen in the womb of the commonwealth is his education' (Harrington, 1992: 197). Civic education pre-empts the dangers of clerical influence. All citizens are to receive a free education up to the age of fifteen. Thereafter specialised professional and religious training in justice, wisdom and courage are given state support in the law courts, university and militia.

Civic militia   In practice the central part of education is training in the militia, to encourage citizens to be brave and energetic and seek glory on behalf of the republic (Harrington, 1992: 206). Harrington's citizen, like Machiavelli's, has a duty to defend the republic. This is at least in part an armed citizenry, which chooses its political representatives when mustered locally for military drilling. But, although he envisages expansion, he does not value war and military virtue for its own sake as much as in the interests of maintaining peace.

Intensity and scope of the republic

The republic is a necessarily specific solution to the human predicament for one group of citizens. The citizens recognise that they share a common good, which they will be prepared to defend. It is a moral community, or 'stopping point', which forms a natural limit to loyalty and obligation: 'A man may devote himself to death or destruction to save a nation, but no nation will devote itself to death or destruction to save mankind' (Harrington, 1992: 286–7).

Thus the bonds that exist between citizens are to particular others; there can be no republic of all mankind. But while the republic requires unity and loyalty, it does not depend on a pre-political uniformity of religious belief or cultural homogeneity. And Harrington believes (like Machiavelli) that the commonwealth must expand, be a 'commonwealth for increase': 'If your liberty be not a root that grows, it will be a branch that withers' (Harrington, 1977: 329). He expresses this as a mission to extend republican liberty and freedom of conscience to other still-feudal tyrannies. And such expansion can take place without having destabilising internal repercussions. Apart from this, he envisages expansion more through the establishment of colonies in further-flung parts of the world than as a matter of competition for domination or territorial control between neighbouring states.

Classical republicanism

In this phase of republicanism, human interdependence is taken to mean that a good life is possible only in a free state, without external rule or an internal tyrant. Freedom exists and can be sustained only in a republic of virtuous citizens, who are prepared at times to put public good ahead of private interest. This requires active participation in civic life, the performance of duties in the form of military service, some part in decision-making, and a degree of self-restraint. For Machiavelli and Harrington, participation may be for many preponderantly a matter of military service, and a commitment to serving the common good more often than active involvement in decision-making. For Machiavelli, citizen *virtù* is more important than institutional design, though a tension between social classes is a key factor in maintaining the republic.

Where Machiavelli stresses the centrality of a narrow idea of *virtù*, Harrington has a more conventional idea of virtue, but its role is reduced by the greater importance of elaborate institutions which elicit virtue and promote the common good. For both, systems of civic education, religion and military training are essential to virtue. Economic inequality also threatens political freedom and needs to be restricted. Corruption, not conflict or excessive governmental power, is the key political problem from this perspective. The principal safeguard against it is, for Machiavelli, (often heroic) virtue; for Harrington it is the rule of law made by the citizens. But neither saw the citizenry as extending to the whole population. Both assumed that there would be those who were naturally dependent, and thus incapable of citizenship. This included women, and, for Harrington, also those who lacked property of any description.

This phase of republicanism may be seen as 'neo-Roman', having a closer affiliation to Roman than Greek antecedents, but there are many common strands with Aristotelian thought. There are stronger arguments for a degree of popular participation than the Roman example provided; freedom is not just a legal status, but is more explicitly connected with participation, whether instrumentally or more substantially. In addition, the emphasis on the capacity of the people for rule, the role of deliberation and the idea of virtue as the habitual orientation of citizens to the common good, as well as the role of law and education in shaping citizens, display Aristotelian influences.

But virtue, narrowly defined, is here in the service of freedom, which, on one interpretation at least, is guaranteed by, rather than identical to, participation. For Harrington the meaning of virtue is closer to freedom, and consequently corruption is closer to dependence. It is the direct ancestor of the notion of public spirit, an active commitment to duty that goes beyond what is required by law.

Both see expansion as necessary to the success of a republic, though Harrington is more optimistic than Machiavelli on the prospects for enduring republican freedom. Machiavelli wrote when the republics of Italy were about to fall finally under aristocratic control, and Harrington wrote *Oceana* in part as a satire on the autocratic republic of Cromwell's England, which was succeeded by the restoration of the monarchy under Charles II.

After Machiavelli and Harrington

These classical republican thinkers emphasised freedom as politically created through the participation of virtuous citizens. Neither Machiavelli nor Harrington used the language of natural rights in their account of freedom. This contrasts sharply with the emerging contractarian theories which define freedom in terms of the natural rights of pre-social, or pre-political human beings. Social contract thinkers increasingly saw the purpose of government as securing these rights. The emphasis shifted towards the *consent* of citizens *to* government, rather than their active participation *in* government, and towards obedience to law, rather than civic virtue, as the basis of political life.

Yet the age of English republicanism developed after Harrington, especially with the renewed conflicts over kingly powers after the restoration of the monarchy in 1660. But the dominant discourse of natural rights and contract could be grafted on to it. This was notable in the work of Algernon Sidney, whose radically republican *Discourses* led to his execution in 1683. Subsequently, many different combinations of the elements of civic republican and contractarian thought were to be produced. After Sidney, republicans increasingly amalgamated arguments based on natural rights and liberty with arguments for self-rule and virtue.

In practice, however, the most successful republic to which defenders of freedom looked was the Dutch republic of the federated United Provinces which had consolidated from the uprising of the people against Spanish rule. There, a form of mixed government emerged with a quasi-monarchical figure, the *Stadtholder*, or Prince of Orange, at its head. This republic was noted more for its religious and personal freedoms than its participatory character. And it played a significant role in the international 'republic of letters' as the centre of printing for works by thinkers from Locke to Rousseau and beyond, who could not publish their writings in less-tolerant states.

In England after the revolution of 1688, the power of the monarchy was constitutionally limited. Many people were thenceforth prepared to understand freedom as guaranteed by constitutional restrictions on arbitrary power, rather than by participation in shaping the laws. This freedom could be expressed in terms of non-domination rather than mutual self-determination. In the dominant strand of the Whig tradition, freedom gradually moved further away from the idea of participating in shaping the laws. In a sense, the idea that those who are subject to laws should make them was superseded by the idea that those who make the law should be subject to it. Only a minority of diehards, known as 'true Whigs' or 'commonwealthmen', stuck to the idea that freedom required self-rule in the sense of a say in the laws to which they were subject.[11] Such arguments were expressed especially with reference to the subordination of Ireland and Scotland to the English Parliament. Even these sought this participation for a limited class. But republican arguments were deployed also against the increasing power that governments sought to exercise through standing armies, public patronage and the use of financial credit to avoid parliamentary control. Republican issues came to the fore again in the English-speaking world only when some of the king's subjects in the American colonies came to resist what they perceived as the arbitrary nature of the exercise of metropolitan power.

At the same time, an alternative, non-republican account of freedom began to emerge, where the alternative to tyranny requires not the active participation of citizens, but limiting the powers of government. These limits are justified by an account of freedom as a natural property of individuals, rather than being politically constituted and realised. The question becomes what kind of freedom, and how much freedom, a citizen can retain in society. For John Locke (1632–1704) in *Two Treatises of Government*, political society is based on a contractual agreement of rights-bearing individuals with the intention of better securing those rights. They surrender the political right to exercise authority, and entrust it to government. Government is to protect the individual rights of life, liberty and property (in a broad sense); and its legitimacy rests on the *consent* of citizens, not on their participation. On this account, if government promotes the common good, that good is understood more narrowly as the protection of liberty and property (Locke, 1963: 398). Although law promotes freedom, it does so by limiting arbitrary power, not through the virtuous participation of citizens. Moreover, the delimitation of areas of government power and inalienable rights creates the foundations for the distinctively liberal public–private distinction between what may, and what may not, be controlled by the state. This is paradigmatically different from the republican distinction between private and public interest (which we have seen in Machiavelli).[12]

CHAPTER III

Participation and Inclusion in the Extensive Republic

Rousseau, Wollstonecraft and Madison

Introduction

> If the republican past was not to become irrelevant it would have to be imaginatively recreated or to be explicitly replaced by a new expansive republicanism to fit the modern political world.
>
> (Shklar, 1990: 266–7)

By the middle of the eighteenth century, the range of conceivable political alternatives tended to narrow down to despotism and republicanism. Rapid political and economic change had brought about a world of larger, more populous states than those in which republican thought had emerged. Ever-growing commerce was increasingly replacing land as the basis of wealth. It was widely assumed that modern states, like older empires, would have to be governed on autocratic lines; thus despotism was justified on the pragmatic grounds of efficiency or 'enlightened' government rather than in terms of supernatural divine right or natural authority.

In opposition to autocratic governments in Europe and America, however, a kaleidoscope of republican views attempted to grapple with the problem of adapting the republic to modern conditions. The focal issue here is *participation*, or broadening the republic to admit large numbers to equal citizenship. This called for new ways of thinking about how to be free under government. I focus here on a few of the key expressions that laid new ground and decisively changed the shape of future republican argument. These are the foundational ideas advanced by Montesquieu; the work of Rousseau and Madison, whose legacies were two widely diverging strands of republicanism; and the ideas of Wollstonecraft who, though less immediately influential than the others, brought women as active citizens into republican theory for the first time. In all these accounts, freedom is the central value, though its meaning varies from security to autonomy. Virtue is increasingly discounted or identified with freedom, as a less heroic and less militaristic republican ideal emerges.

Rousseau creates a benchmark by outlining an ideal participatory republic of virtuous and equal citizens as the minimum condition for freedom from personal dependence. But he is pessimistic about its feasibility in a modern world marked by progressive corruption, inequality and dependence. Madison in contrast produces a revolutionary and optimistic new model in which the institutional innovations of representation, federation and separation of powers allow a republic of free self-governing citizens.

Historical context: expanding commercial societies

Republican thinking now emerged in a remarkable variety of interrelated contexts, among them England, Scotland, Ireland, the American colonies and France. In each of these the effects of commerce and state power were differently experienced. Debates on commerce were especially focused in France and Scotland. While classical thinkers and symbols were extensively invoked in all these debates, there was a growing sense of distance from the ancient world. The view of history which had now come to prevail was a single uni-directional process, whether of progress or decline (in place of the classical vision of cycles). Moreover, the relationship between society and politics was differently understood; instead of politics constructing society, social developments were seen as specifying the limiting conditions within which politics could operate.

The decline of virtue

There was a pervasive sense that the rise of commerce was incompatible with republics of the kind advocated by earlier thinkers. While commerce leads to increasing material interdependence, it distracts people from political concerns. Citizens should be motivated by the common good, producers and consumers are driven by self-interest or private desires. From Aristotle to Harrington luxurious tastes and an excessive concern with money-making were in themselves clear indicators of corruption. Commerce disrupts the balance of property and independence in society, and provides despotic governments with new resources to exert power, as the early eighteenth-century 'country' party in England realised when they opposed the crown's development of a standing army and financial borrowing powers. The size of modern states also endangers virtue: in a large society the bonds between citizens are thinner, and this weakens their commitment to the common good. So, while arguments for simple agrarian republics were repeatedly advanced in Europe and America, they were matched by fundamental doubts about the possibility of sustained commitment to the common good. Commerce makes virtue impossible or no longer necessary.

Republicans had always been aware that individual virtue was, although crucial, a fragile basis for a republic. Now a sharper tension between self-interest and the common good was suggested. Thinkers such as Hobbes had argued that, since humans are naturally motivated by passions, republican virtue that means suppressing these is too austere and demanding of citizens. In response some republicans attempted to conceive of virtue as less heroically demanding. They defined it in terms of reason (Harrington), or as an inbuilt 'moral sense', which makes people sociable, and is at least as natural as self-interest (Hutcheson). Others developed their own accounts of the forces which motivate social and anti-social behaviour. The concept of an 'interest' was proposed as an alternative motivating force, more predictable or reliable than passions. Then the idea emerged that social behaviour is a result of a balance between the anti-social, aggressive passions and the calmer passions, such as the desire to accumulate wealth (Hirschman, 1977). But all these arguments tended to downplay deliberate civic virtue.

One radical argument questioned not the possibility, but the worth of actions consciously directed to the common good. De Mandeville's (1670–1733) *Fable of the Bees* suggested that well-intentioned altruistic acts often lead to disaster, whereas self-interested behaviour under limited constraints leads to the best outcome for all. For example, a vain woman spending extravagantly on luxurious outfits may be seen as corrupt in republican terms, but she creates a living for the tailor, the weaver and the shopkeeper.

They are better off as a result of her self-interest, not her benevolence. So private vice may constitute public benefit. Self-interest is less socially disruptive than the desire for honour and glory. In this view virtue is not just unrealistic, but can be counter-productive. Corruption accordingly becomes a less serious problem.[1]

Thinkers of the Scottish Enlightenment saw commerce as an essential part of progress, albeit one with drawbacks. They tended to redefine 'virtue' in terms compatible with commerce – as industry, honesty and so on – rather than requiring active participation in political life. Adam Smith (1723–90) reluctantly saw republican virtue as no longer an effective basis for society, since commerce and the increasing division of labour had sapped people's courage and martial spirit. He analysed the market as an alternative way of achieving social coordination; one which channels self-interest in a peaceful direction, without the need for virtue. But Smith did not see it as a self-regulating mechanism between purely rational, economic men. The 'hidden hand' first emerges as a substitute for the mutually constraining virtue of citizens, rather than for the activity of government. And, in Smith's view, social approval rather than material self-interest is the primary motivation for commerce: 'It is chiefly from this regard to the sentiments of mankind that we pursue riches and avoid poverty...It is the vanity, not the ease or the pleasure, which interests us' (Smith, 2000: 70–1).

This intellectual change could be summed up as reflecting a shift in social norms from the civic, political and urban life of the city-state to the civil, polite and urbane society of eighteenth-century England, Scotland or France (Pocock, 1975: 64).

Redefining freedom

In this context freedom, too, is under pressure. It is still an issue whether 'free government' is a contradiction in terms. Freedom as participating in making the laws, even to the extent proposed by Harrington, or as Machiavellian freedom through active citizenship, appears increasingly unrealisable.

Variants of social contract thinking came to dominate political discourse in the eighteenth century, and formed the jumping-off point of liberal political theory. While natural rights and republican thought stem from very different basic assumptions, throughout this period many thinkers combined the elements of rights and virtue, natural and political freedom in their arguments without showing any signs of concern for the tensions implied.

Montesquieu

An important figure in this shift in the sense of freedom was Montesquieu (1689–1755). While more an analyst than an advocate of republican ideas, he influenced diverse strands of republican thought. In *The Spirit of the Laws* (Montesquieu, 1900), he laid the foundations for a new expansive republicanism which would be applied in America; in the contrast he drew between modern and ancient republics he provided Rousseau with ammunition for the critique of modern society.

Montesquieu linked the traditional classification of governments with new ideas about the dependence of political forms on the physical and economic conditions of society. Governments fall into three principal categories. In *republics* (which can be either democratic or aristocratic) the people (or part of it) has the supreme power. In a *monarchy* a single person rules in accordance with law. And in a *despotism* the ruler governs entirely according to his own will. Each form of government has its own central motivation or *spirit*. In a republic it is virtue, in a monarchy honour, in a despotism fear. There is a tendency for each to fall away from, and need to be restored to, their basic principles. But the modern commercial world has changed the conditions for political life. Montesquieu adopts an ambivalent view of what he called *doux* ('smooth' or 'gentle') *commerce*; its general effect is civilising, though it produces people who fall short of heroic virtue. It increases interdependence, and restrains outright rapacity; but it also reduces feelings of solidarity. Although formed to live in society, people are not reliably concerned about their fellow humans, and need laws and government to keep them on track.

Civic virtue in a modern republic

A republic of civic virtue is admirable but anachronistic. Ancient republics were small and coherent, so their citizens could be mutually concerned; but they were liable to be overthrown by greater powers, and are no longer possible. People can be virtuous only when concern for their reputation restrains their anti-social behaviour. This is not possible in larger, more impersonal societies. Republics cannot expand without losing their souls. In a commercial society we can expect fairness in dealings with others rather than commitment to the common good:

> The spirit of trade produces in the mind of man a certain sense of exact justice, opposite on the one hand to robbery and on the other to those moral virtues which forbid our always adhering rigidly to the rules of private interest, and suffer us to neglect this for the advantage of others.
> (Montesquieu, 1900: 20.2)

In a modern republic based on commerce people can become rich without being corrupt, because business encourages other virtues such as industry, order and moderation (Montesquieu, 1900: 5.3, 5).

Thus civic virtue plays a very reduced role in Montesquieu's view of a modern republic. He explicitly distinguishes it from moral virtue, and defines it in terms of patriotism: 'virtue in a republic is the love of one's country...it is not a moral nor a Christian, but a political virtue, and it is the spring which sets a republic working'. It is a passion, not an expression of reason. 'It is a sentiment and not the consequence of knowledge: the last man in the state can share this sentiment in the same way as the first' (Montesquieu, 1900: 5.2).

The decline of civic virtue does not mean the death of republics, but the shift to a different kind of republic. In modern society freedom is ensured not because people act virtuously for the common good, but because institutions and laws channel and limit self-interested actions.

Freedom

Political liberty is distinct from both participation in self-rule and independence from rule. Political freedom is no longer understood as active participation in government but as *security* from arbitrary attack or punishment: 'Political freedom is the tranquillity of spirit from the sense each has of his security' (Montesquieu, 1900: 11.6).

Montesquieu acknowledges the attractions of the participatory conception of freedom, and grants that full freedom would require people to rule themselves. In a modern republic this is not possible, though they may be able to choose their rulers:

> [E]very man who is supposed to be a free agent ought to be his own governor; the legislative power ought to reside in the whole body of the people. But since this is impossible in large states, and in small ones is subject to many inconveniences, it is fit the people should transact by their representatives what they cannot contract by themselves.
> (Montesquieu, 1900: 11.6)

As well as the problem of numbers, the danger of violent politics and mob-rule is one of the inconveniences of power resting with the whole people: 'There can be a despotism of the people as well as of a single despot' (Montesquieu, 1900: 11.16). In these situations, 'the power of the people has been confounded with their liberty' (Montesquieu, 1900: 11.2).

But freedom is not the absence of interference, or independence from all rule or law. '[L]iberty can consist only in the ability to do what one ought to desire – and in not being forced to do what one ought not to desire.' This is compatible with obeying laws. People give up some independence for security. Even in a democracy it is not a matter of people doing whatever they like, because each is dependent on the behaviour of others: 'if a citizen could do what [the laws] forbid, he would no longer be possessed of liberty because all his fellow citizens would have the same power' (Montesquieu, 1900: 11.3).

For Montesquieu, freedom depends less on the form of government than on a respect for law, which constrains the ruler's will. Thus, freedom is compatible with any form of government other than despotism. 'Political liberty is only to be found in moderate governments, and even in these it is not always found. It is there only when there is no abuse of power' (Montesquieu, 1900: 11.4). To avoid arbitrary power, making and executing law should be in different hands. The distinction between a republic and a monarchy is less important. Montesquieu finds a 'separation of powers' between Parliament and King in the English constitution, which is effectively a republic in the guise of a monarchy. England shows how freedom can be realised in a large, commercial, non-military state, ruled on the basis of representation and the separation of powers.[2]

To maintain freedom, it is more important that power should be checked by power than that citizens should be virtuous.[3] These countervailing powers may include popular protest, in the same way that factions, for Machiavelli, prevented governments from exercising power in an arbitrary manner. Unity or harmony is not necessarily a healthy sign in a society, if it is produced by despotism.

In addition, Montesquieu argues that the problem of size can be overcome. A republic can extend to a large territory if it takes the form of a federation of small states who can band together for external defence (Montesquieu, 1900: 5.3, 8.2)

Thus Montesquieu's theory legitimated the idea of a commercial republic.

Rousseau

A counter-current emerges in the writing of Rousseau (1712–78). He brings a heightened awareness of new dimensions of dependence and inequality in society; this is not only physical and economic, but also psychological. He reiterates the ideal of a small republic of free, virtuous self-governing citizens in the modern language of social contract theory. Thus Rousseau, often seen as the most backward-looking of eighteenth-century republicans, is in some ways the most alert to central aspects of the modern predicament. He advances many arguments that strike a chord in modern hearts and minds. Balancing interests in the market does not fully resolve the problem of how to reconcile individual freedom with social existence. The key question remains whether there is any way in which individuals can be free in society, or there can be any legitimate government:

> How to find a form of association which will defend the person and goods of each member with the collective force of all, and under which each individual, while uniting himself with the others, obeys no one but himself, and remains as free as before.
> (Rousseau, 1968: 60)

In answer, he offers a resolutely republican vision of a small participatory state, though without much hope of its realisation.

Ultimately Rousseau's theory is torn between two radically divergent alternatives to the problem of freedom – creating either a free citizen or a free man. 'Give man entirely to the state or leave him to himself' (Rousseau, 1964a: 510). He sketches the first solution in

The Social Contract (Rousseau, 1968), where free citizens are immersed in society. The second solution is presented in *Emile* (Rousseau, 1974), the story of a young boy's education to independence and self-sufficiency. Both rule out dependence on particular others, in a way which makes Rousseau a forerunner of contemporary accounts of liberalism as well as of republicanism.

Historical context: Geneva and France

Rousseau was familiar with both sides of the opposing perspectives, and this is reflected in the tensions in his thought. He was a displaced citizen of the Calvinist republican city-state of Geneva. At odds with his native city, he lived for many years in exile in France, where he mixed with the leading figures of the Enlightenment, acting as a secretary and diplomat, writing operas for fashionable society and articles for Diderot's *Encyclopedia*. But his political theory represents a reaction to this life and to the ideas of progress and rational freedom as developed by thinkers such as Voltaire. It was inspired as much by an idealised portrait of Geneva as of Sparta or Rome. While his book established the term 'social contract' in the language of political theory, Rousseau is fundamentally not a contractarian, since he does not believe in effective natural rights that can be used to limit governmental power. It is Machiavelli he admires above all, and whose republican themes he develops in his own way. He intends his account of a republic as a yardstick, not as a programme for revolutionary change, but after his death he was adopted as a kind of spiritual leader of the French Revolution.

For Rousseau, applying reason to social institutions will not be enough to bring about freedom, because the problem is not just autocratic government, but corruption, which has roots deep within individuals in society. He contrasts present corrupt society with the virtue of ancient city-states and the innocence of a primitive state of nature. In the *Discourse on the Arts and Sciences* (Rousseau, 1993) he criticises not only commerce, but also the desire for knowledge and skills that make it possible, which lead him to the more fundamental problem of inequality. In the *Discourse on Inequality* (Rousseau, 1993), he examines social contract arguments to show that such inequality is contrary to human nature. Thus the inequality of political power justified by previous contract thinkers (including both

Hobbes and Locke) is based on inferences drawn not from natural man, but from socialised, corrupt man. His use of social contract undermines their arguments for a transfer of power away from free and equal human beings, through a radical critique of their accounts of natural man, rights, the contract and the sovereign.

Interdependence and the historical account of corruption

Interdependence and the problem of corruption have to be seen as a single, specifically historical development.[4]

In the distant past, humans may have lived as isolated individuals outside society, independent of one another. But they were, like very young infants, barely or only potentially human. They had a basic instinct of self-preservation (*amour de soi*) and, like other animals, were reluctant to harm another of their species (*pitié*). What distinguished them from other animals was their freedom and open-ended potential for development (*perfectibilité*). The qualities considered basic by contract thinkers, including reason, passions, imagination, memory, sexual jealousy and honour, have developed in the slow and steady growth of society. Thus Rousseau sees humans as more deeply interdependent than does any other contract thinker. But only when people live together in settlements, engaging in agriculture and industry, does the full range of what we now think of as basic human capacities and characteristics begin to develop. If humans were ever in such an isolated state of nature they were not moral beings; they were just innocent.

As people come to live together in society, the capacities of civilised humans are developed, and this natural innocence is corrupted. They become more dependent on one another, both materially and psychologically. They begin to compare themselves with others, and seek their approval or regard. Initially, this is benign; there may have been a 'golden age' of simple families living together, but comparisons inevitably lead people to rank others, and to seek to be recognised as superior. Natural inequalities of reason, strength and beauty that are harmless in themselves become the basis of other inequalities of power and wealth. Conflict results from the passions and powers of reasoning and imagination that develop with society.

Rousseau also contrasts modern corrupt society with another, intermediate stage in the development from the peaceable primitive world. In the ancient city republics, Sparta in particular, people had just enough concern for their own welfare and each other's opinion to live freely and virtuously. They valued action more than words, and simplicity more than the sophistication and learning of Athens. Their citizens displayed virtue. Such virtue is based neither in the rule of reason (Harrington), nor in a passion (Montesquieu), but on *conscience*, a more natural hybrid sentiment, rooted in *pitié*. But as states grew larger and more powerful, they tended to become more concerned with wealth and grandeur.

The point here is that there are different kinds of self-interest, some of which are more anti-social than others. The simple instinct of self-preservation does not lead to a conflict which requires men to surrender their rights to a community. Serious conflict is a result of the distinct, socially generated passion of vanity or *amour propre*. This leads to the desire to achieve superiority over others.

> Vanity is only a relative sentiment, artificial and born in society, which inclines each individual to have a greater esteem for himself than anyone else, inspires in men all the harm they do to one another, and is the true source of honour.
>
> (Rousseau, 1964b: 222)

> To this ardor to be talked about, this furor to distinguish oneself, which nearly always keeps us outside ourselves, we owe what is best and worst among men, our virtues and our vices, our sciences and our errors, our conquerors and our philosophers – that is to say a multitude of bad things as against a small number of good ones.
>
> (Rousseau, 1964b:175)

Rousseau measures corruption more in terms of *amour propre* than of material self-interest. People in modern society constantly measure themselves against others, and want to be recognised by them as superior. In this way dependence and corruption go hand in hand. The historical turning point was the division of labour that accompanied the emergence of agriculture and metal-working. The expansion of science, art and commerce in the modern world, rather than smoothing social relations, created further artificial inequalities. Only when people are equipped with reason, passions and capacities in society do human desires lead to the sort of conflict

Hobbes thought inevitable in a state of nature. In these conditions people might well agree to make a contract to create laws that all will observe. But such a contract favours the haves more than the have-nots. Even if it initially creates a collective power, over time this tends to become more centralised, and eventually leads to the arbitrary governments of his own time. Thus all social contracts up to the present have been invalid, as they were unequal exchanges; even if apparently freely made, their outcome was unfair.

In modern society not only are individuals subject to arbitrary governments, but these reinforce inequality and internalised dependence. Corruption has been the inevitable accompaniment of the development of society; it is not a cyclical process but a relentless decline. Thus we cannot aim to go back to a golden age, but we can become aware of the contrast between natural innocence, classical virtue and modern corruption. Yet humans must live in society. Starting from an analysis of corruption, Rousseau finds dependence and inequality as the underlying problems of human society. Having laid out the negative dimensions of interdependence, he turns to consider if there is any way in which people might be interdependent and free.[5]

Freedom

For Rousseau freedom is the most important characteristic of human beings. There are two relevant kinds of freedom. First there is natural freedom – not being dependent on other wills – which people have in the isolated state of nature, and lose when they live in society. It is in this sense that 'man was born free, and he is everywhere in chains' (Rousseau, 1968: 49). Second, there is moral freedom or autonomy, which may take its place. Both senses of freedom are incompatible with subjection to another person. Neither independence nor autonomy is possible in society as it is currently constituted.

Autonomy is a fuller kind of freedom, since it entails not just the absence of interference, but a level of self-mastery. It means living according to a law you make for yourself. This is 'moral freedom, which alone makes man the master of himself; for to be governed by appetite alone is slavery, while obedience to a law one prescribes to oneself is freedom' (Rousseau, 1968: 65).

The task now is to conceive of a political arrangement that would allow people to be free. We should not have to choose between freedom and subjection. Freedom cannot be legitimately alienated: 'by what conceivable art has a means been found of making men free by making them subject?' (Rousseau, 1993: 135). If humans in society cannot be individually autonomous, is there a possibility of establishing collective autonomy? Given the depth of social interdependence, this requires a system of collective self-rule which will allow all citizens to be subject only to the laws that they collectively make, and not dependent on other individuals. Thus real freedom is won only in political society, and exercised by collectively self-governing citizens. Those who live according to laws they make may escape dependence on their own corrupt reason and appetites as well as on the will of others.

Republican institutions in the true social contract

The Social Contract sketches a theoretical resolution of the problem of political freedom in an ideal republic. This is not intended as a blueprint for contemporary societies, most of which are too large and too corrupt. But it provides criteria by which to judge any existing state.

The only way out of corrupt dependence on individuals is to replace it by legitimate dependence on the whole. For Rousseau there are no effective natural rights to life, liberty and property. These are established in society, and 'the power of the state alone makes the freedom of its members' (Rousseau, 1968: 99). To become citizens people must surrender all their natural 'rights' and powers to the community and create a sovereign people. In return they gain effective political rights constituted by the state. Freedom is not alienated, but its form changes: they exchange 'a natural independence for freedom, the power to destroy others for the enjoyment of their own security' (Rousseau, 1968: 77). Thus citizens have moral freedom.[6]

This requires a radical transformation of human beings; it cannot be created from a limited contract based on self-interest. But such change is not unthinkable, since 'it is certain that all peoples become in the long run what the government makes them' (Rousseau, 1993: 139).

> [W]hoever ventures on the enterprise of establishing a people must be ready, shall we say, to change human

nature, to transform each individual who by himself is entirely complex and solitary, into part of a much greater whole, from which the individual will then receive, in a sense, his life and his being. The founder of nations must weaken the structure of man in order to fortify it, to replace the physical and independent existence we have all received from nature with a moral and communal existence.
(Rousseau, 1968: 84)

Though people may be able to form a contract, they cannot themselves determine the form of society before they exist as a people. The figure of the founder or law-giver is required to set up the basic institutions within which they can be self-governing. This is a temporary directive role by someone who does not wield coercive power: 'he must have recourse to authority of another order, one which can compel without violence and persuade without convincing' (Rousseau, 1968: 87). He then leaves it to the people; he is 'the engineer who invents the machine' rather than operating it (Rousseau, 1968: 84).[7]

Participation

The people collectively constitute the sovereign authority. Rousseau appropriates the notion of a sovereign, exclusive right to rule previously claimed by monarchs. Sovereignty is inalienable, indivisible and cannot be represented. This means that power not only originates in the people, but cannot legitimately be alienated by them. As a single sovereign people, they can be both free and governed by themselves, being subject only to laws they have made themselves. Each citizen is dependent on no other individual, but only on the whole. Thus, in contrast to Montesquieu's and Harrington's solutions, there can be no representation and no separation of powers.

The people cannot delegate their power to representatives: 'the moment a people adopts representatives it is no longer free; it no longer exists' (Rousseau, 1968: 143). Citizens are free only as long as all make the general decisions they obey; when citizens and subjects are identical.

Common good and general will A republic is intended to realise the common good through the active and voluntary commitment of citizens; thus it is expressed as their exercising a 'general will', distinct from their particular wills oriented to their own particular goods. Unlike interests, wills cannot be represented, or committed in advance. Thus the general will is reached when each citizen wills the option that is in the common good. It is explicitly distinguished from the 'will of all', which is the aggregate of individual choices of individual goods, which may be represented by popular opinion: 'the general will studies only the common interests while the will of all studies private interest, and indeed is no more than the sum of individual desires' (Rousseau, 1968: 72). The general will is not the will of the majority either; the generality of the general will is derived 'less from the number of voices than from the common interest which unites them' (Rousseau, 1968: 76). Political authority is only legitimate when it is exercised according to the general will, that is, when the citizens choose policies directed towards the common good. Unlike de Mandeville or even Smith, it is only when people deliberately intend it that the common good is realised. This is the condition of their freedom: 'the constant will of all the members of the state is the general will which makes them citizens and free' (Rousseau, 1968: 153).

Laws must be made by all the citizens collectively. To realise the common good, they must decide for themselves, and neither influence nor be influenced by particular others. So debate and discourse do not play a role in establishing the general will. To prevent the distorting influences of sectional interests, decisions are made by secret ballot, and each person consults only himself, without communication or debate. Parties, debates and tumults are a sign of the ascendancy of private interests. Rousseau has a particularly strong version of the republican fear of factions. The decision of the whole people alone is legitimate.[8]

Rousseau recognises that, in drawing up the laws, even virtuous and well-intentioned citizens may have difficulty deciding and agreeing on what is in the general interest. It will not necessarily always be a matter of easy consensus. So there must be provisions for dealing with divided expressions of the general will. Whenever the people, though genuinely intending the common good, are divided in their decision, the majority interpretation of the general will should prevail (Rousseau, 1968: 153). This argument is somewhat more defensible than it initially appears. It resembles Aristotle's epistemic defence of widespread participation in decisions, which was expressed more formally by Rousseau's contemporary Condorcet. On the assumptions that there is a single correct answer, that all are intent on discovering it, and that each has a better-than-even chance of being correct, Condorcet showed that the majority are more likely to be right (what we might call the 'ask the audience' principle). The minority are then regarded as mistaken. They misinterpreted the general will they intended to choose. Putting it into law, this does not damage the freedom of the opposing minority. The decision represents what they really intended to achieve. They will be free in being subject to a law that is congruent with their common good as members of society. While someone may have an interest as a businessman in opposing restrictions on air pollution, as a citizen he has an interest in clean air.

This results from thinking about the point of voting not as opinion polling, or counting the majority of particular wills, but as the majority interpretation of the general will. It must be said that Rousseau does not think that simple majorities alone are adequate; for more serious issues, weighted majorities and even unanimity may be required (Rousseau, 1968: 154). This is not a defence of majority rule; if the majority chooses selfishly, then majority rule should not carry. In practice, of course, it may often be difficult to tell the difference.

The general will is neither a mystical entity over and above the citizens, nor whatever popular enthusiasm happens to arise. It is neither populist nor inherently majoritarian. But as Rousseau was suspicious of all intermediate articulations, it is a *unitary* account of the common good, expressed by 'the people' as a corporate subject.

Thus in Rousseau the idea of popular sovereignty replaces that of balance of forces, or mixed government. Yet decisions made by the whole people according to the general will issue only in *general laws*. This is not a plebiscitary democracy. The people cannot execute the law, as they may be misled or partial in particular cases.

Mixed government To avoid the dangers of partiality and distraction by details, the 'sovereign' must delegate government. So although Rousseau speaks of the indivisible and inalienable sovereignty of the people, it does not mean that all decisions are made and all power exercised by a legislature of the people. Detailed administration must be carried on by an executive separate from the sovereign people, the 'government'. This may take different forms;

depending on local circumstances, it may be more aristocratic or more democratic. Rousseau considers the arguments for choosing the executive by lot and by election, and tends to favour lot because it reduces the opportunity to exercise undesirable influence over voters. In either case the area of government should be limited, and there must be safeguards to prevent the government itself dominating rather than serving. Thus power, while not divided equally among all citizens, is not used arbitrarily: 'power will stop short of violence and never be exercised except by virtue of authority and law' (Rousseau, 1968: 96). Rousseau does not intend the general will to be realised at the expense of individuals. Its power cannot extend beyond the needs of the common good, though that limit has to be politically determined. Its aim is to create equal citizens and to protect their security. They have rights of privacy, although these limits are politically established and interpreted (Rousseau, 1968: 185).

Law Being subject to law is not just compatible with freedom; it is the condition of moral freedom. Laws are created when the people as a whole lay down provisions for the people as a whole in general terms, without specific applications. Thus, under the conditions of a self-ruling republic, law and freedom go together. To be just, it is necessary to be severe, though too many laws are counterproductive (Rousseau, 1993: 142). Law plays a role in shaping the citizens: anyone who refuses to act according to what the general will has decreed must be brought into line. And in this process, in a notorious phrase, he will be 'forced to be free' (Rousseau, 1968: 64). This phrase, above all, has led to Rousseau's being seen as the father of totalitarianism. But such a person is a free rider, who wishes to benefit from the advantages of society without carrying his part of the burden. He continues: 'for this is the condition which, by giving each citizen to the nation, secures him against all personal dependence' (Rousseau, 1968: 64). Rousseau's statement is a more rhetorical expression of the conventional republican belief that being subject to law is the condition of freedom from personal domination, and more specifically of the view that it is possible to be free even while subject to coercion by law. Citizens have a duty to obey the law which guarantees their freedom. This political obligation is based on fair play, the duty to reciprocate for benefits received in a cooperative project, which applies to all residents in a free state after its origin in the social contract (Dagger, 1997: 90).

Shaping citizens

The social contract is not a once-and-for-all solution. Corruption remains an ever-present hazard: 'the body politic, no less than that of a man, begins to die as soon as it is born' (Rousseau, 1968: 134). But because it is artificial there is more hope of extending its life. This depends both on good laws and on the virtue of citizens.[9] As well as actively participating in willing the laws as legislators, the citizens must develop a habitual inclination to act according to them as subjects. Rousseau describes as the most important law of all, that 'which is inscribed neither on marble nor brass, but in the hearts of the citizens, a law which forms the true constitution of the state' (Rousseau, 1968: 99).

The minimum requirements of virtue are that they should 'love their country, respect the laws and live simply' (Rousseau, 1993: 150). Citizens must put their political duties before their private interests. They must 'fly to the assembly' and serve in the citizen militia. 'The better the state is constituted the more does public business take precedence over the private in the minds of the citizens.' The way in which people are preoccupied with profit and comfort, and appoint deputies to serve politically and militarily, indicates clearly the level of corruption (Rousseau, 1968: 140). True citizens are participators in, not spectators of, public life.[10]

Rousseau's diagnosis of corruption as *amour propre* might be thought to convey that any concern for the opinion of others is necessarily corrupt. But this is not the case. Rousseau ultimately distinguishes between exclusive, hierarchical honour that depends on inequality, and honour which can be equally shared. Honour without virtue, like Machiavelli's false glory, is corrupt (Rousseau, 1964b: 180). But concern for the good opinion of others is one way of keeping citizens virtuous.

> The wise man does not chase after riches, but he is not insensitive to glory, and when he sees it is so poorly distributed, his virtue, which a little emulation would have animated and made useful to society, languishes and dies out in misery.
>
> (Rousseau, 1964b: 58)

Citizens should live 'under the eyes of their compatriots, seeking public approbation' (Rousseau, 1964a: 968). Virtuous behaviour is encouraged through a system of 'censors' who reward and punish them by honour and ridicule, instead of prohibiting certain kinds of behaviour. In addition, a republic can give honours, but not exemptions from the law, to eminent citizens who furnish an example for others.

Civic education A civic education is the most essential part of shaping citizens. 'It is not enough to say to the citizens, "be good"; they must be taught to be so' (Rousseau, 1993: 142). They must be formed from the time they are children to love their country, to respect the laws, to cherish one another as brothers, and to live simply. But physical exercise and athletic contests play a larger role in this account of civic education than does military training given priority by Machiavelli and Harrington.

Civic religion Rousseau believes that commitment to the state also requires a civic religion. He saw the Christianity of his time as unrealisable in its pure form, a cause of conflict, and a support for absolute power. His civic religion, in contrast, is designed to unite the citizens in loyalty, and to establish respect for the laws. It involves no major doctrines of faith; instead, a minimal recognition of the existence of God and some socially useful precepts. It is observed mainly in celebrations of republican unity (Rousseau, 1968). Although a deliberate construct, it is not, unlike Machiavelli's civic religion, designed to overawe or deceive, but to encourage 'sentiments of sociability' (Rousseau, 1968: 186). Other religions should be tolerated, as long as their members accept also the basic tenets of the civil religion.

Material pre-conditions of political equality

We have seen that Rousseau highlights the implications of all kinds of inequality for freedom. There are natural inequalities in strength, intellect, beauty and charm. These are inherently innocuous, but become invidious when they are given additional social significance as a means to power and wealth; and inequalities of wealth undermine political equality.

Since virtue is incompatible with luxury, a degree of austerity is needed in a republic. Extremes of wealth and poverty that give some people power over others must be avoided. Property is not a natural right, but one developed and recognised in society. This does not mean that property should be abolished or equalised, but that the extremes of inequality should be limited. Thus: 'no citizen shall be rich enough to buy another, and none so poor as to be forced to sell himself' (Rousseau, 1968: 96). The politically guaranteed right to property is distinguished from natural possession, and is not a right to unlimited accumulation. To the objection that limiting inequality is an unstable arrangement, as property will always tend to accumulate in fewer hands if the market is left to itself, Rousseau responds that this is not an adequate reason either to abandon the attempt to equalise, or to abolish property. Precisely because 'the force of circumstance tends always to destroy equality, the force of legislation ought always to tend to preserve it' (Rousseau, 1968: 197). This response reflects Rousseau's conviction that even well-constituted states are always subject to corruption, and cannot survive indefinitely.[11]

Intensity and scope of the republic

In the republic citizens are bound by a strong sentiment of patriotism, love of their country, which is grounded in their dependence on the social whole. This identification lies between selfishness and altruism. It is modelled on the close face-to-face relations of the family: love for the motherland, and *fraternity* between citizens.[12]

The unity of the republic requires that citizens should be similar, and that other associations and intermediate groups in society should be weakened. Within the republic itself, although the equality of citizens is a key principle, there may be different orders of citizens, from more to less 'active', as in his own Geneva.

The state is a moral community of responsibility, which is particular and bounded: 'every patriot is harsh to foreigners. They are only men. They are nothing in his eyes...The essential thing is to be good to the people with whom one lives' (Rousseau, 1974: 7).

For Rousseau, the scope of the republic is necessarily limited. Taking a different tack from Montesquieu, he insists that it must be small enough for each person to have a significant voice in the expressions of the general will, relative to his position as subject: 'the more the state is enlarged, the more freedom is diminished' (Rousseau, 1968: 104). This is also necessary to develop loyalty to the state and commitment to fellow citizens. Large states are absolutely incompatible with the fellow-feeling natural to a republic and necessary for virtue. 'The more the social bond is stretched, the slacker it becomes' (Rousseau, 1968: 90). 'It appears that the feeling of humanity evaporates and grows feeble in embracing all mankind....It is necessary in some degree to confine and limit our interest and compassion in order to make it active' (Rousseau, 1993: 142).

His is a more peaceful, less militaristic republic. It will not be militarily aggressive or seek to build an empire. As well as the difficulties in knowing and feeling attached to citizens, there are difficulties in administering large territories. Republics may have reason to expand, but these will usually be countered by reasons to remain small. As a result, he held out limited hope for the practical realisation of republics in his own day. In Corsica it might be possible. When advising the government of Poland, he stressed that stronger measures would be needed to create and maintain community in a larger state than would otherwise be desirable.

The scope of citizenship is restricted in another respect. Where previous republican thinkers hardly addressed the question of women, taking it for granted that they were excluded, Rousseau makes it explicit that women are excluded from active citizenship. The freedom of men requires the dependence of women (Grant, 1997: 82–3). Men and women are different and complementary. Women are incapable of civic virtue and freedom. He holds two ideals of women, neither of which are active citizens. The first is the patriotic Spartan mother, who rejoices at the army's victory in battle, although her sons have died (Rousseau, 1974: 8). The other is the modest wife who maintains a domestic haven for the free man, Emile. Though Rousseau's republic may be less militaristic than some of its predecessors, its citizens must be men who participate in public, and who can retire to a private realm where a wife supports them and raises their sons as citizens. The powerful passions aroused by sexual relations are one of the major sources of dependence. They can be used by women to weaken men. To avoid men being dominated, women must be contained within the clear limits of domestic life, where they remain dependent on their husbands. It turns out that what is corrupt for a man counts as virtue for a woman. '"What will people think?" is the grave of a man's virtue and the throne of a woman's' (Rousseau, 1974: 328). 'The man should be strong and active; the women should be weak and passive' (Rousseau, 1974: 322). Their virtue rests in silence and obedience, and they must be concerned about their reputations. In fact the very possibility of a return to civic virtue rests on women becoming more specifically domestic. 'When mothers deign to nurse their own children, then there will be a reform in morals; natural feeling will revive in every heart; there will be no lack of citizens in the state' (Rousseau, 1974: 13).

Participatory republicanism

In Rousseau's reworked republican theory political participation becomes central to a conception of individual freedom richer than that of his republican predecessors. The problem of virtue and corruption is identified with that of freedom and dependence. This involves an internal tension within the self, as much as between self and society. Rather than rejecting all dependence, what is important is to distinguish legitimate from illegitimate dependence. 'In place of clashing individual interests and hierarchical dependence Rousseau seeks mutual dependence and a common subordination to the demands of virtue' (Grant, 1997: 167). Rather than his arguments constituting a defence of totalitarianism, his concern for individual freedom makes him a precursor of contemporary liberalism as well as of republicanism.[13]

Rousseau sees virtue as being much more widely distributed in society than earlier theories, breaking with the anti-democratic intention of theories of mixed government. Thus Rousseau transmutes the aristocratic concern for differential honour into the human need for equal recognition, which later becomes central to republican thought. The political solution is to create a republic in which all virtuous citizens are equally honoured. He is far from naive about the difficulty of creating any such republic. If corruption is a historical process of decline, it is even less tractable than in earlier cyclical views. Thus the degree of transformation required of citizens is much more radical. What Rousseau offers is, in any case, more a critique – that can be applied to any modern corrupt state – than a programme for change.

But even at a theoretical level, Rousseau does not resolve the problem he sets himself. He attempts to defuse the problem of dependence by locating it in the whole republic, thus creating a larger subject rather than an articulated citizenry. This requires a homogeneous people, among whom differences of opinion are taken to be seditious. Thus he is the republican most open to Berlin's critique of the positive conception of freedom (Berlin, 1958). But the primary problem with his theory is not that he thinks government should impose laws on anyone in the name of freedom, but that he takes the common good to be unitary. The majoritarian interpretation of the general will and the masculinist exclusion of women constitute further difficulties. The institutional solution he offers remains caught in a dilemma between the alternatives of individualism and corporatism.

Mary Wollstonecraft

At the time of the French Revolution there were many other hybrid expressions of republican virtue and natural rights arguments. Tom Paine, author of *The Rights of Man*, and Mary Wollstonecraft (1759–97) were particularly prominent as defenders of that revolution. But while the former combined elements of natural right and republican virtue to great political effect, the latter made a more original contribution to republican thinking.

A radical supporter of the French Revolution in the name of equality and freedom, Wollstonecraft did not develop a comprehensive political theory, and is often misrepresented as a confused liberal. But in countering the conservative romantic arguments of Burke and the sexist arguments of Rousseau, she outlines a republican theory of virtue and freedom which includes women as equal citizens.

A great admirer of Rousseau's republican writings, she took exception to his exclusion of women from social and public life. In the *Vindication of the Rights of Women* (Wollstonecraft, 1992) she responds to Rousseau on his own terms. In dealing with women, he makes exactly the mistake he condemns in Hobbes and Locke, describing as natural what is conventional, the result of artificial restrictions on women's opportunities in a corrupt society. The problems that women experience are in many ways just an exaggerated version of the corruption of society in general. Thus virtue and corruption should be understood as the same for men and women.

Interdependence and corruption Human beings in modern societies are shaped by political, commercial and personal relationships of domination and dependence, which limit their possibilities of independent self-direction. In an unequal society, aristocrats and commoners, wealthy and poor, men and women alike are all rendered dependent and degraded by their passions. Corruption is most conspicuous in the idleness, luxury and refinement that are characteristic of the aristocracy and cultivated among middle-class women. Like Rousseau, Wollstonecraft takes seriously the dependence created by sexual relationships; unlike him, she concludes that this should be countered by a system of rights for women, whose legal and conventional position makes them completely materially dependent.

The answer lies both in developing virtue and in establishing laws which allow women to be educated, to own property, to work and to have a say in politics as independent citizens.

Virtue and freedom A reformed society needs virtuous, self-directing citizens. Like Rousseau, Wollstonecraft sees virtue and freedom as almost identical, but she gives a greater role to reason. Virtue is not solely a matter of feeling or sentiment; it requires experience and the free exercise of reason to shape developed and reliable behaviour, and a degree of self-restraint that is essential to civilised society. Virtuous people are able to act as independent beings, while taking account of the needs and rights of others. But being virtuous is not so heroic in a society that is rationally organised, where good laws make it in the interest of all to be virtuous.

She contests the notion that men and women have separate virtues:

> It is a farce to call any being virtuous whose virtues do not result from the exercise of its own reason. This was Rousseau's opinion regarding men; I extend it to women, and confidently assert that they have been drawn out of their sphere by false refinement.
> (Wollstonecraft, 1992: 103)

She warns against confusing virtue and reputation (Wollstonecraft, 1992: 246). 'Public spirit must be nurtured by private virtue or it will resemble the factious sentiment which makes women careful to preserve their reputation and men their honour' (Wollstonecraft, 1992: 256). Women confined to domestic life are liable to focus on concern for their own families at the expense of the common good, 'for the sake of their own children they violate the most sacred duties, forgetting the common relationship that binds the whole family on earth together' (Wollstonecraft, 1992: 271). Those who are given no responsibility for wider concerns are liable to become preoccupied with a very limited interpretation of their own interests.

Virtue and freedom go hand in hand. In order to be free, it is not enough that people are not dominated by or dependent on others; they must also share in determining their future. Wollstonecraft implies a positive conception of freedom as self-mastery. In her response to Rousseau's point that educating women to make them like men would give them less power over men, she replies: 'This is the very point I aim at: I do not wish them to have power over men, but over themselves' (Wollstonecraft, 1992: 156). Thus, in order to be free, 'instead of being arbitrarily governed without having any direct share allowed them in the deliberations of government', women must be allowed to participate in public life, if only through their own representatives. 'To render their private virtue a public benefit [they] must have a civil existence in the state, married or single' (Wollstonecraft, 1992: 264, 267). They should be able to own property, work and take up professions; in this way they will contribute to society, and make men more independent also; 'if women are not permitted to enjoy legitimate rights, they will render both men and themselves vicious to obtain illicit privileges' (Wollstonecraft, 1992: 89). Likewise they will exert a more positive influence on their children: 'till women are more rationally educated, the progress of human virtue...must receive continual checks' (Wollstonecraft, 1992: 127).

Wollstonecraft presents only a sketchy account of the political institutions her theory entails. It is clear, however, that there is no rigid distinction between the public and the private, or between the domestic and the political aspects of life. Reforms of society and character play a large part: 'till men mutually learn to assist without governing each other, little can be done by political associations towards perfecting the condition of mankind' (Wollstonecraft, 1994: 319).

But legal rights are a necessary part of all this. People are born with unequal strength and other capacities. Therefore government should protect the weak (Wollstonecraft, 1994: 289). Wollstonecraft opposed what she saw, in Burke, as a defence of unequal property rights, especially in inherited aristocratic property, at the expense of liberty. This does not mean creating complete equality, or resisting commercial society. Commerce should be developed, but the extremes of wealth and poverty should be removed, and a more equal distribution of land arranged. Inequalities degrade both rich and poor; 'virtue can only flourish among equals' (Wollstonecraft, 1994: 59).

One of the most important aspects of government is the shaping of citizens through education. Like Rousseau she devotes considerable attention to a broad theory of education as the development of character through experience and socialisation. Education is intended to develop reason rather than instilling specific ideas or training in skills, 'to enable such habits of virtue as will render it independent' (Wollstonecraft, 1992: 103). As society and the family are so closely interlinked, they must be transformed together. Public education to form citizens is as necessary as private moral education. In this context she proposed a national system of schools, in which boys and girls would be educated together. 'Public education of every denomination should be directed to form citizens' (Wollstonecraft, 1992: 285).

The ideal relationship and the fundamental bond between citizens is one of friendship. Friendship is not a passion, but a rational form of affection between equals: 'the most sublime of affections, because it is founded on principle and cemented by time'. Unlike the passions, this is not necessarily exclusive; it is the ideal relationship between men and women, and is extensible as 'the common relationship that binds the whole family on earth together' (Wollstonecraft, 1992: 271).

Though Wollstonecraft's ideas were in the short run even less influential than Rousseau's, a quite different strand of republican thought was becoming more prominent across the Atlantic.

Madison: the *Federalist Papers* and the United States

By the 1770s other theories of freedom, both natural and political, fell on more receptive ears, as American colonists felt increasingly alienated from, and oppressed by, the government in England. Intertwined in the American revolution were arguments of natural rights and limited government on Lockean lines, along with republican arguments that the British government was corrupt, and that revolution was necessary to restore the virtue of an autonomous citizenry. The revolution was driven by fear of corruption as much as by opposition to tyranny.

Madison (1751–1836) was one of the leading architects of the new republic. In the propaganda debates that took place around the shaping of the new constitution in the 1780s, he was one of the principal authors of the *Federalist Papers*, a series of newspaper articles written to support the new constitution. These appeared under the pseudonym 'Publius' (after a founder of the Roman republic). Madison and the other founders were conscious of innovating, at the same time as seeing themselves as the inheritors of Rome. Along with a classical training and the ideas of Locke, they were strongly influenced by the works of Harrington and Montesquieu. But they also saw themselves, and were seen, as trailblazers creating a new order of the world.

Interdependence Madison addressed a society which had hitherto understood itself as a loose confederation of states of independent property holders, who were less dependent than the inhabitants of semi-feudal societies in the Old World. Individuals are born with natural rights to life, liberty and the pursuit of happiness; humans are motivated by passions and self-interest. They are not naturally good, and cannot live together harmoniously without government, which he describes as 'a reflection on human nature' (*Federalist Papers*, 1991: No. 51, 290). But human character can be improved, and institutions can be developed to preserve the natural rights and liberty of all.

Freedom Though now often portrayed as the author of a constitution designed primarily to reconcile private interests, Madison saw himself as providing for the realisation of common interests, and he saw particular interests or factions as one of the main threats to the peace and freedom of citizens. He wanted to preserve both freedom and virtue through these institutions. And he sought to preserve the public freedom of the people to rule themselves as well as the private freedom of individuals, understood mainly as the security of individuals from arbitrary interference through constitutional and legal means. This should include freedom of speech and of the press, and of religious worship, jury trial, and laws against arbitrary confiscation of property. But constitutional bills of rights alone are too weak; they are only 'parchment barriers'. A broader structural framework is needed to guarantee freedom. Rather than requiring active participation by all, however, preserving freedom is a matter of ensuring clear boundaries between the spheres of power.

Where Rousseau considered the problem of reconciling freedom and rule at an ideal level, Madison addresses the immediate practical problem of shaping a republican constitution to unite diverse and independent former colonies. He argues that freedom and virtue can be combined through a system of government that combines federalism, separation of powers and representation. America at least, away from the corruption of Europe, can create *ab initio* a large republic of free self-ruling citizens, which may be able to escape the Polybian cycles.

New institutions   The idea of a single documentary written constitution as a higher law above those made by the legislature was itself an innovation. This could be interpreted either as the construction of a social contract, or as the act of legislator figures laying down the fundamental law. But, for Madison, the power of the constitution itself came from the agreement of the people, as originators of all authority. It was designed to provide an institutional guarantee against both despotism (by dispersing power) and corruption (by balancing rival ambitions).

Madison argues that an extensive territory can be a republic if it is constituted as a federation of smaller states. To unite thirteen disparate former colonies, and to secure them against external enemies, he proposes a strong federation – against the anti-federalists who feared central government power and recommended leaving more power with the states. Moreover, he argues, size can be turned to advantage in addressing the perennial problem of particular interests, which threaten the stability of any republic. Even in a country with no hereditary ranks of nobility, different classes, groups or factions will always be present. These give rise to particular interests at odds with one another or the public good. But repressing private interests infringes on liberty. Instead of trying to remove factions, as Rousseau did, Madison believes that their ill effects can be minimised. In a large republic, they may be so numerous that each will be relatively insignificant, and they will tend to cancel one another out. A well-structured republic will 'supply by opposite and rival interests the defect of better motives in such a way that the private interests of every individual may be a sentinel over the public rights' (*Federalist Papers*, 1991: No. 76). There remains, however, the problem of the misguided or self-interested populace (the will of all) – referred to by Madison as a faction of the majority. The majority may sometimes support policies that are damaging to the common good and to minorities:

> As the cool and deliberate sense of the community ought, in all governments, and actually will, in all free governments, ultimately prevail over the views of its rulers; so there are particular moments in public affairs when the people, stimulated by some irregular passion, or some illicit advantage, or misled by the artful misrepresentations of interested men, may call for measures which they themselves will afterwards be the most ready to lament and condemn.
> (*Federalist Papers*, 1991: No. 63, 352)

The problem that collective self-government may threaten minorities, and that individuals may be pulled in multiple directions, becomes a keener concern the more freedom is identified with individual security. But in a large republic it may be harder for a majority faction to coalesce.

Participation or representation? Representation plays a central role in this solution. It serves two purposes. First it provides a way of dealing with large numbers, the other dimension of the size problem. Second, and at least as important, it is a way of appointing virtuous men and thus preventing the emergence of a majority faction. While Montesquieu had advocated representation, most republicans considered that any departure from more democratic political participation needed considerable justification. But Madison pre-empts the debate by making a crucial new distinction between a republic (where people are governed by their own representatives), and a democracy (where they rule themselves directly). Modern republics are distinguished by 'the total exclusion of the people in their collective capacity' from any share in government (*Federalist Papers*, 1991: No. 63, 355). The citizenry must consent to government rather than serve in office.

So Madison adopts representation as a positive principle to minimise the effects of ignorance and corruption and the difficulties of size. It not primarily adopted, as it was for Harrington, because the people is too large a body to bring together. Moreover, when it comes to the method of choosing representatives, he plumps for election, which had always been considered an aristocratic process, rather than the democratic process of lot. What is new here is not representation in itself, but its identification with election. To ensure the selection of virtuous representatives, various types of indirect election through states and electoral colleges should act as successive filters of opinion (Manin, 1994).

Mixed government: the separation of powers Excessive accumulations of power are also combated in a new elaboration of the idea of mixed government. This balances power against power, and interest against interest, among institutions as well as sections of society. The freedom of the citizens is secured by constituting government on the basis of the *separation of powers* – between legislature (Congress), executive (President) and judiciary. In fact, this idea of the separation of powers, influenced by Montesquieu's interpretation of the British Constitution, provides not so much for a clear separation of functions, as for a balance between three institutions whose functions in fact overlapped. Thus it provided a system of checks and balances parallel to the balance between factions afforded by a large republic, but a narrower conception than the traditional sense of mixed government as a balance of interests.

The bicameral arrangement of Congress (the Senate and the House of Representatives) was not a carbon copy of the British Parliament. Indeed, as there was no aristocracy to be represented, there could have been an argument for a single assembly. But, influenced by Harrington's distinction of two houses of deliberation and decision, the two houses not only gave expression to the federal structure of the republic, but created a further element of balancing powers.

Virtue These elaborate institutional arrangements are not, however, designed to replace virtue as much as to sustain it. However, the whole relies less on the exercise of civic virtue by the citizenry in general, and more on that of the political elite:

> [T]he aim of every political constitution is, or ought to be, first, to obtain for rulers men who possess most wisdom to

discern, and most virtue to pursue, the common good of society; and in the next place, to take the most effectual precautions for keeping them virtuous whilst they continue to hold their public trust.
(*Federalist Papers*, 1991: No. 57, 318)

Madison does not abandon the notion of citizen virtue. His notion of virtue, more like Harrington's than Machiavelli's or even Montesquieu's, owes a good deal to the puritan ethos. Virtue is more than simply patriotism, or the feeling of love of country, but a more rational quality including a sense of honour and justice (Howe, 1988). He thinks that other (not specifically republican) virtues such as industry are important for ordinary people in a commercial republic.

The point of the republic is still a commitment to the public good, which is greater than a collection of individual interests. Representation is intended not just to reflect interests but to:

refine and enlarge the public views by passing them through the medium of a chosen body of citizens, whose wisdom may best discern the true interest of their country and whose patriotism and love of justice will be least likely to sacrifice it to temporary and partial considerations.
(*Federalist Papers*, 1991: No. 10, 50)

Virtue can be elicited through the desire for honour and approval, which Madison considered to be as strong a motivation as material interest.

Thus Madison is still seriously concerned about corruption in the sense of behaviour contrary to the public good. But the larger sense of corruption, the fear that laws and institutions are immensely fragile and will inevitably decline, is less salient. He hopes to bypass the problem of corruption, or the unreliability of civic virtue, by the mechanisms which balance ambitions, separate powers and check institutions, as well as by keeping society simple.[14]

Shaping citizens Madison attaches great importance to creating virtuous citizens, but he gives the state less responsibility in this process than his predecessors did. Even more than Harrington, he relies on incentives and political institutions to produce virtue and screen out self-interest, rather than seeking to educate desire. The education of citizens in virtues remains an important, if general, role of government. Rather than instituting a civil religion, however, the constitution rules out the establishment of a national religion. None the less the constitution calls on God, and the state sponsors ceremonials to elicit respect and reverence for its institutions. A citizen militia is still needed to defend the republic, when the idea of a standing army is subject to considerable distrust. The now-controversial second amendment to the US constitution, the right to bear arms, originated in a *duty* to bear arms: 'a well-regulated militia, being necessary to the security of a free state, the right of the people to keep and bear arms shall not be infringed'.

Material pre-conditions for political equality Madison sees the United States as a new order of society, made up of free agrarian citizens, and, in the absence of ranks, marked by less social inequality than the Old World. But he lays more emphasis on providing equal representation than on creating the economic preconditions for political equality. He recognises that the unequal distribution of property is a major cause of faction, but does not directly address the effects of economic inequality on political equality. He does not draw from the 'truth that all men are created free and equal' expressed in the Declaration of Independence any conclusions affecting the issue of slavery or the exclusion of women from citizenship. Though those without property are a potentially dangerous faction, this appears to have none of the redistributive implications it possessed for some in the tradition from Aristotle to Harrington.[15]

Intensity and scope The modern large republic is diverse rather than homogeneous. Madison thought of citizens as bound by contractarian consent or loyalty to the institutions which provide liberty and happiness. But closer ties are to be expected to the constituent states, where most people's interactions and experience will be confined, and which will affect their lives more directly (*Federalist Papers*, 1991: No. 46, 262–8).

We have seen that Madison, far from having reservations about the possibility of extension of a republic, introduced the idea that a free republic needed to be extended. The United States, albeit a federation of thirteen states, was a very large territory. Although a matter of considerable debate in the years that followed, the republic proved capable of extension, first to include new territories to the west, and then to incorporate culturally very different populations of immigrants. But there were those who felt that such extensions undermined its founding principles.

Institutional republicanism   Madison's republican theory combines concerns for individual freedom and civic virtue. He designs a free republic in a large territory by balancing interests, powers and national and state governments. Contrary to some later interpretations, the institutional solution does not exclude considerations of virtue, or substitute for it an emphasis on individual interests and rights. The Bill of Rights was added to the constitution primarily to limit central government power over the states, not in the name of individual rights against government power in general. Madison's is not a purely procedural republic processing interests taken as fixed, but envisages the shaping of virtuous citizens. But popular participation in self-government is consciously pushed to the sidelines when limited to voting for representatives in elections. This establishes what is in traditional terms an aristocratic process of selecting rulers as the norm for modern republics.

Madison's political opponents, the anti-federalists, also espoused republican principles. In some respects, indeed, they adhered more closely to the previous republican tradition, as when they argued for giving more power to the states, for clearer separation of functions, and for a more equal balance between the institutions of government (Manin, 1994). They were not convinced that a republic could extend without becoming a tyranny. While they did not have enough faith in the people to argue for more widespread participation, they were also less prepared to trust the political elite. To limit corruption, they wanted greater accountability through more accurate representation and clearer allocations of responsibility. With hints of Aristotle, they saw the common man as a better judge, and virtue as more widely distributed among rural than urban dwellers. Thomas Jefferson advanced a vision of a frugal and virtuous republic of farmers and independent artisans, in which power would be more decentralised below the parish to the ward level, and frequent reforms would restore the republic to its originating principles. On the other hand, a powerful movement represented by Alexander Hamilton favoured radical modernisation and the extension of commerce.

Between these two poles, Madison combined the elements of individual freedom and civic virtue, and embedded them in the constitution, which has thus been interpreted both as a framework for individual interests and rights, and as an expression of self-governing citizens.

Conclusion

In this chapter we have seen how the eighteenth century gave birth to two new and radically divergent strands of republicanism. One was essentially representative and rested principally on an institutional solution. Freedom was understood as security of life, liberty and property, protected by a form of representative government in which interests and power were separated and balanced. The other was participatory but difficult to institutionalise in any way in contemporary society. In this image the freedom of citizens depends on their being active, united and virtuous participants in their own self-government.

Republics were set up in the course of revolutions against tyrannical government in the United States and France, amid heated debates on their legitimacy and construction. The experience and example of these republics was to be a major influence on the later development of republican thought.

Madison's writings underpinned the new United States constitution. Though Rousseau thought the age of despots was doomed, he himself was opposed to revolution: 'the liberty of the whole of humanity did not justify shedding the blood of a single man'. When the French Revolution took up the themes of liberty, equality and fraternity, Rousseau had been dead eleven years. Both the success of the American revolution and Rousseau's stinging critique of arbitrary and corrupt rule inspired a revolution in the Old World. But the Terror which was part of that revolution discredited the participatory strand of republicanism, while the institutional strand became a model for many modern republics and their constitutions.

CHAPTER IV

Roots of the Republican Revival

Arendt and Taylor

Introduction

In the middle of the twentieth century civic republican ideas emerged again in reaction to the traumatic experience of both right- and left-wing versions of totalitarianism, and the distrust of politics in general which succeeded this experience. The issue now was whether liberal institutions can meet the political needs of citizens, and indeed whether they can even reliably protect individual freedom.

Two thinkers who have set the terms of debate for the republican revival are Hannah Arendt and, more recently, Charles Taylor. Reacting to totalitarianism and neutralist liberalism, they stress the expressive dimension of politics, in which people seek not only to be treated as legal and political equals, but to have the value of their projects and identities confirmed in public. Arendt and Taylor justify the revaluation of political action in three dimensions. They draw attention to the ways in which self-realisation requires public recognition, they see freedom in positive terms as realised in political action, and they reaffirm the role of politics in realising shared goods.

Contemporary republicanism is a contested terrain; we shall later encounter another influential account of republican theory, one that is more instrumental, in which participation is understood as a means to guarantee individual freedom. Its exponents take up the threads of the argument more directly from their seventeenth- and eighteenth-century predecessors. But Arendt and Taylor open up themes and elaborate positions which all contemporary republicans have had to take into account.

In this articulation of republican thought, the focus comes to be on *recognition*. This is used here in quite a broad sense to indicate that politics is an arena of personal expression and self-realisation. For individuals to flourish, their most central concerns need some kind of confirmation in the public arena. This is in contrast to the widely prevailing view which sees politics as a mechanism for reconciling diverging interests more or less peacefully, and for which self-realisation and recognition are private or social, not political, matters. But, republican critics argue, that fails to acknowledge the nature of the need for recognition and the importance of public confirmation of validity. It marginalises personal concerns from political consideration, alienates citizens from politics, and privileges some over others. For these republicans recognition is not an entirely new dimension of politics. It has simply come to be a focus of concern because it is now more *problematic*. Hitherto values and identities were, for better or worse, confirmed through social hierarchies and homogeneous communities. It becomes an issue in societies marked by increasing diversity. This need is most clearly highlighted when it is denied – when people or their concerns are excluded, ignored or misrecognised in being assimilated to others. The key question now is whether politics should be considered as a 'thin' procedure to guarantee equal rights and fair distribution to citizens, as neutralist liberals contend, or should somehow express the deepest concerns, values and even the identity of citizens.

The theme of recognition picks up what was understood in the historical tradition in terms of honour. This was rejected by the contractarian tradition as factious; and by others in the modern world as hierarchical. We saw that Rousseau understood a concern for the opinion of others in conditions of inequality as the basis of dependence. But the contemporary concern for recognition stems from arguments for equality. Recognition is a dimension of human life as important as material welfare. It remains to be seen whether and how recognition can be granted on equal terms to citizens in a republic.

If the eighteenth century saw a *broadening* of republican politics to take in a wider range of people as equal citizens, the issue here is one of *deepening* it to take account of a wider range of their personal concerns.

Arendt outlines a portrait of politics in which individual freedom and recognition are uniquely achieved through participation in the public realm of politics. A republic is a community of diverse individuals related through a common world and public spaces. Rather than facing a choice between individual and collective freedom, individuals realise their distinct identities in political action. Taylor develops a more systematic argument for the ontological interdependence of individuals, and a positive conception of freedom as political participation. He addresses the expressive dimension of politics which makes the recognition of culture and collective identity an important political issue.

Historical context: the nineteenth-century decline

First we should note the decline of republican ideas during the nineteenth century. The ideas of widespread active public participation in politics, of freedom as political activity and the importance of civic virtue were sidelined. The violence of the Terror had discredited the notion of a virtuous self-ruling citizenry along with the name and ideas of Rousseau as invoked by Robespierre and other French Revolutionary leaders.[1]

Moreover, the prevailing sense of history as a single unrepeatable process undermined the idea of political life as a cycle of corruption and return to virtue. More specifically it became almost axiomatic that the modern world is so radically different from that of Greece and Rome that their example can no longer be directly applied, in the way that classical republicans (including even the Americans) had though of themselves as doing. In particular, freedom cannot be identified with participation in politics. Benjamin Constant, who had lived through the French Revolution, expressed this idea powerfully and influentially when he wrote in 1819:

> We are no longer able to enjoy the liberty of the ancients which consisted in an active and constant participation in the collective power. Our liberty for us consists in the peaceful enjoyment of private independence...The purpose of the ancients was the sharing of the social power among all the citizens of the same fatherland. It is to this that they gave the name liberty. The purpose of the moderns is security in private enjoyment, and they give the name liberty to the guarantees accorded by the institutions to that enjoyment.
>
> (Constant, 1988: 316–17)

(It should be noted that Constant went on to argue that civic liberty was an addition to, not a replacement for, political liberty; however, he believed that political liberty could be exercised by citizens in being vigilant over their representatives. [2])

The gulf between the liberty of the ancients and that of the moderns was held by many to make republican ideas obsolete. The political spectrum came to be dominated by liberal theory, based, for the most part, on individual freedom, understood as the absence of interference, and politically guaranteed by systems of legal rights rather than political participation and civic virtue. The success of the American republic, although initially seen as exceptional, meant that its institutional model became a standard for others to follow, and this was interpreted in increasingly liberal individualist terms. As more people received the vote in representative democracies, widespread active participation seemed unrealistic or undesirable.[3]

Tocqueville and Mill

Yet republican ideas persisted in combination with other forms of political thinking through the mid-nineteenth century, notably in the thought of Alexis de Tocqueville (1805–59) and John Stuart Mill (1806–73). These are normally seen as classical liberals, whose theories focused above all on individual freedom and the threat of governmental power. But both also sought to promote active participation and civic virtue against the political passivity which they saw as a drawback of modern democratic and commercial societies.

Tocqueville was a modernising aristocrat, who took part in attempts to establish a liberal political movement in France during the unstable years of the 1830s and 1840s. He emphasised the effects of radically new social conditions on all future forms of politics. After the French Revolution the age of aristocracy is over; it is gradually and justifiably being superseded by democracy, which embodies the values of equality and freedom. But the problem of excessive central government power has to be addressed. In the old regime, this was tempered by the counterweights of aristocratic rank and local privilege. When these are abolished, they create a gap in the political landscape, and there is a danger that an atomised society of individuals may be overwhelmed by the power of the centralised state.

In modern commercial society, there is a real threat that people will become indifferent to politics, or lack political energy. This, rather than ambition or actively sectional self-interest, may be the core of modern corruption. Social life will be characterised by a sort of civic privatism that he calls 'individualism':

> a reflective and peaceful sentiment that disposes each citizen to isolate himself from the mass of his fellow men and to draw himself off to the side with his family and his friends, in such a way that, after having thus created for himself a small society for his own use, he willingly abandons the larger society to itself.
>
> (Tocqueville, 2000: 205)

In *Democracy in America* (Tocqueville, 2000), Tocqueville reports on the way in which the United States, the precursor of trends to come in Europe, seems so far to have avoided this danger. He describes a democracy where strong individual interests are united by the local political institution of the township, which encourages vigorous participation, and by robust forms of political association. The danger of over-bearing central government is limited because the federal structure leaves much to the states and local government. This encourages local initiative, and sustains traces of republican activity. Citizens identify with the law, and know they are capable of changing it. They become aware of their mutual dependence and their collective power through local participation and jury service; civic spirit is inseparable from the exercise of political rights. While political associations are central to this, their social energy spreads into voluntary associations such as churches, schools, charitable organisations and so on. The abundance of associations of all kinds is the key to the American solution to the atomising threat of equality. The character, or *moeurs*, of citizens, based in broadly common religious beliefs rather than shaped by government, is as important as law in sustaining a free society. This kind of civic virtue is different from the heroic action of the past; it is less a matter of disinterested self-restraint than of rational, 'enlightened self-interest':

> Taught its true interests, the people would understand that in order to profit from society's goods, one must submit to the costs it imposes. The free association of the citizens would be able then to replace the individual power of the nobles, and the State would be protected from tyranny and from licentiousness.
>
> (Tocqueville, 2000: 9)

Yet equality tends also to encourage conformity to social opinion. If ostensibly sovereign citizens are more interested in prosperity than glory, lose their drive to participate, and converge towards a mediocre public opinion, they may be governed tyrannically, if benignly, by a bureaucracy.

Thus, however democratic its origins, the power of government needs to be constrained. Even if modern citizenship cannot be modelled on ancient lines, it should not be reduced to electing representatives and enjoying private liberties. Citizens must be educated through local institutions and freedom of political association so as to develop the self-reliance and political energy that can resist social and bureaucratic conformity.

This form of politics is less centralised and less coercive than Rousseau's vision of a republic, but calls for more political activity than Constant's. Although Tocqueville emphasises the fundamental importance of political institutions, he also emphasises the value of voluntary social associations. Thus his theory is less specifically political than earlier republican ideas. In consequence it can be invoked by theorists of an independent civil society as well as by republican advocates of political freedom.

John Stuart Mill was deeply influenced by Tocqueville's analysis. He followed intellectual and political developments in France closely, supported moderate republicans in France in 1848, and hoped England would become a republic one day. But, writing in the context of a Britain which was marked by far greater social and political inequalities than the United States, he saw the potential danger of despotism as lying more in the pressures of commercial society than in increasing social equality. He combined a utilitarian concern with efficient government to maximise the welfare of citizens (which had been central to the theories of his father, James Mill, and of Jeremy Bentham), with a deep concern for freedom as individuality, which he developed in response to the potential despotism of government power and popular opinion (which they had underestimated).

Addressing the problem of government in increasingly complex societies in *Considerations on Representative Government* (Mill, 1991), he advocated a form of representative government with more or less universal suffrage (including women) through proportional representation. Participation in national politics should be mainly through representatives. Government is designed to promote the welfare of the people, but this cannot be achieved through enlightened administration by a technocratic elite. Some degree of self-government will better provide for the welfare of citizens, and also protect liberties more effectively.

Participation is valuable additionally in encouraging active and energetic citizenship through which people develop and exercise their powers. As well as administering the affairs of society, government is also a 'great influence acting on the public mind' (Mill, 1991: 229). When voting, a citizen should not simply defend his own individual interest, but must become more public-spirited, learning 'to weigh interests not his own; to apply, at every turn, principles and maxims which have for their reason for existence the common good' (Mill, 1991: 255). Thus the development of civic virtue is an important dimension of politics. Citizens must be educated in restraint, by examples of conspicuous virtue and by participation itself: 'It is from political discussions and daily political action that one whose daily occupations concentrate his interests in a small circle around himself, learns to feel for and with his fellow citizens, and becomes consciously a member of a great community' (Mill, 1991: 328).

As well as voting for national representatives, participation will also take place in juries and local government. Jury service and military service should be compulsory, though voting should not be legally required. To avoid the tyranny of an ignorant majority, there should be a plural voting system which gives greater weight to the votes of the more educated, and a system of proportional representation to protect minorities. The content of legislation should be drafted by a legislative commission.

Thus Mill advanced a very strong argument for participation and civic virtue, but applied it in a rather limited manner. In addition, while it is important to promote common interests, Mill argued that governments could not be entrusted with extensive powers. Freedom is the most vital common interest, which is threatened by state power. Ultimately Mill places less emphasis on self-government than on the limitation of bad government: 'Men, as well as women, do not need rights in order that they may govern, but in order that they may not be misgoverned' (Mill, 1991: 342).

One of the reasons why the republican elements in Mill's thinking tend to be overlooked, despite his emphasis on active participation and civic virtue, is that, in *On Liberty*, he approached freedom not by defining it in political terms, either as a system of laws preventing domination, or as participation, but as a form of individuality: 'the only freedom which deserves the name is that of pursuing our own good in our own way, so long as we do not attempt to deprive others of theirs or impede their efforts to obtain it' (Mill, 1991: 17). While the point of freedom is the development of individuals, which is not at all the same as licence, Mill expresses this politically in radically negative terms of non-interference, because of his concern with the growth of power. He argues that it is no longer enough to limit government by a balance of powers, and aims to determine where exactly the line should be drawn between the power of government and society and the independence of the individual. This is expressed in the 'harm-principle' which makes harm to others the only justification for interfering with an individual's actions. The sharp line that is implied (though more difficult to apply in practice) has the effect of entrenching more deeply the distinction between public and private as areas properly subject to, and independent of, the control of the state.

Though aware of the ill effects of economic and social inequality he does not look to the state to transform society radically; he fears the power that redistributive welfare provisions give to the state. The dependence and inequality of women, subject to the will of their husbands, and of workers, subject to the power of capitalists, are not to be cured through the positive intervention of a strong state. In the first case reforming marriage and property law, educating women, and changing the attitudes of men are the central elements of a solution. In the second case abolishing legal privilege and extending the principle of democracy will progressively bring about the replacement of capitalist firms by cooperative enterprises.

Rather than republicans, these two thinkers may thus be thought of as civic liberals, who combined ideas of active citizenship and individual freedom with the concern for limiting government power that is more characteristic of the liberal mainstream (Miller, 2000).

Nineteenth-century socialist thinking also took up some core republican ideas, including the social nature of individuals, the idea of a more positive freedom, and the effects of economic inequality on political equality and freedom. But these were reworked in different directions. Marx, for example, shared many republican concerns, but saw the economic foundations of society as the crucial determinant of political activity, and, since he understood politics as a part of class struggle, did not theorise an active political life in future communism.

In the wider political context, nationalist movements arose in which the idea of a republic became intertwined with that of the self-determining nation, whose political power originated in the people rather than a monarch, and could be ruled along more liberal or more collectivist lines. Mill himself believed that, in order for democracy to be possible, citizens need to share a common nationality. Freedom, community and popular sovereignty were interpreted increasingly in terms of the collective nation, whose freedom was now conceivable apart from the active self-rule of citizens.

The twentieth century: historical context

The failure of liberal democracy to prevent the rise of totalitarian governments gave republican thought a new impetus in the aftermath of the Second World War. One influential analysis regarded totalitarianism in Germany and the USSR as a product of the complete politicisation of society, or the permeation of politics into every area of life. It required citizens to put the state before all else, mobilised them into state movements, banned independent associations, controlled schools, religion and every aspect of society. It subjected all citizens to a view of the good life endorsed by the state, and annihilated those who did not fit into this picture. Some argued that this was in part the result of the wave of democratic political arrangements that had followed the First World War. Democratic politics gave rise to deep emotions which were used by demagogues to rise to power, implementing comprehensive political ideologies with disastrous results.

A widespread reaction was to restrict the scope of mass participation in politics; even in democratic polities, it was argued, stability requires that popular participation be limited. Politics is best understood as a mechanism for reconciling interests. Citizens are adequately involved if they can choose between elites in elections for government. A low level of political activity may even be a positive sign of the health of a polity. In the 1950s a theory which saw the balance of plural interest groups as the key to liberal democracy was at its zenith. A neutralist liberal approach also supported limiting the scope of the state to matters which do not interfere with the privacy and freedom of individuals.

Hannah Arendt

A philosopher who, as a Jew, fled from Germany in the 1930s, Hannah Arendt (1906–75) reflected on what she saw as unprecedented political developments of the twentieth century. She argued that the problem of totalitarianism was not the expansion of politics, but its abolition. She portrayed totalitarian rule as the denial of the possibility of freedom by those who represented their deeds as determined by natural forces of race or material history. On this pretext political actors released hitherto unparalleled forces of domination. Instead of extending politics – the debate over how authority should be exercised – they centralised state control in a single organisation. Rather than uniting citizens, they isolated and thereby dominated them. This demonstrated the limitations both of legal and constitutional rights, and of electoral representation in protecting individuals. Without the political status of citizen, first the legal, then the moral personalities, and ultimately the lives of Jews and other minorities were easily forfeited. She concluded that political activity is essential for freedom. But it is more than instrumentally valuable. Apart from achieving concrete purposes, in political activity individual identity is realised and intersubjectively confirmed. Rather than seeing a trade-off between individuality and community, Arendt advanced a theory in which membership of a political community is the necessary condition of individual self-realisation.

Arendt saw dangers in the post-war retreat from politics and the overvaluation of private and intimate life. In the first place the constitutional rights of liberalism may not even guarantee individual freedom. Second, the constriction of politics rules out the possibility of realising freedom in political action. Both are threatened simultaneously by totalitarian regimes. But liberal regimes ignore political freedom.

In response, Arendt outlines a republican theory in which free political activity is the fullest realisation of human nature because it provides recognition of individual identity. This cannot be achieved in the uniformity of a totalitarian state, but is possible among diverse participants in a public sphere. Republican political community is not ruled out by the fact that it is no longer possible to envisage a state in which citizens agree on all moral and cultural values, since for Arendt political community is based on *communi-*

cation rather than commonality. In place of Rousseau's corporate unity, Arendt envisages a community of individuals in articulated relationships. Her ideas are complex and not fully systematically elaborated, and a sketch of the essentials must suffice here.

Interdependence

Arendt's republicanism is based on the ontological and epistemic plurality and interdependence of humans, born or existentially 'thrown' into the world as individuals who are separate and unique, yet similar in many needs and capacities. That 'not man, but men inhabit the earth' is the starting point for her political theory (Arendt, 1977a: 175). Arendt distinguishes three levels of interdependence in different kinds of activities: those driven by biological or social necessity: 'labour'; those concerned with creating objects: 'work'; and finally 'action', in which humans interact and take initiatives directly with others.

'To act in the most general sense, means to take an initiative, to begin, to start something in motion' (Arendt, 1958: 185). It is in this 'action', of which speech is a central element, that people express their individuality most clearly. But this expression realises rather than just communicating a ready-made identity, and actors themselves are not the best interpreters of what they have done or who they are. A secure sense of self and the world needs others to confirm it. By contrast, 'If one is without a deed by which to identify oneself, one's own absolutely unique individuality...deprived of expression within and action upon a common world loses all significance' (Arendt, 1968: 302).

Common world and public space

Through work, people shape an artificial 'common world' of reference. This is more permanent than other activities. This becomes the frame or anchor which is the foundation for all human relations: 'the world like every in-between relates and separates them at the same time'.

> To live an entirely private life means above all to be deprived of things essential to a truly human life: to be deprived of the reality that comes from being seen and heard by others,

to be deprived of an 'objective' relationship with them that comes from being related to and separated from them through the intermediary of an objective world of things, to be deprived of achieving something more permanent than life itself. The privation of privacy lies in the absence of others; as far as they are concerned, private man does not appear, and therefore it is as though he did not exist. Whatever he does remains without significance and consequence to others and what matters to him is without interest to other people.

(Arendt, 1958: 54)

Whereas work creates a world, action is more ephemeral, but creates 'webs of relationships' and gives rise to public spaces. Recognition cannot be realised in the narrow and idiosyncratic confines of family or other intimate relations; it entails a more distant and dispassionate stance, and the multiple perspectives of equals in a public realm. What is revealed in public has a kind of reality and solidity that what we know privately does not.

Being seen and being heard by others derive their significance from the fact that everybody sees and hears from a different position. This is the meaning of public life, compared to which the richest and most satisfying family life can only offer the prolongation or multiplication of one's own position with its attending aspects and perspectives.

(Arendt, 1958: 52)

For Arendt the primary dimension of 'publicity' is visibility – what appears to many. The distance, permanence and objectivity of the public world gives significance to the events that happen within it. The private world is thus less valuable, but it is both the source from which a person can act in public and the shelter to which they can retreat; what is private includes both what needs to be sheltered to survive and what should be hidden because it is not worthy to appear.

Freedom and politics

For Arendt freedom is a matter of action or exercise: 'Men are free, as distinct from possessing the gift of freedom as long as they act –

neither before nor after, for to be free and to act are the same' (Arendt, 1977b: 153). This depends on its spontaneity, not the absence of interference.

People may act freely, but since they are plural, they do not control the way in which their actions unfold – neither their material effects, their social significance nor the 'webs of relationships' they establish. Thus freedom cannot be understood in terms of complete autonomy, self-mastery or sovereignty: 'the ideal of uncompromising self-sufficiency and mastership is contradictory to the very condition of plurality' (Arendt, 1977b: 163–4). Instead of Rousseau's alternatives of individual or corporate freedom, then, Arendt aims to develop the idea of freedom among interacting citizens.

While the capacity for free action is inherent in human beings, who can act spontaneously in most unfavourable contexts, it flourishes when they live in a relatively stable common world, with common reference points, public spaces and institutions. Political freedom emerges in the initiatives taken by citizens interacting as equals in a public realm. 'Political freedom means the right to be a participator in government' (Arendt, 1977a: 218, 268).

Political participation is the expression of the highest capacity of human nature, and achieves 'public happiness':

> the joy and gratification that arise out of being in company with our peers, out of acting together and appearing in public, out of inserting ourselves into the world by word and deed, thus acquiring and sustaining our personal identity and beginning something entirely new.
>
> (Arendt, 1977b: 263)

Apart from its concrete objectives (which may or may not be achieved), the internal goods of political action are interacting with equals, defining one's purposes, realising one's identity and transcending the narrow, transitory and shadowy nature of private life.

There are competitive and communal, expressive and communicative dimensions to Arendt's account of political action. On the one hand it is a matter of individual distinction and identity. But although defining publicity in terms of visibility (rather than interest or control) stresses its aesthetic dimensions, there is more to Arendt's politics than the idea of self-display (Lara, 1998: 10).

While she draws on an idiosyncratic interpretation of the Greek *polis* as the locus of individual distinction, she also has contemporary, less competitive models in mind. The American revolutionaries or the French resistance fighters were exemplars of a kind of political practice in which individual self-realisation in public action and communal benefit were combined. The apparent tension may be partly resolved in understanding politics on the analogy of performative practices in which actors express themselves while also extending social possibilities, for example in art, literature or sport. In political performance citizens interactively define what their collective ends might be, rather than implementing previously determined individual or collective ends.

Although freedom is not individual self-mastery, those who are powerless may join together and realise a fuller freedom in initiating an entirely new train of events. This, and not coercion, or command over others, is the essence of power. Thus power is a common good that emerges among people who act together; not an invariant, or zero-sum quantity, for which people must compete. What Arendt has in mind was surely illustrated when people took it into their own hands to dismantle the Berlin Wall. Only rarely and temporarily do people achieve this kind of joint action. Yet its importance rests not only in the concrete results, but also in the example that their actions set. The Hungarian uprising of 1956 and the Prague Spring of 1968 were suppressed, but they left a memory and testimony to the possibility of joint action. Sometimes the main effects of political actions are in the stories told. But on other occasions people – as in the case of the Americans in the formation of the United States – may constitute entirely new political institutions and practices.[4]

Those who share a public realm become a political community, in which citizens are bound, not by common identity or shared cultural values, but by concerns arising from living in a common world and by participation in a common public realm. Against Rousseau's claims, they do not come to form a common will, but face common concerns and a common world. Rather than merging with a larger whole, the citizen interacts with others within public spaces. In modern politics action will often take the form of political debate between those with different perspectives. The problem in politics is not when people are different, but when they are unable to communicate.

Participation and institutions: the public realm

Arendt's argument leads her to value political participation as the highest expression of human freedom. Human plurality implies the capacity for action and speech between equals, which is possible only in politics. If freedom is to be significantly realised in political participation, there must be wide-ranging opportunities for political participation by citizens. A purely representative politics fails to provide these opportunities.

Formal institutions are of secondary importance. Public spaces can spring up independently whenever people come together in action. The existence of representative institutions has not prevented the attenuation of the public realm in contemporary societies where politics is understood in terms merely of efficiency in providing services. The liberal democratic system of representation, two-party systems and lobbying may give security, but does so at a price.

> [W]hat we today call democracy is a form of government where the few rule at least supposedly in the interest of the many. This government is democratic in that popular welfare and private happiness are its chief goals; but it can be called oligarchic in the sense that public happiness and public freedom have again become the privilege of the few...
>
> (Arendt, 1977a: 269)

To restore public space and promote free political action she proposes a pyramidal system of ascending levels of political institutions. She points to the small-scale spontaneous councils that have arisen repeatedly in the course of revolutions, only to be dissolved by centralising governments. She cites Jefferson's advice to break down power into a ward system of 'elementary republics' to forestall the ossification of institutions and sustain political energy and initiative. Both the American and French revolutions, despite their intentions, left a legacy of centralised institutions rather than public spaces.

For Arendt, politics is primarily a certain way of carrying on debate about collective affairs to which authoritative decision-making is secondary. Thus her emphasis on the intrinsic value of political participation has neither majoritarian nor populist implications. Expanding participation does not mean settling all policy questions by counting preferences, but fostering a process of debate with the widest participation. Yet, even if politics is the most human activity, not everyone will be interested in frequent participation, and she sees no reason why they should be forced to do so. When the obstacles to participation are removed, those who are interested will, in her view, constitute an emerging elite of those more suited to genuine political activity than the elected representatives of present politics.

In fact much of her politics is not directed to state action at all, but is, in Havel's phrase, a kind of 'anti-political politics' (Havel, 1991: 269–71) more about opinions and spontaneous action than coercive authority, and sometimes takes the form of civil disobedience and direct action. This politics constitutes public space, a broader, less structured area of action and debate that forms the context within which the state acts and which is being eroded in contemporary society.

The common good and virtue

Arendt does not use the terms 'common good' and 'virtue' in the way previous republican thinkers did. She uses the Greek term *arete*, or excellence, more often than virtue. But her ideal of political action makes freedom and virtue more or less identical, as they were for Rousseau. Yet virtuous citizens display an orientation to the common good, a concern for the common world and a sense of responsibility for the public spaces shared with others.

Her emphasis on the immediacy and novelty of political action brings it back closer to virtuosity, and differentiates it from acting from habitual disposition, as virtue was understood in much of the republican tradition.

Action and speech are addressed to others, and implicitly seek their recognition and agreement; they are not simply self-expression. Individuals distinguish themselves by exemplifying courage, love of equality, moderation, commitment to promises, and readiness to forgive that transcend their personal experience (Arendt, 1958: 170). If Arendt's conception of virtue is in a sense heroic, it is not entirely removed from ordinary lives, as actions have 'exemplary validity', expanding all our understandings of human possibilities. This emerges most clearly in her analyses of the nature of political debate and judgement. Those engaging in politics should be prepared to persuade and be persuaded, rather than seek to impose their opinion on others. What is involved in politics is 'the judicious exchange of opinion about the sphere of public life and the common world, and the decision of what manner of action is to be taken in it' (Arendt, 1977b: 223).

Political actors are not bound to express their own narrow interests, but should take into account the position of others, to develop what she calls 'representative thinking' or 'an enlarged mentality' that considers continually wider sets of perspectives. Rather than simply empathising with others, this involves exercising judgement from different standpoints to reach a more generally valid view. 'Our thinking is truly discursive, running, as it were, from one place to another, through all kinds of conflicting views until it finally ascends from these particularities to some kind of generality' (Arendt, 1977b: 242).

This is different both from following her individual conscience and from pursuing self-interest. She does not sacrifice herself altruistically for the larger whole, but takes an increasingly broad view of the community of which she is part. But she always sees herself as related to, and responsible for some community.

Corruption and dependence

Political life, public spaces and institutions are all extremely fragile. The novelty of action itself tends to undermine them, although the common world provides some kind of lasting framework. Free communicative action is undermined by several dimensions of corruption, which for Arendt seems to hinge on the systematic blurring of distinctions between the political and the non-political. First, material concerns, or economic and social policy – what Arendt called 'national housekeeping' – have become the predominant concern of modern politics. The expansion of interest-group politics, and the decline of public realms of debate on common concerns, turn politics into bureaucratic administration. Second, intimate private, or impersonal social modes of relationship have expanded into the public realm. In these contexts, politics lacks either the distance or the communication necessary for free action.

For Arendt, the intrusion of private interests and social forces into politics is a more serious threat to freedom than the expansion of political power *per se*. This danger is exacerbated in democracies where the people nominally rule but are given no opportunity to act as citizens.

An important aspect of corruption emerges when the motivations appropriate to private life and intimate relationships – love and compassion – spill over into the public sphere, where relationships are properly characterised by respect, equality and solidarity between those who are relatively distant from one another. When political relationships are modelled on private, people lose their vision of what may and may not be feasible. For Arendt, the French revolutionaries were overwhelmed by compassion for the social problems of their countrymen. Identifying totally with the people, they replaced self-interest with altruism, and understood virtue in terms of self-effacement. The people then became a hypostatised entity above all individuals. Instead of realising freedom then, they created the Terror.

But in the contemporary world it is the model of *impersonal* relations prevalent in the social sphere that threatens freedom most seriously. People in mass societies may be isolated, yet conformist. 'They are isolated in their own experience, which does not cease to be singular if the same experience is multiplied innumerable times' (Arendt, 1958: 53). As well as being overwhelmed by the needs of survival, people may be incapable of free political action, if they are driven to conform to social pressures or follow bureaucratic rules, or abdicate the capacity to act in a variety of ways.[5] The example of Eichmann, who followed the line of least resistance into participating in the attempt to annihilate the Jews, shows how a banal failure to think can lead to the greatest evils (Arendt, 1994).

Thus, where Rousseau saw disagreement as an indicator of corruption, Arendt sees the conformity that can coexist with isolation as more serious, and as the ground in which oppression can take root. The abdication of responsibility in politics is powerfully reinforced by the prevalent view that all human behaviour is determined either by greater social forces or by natural self-interest. This makes the idea of citizens taking collective charge of their destiny seem a remote illusion.

Shaping citizens

Because action is characterised by spontaneity, institutional shaping of citizens plays less of a role here than in the republican tradition.

Moreover, as no contemporary political realm can rely on the common authority of shared values, education passes no authoritative values down from one generation to the next. It is essentially a matter of introducing new citizens to 'taking responsibility for the world'. If anything can help to create citizens, it is the availability of spaces for political action.

Material conditions and economic inequality

Just as political action can arise anywhere, but is fostered by institutions, anyone is capable of action, but it will come more easily to those who have some security. Arendt translates the republican concern to limit the effects of inequality of property into spatial terms. 'What is necessary for freedom is not wealth; what is necessary is security and a place of one's own shielded from the public' (Arendt, 1977c: 108). Against absolute property rights, she identifies a need for property in the sense of security and independence. These have been undermined by capitalist growth and mobility, which have expropriated many (Arendt, 1958: 95). Arendt does not develop the practical requirements of such a need very far. But we may note that guaranteeing citizens the security to act politically provides a ground for government intervention in economic and social affairs other than compassion for suffering.

Intensity and scope of political community

For Arendt citizens are bound by concerns arising from living in a common world and participation in the public realm, not by common identity or shared cultural values. As she puts it, 'the revelatory character of speech and action come to the fore where people are *with* others and neither *for* nor *against* them' (Arendt, 1958: 160). The ties between citizens are characterised by equality, difference and relative distance. Yet this is a community; the obligation of citizens to take responsibility for the public sphere is owed to fellow citizens, not to government.

The appropriate feelings towards other citizens are respect and solidarity, which are marked by distance and allow for the possibility of difference. Respect is 'a friendship without intimacy or closeness: it is a regard for the person from the distance which the space of the world puts between us, and this regard is independent of qualities which we may admire or achievements we may esteem' (Arendt, 1958: 218). Love and compassion are appropriate only in close-knit face-to-face private relations. When criticised for acting in a way that showed a lack of love for her own race, the Jews, she famously responded that love was a matter for persons best kept out of politics. The state cannot be modelled on the family and intimate relations; religion and cultural identity are not the basis of political community. The ties between citizens are not based on their similarity or commonality but on their interacting and communicating in the public realm.

Political relationships are personal even though they are indirect, as distinct from private personal and direct relationships of friends or lovers. They are also to be distinguished from social relationships, which may be direct and impersonal (like travelling on a bus) or indirect and impersonal (like a credit-card transaction). Those who share a public realm, and can act in concert as equals, may develop relations of *solidarity*. Unlike love or compassion between individuals, this is capable of extension beyond face-to-face relations: 'solidarity, because it partakes of reason and hence of generality, is able to comprehend a multitude conceptually, not only the multitude of a class or a nation or a people, but eventually of all mankind' (Arendt, 1977a: 88).

But the state has to be a particular community marked by boundaries. 'Territorial boundaries make possible the physical identity of a people' (Arendt, 1958: 170). A community must be defined in terms of a public sphere which is shared. But political communities are not necessarily distinguished from one another in terms of opposition or enmity. And the limits of states are not ethnically determined, since commonality is not the issue, but the sharing in a common world and common space.

Arendt's account points towards a form of politics that allows for individual recognition among those who are different. Unlike Rousseau's alternatives, her account of freedom is neither purely individual nor wholly corporate. In her account a political community can be based on interaction in a public space growing out of a common world, which provides salient reference points even where people understand the goals of the polity in very different ways and disagree on what policies should be implemented. Politics is not a unitary common enterprise, but the interaction of those with common concerns. This political community is not modelled on direct face-to-face relationships, but on indirect but still personal relationships established in the public sphere. These should not be confused with the impersonal 'social' relationships of conformity that she sees as responsible for the abdication of responsibility in the modern world. Thus Arendt argues for a conception of political community that accommodates difference and fosters freedom.

Arendt's conceptual distinction of labour, work and action powerfully challenges materialist accounts of social interaction and instrumental accounts of politics. It acts as the foundation for an inspiring vision of human self-realisation and freedom in politics. But her insights are accompanied by many difficulties. She does not develop her arguments fully. Moreover, she overvalues political life in seeing it as the highest fulfilment of human nature. She undervalues other relationships, and contrasts a heroic, existentialist politics and other aspects of life too sharply.[6] She applies her conceptual distinctions as if they correspond exactly to areas of real life. Thus the boundaries she establishes between politics and economics, and public and private, are too exclusive. She seems to assume that if political participation is to be of intrinsic (indeed ultimate) value, it cannot also be of instrumental value. In consequence she undervalues both private life and the political institutions of rights and representation. Her account of political recognition is individualised, if not individualistic, and she does not address its social and cultural implications. Finally her theory does not make clear what a republican polity would look like in practice, but remains at a very abstract level. But her theory has provided rich resources for further development by other thinkers.

Charles Taylor

The expressive dimension of politics was explored further by Charles Taylor in the 1970s and early 1980s, when the most heated debates in political theory concerned issues of distributive justice between libertarians, social democratic liberals and socialists. Taylor argued that issues of recognition were at least as important. In a broad-ranging critique of atomistic social ontologies, negative freedom and neutralist liberalism, he set the terms for much of the contemporary debate on the revival of republican politics.

For Taylor the importance of recognition is conveyed in a non-atomist understanding of society, a positive and political conception of freedom, and an expressivist account of politics.

It should be noted that Taylor describes his position as both liberal and republican, understanding liberalism in a perfectionist, rather than a neutralist way, as 'trying to maximise the goods of freedom and collective self-rule, in conformity with rights founded on equality' (Taylor, 1995: 258). He understands contemporary civic republicanism as a strand of liberalism which values participation in collective self-government, and the realisation of common goods as well as individual freedom. Alternative strands of liberalism see freedom as negative, political participation as optional and government as properly neutral with respect to the substantive goods which individuals pursue.

For Taylor, this reflects the coexistence in contemporary society of two principles in increasing tension: individual freedom and collective self-government. There is an implicit republican dimension to contemporary liberal democracies. But individual freedom is more widely espoused, and the dimension of self-government is threatened.

Taylor's critique of neutralist liberalism is rooted in two positions. First, individual development and self-expression depends on a social and political context. Second, people distinguish more and less central purposes in pursuing self-development. Freedom is a matter of realising ourselves according to our most central purposes, not the absence of interference. Thus politics is an arena for self-expression and public recognition of identity and values, and not just a framework for maintaining order and just distribution.

Interdependence and common goods

For Taylor, much modern philosophy and social science is based on 'atomistic' assumptions that exaggerate the separateness of individuals. It thus fails to see how individual development and flourishing depends on engagement in social practices and the communities which sustain them. These are not instrumental to, but constitutive of, individual identity.

Taylor has drawn on Hegel's attempt to elaborate the idea of a community which would allow individuality, synthesising and transcending both the community of the Greek city state, and the individualist society of the modern world. But Hegel's solution, although not a totalitarian state, did not provide for political action. Taylor sees in Hegel's account that humans are happiest when 'the norms and ends expressed in the public life of a society are the most important ones by which its members define their identity as human beings' (Taylor, 1989: 185). This picture creates difficulties for the idea of a neutral public realm advanced by some liberals, which is justified as universal, not in terms of any particular ideal of the good life.

In Hegel's account of the development of self-consciousness, while an 'I', a human consciousness, may assume an objectifying attitude towards the inanimate world, this is problematical where two consciousnesses interact. Each takes himself, and seeks recognition, as the only centre of consciousness or focus of significance, but treats the other as an 'it'. In the struggle for recognition, self-consciousness is achieved only if the protagonists avoid mutual destruction and move beyond victory and defeat to some kind of mutual recognition as equals. Mere victory, or mastery gives only a devalued recognition by a slave, who is by definition unequal. This 'master–slave' episode in the *Phenomenology of Mind* (Hegel, 1967: 228–40) has exerted diverse influence on later thinkers. It symbolises the importance of intersubjective recognition for individual identity. For Taylor it shows that humans have as great a need for interpersonal recognition as for material resources, and denying this not only causes psychological damage but constitutes injustice.

Taylor argues more broadly that many contemporary liberals exaggerate the extent of individual self-sufficiency. The human capacities valued today – survival, self-expression, developing convictions and exercising choice – all require a context of social relations. They are not temporary scaffoldings which can be succeeded by voluntary and limited relationships in adulthood, but form the continuing horizon of their activities. This extends beyond smaller communities such as the family, as these do not develop the capacity for autonomy across the broad range of a whole civilisation. This dependence is true of the autonomous individual in a liberal society as much as of someone pursuing a more traditional life. Only through direct engagement with others in a culture with a range of activities from arts and sciences, a legal culture, and especially public debate about moral and political questions, can people come to be capable of, and to exercise, autonomous choices. 'The free individual of the west is only what he is by virtue of the whole society and civilization which brought him to be and which nourishes him' (Taylor, 1985: 206). 'This self-understanding is not something we can sustain on our own, but...our identity is always partly defined in conversation with others or through the common understanding which underlies the practices of our society' (Taylor, 1985: 209). As it was for Arendt, identity is dialogically construed; it is not defined unilaterally.

Pursuing individual self-realisation requires a social framework at two levels. To pursue some activities at all – to be a lawyer or a professional footballer, for example, requires a whole range of social structures. But it is not just the possibility but the validity and worth of these pursuits that are at stake. For example, it seems that to be homosexual was not regarded as a distinct way of life in ancient Greece. In nineteenth-century Britain, by contrast, it was recognised but condemned. Activities gain their meaning in contexts of social practices and understandings. The significance of a pursuit depends in part on its public recognition. As is clear in debates about homosexual marriage, there is a difference between private actions and those which are publicly recognised.

So, individual goods depend on socially recognised meanings. Some of these are simply *convergent* – where people happen to value the same things. Others are more significantly *common meanings*, which form the basis for interaction. Language is the paradigm example. At the very least the language they use conveys common structures of meaning between speakers, but it also frames culturally particular practices, for example of family relations, or of negotiation and voting, which depend on a range of cultural assumptions and are not universal among human beings (Taylor, 1985: 39; 1995: 139). This understanding does not always involve agreement; in fact the bitterest disagreements – for example, between Protestant and Catholic, Israeli and Palestinian – depend on common meanings between the rival groups, who see the issues in a way that outsiders fail to grasp.

But a third kind of *shared meaning* is present when people jointly value something, and their valuing the good is mutually recognised. The difference is like that between listening to music in your home and going to a concert. It is not just that the concert is live; part of the value is in the presence of other people and their enjoyment.

Some such common or shared goods are indivisible, not distributed across individuals: they are 'irreducibly social goods' (Taylor, 1995: 188). And sometimes they may be implicit in institutions even if not consciously recognised. For Taylor, public space and the practice of self-government currently falls into this category.

What normative conclusion should be drawn? Does this mean that government should promote such shared goods? Taylor has more recently clarified what is at stake here by distinguishing issues of 'ontology' and 'advocacy'. One concerns the relationship between individual and society; the other the normative position we adopt. On the first dimension, society can be understood *atomistically* – as made up of strictly separate individuals – or *holistically* – as individuals deeply embedded in social relationships. On the second dimension, giving priority to individual or collective goals distinguishes *individualist* or *collectivist* advocacy positions respectively. On this basis, libertarians are both atomists and individualists; Marx was a holist and a collectivist. But, although it narrows down the range of meaningful options, being a holist does not directly imply any particular normative outcome (Taylor, 1995: 183). Thus Taylor describes himself as a holist individualist, who sees a social framework as essential to individual pursuits but attributes ultimate value to the fulfilment of individuals. This means, however, that individuals should be committed to sustaining the common goods that are the precondition of their flourishing. They are engaged selves in a dual sense, their lives are embedded in social practices, and they consciously negotiate the terms of these practices.

Freedom

Freedom is the capacity to be self-directing, but since people are deeply engaged in society it cannot be conceived of solely as individual independence.

Negative and positive freedom Accordingly, Taylor advances a critique of the negative conception of freedom as the absence of interference, and of Isaiah Berlin's influential argument that a positive conception of freedom as self-rule starts on a slippery slope to tyranny.

For Berlin politics should protect negative freedom, freedom from interference (Berlin, 1958). This understanding of freedom may be understood as answering the question, over *what area* am I master? Positive freedom answers the different question, *who* is master? It thus involves self-mastery, or adhering to a true or higher nature, rather than immediate inclinations. Although Berlin recognises that there is no inherent connection between self-mastery and political oppression, he identifies a pervasive historical connection. The Jacobins in the French Revolution ruled violently in the name of true freedom. Classical Marxists spoke of the higher interests of the working class. Communist elites claimed to realise such interests on their behalf, even if the workers preferred to pursue more immediate goals such as higher wages or better working conditions. Arguments for positive freedom thus enter a slippery slope towards domination in the name of a higher nature.[7]

For Taylor, the social interdependence of human beings makes defining freedom in strictly negative terms – of the absence of interference – problematic. He distinguishes an *opportunity* from an *exercise* concept of freedom. Negative freedom requires only the absence of interference, but does not imply that we do anything with it. Positive freedom is an exercise concept – realised only in actively determining oneself and the shape of one's life. Negative freedom does not discriminate between kinds of interference that are more or less damaging to the projects of individuals. Nor does it take account of internal obstacles to freedom. A person whose life is dominated by an addiction to alcohol is free in the negative sense, but not in the positive sense. 'Doing what you want' is not fully free if what you want is out of your control. Freedom involves being able to act according to what you understand to be your most important purposes.

Against the prevailing utilitarian view that politics is concerned with reconciling individual preferences, all of which carry equal weight, Taylor argues that humans have first- and second-order preferences: those they happen to adopt at any moment, and those they endorse and feel more fundamental to their life-projects. People attach significance to life-goals such as integrity, freedom, self-reliance, caring, 'making a difference', or material success. While individuals in the modern world pursue many diverse goods, they characteristically rank these according to their worth in relation to their most central life-goals. And in the modern world those purposes are humanly defined, as a matter of authenticity to the individual's identity. Now, the higher self is a matter of determination as much as of discovery. Freedom is a matter of realising oneself according to these most authentic purposes. So positive freedom as self-mastery does not necessarily imply congruence with an existing template. It is essentially a matter of being self-directed, rather than determined by forces that do not express our reflective selves.

For people whose development depends on social practices, self-mastery has to be undertaken in a social context, not on terms set by each individual. And because there are more and less central motivations, we may not be free when we act according to our immediate inclinations. This does not mean that anyone else, or the collective, can step in; the ideal of autonomy cannot be realised by 'forcing' anyone to be free, on the one hand. But 'interference' of some kind is inevitable in participating in social practices. Such interference may be more or less harmful to freedom, depending on the relative significance of the action in a person's life-project. Being stopped at traffic lights is less significant than having to pay inheritance taxes, and that is less significant than being forced to recant religious beliefs, or being forbidden to work or to marry. Interference *per se* is not the main obstacle to freedom.

So, for Taylor, Berlin's criticism misrepresents the positive conception, and, furthermore, the slippery slope argument is itself open to criticism. It is one thing to see freedom as autonomy, a matter of realising your deeper concerns; it is quite another to identify these with a particular social whole, and yet another to say that anyone else can make you free by imposing any way of life on you. This is not necessarily a slippery slope.

The contemporary aspiration for freedom is implicitly motivated by the desire to remove impediments to achieving what is significant to us. Freedom is an issue in, for example, debates on aspects of parenthood such as surrogate motherhood, child-care, rights of adoption for gays and lesbians – issues which arise because people take being a parent to be a valuable part of life. Liberal rights embody the social recognition of values that have been established as particularly significant in our society.

A positive conception of freedom as self-realisation implies that individuals should be able to shape practices, and participate in collective self-rule. Even Mill's 'pursuing your own good in your own way' cannot best be realised on the basis of non-interference.

Participation in self-government

Because individual self-development requires the context of social practices, freedom is exercised in part through political action, where people have a say in the shaping of the wider society.

> If realising our freedom partly depends on the society and culture in which we live, then we exercise a fuller freedom if we can help determine the shape of this society and culture. And this we can only do through instruments of common decision. This means that the political institutions in which we live may themselves be a crucial part of what is necessary to realise our identity as free beings...In fact men's deliberating together about what will be binding on all of them is an essential part of the exercise of freedom. It is only in this way that they can come to grips with certain basic issues which will actually have an effect on their lives. Those issues, which can only be effectively decided by society as a whole and which often set the boundary and framework for our lives, can indeed be discussed freely by politically irresponsible individuals wherever they have licence to do so. But they can only be truly deliberated about politically. A society in which such deliberation was public and involved everyone would realise a freedom not available anywhere else or in any other mode.
>
> (Taylor, 1985: 208)

Political participation has both intrinsic and instrumental value. It achieves recognition at two levels: first, through civic participation itself; second, through the other practices and values realised through politics. So political life is both an important part of identity, and an opportunity to realise further purposes. Gaining a hearing is itself a level of recognition (Taylor, 1995: 277). If the values realised in public life cohere with the goals of citizens they thereby gain another level of self-realisation.

Politics has an expressive dimension; it is not just a procedure for reconciling or realising private, previously determined interests. It is the site of conflicts over meaning as well as over material resources. In a republic citizens publicly recognise that they share the good of the laws and practices of the republic. 'Public space is a crucial category for republicans' (Taylor, 1995: 96). When a practice is public it gains a special status. People do not just marry and have families, but their doing so gains public recognition.

In a modern liberal democracy shared goods are more latent than explicit. Today people value ordinary life as well as collective self-government, and are less interested in military honour or glory than fulfilment in personal relations. Thus their appreciation of political recognition is at risk, as they identify an emphasis on political action with aristocratic society (Taylor, 1995: 144). But they too have higher-order concerns, such as integrity, care or self-reliance. In a world where there are diverse views on what is important, realising the practices which allow individuals to pursue their goals needs deliberation and debate.

Institutionalising common goods

The activities within which we pursue our goals need institutions ranging from art galleries to football leagues to law courts and representative assemblies. And sharing these political institutions brings about further interdependence (Taylor, 1985: 310).

The central activity of politics is deliberating on questions concerning everyone; this entails acknowledging interdependence on these practices and institutions. Participation is meaningless without an underlying common purpose within horizons of shared meaning. In consequence, politics and the state cannot be neutral about questions of value. The state expresses and sustains the shared values of the political community. Thus, against neutralist or procedural liberals, Taylor argues that politics realises shared goods, rather than only individual or convergent goods.

Thus Taylor criticises the idea of liberal neutrality – that the state treats all citizens equally by being neutral with respect to conceptions of the good life. Even in a liberal society this is not the case. 'Liberal society itself cannot hold together just by satisfying its members' needs and interests; it requires a common or widespread set of beliefs which link its structures and practices with what its members see as of ultimate significance' (Taylor, 1989: 459). Freedom is the shared good which liberals value – 'freedom and individual diversity can only flourish in a society where there is a general recognition of their worth' (Taylor, 1985: 207). As a shared good, because it is often implicit instead of fully perceived, it tends to be undermined (Taylor, 1985: 97).

For Taylor, the republican commitment to participatory self-rule and shared values need not mean that there must be a single expression of common values in a diverse society in a way which excludes or oppresses minorities. Pursuing shared meanings in politics is itself a common project. For example, in Canada, national life is based on diversity, and the deliberative political resolution of difference is itself a significant part of the national identity.

Civic virtue

A collectively self-governing polity requires a high level of commitment to the polity. In order to sustain politics, citizens need not just to be law abiding but to identify with the institutions of the political community (Taylor, 1993: 41). For Taylor, political obligation is not a matter of voluntary consent to obey just institutions, but the acknowledgement of interdependence in social practices. Every political society requires some sacrifices and demands some disciplines from its members. In a free society, 'this can only be a willing identification with the polis on the part of the citizens' (Taylor, 1995: 165). Civic virtue is not understood in terms of self-interest or self-sacrifice, or egoism and altruism: 'It transcends egoism in the sense that people are really attached to the common good, to general liberty. But it is quite unlike the apolitical attachment to universal principle that the stoics advocated or that is central to modern ethics of rule by law' (Taylor, 1995: 187).

Citizens must have a sense of belonging to a particular community if they are to support the political community actively. 'Unless there is a common sense of a determinate community whose members sense a bond between them from this common allegiance, an identification with the common good cannot arise' (Taylor, 1993: 98).

Taylor also highlights the original sense of the term patriotism, as loyalty to the communal over private interests, rather than in its current sense of loyalty to one's own country as against others. This commitment to the common good comes from identifying with others in a particular common *enterprise*, though one based not on similarity but on a common history. Republican solidarity underpins freedom because it provides the motivation for self-imposed discipline. And the concern takes the form of supporting those institutions in quite general terms. It is not narrow obedience to whoever happens to be in power; in fact civic virtue is often exemplified in outrage at political malpractice.

Corruption

Conversely Taylor describes corruption in terms of failure to support the institutions of the polity. This arises from a blindness to the shared goods implicit in the modern practice of self-rule. But contemporary corruption is reflected less in the failure of individual citizens than in institutional failure to provide opportunities to participate, and in the alienation of citizens from bureaucratic rule. In this context the state comes to be seen as a provider of services, and politics as a clash of individual interests.

Taylor devotes less attention to ways of overcoming personal corruption than to the need to provide opportunities to participate and deliberate, to create a wider awareness of social interdependence, and to strengthen commitment to self-government. Greater political participation, especially at local levels, will itself generate the sense of identity needed for a flourishing society.

Material conditions for political equality

The importance of common citizenship suggests strong requirements for equality of resources. Yet in modern society people value individual prosperity as well as collective liberty and deliberation. If society is conceived of principally as an association of property holders, it may be hard to justify redistribution. But if it is a community of self-determining citizens, the importance of political equality justifies a significant level of redistribution, to address injustice and also the 'failure to embody or allow for certain excellences of the good life' (Taylor, 1985: 316). While freedom and inequality may seem compatible to libertarians, a sense of freedom can be sustained and reproduced in deliberation and interaction only among citizens who are relative equals.

Intensity and scope of political community

For Taylor citizens identify with a particular community of self-governing citizens, united by a sense of solidarity thicker than an agreement on principles of universal justice. 'The bond of solidarity with my compatriots in a functioning republic is based on a sense of shared fate, where the sharing itself is of value' (Taylor, 1995: 192).

Patriotism is a loyalty to a specific set of practices and institutions: 'modern democratic states require much greater solidarity toward compatriots than toward humanity in general' (Taylor, 1996: 120). This lies somewhere between friendship and family feeling, on one side, and altruistic dedication on the other (Taylor, 1995: 188). Like friendship, it is compatible with difference: 'A long history together can make the interchange with some partner, precisely in his/her difference, internal to one's own identity' (Taylor, 1994: 255). So although the relationship between citizens is based on a shared identity, this does not mean that they must be homogeneous. Citizens may have multiple nested identities.

Yet, while autonomy requires the engagement of individuals in social practices, Taylor goes further than this to say that, because culture sustains identity and meanings, cultures should be given expression in politics. Not just language in general, but specific languages are the bearers of common meanings and communication. If citizens have an 'obligation to belong', membership itself, and not simply interaction in the public sphere, is the ground of political community (Taylor 1985: 198). This reflects a more specific attachment to particular social practices than Arendt's 'taking responsibility' for the common world. So, although he endorses a liberal politics, he adopts a thicker model of political relations than Arendt. It may not be enough to speak a language to support it, but it may be necessary also to provide for its survival for future generations. In the case of Quebec, he defends legislation requiring all francophones and (non-English speaking) immigrants to send their children to francophone schools, and requiring the exclusive use of French by all except small businesses.

Taylor has extended his discussion of recognition in politics to apply to the currently much-debated issues of pluralism and multiculturalism. The multicultural nature of many modern societies makes problematic the public recognition of the values and practices of a single culture. Members of minorities, even if they have individual civic and political rights, are not being treated as equal citizens if their culture is overlooked or disparaged in society. If politics is to express citizens' values, how can it meet the conflicting demands or needs of two different cultures in a society? Those whose deepest values are not recognised suffer harm. In order to overcome the risk that minority cultures will be diminished, Taylor suggests that we should start from a premise that recognises enduring cultures as of equal worth, and seek out ways of providing more inclusive recognition of different identities.

So culture becomes a focus for politics. In fact Taylor, unlike Arendt, comes to see republican self-rule as taking the form of national self-determination in contemporary politics. National linguistic cultures are the domains of political community. Nationalism has a distinct origin and no intrinsic connection with republican self-government, so that it can be realised though despotic as well as democratic governments (Taylor, 1995: 142). Yet he believes on pragmatic grounds that nationality is today a condition of self-rule: 'civic humanism requires a strong identity with a community and the nation is the community of modern times' (Taylor, 1993: 42). This has come about as local and regional loyalties and powers are eroded and other communities bureaucratised to the level of 'service stations' that meet the consumer needs of citizens (roads, water-supply, health care, education or social welfare), but do not allow self-government.

It is not quite clear how the claims of national self-determination and recognising minority cultures are to be reconciled. There is at least an apparent tension between affirming the equal worth of cultures and endorsing the priority of a rather thicker-than-public culture of French in Quebec; which might suggest that the '*survivance*' of their culture has to be at the expense of immigrants.

Taylor redescribes the republican project in a way that makes it appear in many ways more attractive and less alien to modern aspirations than earlier expressions of the tradition. He demonstrates how deeply individual fulfilment is rooted in social practices. He gives an account of human beings as doubly *engaged* selves in that they both depend on social frameworks, and contribute to shaping those frameworks. He shows that the opposition between negative and positive conceptions of freedom is not as straightforward as it may initially appear, and that it is possible to invoke an active political dimension of freedom without leading to a justification of tyranny. Political participation can be both intrinsically and instrumentally valuable, without being the highest realisation of human existence. This is a less heroic politics than Arendt's, which makes room for the ordinary concerns of modern life that she undervalued.

Similarly, Taylor, unlike Arendt, acknowledges the importance of rights, and the practicalities of representation. He describes himself as a liberal–republican, but, although he speaks of republican self-government as a latent dimension of our society, he does not make it quite clear exactly how his liberalism and republicanism are related.[8]

The fact that individual fulfilment depends on cultural practices does not necessarily mean that all or any particular social practices or communities should be supported. In discussing the politics of recognition, however, Taylor comes almost to treat culture in a holist sense. Individuals appear to be more closely tied to prepolitical, cultural goods than their political autonomy might suggest. It is also not clear whether or how far the premise of the equal worth of all cultures can be institutionalised in practice. Whether the relations of solidarity between self-determining citizens subject to a common fate should be identified with those of members of a particular pre-political culture is an issue explored in Chapter VIII.

Conclusion

Arendt and Taylor emphasise the value of participation in politics. They highlight the limitations of negative freedom, and rehabilitate the idea of political freedom in the light of modern concerns with recognition. Individual identity is in part constructed through life in the public world. And political life is intrinsically more valuable than liberal theorists took it to be for most of the twentieth century. But specific questions remain unanswered about the priority of individual and common goods, the conditions for civic virtue, the nature of freedom, the feasibility or desirability of widespread political participation in the twenty-first century, and the possibility of universal recognition through politics, as well as the specific institutional structures these require.

PART II

Contemporary Debates

Introduction to Part II

What I aim to do in Part II is not to stipulate what is the essence of republican theory, but to explore how best to address current problems, and how to avoid the difficulties encountered by historical accounts of republicanism and by existing liberal and communitarian accounts. Republicanism is a theory still under development, rather than one that exists ready-made for application to contemporary issues.

In this part of the book, I discuss the issues that arise for a contemporary articulation of republican political theory within the framework of the four focal concepts: civic virtue, freedom, participation, and recognition; and I examine the problems and criticisms they encounter. These could be considered as four dimensions of modern citizenship which have to be addressed. Civic virtue and political participation are sometimes combined in the idea of active citizenship, but they are conceptually distinct, and so I treat them separately here.

Chapter V discusses the nature and significance of the common goods of a political community, how *civic virtue* is implied in sustaining these, and what it means to put public before private interests. Is this oppressive or simply too demanding of citizens? How can civic virtue be elicited in citizens?

Chapter VI analyses debates about the nature of *freedom* in civic republican theory. What is freedom for republicans? Is it a matter of self-mastery, of non-interference, of non-domination, or of some kind of mutual self-determination? What are the material preconditions for freedom? What is the extent of state action and justified coercion? Is there any place for rights in republican politics?

Chapter VII discusses the role and form of political *participation*. How is political equality best realised? Can a deliberative form of democracy be more inclusive and legitimate than existing forms? What is the scope of deliberation? What institutions and procedures does this require? Can this kind of politics deal with the size, complexity and diversity of cultures in a modern society?

Chapter VIII considers issues arising from understanding politics in terms of *recognition*. What at is at stake in the claim for equal recognition, and to what extent can republican politics deliver it? What is the intensity and scope of the republican political community? Should a republic be based on common nationality? Does the internal community of citizens depend on external relations of enmity or exclusion, or radically limit obligations to outsiders?

CHAPTER V
Common goods and public virtue

> Is there no virtue among us? If there be not we are in a wretched situation. No theoretical checks, no form of government can render us secure. To suppose that any form of government will secure liberty or happiness without any virtue in the people, is a chimerical idea.
>
> (Madison)[1]

Introduction

While people often acknowledge that they have responsibilities, as parents and children, as friends or neighbours, the idea of civic virtue, of an extensive responsibility to the larger political community, does not chime easily with contemporary ways of thinking. The very word 'civic virtue' connotes, if not authoritarian Jacobin austerity, then nineteenth-century municipal preoccupations with tidy parks and street furniture. 'Public spirit' is a little less alien. 'Civility' is more acceptable, perhaps because it sounds less demanding. Likewise the term 'the common good' is no longer popular, because it has been used to justify overbearing power over individuals, and can be invoked to promote thinly veiled self-interest.

The idea that citizens need to be concerned with the common good and to take some personal responsibility for realising it is one of the longest-standing themes of civic republicanism, which flows from understanding citizens as engaged in a political community. The obverse, corruption, is at one level an excessive concern with particular private interests, but, more generally, it represents the inherent fragility of political systems.

This chapter examines the grounds for civic virtue, and addresses some of the issues that surround it. Is there a problem of corruption today? Does society need public-spirited citizens? What are the common goods of citizenship which justify such a commitment? What does it mean to put the public before the private? What, specifically, does civic virtue require? Is it oppressive or moralistic? Are there ways in which civic virtue can be elicited, or in which the character of citizens can be shaped, that are compatible with freedom?

Any commitment to civic virtue and the common good may be seen as subordinating the individual to society, or private life to public life, in a way that is incompatible with modern concerns with individual fulfilment. The requirement of civic virtue may be seen to be *anachronistic, oppressive, moralistic* or *unrealistic*. It may seem a throwback to small, weakly institutionalised ancient democracies, where there was no separate state to carry out collective decisions. In some interpretations at least, the historical notion of civic virtue oppressed citizens by requiring uniform standards of behaviour. Even if not oppressive, it conveys a political world dominated by obligations rather than by rights; it may be too morally demanding of citizens, and therefore both unrealistic and undesirable.

Liberals for long resisted the idea that common goods require extensive civic virtue among citizens. While it is widely agreed that citizens should obey the law and pay taxes, it is often argued that this political obligation is the limit of a citizen's duties in a representative, law-governed state. It may be seen as unrealistic to expect any degree of commitment to what is shared, given the loosely connected societies we live in today, in which it may be difficult to see the impact of any personal effort in the larger social picture. In this way even voting, to say nothing of larger sacrifices of personal interests, may appear not to be worthwhile.

Feminists have argued that the demands imposed by civic virtue discriminate against women; first it was defined in militarist and masculinist terms which depended on their exclusion. Subsequently they were given a gender-differentiated citizenship that prescribed for them a distinct civic virtue devoted to rearing male citizens and soldiers (Pateman, 1988; Vogel, 1981).

Do we need public-spirited citizens? Corruption and threats to common goods

The argument underlying the idea of civic virtue is that the freedom of interdependent citizens ultimately depends on their active commitment to the collective goods they share. Political institutions that provide some degree of control over our destinies are still a fragile creation that cannot be taken for granted. This is underlined by the difficulties in establishing a flourishing political and social life in the former socialist states where liberal–democratic political, legal and economic institutions were set up after 1989. And established liberal democracies also experience financial scandals, tax revolts, voter alienation and increasing head-on conflicts of rights claims between citizens and the state; Western societies imprison an increasing number of people, but have not put an end to crime. For a society to flourish, a significant fraction of the population must act in socially responsible ways even when they are not subject to law. Volumes of legislation on campaign finance and public ethics have not solved the problems of unequal access to power and lack of accountability. Contrary to assumptions, we cannot safely leave politics to the politicians. Madison's hope that institutions would balance out interests and bring the virtuous to electoral office seems to have been unfounded. Without vigilant citizens, we cannot be sure that our institutions will not be taken over by sectional interests and used to act against our interests instead of for them.

In the meantime common goods that people in Western societies have tended to take for granted are now under threat – for example, clean air and fresh water. And certain common bads or risks have emerged, that there is great difficulty in addressing collectively, such as unsustainable development and societies with an increasing threat of violence.

Many states described as liberal democracies or even republics today provide services from defence through economic infrastructure to health care and education. But the state is portrayed as supplying these mainly as individual interests, rather than as common goods. People understand the worth of citizenship more readily in terms of rights than duties. The average citizen typically recognises as duties no more than to obey the law (including payment of taxes), and possibly, though decreasingly, to vote. In voting, political rationality is defined in terms of pursuing self-interest. Successive elections in industrialised countries show that citizens are increasingly likely to be politically segmented along cultural, economic and geographical lines. Without a commitment to some common interests, willingness even to obey laws and pay taxes comes under strain. And people who have lost faith in government do not set up alternative networks, but tend to disengage further. Even well-intentioned people feel powerless, and see no point in being apparently the only ones who are prepared to exercise restraint. The deterioration in public services and the degradation of the environment prompt the suggestion that the issue is not whether we can afford any kind of civic virtue, but how we might survive without it.

We shall see that two kinds of arguments can be derived from this. One is that institutions and laws alone cannot guarantee a democratic politics and a flourishing society. The other is that if politics is structured around individual interests, we lose sight of common goods important for human self-realisation. Following the first (essentially liberal) argument, civic virtue is needed to guarantee individual interests. The price of freedom is eternal vigilance. As in the instrumental interpretation of Machiavelli's civic virtue, citizens must be prepared to take an active role, restrain their claims of rights, and support institutions in order to realise their individual interests in the longer term (Skinner, 1990, Spitz, 1994). On the second (more distinctively republican) argument, we might go further to say that civic virtue is needed to sustain common goods. Self-governing citizens, who take a wider view of the purposes of politics and consider common as well as individual goods in their political demands, enjoy a fuller freedom.

Neither individual freedom nor a wide range of common goods can be secured exclusively through deregulated market exchanges of individual interests, or through state provision and legal regulation. This needs the goodwill and active contribution of a substantial number of citizens who in some sense identify with the institutions and laws, and are actively concerned with the common goods of their society. Otherwise laws are flouted, and institutions from which people are alienated cease functioning. This suggests that the idea of citizen commitment to the common goods of society is not anachronistic in itself. But we need to consider what form it might take that will not be oppressive or unrealistically demanding.

The common good

The common good is a concept that is not popular today. The introduction of even the notion of the common good of a political society may be resisted as collectivist and potentially oppressive.

However, there are a number of different senses in which it can be used. These need conceptual clarification. There are senses of the common good which are not inherently oppressive, and which represent important dimensions of human life. Without a concept of common good only quantifiable benefits distributable among discrete individuals can be considered part of the good that politics provides.

The common good may be understood in at least the following senses:

The corporate good of a social group The common good has historically often been used in the sense of the unitary good of an organic or corporate whole directed to a single purpose. This includes Aristotle's *teleological* conception based on human nature, and Rousseau's collectively determined conception, the General Will, as well as some communitarian interpretations of the national interest or shared values of cultural and ethnic groups. This sense has been justly criticised as intrinsically hostile to individual freedom and self-determination.

The aggregate of individual goods Accordingly it has been suggested that the only legitimate sense of the term is a simple *aggregative* one, as the sum of individual goods. On this basis, if benefits to some are offset by losses by others, we cannot talk of the 'common' good. There is no sense here in which goods are shared. As Margaret Thatcher might have said, there is no such thing as the common good, but only the good of individuals, families and so on.[2]

But there are other ways of understanding the common good that may be relevant to politics. As Mouffe puts it, 'Our only choice is not one between an aggregate of individuals without common public concern and a pre-modern community organised around a single common good' (Mouffe, 1992: 231).

If there is not a single common good, or goal of society, there are *common goods*, that can be achieved – and harms avoided – only through cooperation.

The ensemble of conditions for individual goods A more complex understanding sees the common good as the ensemble of conditions for individual fulfilment. This is the sense of the common good which liberals from Locke to Rawls recognise. Here it refers to goods from which everyone benefits (and correspondingly, common bads are those from which everyone suffers).[3] We may all benefit from peace or improved traffic flows, and suffer from increased output of greenhouse gases, but it is mainly as separate individuals with our own priorities and purposes that we do so.[4] If such common goods benefit all, it is as individuals for their own diverse purposes, an *individualist–instrumental* use. (So these are like Taylor's convergent goods.) This is the principal sense intended by contemporary 'instrumental republicans', who argue that these goods cannot be realised effectively by political institutions alone, but need greater commitment of citizens to support them. Political participation and civic virtue are then the necessary *precondition* for realising diverse personal goods or life plans, if not intrinsically valuable activities (Skinner, 1990). While this can be expressed as putting the common good first, it might also be expressed as pursuing long-term interests, or exercising more foresight in realising individual interests. This entails an instrumental account of civic virtue.

Even these examples of common goods may not be valued exclusively as a matter of individual distribution, or be immediately distributed across individuals. It may be a matter of keeping positive possibilities open, and minimising common risks; for example, the environmental goods of clean air, water and sustainable growth. The significance we attach to them may be greater because we may be concerned for their survival for the future for individuals who are not yet born or may not yet be identifiable. Those who are vulnerable in common to such dangers may be seen as living in what Arendt calls a *common world*, and thus share at least a frame of reference. At this level, it may be more appropriate to speak of common concerns than of shared goods.

This points towards a further sense of common goods.

What is good for each person as a member of a society or group
There is also an *intersubjective–practical* sense of the common good in which people who are intrinsically social as well as significantly separate benefit as members of a group. While we may not be able to speak of *the* common good, understood as a single overarching purpose in society, there are common goods which can be realised only in interaction with others. The republican tradition

has emphasised the interdependence of citizens, in its material, moral, psychological and ontological dimensions. Humans carry on their lives only in a range of practices in which they interact with others, and which give (or fail to give) public recognition to certain goods.

Realising the ideal of autonomy prefigured in the tradition (and further developed in Chapter VI) requires collective or common goods. We saw that for Taylor, freedom depends on engaging in social practices through which people exercise their capacities and relate to others. These practices exist in and through the actions of individuals, and their value depends on the opportunities for self-realisation they offer them. But this means that individual self-realisation depends on common goods, and is constricted by common bads in a way that cannot be understood wholly instrumentally. These are 'irreducibly social goods' in the way that, without a group of common language speakers, you cannot communicate through your native language.

But the existence of such common goods does not always rely on consciously shared values. People tend to use their native language unreflectively. It becomes a consciously shared value only when threatened with extinction, when language preservation or revival movements are set up. The idea of the common good does not translate directly into shared values.

Yet, as we have seen, shared goods, as distinct from convergent ones, depend on common meanings. Social institutions not only create the possibility of certain kinds of life, but also confirm their value. As Raz puts it, 'a person's well-being depends to a large extent on success in socially defined and determined pursuits and activities' (Raz, 1986: 309, 162). You cannot, for example, be a monogamist in a society of polygamists; you are just someone who so far has one wife.

Some, but not all, socially recognised activities gain part of their value from their being joint activities, participated in *with* others, like the enjoyment of a party or a concert, where 'the individual experiences are unintelligible apart from their reference to the enjoyment of others' (Waldron, 1993b: 355).

Instead of seeing people as quite distinct entities we have to recognise how they are interconnected, and how the good of one is often dependent on the good of others. The common good is realised in the activities of participants for whom membership in the community of the practice is part of living a worthwhile life. (Conversely, there are common harms which cannot fully be avoided by separate individuals. Thus feminists have argued that the harm of sexual harassment, for example, cannot be understood in individual terms, but represents a wider social practice with effects on women in general.) The common good towards which members are oriented is the flourishing of those practices, and this depends on the quality of participation by members. Thus there are common goods which are not decomposable into individually distributed goods, and cannot be understood wholly instrumentally. These goods are neither a property of the whole, nor determined by the goal of an organic entity. Thus, in this context, it is more appropriate to speak of common goods than 'the' unitary common good.

Some common goods have a certain priority over individual goods because they consist of practices and possibilities through which individuals realise themselves in many dimensions essential to human fulfilment. But common goods should not be thought of as inherently in conflict with the good of individuals, but as part of the good of individuals. Nor are they essentially in tension with freedom, if it is understood in terms of autonomy. Autonomy is a matter of acting according to one's most significant purposes, and needs some social framework of support. 'The provision of many collective goods is constitutive of the very possibility of autonomy, and it cannot be relegated to a subordinate role, compared with some alleged right against coercion in the name of autonomy' (Raz, 1986: 207).[5]

Common good and the political community

But, it may be argued, the constituency of concern for common goods is not necessarily that of a political community. Common goods relate groups which are not coterminous with state boundaries; common cultural and environmental concerns may be both more local and more extensive, in families, religious groups, nations and continents.[6] As individuals and groups, citizens may have conflicting goods and ideas of what constitutes the common good. However, those who are citizens of a modern state share a significant range of social practices and common concerns by virtue of being subject to the jurisdiction of a common sovereign authority.

Common Goods and Public Virtue

They are thrown together by the fact of birth or residence in the same polity. Even in a globalising world, independent states still exert great authority. They have coercive, fiscal and symbolic power, and they bound overlapping ranges of practices and interactions to a very significant degree to create multiply reiterated interdependencies. The differential experience of East and West Germans up to 1990 provides a good illustration. Even in the case of the Republic of Ireland and Northern Ireland, where the border has been more permeable to movement and media, where one state has been deeply divided and many nationalists in Northern Ireland have felt deep affinities with the South, the existence of separate states has strongly determined the bounds of interactions in practice (Whyte, 1983). Accordingly, the interdependence of citizens, if largely involuntary in origin, is particularly significant. They live, in something like Arendt's sense, in a common world. They share at least common concerns and a common fate. They are vulnerable to one another. And, for good or ill, things that appear in public acquire a significance which affects the possibilities of its members. The state significantly frames the constituency of concern of important common goods.

Those who live in a modern liberal representative democracy are subject to an authority that they may potentially hold to account. If they can make it accountable at all, they are jointly responsible for the direction it may take. But republican citizenship, being a member of a non-dominated or self-directing political community, is understood as in itself a *common good* in the intersubjective practical sense; the good of citizenship, as well as a means of realising other individual and collective goods. It is common in the sense that it is realised to the extent that all other citizens enjoy the rights and support the practices that it entails. We shall see that one way of understanding the common good shared by members of the republic is as *freedom as non-domination*, constituted by the intersubjectively secured status of equal citizenship, which no one can achieve for themselves unless others in the same category enjoy it (Pettit, 1997a: 259). On a stronger republican theory, the good of citizenship lies in active participation in collective self-determination. 'When politics goes well, we can know a good in common...that we cannot know alone' (Sandel, 1982: 183). In both cases the political common good is not just a precondition for individual good, but *constitutes* it.

155

Different claims need to be distinguished here. To say that membership of a self-governing political community is an *intrinsic* (or non-instrumental) good is distinct from saying that it is the *ultimate* good, or the highest realisation of human nature (Mason, 2000: 43–5, 111; Raz, 1986: 177–8). While Arendt regarded the practice of self-government as the ultimate good, it is better to see it as an intrinsic good which realises freedom in self-government. It is particularly important in so far as it shapes other social practices within which people pursue their lives. Thus it can be seen as a *framing* common good, different from an instrumental good in so far as it has value in itself (Raz, 1995: 37). Of course, in a more mundane way political life is also instrumentally valuable in achieving material purposes such as security and economic welfare. It is in so far as citizenship has this framing status that it makes any sense to give it priority.

The model of common good central to republican politics is that of intersubjective recognition in the joint practice of self-government by citizens who share certain concerns deriving from their common vulnerability. Thus it should be distinguished from the idea of a common good as a set of shared pre-political values, and from more general senses of belonging to a community. First, values that happen to be shared within a group may not fully realise or sustain their common goods. Those who share common goods may mis-identify them, or fail to coordinate, or otherwise fail to realise them publicly. Second, the recognition and empowerment provided by political activity and the status of citizenship are distinct from feelings of belonging *per se*.

While some communitarians see shared values as the basis of the republic, we shall see that a republic does not necessarily start from clearly agreed purposes but from sharing a common world and common fate. Because there may be multiple perspectives on common goods, the political community is only in a loose sense a collective enterprise. Citizens may not share a clear single goal or deep values, and they may understand the goals of the polity from different angles, and value citizenship for different reasons.[7] That they share a common good may be more easily recognised in negative instances of common 'bads', or risks that face members of a community.

Because citizens may adopt multiple perspectives, their common goods are better understood in intersubjective–practical rather than in teleological or unitary terms. It is possible to share a political common good without a comprehensively shared conception of the good life.

As common goods do not take determinate form until specified in relation to concrete policies, it is better to think of them in terms of common concerns. *The* common good is a horizon of meaning, or a regulative idea to be taken into account in actions and decision-making, rather than a fixed goal.

This needs to be specified in interaction in a political community, where shared values may emerge. When social practices are publicly recognised, certain common goods are given priority. Thus a central common good is the existence of public spaces in which citizens can act and deliberate on the shape of their society and its social practices. None the less, even when politically and inclusively determined (as in the fallibilist account to be developed here), the way the common goods of a society are specified will favour some practices rather than others. To this extent it is true that 'the republican tradition seeks to shape a public culture of a certain kind, even where doing so privileges certain conceptions of the good life over others' (Sandel, 1998: 329). But in a republic these are not understood as replicating the values of a pre-political community, or based on an existing consensus, but as determined in politics.

The dangers of hypocrisy and fanaticism are often advanced as arguments against the use of language of the common good in politics. The common good may be invoked politically to lend individual or sectional interests a spurious respectability. Thus today dam projects that benefit international engineering companies and hubristic political leaders are defended in the name of the 'greater common good' (Roy, 1999). And even those who sincerely intend the common good may be excessively righteous, and see themselves as its best, or only, legitimate interpreters.[8] But these arguments constitute a case not against the idea of the common good, but in favour of its political definition and scrutiny of actions justified in its name.

The common good of freedom and membership in a political community needs the active engagement of citizens if it is to be realised. Civic virtue is important because active membership supports social practices in which people realise other common goods, and the political community is a crucial frame for these social practices. While the common goods of members of a polity partly depend on the state, the state depends on the active support of citizens.

Is civic virtue oppressive? The republican public–private distinction

Citizens should act to put public interests before private. But this is not to say that these are centrally interpreted and imposed by the state.[9] Thus a pervasive critique of republicanism is misdirected. There is an important difference between the republican and liberal understandings of the nature of public and private that is crucial here. In liberal thought public and private are distinguished primarily on the dimension of *control*. What is public is what is controlled by all or many; what is private is controlled by one, a few, or specified individuals. In political terms, the public is identified as what is controlled by the state, and the private as what is not controlled by the state, and these are mutually exclusive (Benn and Gaus, 1983; Pitkin, 1981). It may then be assumed that the republican concern that common goods should be put before individual interests unpacks to mean that these are to be realised or imposed by the action of the state. But republicanism does not simply reverse the priorities of liberalism or redraw the boundaries of private and public. The republican distinction between public and private is paradigmatically different. For republicans the most salient dimension of the public is *interest* or relevance; what is quintessentially public is in the interest of all; what is private is in the interest of or relevant to one, a few or specified individuals, or sections of society. This does not map directly on to the state and the non-state. Thus there is a less clear-cut opposition of private and public (Honohan, 2000).

Public and private are not primarily opposed as two separate spheres, but as different orientations within individuals. This highlights a tension *within* each person between the immediately perceived particular advantage of each and the general interest of the citizen as an interdependent member of the polity, and requires each to be active in pursuit of the common good, to have *public spirit*, and to participate in public service.

If it is defined in terms of interest, the public is seen as rather diffuse, extending throughout the citizenry rather than necessarily being concentrated in a single agency or institution such as the state. The dimension of control is not immediately entailed. Characterising something as being in the public interest does not directly imply its enforcement by the state.

The common good is not that of a corporate entity *over and above* any of the citizens but the good of the citizens themselves as members of a political community, as distinct from their good as singular individuals. In this perspective the considered good of citizens takes priority over desires, preferences and values that are separable from their characters as members of this political society.

The primacy of the public over the private reflects not the good of the *majority* over the minority, but a division within each citizen. For everyone has both a public and a private interest; even the industrialist *qua* citizen has an interest in breathing clean air. Heteronymous private preferences are self-destructive when they put immediate purely individual advantage ahead of the advantages enjoyed as a citizen. Those who put private before public interest are not just short-sighted; they suffer from serious blind spots, and fail to see where their real advantage lies, and the importance of questions of who they are as well as what they want.

Not all individual interests are defined as inherently corrupt. But it is important to focus on common goods because under current social conditions they are less visible and therefore more vulnerable. We become aware of the importance of the ozone layer only when the pursuit of individual goods begins to destroy it, and of languages when they are dead or dying. We regret the loss of countryside or wilderness only when these have been dramatically reduced by urban and industrial expansion. And regretting does not itself counter the market forces that may have produced such results. Markets that are shaped by individual interests are good at providing individual goods; they are notoriously inadequate at providing – indeed tend to erode – public goods. To achieve these requires that certain individual interests be limited.

Civic virtue is, like the classical idea of virtue from which it derives, an established disposition to act in certain ways, not a matter of acting in accordance with law or duty. It represents internalised inclination, closer to what Tocqueville called 'habits of the heart', or Aristotle saw as the education of desire, than the triumph of reason. It involves developing and modifying perceptions of where our interests lie. It is not a matter of choosing to be wholly altruistic or wholly selfish, but of identifying with an expanding range of others through action and experience. Civic virtue is a second nature, a predisposition to act voluntarily in some wider interests; it cannot satisfactorily be enforced by the state, and is not inherently in conflict with individual self-realisation.

Thus the idea of civic virtue itself is not inherently oppressive. But any attempt to impose it under unfavourable conditions, as in one interpretation of the French Revolution, or in contemporary Cuba, for example, will lead to oppression. The problem is not the introduction of the idea of civic virtue but the attempt to impose it by force (MacIntyre, 1984: 238).[10] But it should be noted that there is a difference between enforcing obligations and fostering the capacities which dispose citizens to fulfil these special obligations; republican politics may still be concerned with eliciting civic virtue (Mason, 2000: 112–13).

Although virtue and rights are often seen as contrasting principles of republican and contractarian political theory, freedom is a central concern of contemporary republicanism, and the emphasis on the common good and virtue can accommodate a range of individual rights (as we shall see in Chapter VI).

Specifying civic virtue

A further criticism of the idea of civic virtue is that, as currently advanced, it is too vague to give any understanding of its practical implications, and therefore may have very diverse political implications (Pangle, 1998; Galston, 1998).

So in what follows I try to specify some of the dimensions of civic virtue necessary for a self-governing citizenry who share concerns for the common world. Virtues and civic virtue are not discrete qualities, but dispositions which support practices and ways of life – in this case the practice of self-government. It should be noted that virtues, unlike legal duties, are not absolute requirements, but are realised to a greater or lesser degree.

Awareness Citizens become *aware* of the interdependencies and common economic, social and environmental concerns of the polity. They recognise how they are related to other citizens in being dependent on practices supported by them, and affecting them by their actions. Since the possibility of self-government depends on the equal opportunity of all to be self-governing, they inform themselves of the social conditions of their fellow citizens. This is civic virtue as orientation to *fellow citizens*, based on multiply reiterated interdependencies, rather than commonality of race, culture or religion. Citizens pay *attention* to political issues, and contribute to policy decisions directly or indirectly.[11]

Self-restraint They exercise some *self-restraint* in pursuing personal interests in wealth, power or status; this corresponds to the classical idea of accepting duties and putting the common good before the individual. Recognising their interdependence with other citizens, they accept the justice of some redistributive measures designed to maintain political equality, so that all can participate. They do not support common goods only when this converges with their individual interests; indeed they do not continuously calculate the balance of interests. They accept individual costs which will range along a continuum from, for example, taking time to recycle, to sacrificing wealth, through giving time and energy for political concerns, up to, in some circumstances, risking death. This suggests significantly limiting expectations of growth in the direction of sustainable development, and revaluing work partly in terms of the common goods (or bads) it realises, rather than solely in terms of the individual market-determined rewards.[12] Political participation itself may take forms from the very minimal and familiar voting and serving on juries to attending hearings, engaging in deliberative processes, up to serving in public office. This is implied in taking responsibility as a citizen for what happens in the common world rather than focusing on personal integrity alone.

Deliberative engagement When *engaged in politics* virtuous citizens adopt an approach which recognises the multiplicity of perspectives. We shall see in Chapter VII that deliberation is central to participation; thus a crucial part of civic virtue is *willingness to deliberate*; to reflect on opinions and communicate with others. They regard politics not primarily as a means of realising individual interests, but as a process of communication through which common interests may be defined and realised. This involves more than tolerance. Citizens listen to other points of view, are prepared to explain their own position and to revise it in deliberation. But it does not presuppose consensus; there will be strong differences on how to interpret, prioritise and realise common goods. Learning to deal with conflict is itself an important part of civic virtue. Citizens need to be able to exercise independent judgement, but accept decisions when made in a fair public procedure. But they are vigilant with respect to abuses of power, public or private. They are prepared to raise and support others who raise issues of concern in the public arena, and to defend the interests of fellow citizens subject to injustices as well as defending themselves. This may involve opposing laws which undermine freedom, including civil disobedience and direct action (Kostakopoulou, 1996; Parekh, 1993).

Civic virtue, then, entails active *solidarity* with other citizens – sometimes against government and institutions – rather than passive obedience to laws. But this does not require continuous frenetic political activity by all the citizens. Political participation is only one aspect of active citizenship; civic virtue is an attitude displayed by citizens in their interactions within the framework of the polity (Philp, 2000).

Conversely, just as civic virtue goes beyond formally obeying laws, corruption is not found only in illegal activities, but in engaging in political interaction to realise only individual or sectional interests in wealth, power or status; in ignoring political and social affairs, or refusing to take account of, or deliberate with the views of others. It is exemplified by those who turn a blind eye to political wrongdoing, leaving it to others to report or protest against it. There are obviously many degrees of corruption, some much more serious than others. But systemic corruption is present when political institutions are structured in terms of bargaining between individual interests. This is broader than the more conventional and obvious forms of corruption of using wealth to buy political influence and political power to enrich oneself (Shumer, 1979).

Is civic virtue moralistic?

Even if civic virtue is not oppressive, it may still be regarded as too morally demanding and as requiring citizens to conform to a uniform model that places excessive burdens on at least some (Habermas, 1996). On this account the demand may be seen as unjust or unrealistic. The notion of civic virtue entails only some

Common Goods and Public Virtue

elements of a wider moral theory of the virtues. In acknowledging the role of this kind of established disposition in sustaining political life, civic republicans are not alone. Many liberals now agree (contrary to some earlier formulations) that a liberal polity cannot be sustained on the basis of legal institutions and safeguards alone, but requires the support of citizens who practise certain virtues; for example, of tolerance, honesty, and promise-keeping. But these liberal virtues may be seen as 'thin', as a minimal commitment to fair procedures, or vigilance in protecting one's own interests, whereas republican virtues are more substantial, more communally directed, and thus may seem to be more demanding (Galston, 1988; Burtt, 1993).

The list here is neither as demanding or as general as might appear at first sight. It does include virtues specifically excluded from some accounts of liberal civic virtue. Political participation, putting the public before the private, and subordinating personal interest to the common good are absent from Galston's listing of liberal virtues. But it does not express a general requirement to be 'good'. Its norms are not for saints but for 'good enough' citizens. In the current context of expanded private interests, it may seem more heroic than it really is.[13]

It does not concern the whole of morality, but only a political morality, the virtues needed for self-governing citizens.[14] These are entailed by a commitment to a political society of mutually self-determining citizens and the common world in which they interact. It does not directly concern the intimate lives of citizens and politicians alike in areas which are not relevant to their attention to the common good. In the modern world there will be a difference between the requirements for the good citizen and the good person. 'One need not believe that civic virtue constitutes the whole of virtue in order to view it as an intrinsic good, an essential aspect of human flourishing' (Sandel, 1998: 325).

It may also be useful to draw attention to the features of many traditional accounts of virtue that are not included (though these may or may not still be valued on other grounds). It does not include Machiavelli's warrior virtues of ambition, ruthlessness or glory, Rousseau's intellectual simplicity or submergence in common will. It does not elevate political activity above all others, unlike the Athenians or Arendt. Nor does it require silence or modesty for women. It is not as demanding as the Christian message of universal love, or many other religious messages. It does not require general charity to the disadvantaged. It is not dependent on any understanding of the place of humans in a cosmic value scheme. It does not require citizens to take up responsibilities which the state already carries out more effectively, or which only the state can carry out.

The focus of republican civic virtue is, moreover, notably narrower than the call for virtue advanced by some communitarian theorists, who argue for much more sweeping reformation of character (Etzioni, 1995a; Sacks, 1997; Selbourne, 1997). It has nothing to say about the accounts of family values, marital fidelity, religious belief, punctuality, industry or self-sufficiency, that have been emphasised by moral communitarians. Some of these may be independently important elements of morality, but they are not directly entailed in the civic virtue needed by self-determining citizens. The citizenry may establish social practices that require other virtues, but that is a separate matter.

Political obligation and civic virtue

While civic virtue may be specified to some degree in response to the vagueness objection, there is no fixed 'standard' or intensity of virtue that is demanded of all. There are many different forms which it may take for different people, because supporting mutual self-government has multiple dimensions (Philp, 2000; Wolff, 2000). The circumstances of the republic and the individual also affect the level and kind of civic virtue which can be expected from citizens. Unlike legal obligations such as paying taxes or observing speed limits, there is no clear metric for how active, tolerant, respectful, etc. a citizen should be, in taking on responsibility for mutual self-government.

It is a less *heroic* account of virtue than that advanced by Machiavelli or even Arendt. Rather than putting glory and greatness before material interest, a virtuous citizen puts the opportunity to be self-governing and to shape social practices before more specifically individual interests, and identifies with a broader rather than a narrower dimension of the self. There are benefits (both internal and external) that are realised in practising civic virtue. It resembles other responsibilities whose observance are regarded as benefits rather than costs – as the duties of friendship or parenthood can be (Raz, 1989: 19; Scheffler, 1997: 193; Mason, 2000: 110). Some of the pressure for parental leave reflects the fact that, under favourable conditions, the duties of child-rearing are part of the good of parenthood. Again, under favourable conditions, the sense of self-worth, achievement and significance achieved in contributing to a polity may be so regarded. These are special obligations justified by the good of citizenship (Mason, 2000: 100). It is thus different from contributing to benefits received in a system of fair exchange, if those are understood as individually distributed and realised. Many of the benefits are more potential than real, and the effect would be lost if parents or citizens were to calculate the exact costs and returns. This means it is not always irrational to be unilaterally virtuous. Civic virtues often promote the good of the individual along with that of the wider society.

This responsibility is broader and more fluid than political obligation in the narrow sense of obedience to law, as a commitment to shared goods and the possibility of collective self-determination. Political obligation is here understood as being based on the engagement of citizens in a polity, rather than on voluntary contract, individual utility or natural justice. People have obligations to those who are systematically vulnerable to their action, as are citizens interdependent in multiply reiterated practices. They can either cooperate in political interaction, or jeopardise their chances to shape their inevitably common future. They can realise, or fail to realise the good of citizenship and the valuable relationships which constitute it. They owe these obligations to people they may never know well, feel emotionally attached to, or even meet.

Interdependence grounds bonds and obligations between those who find themselves in a polity and are thereby vulnerable to common risks and have the potential opportunity to be mutually self-governing. Jointly self-governing citizens, who are significantly equal though different, have special obligations to one another that are not self-assumed and are not reducible to observing laws or loyalty to the state. Obligations to fellow citizens can be justified despite theoretical difficulties in grounding narrower political obligation and the practical suspicions of uncritical patriotism to contemporary states (Simmons, 1996; Horton, 1993, Parekh, 1993).

The nature of this relationship, and of the commitment possible among large and diverse bodies of citizens, will be discussed further in Chapter VIII.

As we have seen, civic virtue takes various forms, from more passive self-restraint to active public service and even to resistance. It does not mean simply more *obedience or deference to authority* than in a liberal system. It should be noted that it is an obligation owed between citizens rather than to any central authority. As Parekh puts it:

> as members of a polity citizens owe it to their fellow members and not to the civil authority to expose its wrongdoings, to participate in the conduct of public affairs, to highlight prevailing injustices and in general to promote the wellbeing of their community.
>
> (Parekh, 1993: 244)

This requires acting independently in the interests of the common world and political sphere. If it is an obligation to 'belong', as Taylor puts it, it is in the sense of engagement with matters of common concern, not of adhering to the current interpretation of the common good, or of conforming to social expectations.

Feminist objections

The traditional notion of civic virtue has been criticised for its militaristic nature. This was particularly pronounced in Machiavelli's account, though less so in other expressions from Aristotle to Rousseau. The content of civic virtue depends on historical circumstances and the nature of the threats to freedom or self-government. In the Italian city-states these came from internal or external seizures of power by force. There need be nothing quite so martial about civic virtue in a republic which is not under constant threat of external attack; and we have seen that the modern republican tradition has become progressively less militaristic. When the principal threat to the republic is external attack, it may be more appropriate to understand civic virtue in military terms, but to the extent that the threats are identified as political corruption, commercial power and consumerism, environmental degradation, social exclusion or fragmentation, the requirements of civic virtue will vary accordingly.

The feminist critique of civic republican politics was based not only on its militaristic origins, however, but also on its demand of uniformity from the citizens. The emphasis on political participation by active citizens was defined in masculinist terms of strength, rationality, courage, impartiality and fraternity which made republican politics as alien as its liberal counterpart.

> Founded by men, the modern state and its realm of citizenship paraded as universal, values and norms which were derived from specifically masculine experience: militarist norms of honour and homoerotic camaraderie; respectful competition and bargaining among independent agents; discourse framed in unemotional tones of dispassionate reasoning.
>
> (Young, 1990b: 120)

A woman's virtue was defined in terms of emotion, weakness or silence, and this notion was used as a pretext to confine her to domestic life. Republics exalted public relations and identified the private as corrupt, and were contemptuous of private concerns in the family. When women were incorporated into citizenship it was on different terms from men, in a separate sphere – as private wives and mothers to public citizens and soldiers. Republicans from Athens to Rousseau's Spartan mother, and even to Arendt, see domestic life as, at best, a foundation for public action. In practice too, the French and Swiss republics were among the later democracies to enfranchise women.

Feminists have been suspicious of the very language of 'virtue', which, by the mid-twentieth century, had mainly sexual connotations, and functioned to constrain what a 'respectable' woman, as distinct from 'a lady of easy virtue', could do. But republican civic virtue is not essentially gendered; it is a concern for common goods, which may take different forms. And Wollstonecraft pointed to the way in which a republican account could include women as equals, in defining virtue in terms of self-reliance rather than grandiose public action.

Feminist politics has been developed around the maxim 'the personal is political', which may seem to be at odds with the republican emphasis on civic virtue and the priority of public to private concerns (Phillips, 2000: 291). Against this, we have already seen that the republican public–private distinction is not as sharp as the liberal one, but, more importantly, it does not map directly on to the public–domestic distinction. The conception of civic virtue advanced here does not align the public with the non-domestic, or the private with the domestic spheres, but with broader and narrower interests. The contemporary republican revaluation of common goods and public life in relation to *particular* interests does not exclude women or their interests from public life, nor devalue intimate or domestic life. In this account it is not the domestic but the purely particular which must cede some ground to common concerns. Public political participation requires us to *translate* the concerns of ordinary life into public terms, not to detach ourselves from them (Pitkin, 1981: 346–7).

There is still an issue here. Requiring people to transcend their own personal interest may be seen as inadmissible. Feminists, postmodernists and multiculturalists especially have seen this as imposing universalist conformity in a way that fits ill with the diversity of modern pluralist societies. The ideas of community and civic virtue and 'that old chestnut, the common good' (Phillips, 2000: 285) require people to transcend concrete material relations, often with the effect of masking inequalities and domination (Young, 1987; Frazer, 1999). 'Feminism has always, in some sense, been about challenging false unities' (Phillips, 2000: 287). This highlights the necessary conditions to justify invoking the common good. The more unequal are power relationships between people, the less plausible it is to talk of any but the most basic common goods. In a radically unequal society, invoking the idea of a common good to advance a policy may indeed be oppressive.

The broader account of civic virtue advanced here does not impose a single standard of behaviour on individuals in a way that is inherently oppressive to minorities. In addition, it should be emphasised that what is transcended is not what is culturally or morally different *per se*, but purely particular preferences which are somehow arbitrary, limited or unreflective, and do not take account of interdependence (Sunstein, 1993c). So we may try to minimise our own tax payments even when we agree on values and principles such as, for example, that there should be public health care and education provision. But immediate particular preferences are subject to transformation. Virtuous citizens are aware of their considered interest as interdependent citizens, and are capable of transcending their particular positions, or progressively enlarging their viewpoints (as suggested by Arendt, and developed in Chapter VII). The idea of a common good requiring people to transcend their narrow viewpoints is not necessarily oppressive unless it is seen as setting a predetermined end point (Squires, 2000: 184). In a deliberative republican politics, however, it is understood as a horizon of meaning. This is compatible with feminist concerns about premature consensus under conditions of inequality. Indeed one of the strengths of feminist arguments has been their insistence that what may appear as individual problems (for example, how to combine work and child-rearing) can be translated into issues of equality that are of public concern. While feminists have insisted on politics addressing women's interests, in so doing they have shown how these are public issues and have thereby revitalised the public sphere.

Civic virtue and citizenship are now conceived as taking a variety of forms and levels of concern among those whose goods are interdependent (rather than the historical connotation of militarism, masculinism and conformism). This is more congruent with the practices of care – of children, old people and the disabled – which, historically, have largely been the province of women, and carried on in the domestic (non-state, non-market) sphere. Such practices, it has been argued, reflect the deep dependency of individuals, which political thought of all kinds has overlooked (Kittay, 1999; MacIntyre, 1999: 6–7). Instead of idealising the masterful man unable to recognise dependence, republican politics seeks to provide a space for freedom within interdependence. In the context of recognising deep dependency, MacIntyre has argued for the importance of norms of 'just generosity', which has much in common with the open-ended character of civic virtue as presented here. But, for MacIntyre, this has to be focused at the level of the local community rather than that of the state (MacIntyre, 1999: 123). From the republican perspective, one way of recognising such dependence would be to give such practices of care a public role in citizenship. This approach may help to displace the polarisation of public and domestic spheres. At the same time we need to emphasise the continuing importance of mainstream political activity, as well as informal, particular or local social networks of family and friendship (which are potentially hierarchical or self-denying). Recognising the public dimension of personal concerns needs public structures (Dietz, 1992; Squires, 1999: 186–8). This is a better approach than taking a role model based on mothering, which simply reverses the public–domestic distinction to revalue the private care performed by women, as some 'maternalist' political thinkers have suggested.

It may still be argued that even an ostensibly gender-neutral account of civic virtue places demands on citizens which exclude or relegate to second-class citizenship women who cannot attend political meetings, serve on committees and so on. Certain kinds of obligations fall disproportionately on women, and have inhibited their participation in political decision-making. Finally, if civic virtue imposes social obligations without the corresponding conditions for observing them, this will reinforce inequality (Phillips, 1999; Squires, 1999). The feminist critique highlights the need to match demands for civic virtue with resources of time and money. The exercise of civic virtue requires a say in decision-making, which means that there must be different kinds and levels of participation available to citizens. These material pre-conditions for freedom and civic virtue are discussed in Chapter VI, issues of equal participation in Chapter VII and of differentiated citizenship in Chapter VIII.

Shaping citizens

If civic virtue is so important, how can it be generated among people who may neither know nor immediately feel for one another?

Before addressing this, we may challenge the underlying assumption that in large modern states it is hard to motivate citizens because the impact of any individual's actions is so small. If that were the case, then indeed the exhortation to virtue, which is one part of republicanism, would be pointless. One vote in millions may well seem inconsequential. The aftermath of the 2000 presidential election in the United States suggests otherwise. In any case it can be argued that a person is morally responsible, not only if their act has been the sole cause of a particular result, but also if it has been one of a set of acts which bring about that result (Parfitt, 1984: 73–5). But more specifically, the effects of civic actions other than voting are not infinitesimal. Someone who, for example, carries on a small but persistent project to teach adults to read may have far-reaching effects; even participating in a public debate may inform or influence many. Apart from its direct effects, it may make people aware of others in their societies whose claims need to be considered. Such activities create powerful examples of the possibility and worth of civic action for other citizens. But they are also valuable in themselves; these actors realise themselves in extending their own horizons of concern and achievement.

By definition civic virtue cannot be elicited by force, by banning or burning luxuries, or by requiring people to perform certain duties. So specifying civic virtues is distinct from justifying their enforcement by authority. We shall see that republican theorists do allow some level of coercion to realise common goods, as well as promoting freedom, when the range and limits of justified coercion are discussed in Chapter VI. They have emphasised what has been called the 'formative project' of shaping citizens (Sandel, 1996: 323). Critics have accused contemporary republicans of being squeamish about addressing this issue. So here I consider the arguments for measures to elicit civic virtue.

First we might note that this is not as much of an uphill struggle as is sometimes depicted. Many people do have a sense of responsibility and commitment to wider groups of people at different levels of society. Even in the notoriously individualistic and commercially competitive area of computer technology, the practice of open source software creation has emerged, in which people recognise that individual achievement and common good are promoted together.

What is at stake here is to extend this to the level of the polity and its multiple reiterated interdependencies. This may be encouraged by broader public engagement, as we will see in Chapter VII, and should not all be seen as sponsored by the state. But it cannot be left entirely to the associations of civil society. Families, churches and ethnic or cultural groups have a different rationale from the self-governing republic, and they can be hierarchical and parochial in ways that fail to generate the sort of civic virtue needed by citizens.

Identification

Citizens may take responsibility for the polity because they identify with it. It can be argued that citizens will identify more with a republican than a liberal state since it provides the common good of freedom as non-domination (Pettit, 1997a: 260). If laws are seen to track their interests, citizens will be more trusting and trustworthy in their political interactions, and more confident that others too will be prepared to undertake their responsibilities.

There are various ways of creating structures with which people can identify. It is often easier to feel responsible for smaller than for larger groups. This is at least as important as cultural homogeneity in determining people's commitment. The larger size of modern states is often advanced as a reason why civic virtue is not possible today. But this may equally be a reason to articulate existing states internally into smaller, nested or parallel units, in which interaction is crucial in eliciting civic virtue. Where efficiency may suggest centralising government into larger units, in the long run moving too far in this direction may be counterproductive, creating the sense of powerlessness, dependency or disengagement identified in contemporary society by social critics of right and left. However, it then becomes necessary to consider how to integrate local and intermediate units, so that they do not become wholly particular and parochial in their focus.

An alternative form of identification is based on cultural or national commonality. But while a shared culture may give people a sense of belonging to an abstract or 'imagined' community, it does not necessarily elicit the active commitment to the mundane concrete reality that civic virtue entails.

On one view, stronger structures of accountability and the possibility of contesting decisions could strengthen the legitimacy of the polity, and thereby elicit more voluntary commitment for the polity (Pettit, 1997a: 253). On another view, however, greater participation in political decision-making is needed to generate the level of identification necessary to elicit civic virtue: 'The procedural republic, it turns out, cannot secure the liberty it promises because it cannot inspire the moral and civic engagement self-government requires' (Sandel, 1996: 323). Under current conditions, however, participants are not necessarily more public-spirited than others. The structures of participation, the level of engagement and the quality of information available may also determine whether participation will generate civic virtue.

Incentives

As well as identification, civic virtue can be elicited through incentives of various kinds. From Cicero through Machiavelli and even

Rousseau, honour was regarded as the incentive and reward for virtue. While honour had a hierarchical structure, it has a more egalitarian equivalent in recognition. Can recognition, or its obverse, something like *disapproval*, generate civic virtue today? It is sometimes assumed that social approval or disapproval are ineffective sanctions in an individualistic society in which material success is the most valued goal. But Adam Smith was as aware as Rousseau that one reason people strive to become wealthy is to impress, or feel superior to, others. The contemporary emphasis on intersubjective recognition suggests that social sanctions can be influential even in modern society. Thus Pettit speaks of the influence of an intangible hand of opinion, between the iron hand of the state and the invisible hand of the market. This can be effective even in large and relatively anonymous societies: 'While we may each lack a name on the street of a big city, that namelessness is quite consistent with being well known in a range of the interlocking circles that fill the space of the modern world' (Pettit, 1997a: 228). Civic virtue can be elicited in citizens when it becomes the widely expected and approved norm.

This positive recognition of public spirit need not necessarily be embodied in a formal system of honours. Some republics, such as Ireland and Norway, have ruled out systems of public honours, whereas republican France has numerous categories up to the *Légion d'Honneur*. On one argument such honours are incompatible with the equality of citizens, and informal recognition should constitute an adequate reward. But looked at another way, they highlight the example of virtuous citizens, and create an alternative focus to the celebrity of wealth and entertainment. To be effective, however, such a system of honours needs to remain independent of, rather than superimposing honours upon wealth or power, as existing systems often tend to do.

In any case such incentives can be only of limited effectiveness. As Rousseau pointed out, citizens are not made in a day; civic virtue must be internalised from an early age. The stronger republican tradition has recurrently envisaged civic education, civic religion and military training as means of inculcating virtue in citizens. What kind of institutions may be envisaged to foster values of public service? Can any of the traditional republican schemes for shaping citizens be employed today? This is a very contentious issue, where republican tradition seems to run counter to many liberal intuitions.

Contemporary Debates

Civic education

Education in civic virtue has been advocated to unite citizens and to train them in the capacities needed for public service. Civic education has often been employed to inculcate national values or 'manufacture consent'. But some liberals, and democrats too, have come to acknowledge the role of education in creating citizens who are autonomous (Gutmann, 1987; Callan, 1997). If civic virtue is not natural but none the less necessary to sustain a society that provides the condition for self-fulfilment, education to cultivate this may be necessary and justified. On the interpretation of republican civic virtue advanced here, civic education has two principal dimensions: awareness of interdependence and capacity for deliberation. A civic education based on these dimensions is not inherently in contradiction with the idea of free, self-governing citizens.

This civic education is less a matter of instilling doctrine than of creating an awareness of interdependence: a knowledge of the condition of other citizens, and the history and development of the republic. It comes about through experience and interaction with people in different sections of society as well as in formal classroom settings. Instead of conveying a unified national history, it needs to highlight the complexity of that history and of the concerns that confront society now. By contrast, other approaches to political education stress either commonality or difference. In France, for example, education in a uniform national curriculum through the single national language has been seen as essential to create citizens. By contrast, cosmopolitan liberals argue for a multicultural education to foster an appreciation of difference. But education to acknowledge interdependence may be more important in creating virtuous citizens than an emphasis either on commonality or on difference. (This would suggest, for example, that while minorities may be taught in their own languages, majority students should be encouraged to learn these minority languages.)

The second important dimension of such an education is developing an understanding of the effects of private and public actions, and the ability to form judgements, consider other points of view, and deliberate; to create trust, and learn to take responsibility not just for oneself but as a member of society. This would prepare future citizens to take up a concern for a common world and participate in deliberation and decision-making. Some of this comes about through the experience of participation, which may be introduced in small groups. Some of the shaping of citizens through education occurs through the structure of education rather than the curriculum. A strong system of state schools in itself can go some way to bring diverse citizens together. Smaller schools establish a firmer basic sense of engagement and responsibility in young people. It may not be possible to know everyone in the modern state, but school is the institution through which children usually first enter the larger world and form their basic sense of relationship to that world.

Does this mean that the state should have the monopoly of legitimate education (Gellner, 1983: 32)? In recent years there has been an intense debate among political thinkers on the nature of education, its role in creating autonomous citizens, and how to address this in a multicultural society. Some suggest that education must be public and secular, and requires a national curriculum. There are broader issues in these debates which cannot be addressed here. But the need to foster civic virtue in citizens may require less stringent conditions than many of these arguments suggest. Civic education understood in this way may not necessarily have to be public, secular, nor provided through a wholly national curriculum. In different contexts, different solutions are possible and desirable.

Civic religion

While some contemporary communitarians stress the importance of religious belief and practice in supporting an ordered society, this invocation of religion is not an intrinsic element of contemporary republicanism. Even in the republican tradition, a civil religion served mainly as an extension of civic education. It was less a set of religious beliefs or spiritual practices than an attempt to exclude supernatural or hieratic claims from politics, to borrow the awe or respect they engendered, or to bind the citizens through a common story of origins and history, ceremonies and festivals.[15] These uses are distinct from what the adherents of religions take to be their central purpose, and are not specific to a republic. In practice, the idea of civic religion may justify the kinds of collective ritual and honour that are given, for example to the Constitution of the United States, to the symbolic opening of Parliament by the Queen, and to commemorations of dead heroes and leaders in the Panthéon. This is less a matter of deep beliefs than a symbol of political unity and respect for political institutions of the polity.

Such modern examples tend to have political institutions or the nation as the focus of respect, but another approach focuses on creating identification more directly among otherwise diverse citizens by providing common experiences and reference points. This may emphasise the value of public occasions and spaces set aside to foster interaction in joint activities, and lay the ground for purely political engagement with one another (Sunstein, 2000).

From another perspective, the solution to the problem that civic religion was initially intended to address is to make the separation of church and state a fundamental principle. On one interpretation, this means that a republic must be wholly rational and secular, and that there must be no public role or support for any organised religion. In France, in particular, secularism, or *laïcité* is held to be a central tenet of republicanism. But the implications of such arguments are differently interpreted. In the USA, but not in France, it rules out state support for religious schools. In the USA, while the words 'under God' were added to the pledge of allegiance of the United States in 1954, prayer is forbidden in schools. The proper place of religion in politics will depend on the inequalities of power that arise in particular societies.

Civic service

For Machiavelli, Harrington and others, military training and service was an important way of forming citizens. Some kind of compulsory military service was common in states of all kinds until recently. (And even liberal theory can recognise that there are circumstances in which a liberal state may require its citizens to risk their lives in its defence.) If a republican polity is neither devoted to imperialist expansion or glory nor constantly challenged by neighbours (or if warfare is more capital- than labour-intensive), then an armed citizenry may be anachronistic. (It is somewhat ironic that the right to possess guns is the only universal aspect of a civic militia now remaining in the United States.) Yet military service was valued partly as developing civic virtue and bonding citizens to the republic. The experience of service in the Second World War, for example, appears to have forged a strong sense of duty to the common good (albeit often narrowly defined) in many members of the generation which was engaged in it.

So there are proposals for a non-military equivalent, which establishes the membership of citizens in the republic by requiring them to spend time in some kind of 'civic' service, constituting what William James spoke of as 'the moral equivalent of war' (Dagger, 2000b). This could be chosen from a range of environmental, educational or social projects, including notably the caring activities previously regarded as the sphere of women (Bubeck, 1995). The aim here is not just to create a sense of belonging, but to help to create citizens who are active, responsible and aware of their interdependence on others. But any such programme of civic service is perhaps best understood as a part of civic education for young people, not as imposing compulsory service on adults, since we have seen that civically virtuous action needs to be voluntary. Imposing service on mature adults is unlikely to elicit the sense of commitment envisaged. What may be argued is that, for young people, the experience of such service opens up their perspective to dimensions of life of which they might otherwise be unaware, and may establish attitudes and habits that they will carry through life.

The argument for such a system of civic service is that (like civic education) it would increase the commitment of citizens by making them more aware of their interdependence; by mixing with a broader range of people than they would meet in their everyday life, they will become aware of the spectrum of their fellow citizens and the many dimensions of life in the republic. As a part of education, it would be just one of many compulsory elements that are already required of children, on the grounds of their development both as individuals and as citizens. It has been suggested that requiring up to a year of a citizen's life is little more exacting than a comparable extension of compulsory schooling, and closer to an extension of voluntary service programmes. Alternatively, shorter periods could form a module of university education. It could also be rewarded with credits for further education, in the manner of the United States GI Bill.

Independently of the concrete benefits which they could bring, environmental, educational and social work could contribute a sense of responsibility for the larger world. It may not be the most effective way to carry out such tasks, but this objection is less substantial than it may at first appear. Of course they will be done badly in some cases, as in the case of many first jobs. But it might well achieve better results if, unlike much military service, participants had a range of choice. Such service could help to counter the increasing segmentation of citizens into social sub-cultures, and provide a clearer perspective on the concerns of the political community.

Even if there are strong arguments for such programmes, however, the details of their implementation will determine their success. Civic service would need to be universally required, properly funded and appropriately allocated to promote citizenship effectively. A form of civic service which may seem more feasible for adults is for citizens to participate in policy-informing and decision-making bodies such as citizens' juries, to be described in Chapter VII. (The motivation and justification of republican commitment is further discussed in Chapter VIII.)

Does this cultivation of civic virtue under the auspices of the state give it too much power? This is a genuine concern, which suggests the need for very rigorous forms of accountability in any state. But already in practice education policy serves widely to achieve objectives of political unity. The power of most modern states over education means that they exert considerable influence over the values endorsed in society. It may be better if this is made explicit in programmes of civic education and civic service that are open to scrutiny and deliberation. The influence of such programmes may act as a countervailing force to market and other pressures which highlight individual goods, and thereby threaten the social practices and common goods that are essential to the autonomy of citizens.

Conclusion

The republican emphasis on civic virtue is not inherently oppressive or unrealistically demanding. It represents the voluntary commitment of citizens who see the value of their contributions to society. Civic virtue is not a substitute, but a necessary support for institutional provisions. Republican theory does not amount just to exhorting citizens to a concern for the common good. The point of commitment to the common good is the full development of citizens as autonomous, as able to shape their individual and collective lives. Some communitarian and conservative advocates may empha-

Common Goods and Public Virtue

sise virtue and duty without recognising this ground in freedom. In civic republicanism, by contrast, civic virtue is just one dimension of active citizenship. It is in the service of freedom, and requires the opportunity to participate in decision-making. People cannot be condemned as apathetic or politically ignorant if they do not have the conditions and opportunities for effective freedom and participation. To expect virtue from citizens they must have the minimum material conditions for a satisfactory life in the terms of their society; and they must be free from systematic domination. They need institutions which allow them to contribute and have some sense that their contribution counts, and some degree of assurance that others will act virtuously too.

Since what is in the common good of society is neither unitary nor predetermined, citizens must have a say in shaping the common goods of the republic. In conditions of great inequalities of power, it becomes harder to identify any really common goods. Under conditions of moral and cultural diversity, there is no single interpretation of the common good that can claim authority; accordingly, there needs to be wide-ranging deliberation on what the common good requires in any society, and accountability of those entrusted with promoting it. Although the common good does not provide a single clear criterion for judging policy proposals, it is a regulative idea that cannot be dispensed with.

In the next two chapters I examine the nature of republican freedom and participation, which are the context in which civic virtue can be expected of citizens.

CHAPTER VI

Freedom

Non-domination and republican political autonomy

Introduction

Freedom is perhaps the most widely invoked value in contemporary society, though it is understood in many different ways. It should be clear by now that republicanism is more than a call for extended social responsibility. Civic republican thought addresses the problem of how interdependent humans can be free. This has two dimensions – what do we mean by freedom in a social context, and what follows for the shape and extent of legitimate government? But a variety of republican conceptions of freedom have been advanced. Some are closer to the negative conception of non-interference; others, contrasted to slavery, are closer to self-mastery. Political freedom has been expressed sometimes in terms of the rule of law, sometimes in terms of political participation. Does freedom as collective self-government necessarily clash with individual freedom?

In this chapter I consider how three different conceptions of freedom deal with the problems of plurality and interdependence identified by republicans. These conceptions are: non-interference, non-domination and mutual participation in self-government – what I will call 'republican political autonomy'. I argue that republican political autonomy offers a better way of addressing the issues at stake. I examine how different accounts relate political participation either instrumentally or intrinsically to freedom; what socio-economic conditions freedom requires; and whether collective self-government and the common good necessarily conflict with individual freedom. I examine the ways in which freedom may be promoted or impaired by government and law, and explore the extent of justified coercion in a republican polity. Can you be forced to be free? Are there any grounds for individual rights, and for privacy rights in particular?

Rather than having to choose between the 'liberty of the ancients' and the 'liberty of the moderns', we see that this approach deconstructs the radical opposition between these kinds of freedom, and between positive and negative, and personal and political freedom.

Defining republican freedom

Republicanism cannot be distinguished from liberalism on the basis of their endorsing negative and positive conceptions of freedom respectively. Though many liberals adopt a negative conception of freedom as non-interference, by no means all republicans adopt a positive conception as collective self-mastery.

There have been two distinct emphases in traditional republican thought – in terms of participation in politics, on the one hand, and of the rule of law, on the other. In both, freedom is understood in political terms, not as a pre-political property of natural individuals. But they differ on the centrality of political participation to freedom. Freedom may be *defined* in terms of political participation – as sometimes in Aristotle, Rousseau and Arendt – or it may be seen as a *consequence* of participation (on one interpretation of Machiavelli). In a third approach, freedom is *constituted* by legal status (Cicero, Harrington – 'freedom by the law'), and this may or may not require the participation of the citizens in making the law. If political freedom as participation is understood as that of a corporate, or what Habermas calls a 'macro-subject', it may seem bound to conflict with individual freedom from interference. Rousseau recognised this dilemma as much as Berlin, and aimed to overcome it, but no political theory has yet succeeded in unproblematically reconciling the idea of freedom as collective self-government with that of individual freedom.

Republicanism and negative freedom

On one interpretation, republican freedom can be expressed in terms of the negative conception. One reading of Machiavelli suggests that what is distinctive about his theory is the way in which citizens must actively perform public service, or put their duties first, in order to preserve their individual freedom. On this argument it is negative freedom – not to be interfered with in their private pursuits – which individuals secure; this freedom is related closely, but externally or consequentially, to their political participation. On this view, liberals have been mistaken in believing that negative freedom is unrelated to political participation, and can be guaranteed by a frame of rights respected by the state and citizens alike. Republicans see that this is not sustainable. If citizens do not observe their obligations and perform civic duties, the polity will decay into corruption, and their private spaces of freedom will be eroded. None the less, on this account, the freedom they are concerned to secure – personal liberties for citizens to pursue their own lives without interference – is much the same. Freedom is not constituted by, but follows separately as the consequence of participation in political affairs. In contemporary terms, then, the republican message may be that excessive claims of rights without responsibilities are self-destructive, and that those who are concerned with their private rights need to pay attention to their public duties (Skinner, 1990: 308–9). The disagreement with liberals is less about the *nature* of freedom than its *conditions* (Skinner, 1998: 70). In this *instrumental republicanism*, participation and civic virtue are not seen as intrinsically worthwhile, but as the necessary preconditions for the chance to realise other diverse goods or life plans.

Negative freedom is an intuitively attractive and clear conception. It is plausible to think of infringements on our freedom in terms of interference, and, accordingly, of freedom as non-interference. When thought of in this way, however, all law and government, even if justified on other grounds, necessarily encroach on freedom. So negative freedom does not provide as clear a line of defence in political applications as might initially appear. In addition, it is not quite clear in what sense civic virtue is prior to individual negative freedom, as it is instrumentally directed towards the latter. Thus it has been argued that this account of republicanism is not significantly different from liberalism, or merely comes around to the ends pursued by liberalism by a longer route (Patten, 1996; Poole, 1999: 95).[1] And this version of republicanism may not be any more sustainable than the liberal alternative, if people are not sufficiently long-sighted, or are otherwise unprepared to undertake what they perceive as the costs of civic duties.

Furthermore, perhaps this formulates the republican intuition about freedom too narrowly. It can be argued that republicans want to avoid not just specific instances of interference but rather a life lived under the *threat* of interference or coercion (Skinner, 1998: 84; Pettit, 1997a: 63). Republican politics challenges not just acts of interference, but the *status* of subordination which makes such acts possible. We have seen that freedom since Aristotle and Cicero has been contrasted not to interference, but to slavery – being subject to the will of another person. A slave with a humane or undemanding master may suffer relatively little interference, but, being subject to the threat of such interference, is in a condition of dependence or domination. Domination is defined as having the power of arbitrary interference over someone (Pettit, 1997a: 52). Non-interference is compatible with the existence of threatening powers, if not with their use. Even in the silence of the laws, then, we are not necessarily free. Accordingly, those who are not protected by laws preventing their domination by others are unfree – like Harrington's bashaw, the subjects of a king with extensive prerogative powers, a wife in Victorian England, or any prisoner subject to the whim of a prison guard. These people must live in fear, or take precautions against the exercise of someone else's will. They are unfree in so far as they have to curry favour or dissimulate in order to minimise the danger that the threat will be realised, instead of acting according to their own purposes. In so far as the negative conception of freedom fails to capture this, it misses an important social dimension of unfreedom.

Freedom as non-domination

Accordingly, the republican conception of freedom has been defined in terms of non-mastery or *non-domination*. This account of non-mastery picks up the opposition of freedom to slavery present in the republican tradition since Aristotle, and the status of freedom embodied in a legal system emphasised in Cicero (hence it has been called '*neo-roman*' by Skinner (Skinner, 1998: 10–11). It builds on Machiavelli's notion that people may be free in the sense that they 'neither arrogantly dominate nor humbly serve'. This may be seen as a missing middle term in the negative–positive distinction of non-interference and self-mastery: being neither interfered with *nor* master (Pettit, 1997a: 22). On this view it is not interference that is the main threat to living freely but domination – the threat of interference which cannot be prescinded. To be free, it is more important *not to have* a master than to *be* a master. In political terms non-domination can be established by replacing the arbitrary will of a king or monarch with the rule of law. It does not necessarily require being the lawmaker.

The political implications of such a conception of freedom are a system of laws that provide guarantees against illegitimate interference, so that citizens may be able to act independently. It is arbitrary power, not law, that is incompatible with freedom. Individuals cannot single-handedly secure themselves from exercises of power. When they are dominated they are subject to uncertainty, need to ingratiate themselves with the more powerful, and cannot establish their free status publicly. Laws provide security in non-interference, or resilient protection from domination. Freedom is a status, recognised by all, which receives institutional support. For Skinner, this freedom is guaranteed in a general way: law provides the framework for freedom, but those actually coerced by law cannot be said to be free at that specific moment. Coercion by law, as well as dependence on the will of another, infringes on freedom (Skinner, 1998: 82–4). For Pettit the crux is dependence on the will of another; so being subject to a law, properly made and applied, is compatible with freedom. On this understanding, the state is not a necessary evil, providing security at the cost of some freedom, but a real asset, playing a role in promoting the ideal of freedom as non-domination. Because it is an ideal, rather than a constraint, guaranteeing freedom does not mean minimising state activity.

On the non-domination view, freedom is not an external consequence of the laws, but is *constituted* by the institutions of rights and accountability. By creating a recognised legal status that deters interference, these give immunity from interference rather like antibodies in the blood (Pettit, 1997a: 108). This is in contrast to laws that apply sanctions to redress wrongs after the event.

This is a stronger account of freedom than non-interference. It requires institutional safeguards, and takes account not only of public domination by the state but also of areas such as work and the family that have often been understood as private and non-political. Republican politics promotes the non-domination of all individuals in every aspect of their lives. (Liberals do not entirely ignore harms in these areas, as might seem to be implied, but they have been more concerned with specific acts and with abuses of state power, and have drawn the public–private distinction in such a way as to make state intervention to prevent other harms problematic.)

To realise this freedom fully throughout society needs not only the guarantee of law, but also the widespread support of civility or civic virtue. There is, however, no intrinsic connection with participation in political life, so this too can be understood as another form of instrumental republicanism.

Advantages and limits of the non-domination account

There is much to be said for this account of freedom. It translates into more useful and robust criteria for identifying constraints that seriously prejudice human freedom than the negative account. It can readily be applied to the contemporary lives of women in families, prisoners in institutions and students in schools, or anyone whose possibilities of development and independent citizenship are adversely affected by being subject to domination even when they are not actually being interfered with.

It establishes freedom more securely in law and institutions. In identifying a range of threats to freedom, and establishing the equal legal status of potential victims, it gives a degree of recognition not implied by negative freedom. It recognises the capacity of individuals to be independent and self-directing, which is distorted when they are subject to the will of others. This shared status makes freedom a common good, which cannot be enjoyed unless others also enjoy it (Pettit, 1997a: 72, 121; Spitz, 1994).

Yet this account is still closer to the negative than to the positive conception of liberty. It is an opportunity rather than an exercise conception of freedom. It is more concerned with consolidating non-interference than with establishing a fuller notion of freedom:

> This conception is negative to the extent that it requires the absence of domination by others, not necessarily the presence of self-mastery, whatever that is thought to involve. The conception is positive to the extent that at least in one respect it needs something more than the absence of interference; it requires security against interference, in particular against interference on an arbitrary basis.
> (Pettit, 1997a: 51)

In contrast, freedom as autonomy springs from different intuitions from negative freedom. It is an ideal of self-direction. To be autonomous a person must act according to purposes she endorses. This defines freedom in terms of realisation rather than opportunity. The notion of autonomy has developed from Rousseau's idea that freedom lies in obeying a law one makes for oneself. A fuller definition defines autonomous persons as those who 'adopt personal projects, develop relationships, and accept commitment to causes through which their personal integrity and sense of dignity and self-respect are made concrete' (Raz, 1986: 154).

Pettit does not dismiss the idea of autonomy or self-mastery out of hand. He maintains that non-domination is compatible with personal autonomy and that republican institutions facilitate this indirectly:

> Freedom as personal self-mastery, however, is a richer ideal than that of freedom as non-domination; there can certainly be non-domination without personal self-mastery, but there can hardly be any meaningful form of self-mastery without non-domination.
> (Pettit, 1997a: 82)

But he argues that personal autonomy does not have to be a concern of republican politics: 'people can be trusted to look after their own autonomy, given that they live under a dispensation where they are protected from domination by others' (Pettit, 1997a: 83).

But if personal autonomy is understood as an ideal of a self-directed life, led according to purposes a person can endorse, the chances of being autonomous will be affected by many factors apart from domination. Starting from the assumption that no one can ever be completely master of their life, freedom may be better understood as being the 'part-author' of one's life (Raz, 1986: 155). Autonomy may be understood both as a capacity and as an achievement, and is therefore a matter of degree, not an absolute (Raz, 1986: 156, 373; Dagger, 1997: 38). Autonomy may be threatened not only by external interference, but also by being subject to uncontrollable desires or motivations that a person reflectively regrets. To achieve autonomy, individuals need social practices within which to develop their projects and relationships. Autonomy is limited not only by domination, or dependence on the will of another, but also by dependence on the effects, often unintended, of the actions of others. Personal autonomy is affected by our vulnerability to one another. It is promoted when people can coordinate to achieve objectives beyond the capacity of one individual. It is reduced when they fail to do so. We may argue that autonomy is enhanced if people can have a say in shaping the practices through which they pursue their lives in society. Thus political autonomy can be seen as a natural extension of personal autonomy.[2]

A point of clarification is necessary here. Republicans see citizens as independent political actors. But I have emphasised the grounding of republican theory in interdependence. What does political independence mean in this context? Political independence requires being able to think and speak for yourself, not being dependent on or dominated by the will of another. But it does not require realising projects without relying on social practices and assistance or cooperation from others. Thus it is compatible with a more relational ideal of autonomy which has been advocated by some feminists, who have been critical of the liberal conception of freedom as independence (Nedelsky, 1989).[3]

Personal and political autonomy

There may be dimensions of personal autonomy that cannot be politically guaranteed. But if we accept that personal autonomy is deeply reliant on social frameworks, then we may see autonomy as more closely connected with political participation in shaping the collective life, not just being secured from domination.

Thus Habermas sees private and public autonomy as 'equiprimordial':

> It is not a matter of public autonomy supplementing and remaining external to private autonomy but rather of an internal, that is, conceptually necessary connection between them. In the final analysis, private legal persons cannot even attain the enjoyment of equal liberties unless they themselves, by jointly exercising their autonomy as citizens, arrive at a clear understanding about what interests and criteria are justified and in what respects equal things can be treated equally and unequal things unequally in any particular case.
> (Habermas, 1994b: 113)

If freedom is understood as an ideal to be promoted, rather than a constraint to be observed, non-domination appears to point beyond itself, not to full mastery, but to participating in determining the conditions of social life. We could see non-mastery as a precondition for some degree of mutual self-determination in 'republican political autonomy'. The way in which not only domination, but also powerlessness, tends to undermine autonomy has recently been highlighted by feminists and others. This is hinted at in Wollstonecraft's response to Rousseau: 'I do not wish them to have power over men; but over themselves' (Wollstonecraft, 1992: 156). Autonomy may not be fully realised in politics, but it needs a political expression, and cannot be fully realised outside politics either. It has personal and political dimensions. Personal autonomy points forward to political autonomy.[4]

Republican political autonomy: freedom and participation

Republican political autonomy means that citizens engaged in practices follow purposes that they can endorse as theirs, in so far as they have a say in shaping and sustaining them. Political decisions affect the range of possibilities open to individuals, and to the extent that they lack any say in these decisions, their autonomy is reduced. 'Together we can take charge of the social conditions that we collectively create, that would otherwise constrain our individual lives as alien powers' (Pitkin, 1984: 325). For republicans from Machiavelli to Taylor, the freedom achieved in a republic gives citizens some ability to control the conditions of their collective life.

Thus a number of thinkers have proposed a closer connection between freedom and political participation. Whereas non-domination is secured by having a government that tracks the interests of citizens, autonomy can only be realised by people acting themselves. Accounts of freedom as participation pick up the strand of republican thought from Aristotle's freedom as 'ruling and being ruled in turn' to Rousseau's moral freedom of citizens who are subject to the laws they make for themselves. Their views range from Arendt, for whom freedom was more or less definitionally equivalent to political participation, to contemporary 'strong' republicans who, following Arendt and Taylor, see participation as an intrinsic part of freedom.

Freedom

On this understanding of freedom, the relationship between freedom and participation is intrinsic; one dimension of citizens' freedom *is* participating in self-rule, not an external consequence of so doing. Barber, Pitkin and Sandel offer accounts of politics in which participation is intrinsic, though not definitionally identical, to freedom.

> Men who are not directly responsible through common deliberation, common decision and common action for the politics that determine their common lives are not really free at all, however much they enjoy security, private rights and freedom from interference.
>
> (Barber, 1984: 145–6)

> I am free insofar as I am a member of a political community that controls its own fate and is a participant in the decisions that govern its affairs...the republican sees liberty as internally connected to self-government and the civic virtues that sustain it.
>
> (Sandel, 1996: 25–7)

> The distinctive promise of political freedom remains the possibility of genuine collective action, an entire community consciously and jointly shaping its policy, its way of life...Only citizenship enables us jointly to take charge of and to take responsibility for the social forces that otherwise dominate our lives and limit our options, even though we produce them.
>
> (Pitkin, 1981: 344)[5]

In different ways each of these expresses the idea that freedom as autonomy requires contributing to shaping collective social practices. But this cannot be achieved through a simple unitary process. Although Rousseau's attempt to extend autonomy to the level of society foundered in positing a unitary, corporate subject, developing a conception of political autonomy remains a worthwhile objective.

We saw above that Habermas also advances a theory of political autonomy as part of collective self-government, in seeing it as parallel to private autonomy as two irreducible dimensions of freedom. 'Political autonomy is an end in itself which can be realised not by the single individual privately pursuing his own interests, but only by all together in an intersubjectively shared practice' (Habermas, 1996b: 498).[6]

These thinkers raise the question of how freedom as participation in mutual self-government can be realised, and how different contributions may be combined so that people may act still according to purposes they can endorse. If participation and freedom are to be connected, it must be in some way that maintains personal freedom in individual lives while allowing for collective self-government.

To leave room for personal freedom, a more positive conception of freedom cannot be based on a fixed account of human nature, or require citizens to act according to a pre-determined ranking of goals and purposes. It cannot define political activity as the highest good of a human life, nor assume that there is a unitary common good of society. If autonomy is a matter of acting according to goals a person can endorse, someone cannot be 'forced to be autonomous' by being coerced into behaving in a certain way, though he may perhaps be prevented from acting in ways that would further reduce his autonomy in the future. Political equality is central to the idea of freedom as participation in collective self-government.

At this point we should note that any process of collective self-government needs to be accompanied by a close scrutiny of the dynamics of non-political relations. It is precisely this that the idea of non-domination supplies. Non-domination is an essential complement to the idea of freedom as participation in self-government. While classical republicans were aware of the distortions that result when participants are subject to the will of others, they have often been accused of being blind to other exercises of power. A system of collective decision-making without guarantees against domination may just translate the will of those in socially dominant positions into political effect, and further strengthen their power to realise their own interests. Even what appear to be common goods may become club goods, which benefit those who have the capability, time and resources to make use of, for example, political participation, or public spaces such as art galleries or museums.[7]

The issues concerning the way in which many different contributions can be combined in participation through deliberative decision-making are discussed in Chapter VII. In the remainder of this chapter I address the more immediate issues concerning freedom.[8]

The material preconditions of political equality and freedom

The first issue to be considered is what socio-economic preconditions freedom requires. Both non-domination and political autonomy require more stringent material conditions of freedom than non-interference. Citizens need a material basis, not just 'social capital' or civic virtue to be able to act as active and independent citizens. Extremes of economic inequality present a serious obstacle to the possibilities for political equality and freedom.[9]

In the socialist tradition these material conditions for political equality were sometimes identified with positive freedom itself. But for republicans, reducing economic inequality is primarily understood as a condition of equal opportunities for self-government. Thinkers in the republican tradition argued that only those who could be independent should participate. While they were concerned about the corrupting effects of the desire for wealth, they also feared the effects of poverty and economic inequality on the political equality and independence of citizens. They saw property ownership as a way of guaranteeing independence, rather than as a natural or absolute right, and did not see this as extending to a right to unlimited accumulation.

One approach to ensuring the independence of citizens was simply to exclude those deemed incapable of it (those without property, women, servants, children, etc.). But republicans also proposed substantial redistribution measures, ranging from limiting inheritances to actively redistributing land. The grounds for exclusion have been whittled away, as land and property ownership, masculinity or marital status have come to be no longer regarded as an essential basis of citizenship. But there are still genuine concerns about the effects of material inequalities on political independence. The issue now is not 'property' in itself. Unlike in Rome or seventeenth-century England, a small land holding (or a trade) is not what it takes to be a political equal. Thus Arendt tried to define property more abstractly as a guaranteed place in the world, or the degree of *security* necessary for citizens to develop certain capacities and take up opportunities for participation.

Republicans (in contrast to many communitarians) have addressed the issue of the economic conditions of freedom, civic virtue and community. For example, Pettit identifies the problem of domination of the needy and of employees, and Sandel the effects of such dependence on political independence of mind (Pettit, 1997a: 161; Sandel, 1998: 326).

For Pettit, to enjoy non-domination a person needs the resources and capabilities to be able to function in society, and to work and live in security without having to placate others, not being subject to the whim of employer, patron or state agency. Thus freedom is undermined not only by absolute poverty or lack of resources and opportunities, but also by extremes of economic inequality.

The degree of equality required may be greater if, as will be argued in Chapter VII, political autonomy means having an equal voice in a deliberative politics. The material conditions for republican political autonomy may be more demanding than those for freedom as non-domination. Otherwise participatory politics may favour the economically powerful, amplifying the existing inequalities of civil society. Equality in deliberation is undermined by the absence of resources and capabilities for participation; for example, the cognitive abilities and language citizens need to put forward viewpoints and to judge alternative proposals. But as well as the opportunity for adequate education, security of employment and health, they need the time to invest in specific political commitments, to consider proposals and their implications. Someone who has no job, who has to do two jobs, or who lacks any security of employment will be at a serious disadvantage in political life.

While freedom may not require complete economic equality, these considerations suggest that it requires more than a basic threshold of resources or capabilities, as economic inequalities tend to translate into possibilities of domination and unequal exercises of political power. It remains to be addressed what political provisions a modern republican government should adopt to achieve this.[10]

Freedom and the extent of governmental activity

The other side of the question of freedom in a republic is that of the extent of legitimate state action. What is the extent of justified coercion in promoting common goods? What may and should governments do to promote autonomy, and can republican theory justify any limits to government action in the name of individual freedom?

While the non-domination and republican political autonomy accounts differ in their view of the importance of political participation, or active contribution to political decisions, they both adopt a more optimistic and expansive view of government action than those liberals who understand freedom in terms of non-interference, and who deny that governments have a substantial role in promoting common goods (Pettit, 1997a: 148).

As well as a strong system of law to prevent domination, government intervention is required to provide the economic and social conditions for resilient independence. We have also seen that republics promote the common goods of their citizens, and thereby favour some practices and discourage others. But it should be recalled that the state is not the entire focus of republican politics. The republican focus on the public is less preponderantly on control – on the central state and its coercive powers – and more on the activity of citizens and their resolution of the tension between particular and general interests. What is in the common good does not automatically become a matter of state control. To a considerable extent it relies on the voluntary actions of citizens. In the next chapter we will see that a good deal of citizen participation in self-determination takes place in a variety of public spheres not immediately engaged in state policy-making.

Second, when the state does act, this does not always take the form of coercive or prohibitive legislation. Collective self-government does not mean that everything considered to be in the common good is the subject of coercive legislation. The state also acts symbolically when, for example, it proclaims a day of remembrance, endorses a practice, or honours achievements. It also exerts its fiscal power through taxation and subsidy; thus, for example, many governments tax cigarettes and alcohol more heavily than other commodities, and subsidise the arts and sport. Although the ultimate threat of force underlies the power of taxation, we recognise an important political distinction between the Prohibition of 1920s USA and the heavy taxes on alcohol that are common in many countries today.

Yet republican political autonomy does entail a significant amount of state intervention. In the first instance this is required to prevent domination. Republicans may give a greater role to government than many liberals would countenance, because, in their view, state agents do not necessarily or always represent the most serious threat to autonomy. Serious threats come from the arbitrary private power of, for example, individual men over women, of large corporations over their employees and consumers, or of established elites in cultural and religious communities. A broader view of the ways in which freedom is threatened requires the state to undertake more responsibility than the minimal government entailed by contrasting freedom and interference.

Coercion and its limits

It is a subject of debate among republicans whether all coercion invades freedom. While any interference reduces negative freedom, on Pettit's view of non-domination, citizens' freedom is impaired only by arbitrary and unjustified coercion, not by laws that follow their interests (Pettit, 1997a: 65). It may seem more intuitively plausible to say that we can be free in a general sense under law, but that all coercion constrains our freedom, even if it does not dominate us (Skinner, 1998: 83 n54). However, if autonomy is not absolute but a matter of degree, achieved in a life as a whole, it is not necessarily undermined by some element of coercion. Some constraints are more significant than others, and some may be in the interests of more important goals. While being stopped at red traffic lights, for example, is not significant, being required to reveal your income and to have it taxed are progressively more significant, but are justified in the name of the greater resources for autonomy made possible in different ways by, for example, the provision of law courts, health care, local authority housing and museums or sports facilities. This does not mean that all state coercion can be justified. We may set limits to state action where it seriously damages the ability of citizens to be politically autonomous. Not all individual goods can be overridden in the name of common goods. Certain *fundamental interests* may be identified which must be taken into account. These may often be protected as legal rights, though, in the republican view, they will not be formulated in terms of absolute boundaries.

This makes republican politics more complex at the level of theory, as it may look more clear-cut to disallow all interference. But this is not borne out in practice, where what constitutes interference is not easy to tell, so that the liberal public–private distinction turns out to be of limited effectiveness. In states which undertake extensive education, health and welfare functions, the distinction between what is controlled by the state and what is not cannot be rigidly sustained, and is not particularly effective in maintaining freedom; as Nedelsky puts it, 'the characteristic problem of autonomy in the modern state is not...to shield individuals from the collective, to set up legal barriers around the individual, which the state cannot cross, but to ensure the autonomy of individuals when they are within the legitimate sphere of collective power' (Nedelsky, 1989: 13).

The state: what is the extent of justified coercion?

So law and government activity include both non-coercive intervention and some degree of justified coercion. If freedom does not exclude all interference, we will need to distinguish between justified and unjustified interference. It thus makes sense to ask what are the limits of justified coercion? I consider government action under four headings: preventing domination, promoting autonomy, overriding distorted preferences, and promoting common goods. This addresses the general grounds on which government may be justified in acting, without providing a blanket justification for any particular instance of intervention. The actual interventions justified will depend on deliberative judgement in the cases that arise in particular contexts.

Protecting citizens from domination

To promote freedom, republican government will undertake a range of activities and intervene in areas that some liberals deem private and therefore outside the legitimate range of government activity, except in the case of specific concrete harms to individuals.

> For republicans whose concern is non-domination, taxation is not nearly so bad or objectionable in itself as the domination it is designed to protect. As long as the taxation is not arbitrary, but in the interests of citizens, it limits their range of action, but does not dominate them. Since non-domination can be social as well as political, the state may intervene between employer and employee, husband and wife.
>
> (Pettit, 1997a: 148–9)

As well as performing the functions of maintaining order, providing basic services, defending the polity, and coordinating markets in ways that are conventionally accepted to some extent also by advocates of negative freedom, this entails regulating a wide range of activities and practices in domestic life, the economy and civil society. This will include, for example, introducing legislation on safety and equality at work that libertarians may see as infringing freedom of contract. Freedom of contract is not regarded as the model of justice (Pettit, 1997a: 164). Other asymmetric relations of private power may need protective legislation: for example, between doctor and patient, between multinational companies and small suppliers and consumers, and between banks and their clients. Such measures are designed to reduce the vulnerability of citizens to employers, officials, parents and so on. If this limits the range of choice, it also strengthens the intensity of freedom from domination. This may tackle not just specific identifiable harms to individuals, but also the threat of such harms which diminishes their independence. For example, the existence of cartels which dominate the news media threatens to limit the access of other voices to public political expression.

To prevent domination, it may be argued, for example, that certain kinds of pornography or hate speech should not be legally protected, if they discriminate against particular groups, undermine their equal status or subject them to other groups to the extent that their political equality as citizens is damaged. Giving offence alone may not be a ground to control speech, and treating people equally cannot dictate that everyone is always equally respected. But if some pornography treats women as objects for the use of men, not only may it subject them to an unequal risk of violence, but it also affects their public status as established and publicly recognised equals, and their ability to interact on that basis (Sunstein, 1991; 1993b). Thus what counts as free speech may be delimited in the interest of their autonomy. This is not to override the right of free speech, but to interpret it differently. The right of free speech may then be interpreted less as:

> a guarantor of unrestricted speech 'markets' and much less as a vehicle for the translation of economic inequalities into political ones, but instead as an effort to ensure a process of deliberation that would, under current condi-

tions, be promoted rather than undermined through regulatory measures.

(Sunstein, 1991: 30)

Promoting autonomy

As well as preventing domination negatively, the state may be justified in promoting autonomy more positively, both directly and through ensuring the structures, status of citizens, and material conditions on which it depends.

Structures, capacities and possibilities For instance, some degree of coercion may be needed to provide the basic framework of participation and deliberation – public spaces in which citizens can contribute, and more equal means of access to participation. In order to promote political autonomy, the state may support much more extensive *public spaces* within which political debate and deliberation over the common good can take place. This entails expense on institutions, meetings, procedures and officials, information, and providing more levels of government than may seem economically most efficient.

We have already seen that education for deliberation and citizenship is important for civic virtue. Requiring this can be justified in part as extending the autonomy of those who are subject to coercion in giving them the capabilities for participation. But it may also involve coercing some to take up their role as citizens in order to promote the autonomy of others. Where the common goods of social practices are regarded as essential to individual autonomy, the activity of other citizens affects each citizen's possibility of autonomy. The state may require parents to allow their children to receive education and health care, and the childless well-off to pay taxes for the education of other people's children. It may intervene when parents impose cultural practices on children which not only restrict their future options (as all forms of education and upbringing do to some extent) but do so radically, and with respect to what may be seen as fundamental interests.

Supporting the public and private autonomy of citizens implies a more active role in providing the means of access to participation to allow greater political equality. The state will implement policies to promote political equality among citizens, so that they can develop independent preferences and beliefs. This may include supporting public-interest media, and giving them some protection from market forces which favour entertaining and sensational programming at the expense of information and education. It may require all broadcasting bodies to broadcast more substantial political and educational programming, and to make space for cultural minorities in deliberation and organisation. Likewise electoral campaign contributions and political advertising may be controlled in the interest of equal political autonomy, when electoral success is demonstrably a function of campaign finance.

To the extent that political autonomy requires more extensive participation, the state may also be granted a role in giving a greater voice to the excluded. In relation to proposals for participation to be discussed later, citizens required to serve on 'citizens' juries' need to be paid and supported with child care; and, for example, employers could be required to grant hours of political or civic leave, or to sponsor voluntary activity among their employees.[11]

Because the market is better at meeting current effective demand than providing for future or collective goods, the state may also sustain possibilities and valuable options currently undervalued by, or under pressure from, the market or other forces in society. This includes supporting dimensions of social life and the natural environment in order to provide options for the future that would otherwise be under threat of disappearing. Examples include restricting development in wilderness areas, preserving historical buildings and cultural heritage, including language. The point is neither to extend the range of undominated choice just for individuals, nor to preserve these as intrinsically valuable. Here these practices are sustained as the horizons within which freedom makes sense, but they are not conceived in terms of teleological common goods, which have absolute and non-negotiable value.

Material preconditions for autonomy The conditions for the autonomy of citizens are in part secured by laws that establish the public status of citizens as equals, and outlaw certain kinds of actions. But the state may also take action to provide the material preconditions for autonomy.

The independence of citizens required by non-domination implies extensive social and economic policies to promote socio-economic independence (Pettit, 1997a: 160–1). To ensure that citizens have the basic capacities and resources to participate as independent members of society, the state can provide and require general education, regulate employment and exchanges, and give some level of entitlements to welfare and health care. But we have seen that this must go beyond providing just a threshold of resources of security, time and education to address the effects of relative inequality upon autonomy. One way of doing this is by making available a wide range of resources, such as education and access to health care, on a universal basis. This not only provides material benefits, but also strengthens political equality and civic identity.

Such interventions may be objected to on the grounds of freedom, justice or practicability. But some interventions are necessary to create a balance between one person's freedom and that of others, and between certain kinds of freedoms and interests and others which are more significant or more fundamental. The fundamental interest in equal political autonomy, which frames the possibilities of personal autonomy, justifies certain limits on economic freedom.

The issue is not whether the state should intervene in the market or not; even the market needs state support to function efficiently. The state protects market exchanges and private property in a wide variety of ways. And the exchanges which take place in the market do not, as some libertarians suggest, adequately mediate the interdependencies they create. In the first place, the wider social costs of provision are only partly reflected in the market price of many goods. The environmental costs of oil production, or the social costs of dioxin production, for example, tend not to be borne by those who are the main market actors. There are arguments that markets should more fully reflect such interdependencies, but, in the short run, government action may, and to varying extents does, limit or compensate for such costs.

At a practical level, it may be argued that the market is more efficient, not only in producing, but also in distributing resources than interventionist states, and that it is unrealistic to talk of major state-sponsored redistribution today, when welfare states are in retreat. Moreover, the reach of individual states over economic activities is diminished by globalisation processes, so that states which raise high taxes to finance redistributive measures risk the flight of capital.

At the other extreme from these libertarian objections, for classical marxists the deficiencies of the market could only be resolved by a complete transformation of society. But the attempt to create political equality by abolishing private property, or, in the short run, centralising it in the state, proved ineffective. It did not provide prosperity, and it tended to undermine all kinds of freedom. It now seems more feasible to regulate employment and exchange than to do away with wage labour of any kind, even if this ameliorates rather than transforms society. As Rousseau argued, it is because there is an inherent tendency towards inequality that it has to be countered politically. Politics is about taking some degree of control over matters that cannot be resolved definitively. In view of communism's encounter with history, and the now almost indisputable functions of markets, other ways of limiting inequality have to be considered.

A variety of approaches may be derived from this. Pettit argues that non-domination requires that the state should act to promote economic prosperity in general, to provide support for the development of capabilities, and to introduce measures to regulate employment conditions that will prevent workers being dominated by employers (Pettit, 1997a: 159–61). But he argues that this does not lead towards a strict material egalitarianism, as, beyond the redistribution needed to ensure that some people are not subject to domination by others, any action taken by the state to increase resources for some must reduce the range of choice of others (Pettit, 1997a: 161, 205). In addition, only those measures which do not create a dependency on the state are desirable.

Some forms of redistribution may in themselves entail domination or lead to debilitating welfare dependency. But not all dependence is illegitimate; and dependence on an accountable state of self-governing citizens may be less inherently dominating than dependence on individuals or corporations. What is necessary is to develop more accountable and less dominating political means of ensuring the conditions for autonomy.

More participatory republicans concerned for political autonomy may need to be concerned for greater equality. And indeed there are arguments for more radical redistribution, which may be more in keeping with republican political autonomy. These aim to harness the dynamism of markets in realistic ways while still distributing widely the resources necessary for autonomy and citizenship. One approach focuses on giving people greater equality of initial resources with which to enter the market. This may be through a one-off cash grant or credits for education, housing and other means of establishing a livelihood (Ackerman and Alstott, 1999). But an alternative proposes a more continuous adjustment of inequalities through, for example, guaranteed minimum, or basic income schemes that provide citizens with a uniform non-discretionary regular grant of money (Van Parijs, 1995; White, 2000a; 2000b). This provides people with more equal resources as a foundation for exercising freedom. These may often be advanced in terms of individual choice, but they can also be defended in terms of promoting the equality and political autonomy of citizens.

Government intervention must be justified in terms of both its necessity and its effectiveness. In any case, what is required will be specific to specific contexts. Measures must be sustainable, non-dominating and non-dependence-inducing. Government measures alone will not achieve a social and economic balance; these will require changes in the attitudes of the more privileged, as well as political policies. But the level of redistribution needed is almost certainly greater than has been envisaged by the neo-liberal programmes of government which have been in the ascendant in industrialised countries since Reagan and Thatcher.

This issue requires a great deal more practical elaboration than can be attempted here. Indeed, it is an area in which republican thinking is in need of considerable development, giving more substance to the proposition that republican politics must address the problem of systemic inequalities as well as personal domination (Phillips, 1999: 113).

Overriding distorted preferences

Government action may also be justified in cases where the expressed preferences of agents appear to damage their autonomy. There are at least two ways in which this may be the case: first, when individuals deviate from their previously expressed and agreed purposes, and second, when preferences are distorted in some way. 'In many settings regulation that apparently overrides private choice is actually a means of facilitating private choice in the light of collective action and co-ordination problems' (Sunstein, 1990: 10).

The state may act to enforce the declared interests and considered views of citizens. In cases of this type the government simply holds citizens to their precommitments, as the sailors refused to untie Ulysses when they passed the Sirens. When the time comes we may be reluctant to take the personal consequences of decisions we genuinely wanted and agreed to. A good deal of tax enforcement comes under this heading. In this case the state enforces, for example, our second-order desire for health care over our first-order desire for greater disposable income. Thus Sunstein characterises the US constitution as a precommitment strategy, through which self-ruling citizens bind themselves to their considered intentions (Sunstein, 1993a: 121).

But there are other cases in which government cannot be construed as holding people to previously espoused purposes, but as constraining them from actions or expressed preferences which seriously diminish their autonomy. In many contexts, and particularly in contemporary society, people are driven or manipulated to act in ways that undermine their autonomy. People adapt their preferences to what is available to them. Those who are in desperate need, under duress, dominated or manipulated by others, or misled through lack of information, may act or fail to act in ways that reduce their own autonomy. Poor people may believe that winning the lottery represents one of their best chances to become financially secure, and are vulnerable to heavily promoted lottery tickets. As Sunstein puts it: 'For purposes of autonomy...government interference with existing desires may be justified because of problems in the origin of those desires' (Sunstein, 1993c: 205). The mere fact that someone acts in accordance with a preference or consents to a proposal does not mean that it must be regarded as their considered judgement that may not be overridden. Compared with intervention to hold people to their commitments, this involves a more debatable kind of paternalism; its extent needs further clarification, and each case needs separate justification.[12] Drug use is a currently controversial example. An example where intervention may gain more support is provided by professional boxing, since those who engage in it jeopardise their health and mental capacities, and typically discount the risks of a job that seems to offers an escape route from a life of disadvantage. But each issue needs to be scrutinised, both in its justification and the likelihood of its success.

This does not provide a blanket justification for government to act in what it takes to be the best interests of citizens against their expressed preferences.[13] Only in the case of distorted preferences might we think of republican government as in any sense legitimately 'forcing' someone to be *free* by countering their own expressed preference. Even in this case, coercion does not make someone immediately free; but it may prevent them becoming less autonomous. It is analogous to stopping someone from selling themselves into slavery.

Realising common goods

We have seen in Chapter V that common goods are essential to autonomy. Many such common goods cannot be realised independently by citizens. As citizens people may choose to realise purposes that for a variety of reasons they do not or cannot express through market processes (Sunstein, 1993b: 208). While some of these may be realised through the actions of virtuous citizens, many may be realisable only through government action. What has to be taken into account here are problems of coordination and size, the assurance that others can be relied upon, and the range of opposing forces that limit the possibility of effective voluntary action by citizens.

Even if individual goods are well-enough provided, citizens have an interest in common goods which are not realised by the market alone. Some argue that, although there are many common goods which can be realised only collectively in society, this power should not be entrusted to governments, as it will result in oppression or distortion (Raz, 1986: 425–7; MacIntyre, 1999: 132). But individuals or lower-level communities typically cannot realise these goods against market forces; they cannot, for example, guarantee the preservation for future generations of valued heritage or common culture. Few communities can match the muscle of multi-national corporations and states. If the precepts of *The Economist* were literally applied, we might live in a world where you could buy only the *Sun*. Pressure for office space and housing may erode public space and collectively enjoyed facilities, the historic layout of a city, the sense of place on which a community depends. Environmental and cultural goods in particular need coordinated action; but so do health, education and welfare.

Governments involved in providing, supporting or regulating the provision of goods in these areas not only lay the grounds for autonomy, but give specific determination to the common goods they represent. Governments then realise (or fail to realise) certain common goods in providing, supporting or regulating, for example, health, education, welfare and cultural activities. These are social practices within which citizens can live autonomous lives, but also more concrete expressions of collective autonomy, which embody specific common goods. In providing these, the state is not and cannot be strictly neutral about values. Governments do business through one language or another; they sanction or do not sanction marriages, provide education which is denominational or secular, monolingual or bilingual, and these provisions embody certain values rather than others. And even the minimalist government of libertarians will have this kind of effect in designating the limits of government in one way rather than another. It is better to recognise that the state will shape social practices and construct the common good, and address how this operates. But republicans see the pursuit of specific goods as not only inevitable but desirable, as concretely extending the range of practices or goods which citizens can enjoy. Thus for republicans liberty may be restricted on grounds other than those of liberty itself.

In politics common goods are specified in ways that express collective self-understandings. But the substance of public life is different in every case. For example, whether education should be run on state or private, secular, multi-denominational or denominational lines is not something that can be decided on *a priori* grounds. It depends on the forms of interdependence and the causes of conflict or marginalisation in a particular society. Denominational education may cause discrimination in one society, where religion is a key point of conflict, but be justified in another. In an Irish context, for example, it may be that joint schooling is needed in Northern Ireland to break down sectarian barriers, while separate Protestant schools are supported in the Republic, in order to sustain the tiny Protestant minority.[14] Francophone schooling may be justified in Quebec because the French language, central to its political community, is marginalised in North America, not because of inherent rights of the indigenous culture. Moreover, this can leave space for diversity; supporting the common good of, for example, religion, does not have to mean supporting a single religion by having an established church, but may be achieved by supporting many churches.

From a republican perspective, these policies are not fully predetermined by a shared conception of the good life. These cannot be justified simply on the basis that they express an already existing overlapping consensus or commonalities. If citizens are to be autonomous, the common goods realised in politics cannot simply reproduce those of a pre-political group or culture. They should be the outcome of extensive deliberation and open to scrutiny and reconsideration. But through them the common goods of the society are provisionally embodied.

This role of government points to a need for deliberation on the nature and form of the practices supported by government. In a plural society, even if it is possible to support a range of common goods, there will be instances where not all values can be embodied; but if there is wide-ranging participation in deliberation on the shaping of social practices, these are more legitimate if every citizen has a chance to express their view, and the whole may express the reflective agreement of the citizens. And part of the recognition that citizens receive will be the fact that these practices express purposes they can endorse. The problem is not a state that is not neutral, but one that fails to take account of voices or potential voices (Cooke, 1997b: 15). (These points will be developed further in Chapters VII and VIII.)

Who will regulate the regulators?

The power entrusted to government to realise common goods gives rise to two kinds of dangers. First, there is the danger that the state may reflect, or even amplify the asymmetries of power in society. Thus republicans need to establish measures to ensure that the political process provides a counterweight to other forms of power.

Second, there is the danger that republican government itself may become oppressive. This is a real concern about any government which is given extensive powers. To see government as holding these large responsibilities suggests a great potential for the abuse of power. Thus, from a perfectionist liberal viewpoint, even if extensive measures are judged to be necessary to provide the basis for personal autonomy, the state should not play a major role in the more specific provision of common goods. As Raz puts it, 'the role of government is extensive and important, but confined to maintaining framework conditions conducive to pluralism and autonomy' (Raz, 1986: 427). And it is one of the greatest fears of critics of republican thought – not only that of liberals, but also communitarians and feminists who see the modern state as a monster which has perpetrated crimes in the name of high-sounding ideals. In more everyday politics, the negative effects of dependence on state bureaucracy support one of the more plausible critiques of social democratic welfare states in the twentieth century. Political autonomy suggests the need to limit the power of government as much as of individuals and groups so that it does not overreach itself and diminish, rather than promote, the autonomy and common goods of citizens.

Thus freedom requires a strong institutional structure of accountability and transparency within which the government exercises its power. This does not undermine the principle of collective self-government, but means that the way that self-government is assured is through the ensemble of government institutions, not just through an apparently mandated legislature or executive of a unitary people. The separation of powers between the elements of government plays a role in constraining parts of government, and balancing one against another. As well as representatives, there may be room for a strong role for the judiciary in self-government. The actions of administrators need to be constrained by statutory guidelines and review processes, such as an ombudsman to check on the exercise of power by departments and branches of government. In particular, no single official should be given the discretion to interpret what is in the common good in dealing with, for example, decisions on entitlements, civil liberties or on admission or citizenship. The less accountable the government the less justified scope there is for coercion in promoting common goods.

There are in principle limits to the power which government can justifiably exercise over citizens. On what grounds and of what kind are these limits? Are there any rights in a republic? In particular is there any republican justification for privacy rights?

Are there any rights in a republic?

In the republican tradition individual rights and privacy have not received the same central emphasis as in the liberal tradition. Theorists in both traditions have tended to contrast liberal rights to republican duties. But we have seen that liberals too believe that citizens have duties, yet for them individual rights, independently derived and justified, constrain the goods which can be pursued through politics. By contrast, republicanism is a theory based on common goods and politically defined freedom. It is not a rights-based theory.

Whether constitutional rights can find a place in republican politics is a further question. It is true that the point of departure for republican theory is not absolute, natural, pre-political rights as moral constraints on a subsequent political order.[15] The idea of rights is an historically developed discourse. Republicans and communitarians are critical of the use of individual rights in contemporary politics to pre-empt debate about the validity of claims, since debates in terms of rights are no less contentious than debates over substantive goals. Republicanism does give a heavier weight to duties as they are better guides to action for citizens (Bellamy, 1993). Some republicans have repudiated rights, as if they were necessarily individualistic; Arendt's contrastive theory dismissed rights along with other features of liberal democracy. Other communitarians admit rights but as a distinct and potentially opposed principle which has to be balanced against common goods (Etzioni, 1995a).

Only if rights are understood as individualistic, natural absolute properties of a sovereign, self-owning person (on the model of property) are they incompatible with republican political autonomy. An alternative political account of rights grounds them in autonomy (Ingram, 1994). Some theorists aim to combine liberalism and republicanism by adding a rights-based theory to a virtue-based one as separate, but compatible, principles (Dagger, 1997: 5). This is one way of approaching the issue, but it is also worth examining if and how rights can be generated directly from the idea of citizens as politically autonomous participators in collective self-determination. The value of freedom that is expressed in the liberal account of rights has an alternative expression in republican autonomy, and the role of rights as a limit on power can be justified on republican terms. Here the existence and acknowledgement of rights is less the essence of liberty than its legal guarantee.

Although Machiavelli and Harrington advanced theories of political freedom without reference to rights, at least since Rousseau rights have been given a place in republican citizenship (though not always in a consistent manner). Rights may be derived from citizens' interests in self-rule, and the social and economic preconditions for equal citizenship. Individual rights are based on the social recognition of individuals. A system of rights may itself be regarded as a common good – available to all citizens as citizens and depending on the state for its realisation (Raz, 1995). These represent the guarantees of individual non-domination and access to the public realm. The notion of freedom as participation in collective self-determination itself can be a strong criterion for which rights are important (Cohen, 1996). In republican theory, rights are constituted and protected politically rather than seen as natural attributes of individuals. The public life of the republic constitutes rights and guarantees liberties. Matters that are guaranteed on private grounds in liberalism are justified as the basis of equal citizenship here (Sunstein, 1988: 1551; Miller, 1995b: 449; Sandel, 1996: 290). A right to free speech, for example, may be defended on the grounds that it makes possible the political debate and deliberation on which citizenship depends. Similarly the right to religious liberty may be defended on the grounds that religious practices and beliefs are important features of the good life and thus worthy of special protection.

Whereas negative liberty is congruent with rights derived from an idea of self-ownership, political autonomy provides a different ground for rights. Republican rights are those of citizens interacting in society, and they set limits to what can be done to, or demanded of individuals. But the list of rights and how they are interpreted will be somewhat different from their liberal counterparts.

Rights may be seen as supporting the political autonomy of social individuals, rather than sustaining the claims of separate individuals against society. Rather than seeing individual rights as a constraint on common interests, 'rights and their boundaries demarcate the degree to which individual *and common* interests...are to be protected when they clash with other individual and common interests' (Raz, 1995: 36; my italics).

Since so much of our lives is spent in socially and politically determined practices, rights understood in this sense may have potentially greater power to defend autonomy than rights conceived as absolute barriers, which have often been criticised as too formal. Those rights which are central will be those necessary to sustain citizens as active participators in determining the social conditions of their lives, and to enjoy equally the common goods made possible through collective self-determination, as well as to give them access to the individual goods necessary to be self-determining citizens.

What sorts of rights can republican autonomy generate?

The first point to note is that, in a republic, equal citizenship requires that all have equal rights and the opportunity to participate in politics. Unless all have equal rights there is no ground for them to respect rights of others or to display civic virtue (Spitz, 1994). Unlike duties, rights are reciprocal; citizens owe equal rights to one another. Thus rights cannot be absolute; they are limited by the equal rights of others.

There is not space here to focus individually on each of the rights which can be justified in terms of the capacity to be a member of a collectively self-governing body of citizens. But it can be suggested that, on the basis of the norm of equal citizenship, a spectrum of rights from the basic rights of life and liberty, through freedom of speech, movement, fair trial, religious belief, and rights against arbitrary arrest and torture can be derived, as well as the more obviously political rights to vote, assemble, and associate (Lever, 1998; Michelman, 1986: 43).

For republicans concerned with non-domination these rights will need to be upheld against a variety of threats other than the state. But the rights which are particularly at issue here are those limiting the power of government to act in the name of the common good. Rights cannot be applied simply but require interpretation in context. Certain *prima facie* rights can be limited if their exercise undermines the capacity of some citizens to interact as equals in politics. This approach may seem to require more judgement and interpretation than the expression of absolute rights as constraints on government. In practice, however, these too involve interpretations which are not neutral with respect to values, as we have seen in the case of freedom of contract.

Some of these rights may be differently interpreted from their liberal expression. Freedom of speech has already been mentioned. Republicans argue for a clear distinction between a right to speech that has clear political relevance and a general right to expression; this is relevant to issues of campaign finance, hate speech, pornography and other areas. Second, rights to property are not absolute or primary. The interest of all citizens in something like property as a basis for independent citizenship limits the justified extent of individual appropriation. Since rights are a less-central motor force in republicanism, the ground for providing for reasonable conditions of living, often described as socio-economic, or positive rights, may be formulated differently in republican theory as preconditions for equal participation in political citizenship.

Because they are not natural and absolute, but politically constructed and guaranteed, rights can evolve in the light of conditions for self-government, through deliberation. Yet the idea of constitutionally protected rights is not intrinsically at odds with the idea of popular self-government. Some rights may be given constitutional status in the light of their importance in assuring republican participation in self-determination rather than by virtue of being natural or absolute (Raz, 1995: 42).

A right to privacy?

The emphasis laid by republican thinkers from Aristotle to Arendt on the primacy of politics and public life over domestic life, and the primacy of the common good over individual interests, may appear to undermine the possibility of privacy rights in republican theory. In the ancient *polis* there was no area of privacy which was definitively outside political control. The idea of a private area beyond government control has been largely a development of liberalism since Locke.

But things whose value we think of as private in the sense of personal or individual – intimate relations, family life, personal success and economic security – are not dismissed in republican thinking. These are variously seen as either the necessary basis for, or the parallel value to public autonomy. For Arendt, for example, privacy is important to give citizens the secure place in the world necessary to be able to become a political actor at all. A life cannot be lived entirely in public. The family and intimate relations are valued as the sheltered basis from which actors can emerge into the public. Privacy rights do not have to presuppose a naturally isolated individual but a social individual, who has interests and a capacity for autonomy that requires sheltered development.

But it is not clear that privacy is best understood in *spatial* terms, as an area outside government control or interference. In the first place the extent of interdependence and externalities of our actions suggests that drawing clear lines is not possible. In addition, feminists and others have drawn attention to the way in which the limits of private spheres are constituted by public decisions, and the spatial understanding of privacy has masked domination within the private sphere, and taken it off the political agenda.

However, this does not mean rejecting privacy rights. Individuals have a legitimate interest in many of the dimensions often subsumed under the term privacy. Privacy may be thought of in *personal* as well as spatial terms. For example, the privacy rights invoked in legalising contraception have been justified variously in terms of spatial access and personal control. The argument that the state should not inquire into private (that is, properly hidden) relations rests on the conception of privacy as spatial access. The argument that the state should not intervene in what is properly a matter of individual agency is a more recent account of privacy in terms of personal control (Sandel, 1995: 73–5). As feminists have argued, privacy may be better thought of as granting respect to personal autonomy than as an area of non-interference. What is private need not be excluded from political intervention by definition, and there should be no rigid boundary around the domestic or other areas. Here again the issue is not whether there is or is not political intervention, but whether autonomy is being seriously undermined by the state or other agents (Nedelsky, 1989; Cohen, 1996; Lever, 1998).

This provides a different ground and range of privacy rights from those currently criticised by radicals as anti-democratic. These include the capacity for self-direction, for autonomy in decision-making and for deliberation. Even rights to privacy are grounded in common life and public discussion (Miller, 1995b: 449). If politics requires a variety of perspectives, privacy may play a role in fostering creative and imaginative approaches, protecting minority views, and giving people time and space to develop.

But the right of privacy has often been used as a way of suspending collective judgement on actions where conflicting values are at stake – in the case of abortion or homosexuality, for example. And such withholding may be seen as out of character with the republican aim to realise common goods through politics. Thus it might be suggested that the US Supreme Court's 1986 (Bowers *v* Hardwick) decision to uphold a Georgia state law against homosexual sodomy supported a republican expression of collective values in law. But it may be argued that this is not an exemplary civic republican judgement. As outlined above, political autonomy requires that the common goods realised in politics do not simply transpose the values of a pre-political community into law, but are based on deliberative determination. Moreover, the Georgia state law in question may be challenged on the basis of its effect on political autonomy. For citizens to be capable of autonomous participation, it may be argued, they must be able to develop autonomous ways of life. While some degree of interference in the lives of citizens is justifiable, laws which obstruct fundamental self-definition and social relationships undermine autonomy fundamentally. Republican political autonomy requires capacities for independence and participation as equal citizens, which are undermined by laws prohibiting homosexuals' development of sexual and social relations, just as laws on relationships between black and white did in the past. This law could be challenged on the grounds of republican political autonomy, which include a right to privacy of citizens' intimate relationships – grounds, it should be noted, that are different from the liberal right to privacy based on freedom in self-regarding actions (Michelman, 1988).[16]

Rights, including privacy rights, can be justified on the basis of republican political autonomy. This is not to say that there will not be practical conflicts between rights and the common good, just as there are conflicts between different rights, and the rights of different people. But in both cases deliberative arbitration is needed. Rights will need to be balanced against rights and rights against fundamental interests deliberatively, in courts and political institutions.[17] While property rights may be limited in the interests of common goods, the common good does not always trump individual and minority interests. For example, the livelihood and survival of a minority may constitute a valid claim to be balanced against a project that is otherwise deemed to be in the common good. (The Indian Sardar Sarovar case of population displacement for a large dam is vividly described in Roy, 1999.)

If republican politics promotes common goods of citizens, a real question arises whether there can be special rights for intermediate groups; this raises a different set of issues which will be addressed in Chapters VII and VIII.

Conclusion

In this chapter I have argued that republican freedom should be understood in terms of political autonomy, rather than of negative

Freedom

freedom from interference. This is a notion compatible with, but going beyond that of non-domination. To be autonomous means to act according to purposes that one can endorse. It requires engagement in social practices to realise the common and individual goods they provide. Personal autonomy extends into political autonomy when citizens can jointly shape the practices within which they live their lives.

The state may have extensive powers to prevent domination, promote autonomy, counter distorted preferences and realise common goods agreed in deliberation. But these powers can be limited by rights of citizens, grounded specifically in their political autonomy.

There is no simple way of determining what is in the common good for a society. The nature and specification of the common goods realised in politics needs to be open to reflection and deliberation by those who are affected by them. In the next chapter I discuss what kind of citizen participation in mutual self-rule is desirable or possible.

CHAPTER VII

Participation and Deliberation

Introduction

Participation in collective self-government has been a key value of republican thought since Aristotle, though its significance, availability and extent have all been contested. Since the eighteenth century at least republicans have been divided into those who advocate representative politics and those who argue for a more direct say by citizens in the direction of political affairs. In a more instrumental account of republicanism, participation is considered valuable in protecting the pursuit of individual ends; in a stronger republican account, it is a good in itself, as well as a means to determine or realise other social goods. In this chapter I consider whether, and under what conditions, widespread participation may be realised in modern societies marked by moral and cultural diversity.

We saw in the last two chapters that republican politics is particularly concerned with realising common goods. If these are to support citizens' autonomy, and they in turn are to be actively committed to these goods, the way in which they are defined is of crucial importance. While some communitarians assume a consensus over the common good, derived from ethnic identity or shared pre-political understandings, for republicans the common goods of society have to be politically determined. This is entailed precisely because citizens have different perspectives on questions of common concern, since such pre-political bases for loyalty cannot be assumed or guaranteed. Most states are made up of heterogeneous people who find themselves thrown together: 'a polity consists of people who must live together, who are stuck with one another' (Young, 1996: 126). The state is not a common enterprise undertaken with an immediately obvious common purpose or shared goals. In the light of moral and cultural diversity, it follows that the political determination and contestation of common concerns or goods is central. The equality of citizens requires that all can contribute to fundamental decisions. There needs to be an expanded public realm of *deliberation*. But it remains to be decided just how widely distributed through society decision-making can or should be. Is freedom and the common good best realised through institutional procedures which prevent accumulations of arbitrary power through processes of accountability, or through more substantial participation by citizens?

In this chapter I consider a range of issues that arise concerning participation. How can modern citizens be politically autonomous? How is political equality best realised? How much participation is desirable or possible? I then consider the nature and justification of deliberative politics. Are deliberative decisions more legitimate than non-deliberative ones? Or does deliberation favour some groups at the expense of others? What is the scope of deliberation? Does moral and cultural difference require political neutrality, or confining the range of issues or viewpoints to be considered in political discussions? Does successful deliberation require or reach a consensus in shared values? What institutional framework and procedures are required by a republican politics? Can a polity of (even) deliberatively determined ends deal with the size, complexity and plurality of cultures and values in a modern society?

Arguments for and against widespread participation

Since the eighteenth century a steadily growing range of people have been admitted to the public realm in the name of political equality, with the extension of citizenship to all adult males, to women and to other formerly excluded minorities and subject groups. Yet the form that participation has taken in liberal democracies has for most people been narrowed down to voting for representatives. Through the example of the United States, representation was hailed as a magical invention to resolve the problem of numbers. But representative politics as currently practised effectively minimises most citizens' active contribution to decision-making. More people have been included in politics at the cost of allowing only a shallow level of participation.

A number of different arguments may be advanced on behalf of more active participation. First, unless citizens participate, governments will not reliably follow their interests. Second, the citizens will value common goods, and be more strongly motivated to act in a public-spirited way when they are involved in making the decisions that shape society. Finally, in participating, citizens express themselves, and may gain the recognition of their peers.

Protecting individual interests

In politics authoritative decisions are made in a wide range of areas that determine the possibilities open to citizens. The potentially arbitrary power of government, the danger of corruption and the limits of institutional safeguards support more active participation in, and oversight of, political decision-making by vigilant citizens. This is a dimension of active citizenship parallel to civic virtue. But on the basis of this concern alone we would not see participation as having any intrinsic value of its own. Strong representation is important, as feminists in particular have argued convincingly that the interests of significant groups are not satisfactorily defended in the absence of their own representatives. If interests can be protected reliably through representatives and constitutional safeguards, we should be content with very limited citizen participation. It may be argued that the power of *contesting* political decisions is more important than *contributing* to them (Pettit, 1997a: 185).

Promoting wider interests

There are strong arguments to suggest that the more opinions brought to bear on a decision, the better the decision may be. The 'epistemic' argument for democracy suggests that, other things being equal, wider participation produces better decisions. More specifically, on the republican account, political outcomes should be directed to the common good, not merely a battle of individual interests. We may argue for more participation because of the range of shared common goods which may be realised, or common bads avoided, by citizens who can come together to determine their collective future through the political process. In addition, participation educates citizens and makes them more aware of the conditions under which the polity functions, and of their connectedness with other citizens; it thus makes decisions more legitimate and increases compliance. Participation gives the sense of ownership needed to generate civic virtue. More specifically, engaging in deliberation with others in political decision-making encourages people to think of interests beyond their own.

Realising an intrinsic good

Participating in decision-making is intrinsically valuable as well as promoting other interests of citizens. Autonomy is an interest in being self-directing, which needs to extend to the frame of historical and social practices, and therefore to take political form. Through participation citizens express and realise themselves, gain a sense of political efficacy or empowerment, and may achieve social recognition of their values. We can see the public as an area of self-development and self-expression, which realises ends not otherwise achievable.

We saw in the last chapter that strong republicans such as Barber and Pitkin see active participation in political activity as a central part of freedom. 'I am not yet fully taking charge of my life and of what I am doing until I join with my fellow citizens in political action' (Pitkin, 1981: 349).

We may see participation as valuable in itself without agreeing with Arendt that it is *the* privileged locus of the good life or the highest realisation of human nature, or characterising it in terms of a performance for individual distinction, which excludes the pursuit of other interests. This reduces citizens to 'posturing little boys clamoring for attention' (Pitkin, 1981: 338). Politics has to be about the material concerns of citizens. But participation is also intrinsically worthwhile; it is not just a matter of securing the interests of citizens. Participation is a matter of self-definition, concerning what you are and do, not only whether your interests are realised.[1]

Indeed this value may be more important in sustaining civic virtue than the instrumental argument that active citizenship is needed to guarantee one's own interests. 'Unless citizens have reason to believe that sharing in self-government is intrinsically important, their willingness to sacrifice individual interests for the common good may be eroded by instrumental calculations about the costs and benefits of political participation' (Sandel, 1998: 325).

So greater participation is supported by arguments for securing interests, for defining the common goods of an historically evolving polity, and for the self-expression and recognition of citizens. But there are influential arguments for limiting citizen participation. The arguments against widespread participatory politics include the problems of numbers, of competence and of the danger of majority tyranny.

Numbers

The large number of citizens in modern nation-states, as republicans from Harrington onwards recognised, rules out continuous participation by all citizens in a single national assembly – what might be called *assembly democracy*. But we can distinguish between direct and participatory democracy. In direct democracy all citizens simultaneously participate in a single forum. In one sense this is clearly infeasible in modern nation states. As Madison put it bluntly, 'The room will not hold all.' In principle, however, there are ways in which large numbers of citizens can have a voice in making a decision – through referendums and citizen-initiatives, as practised to some extent in countries including Switzerland and Ireland, and in some states of the USA. Though these are practically quite limited, modern information technology, in particular the internet, could in principle facilitate a system of virtual assemblies, allowing more frequent consultation at less cost to the state and individuals than frequent referendums of a traditional type.

In any case, citizens may be extensively involved in decision-making, not in a single forum, but at many levels in various kinds of process. Large numbers can be accommodated in various kinds of participatory structure in regions, localities, neighbourhoods or workplaces. These kinds of assembly may be united in some kind of pyramidal structure, and mesh in with a system of representation. Participation and representation do not have to be mutually exclusive.[2] The problem of numbers alone is not a decisive objection to a more participatory politics.

Competence

A second argument against widespread participation is that citizens may have little competence, information or interest in determining the common good. This supports a division of labour in which representatives are more knowledgeable, or more civic-spirited, as Madison envisaged. This assumes that representatives are more insulated from particular interests and bias than citizens. But we know that professional politicians are exposed to all kinds of pressures; for example, to represent the interests which provide campaign finance, and to follow opinion polls in order to gain popular re-election. Both these pressures dilute the deliberative consideration of the common good. We do not have to believe that representatives are concerned only to further their private interests, merely to believe that they experience similar tensions between particular interest and the common good as other citizens. The contrast between passionate, ignorant and sectionally interested citizens and rational, informed and disinterested representatives may well seem overdrawn in the light of contemporary scandals. It is true that each voice is only one in millions, and that mathematically speaking the opinion of each counts for less, the larger their groups become. Yet if citizens lack interest in politics today it is in large part because they feel that they are faced with limited choices of parties, representatives and policies, and more limited opportunities to participate. Citizen apathy is partly a rational response to current political conditions. The fact that, despite this, significant numbers of citizens still do vote, suggests that participation of some kind is valued for its own sake. The increasing range of alternative forms of political activity suggests that a good deal of political energy is channelled into community and environmental politics, and into protest movements from animal rights to anti-globalisation, or the so-called 'new social movements'.[3]

The danger of majority tyranny

The final and most serious argument against widespread participation is that participatory democracy has a strong tendency to lead to majority tyranny. Participatory self-government has been rejected repeatedly on the grounds that it leads to oppression. It tends to be identified with direct democracy, or the rule of a majority that is either ignorant or emotional, will oppress individuals or minorities, and will support demagogues in power. Thus Pettit dismisses arguments for strong republicanism on the grounds that they are associated with direct democracy. 'Direct democracy may often be a very bad thing, since it may ensure the ultimate form of arbitrariness, the tyranny of a majority' (Pettit, 1997a: 8). Popular sovereignty equals populist sovereignty. This argument is supported by evidence that popular views expressed in opinion polls on subjects such as immigration and the death penalty seem more intolerant than members of political elites. Thus a political system which makes participation a key value is likely to endorse the death penalty and harsh measures against immigrants and asylum seekers. To prevent this, certain topics should be kept off the popular political agenda entirely.[4]

But the connection between majority tyranny and participation is not as clear as this argument suggests. Majority tyranny does not require popular participation; elected representatives too can adopt intolerant policies promoting majority interests at the expense of minorities, even if they appear deliberatively indefensible or discriminatory. The popular views described above are those expressed by citizens under political conditions where active participation is rather limited. Indeed majority tyranny can also result from an apolitical perversion of communitarianism, in which an elite determines community values which are established without any significant degree of political debate or participation (as in Nazi Germany or Soviet Russia, among other examples). Other evidence suggests that elites may often be more extreme than popular opinion, and that popular extremism is often elite-manipulated.

If we had to conceive of participation in collective self-government on a holist unitary Rousseauian model of a single expression of the general will on every issue, where all dissent is subversive, there would be a genuine difficulty. However, collective self-government does not have to be considered on a unitary model. That would be to commit the 'aggregative fallacy'. Elections or referendums do not generate a 'people's will', simply an aggregate derived from adding and subtracting the responses to the choices offered. These responses, both the majority and minority, may reflect a wide range of reasons and opinions which are not recorded by the election process. The idea of popular sovereignty cannot be applied coherently to interpret electoral results as expressing a single sovereign will. Of two recent examples – the 2000 US Presidential election and the 2001 Irish referendum rejecting the EU Treaty of Nice on EU enlargement – it has been appropriately said that if 'the people' have spoken, it is hard to know just what they meant; one because it was so evenly divided, the other because of the variety of opinions dissenting from different elements of the Treaty package.[5]

With or without such a unitary metaphor, majority tyranny can result if all decision-making is organised on the basis of majority voting. But we can distinguish participatory politics from a system of immediate direct democracy, operating according to the principle of majority rule. The politics of a republic in which participation is widely practised may be more articulated, and decision-making more diffuse than the analogy between individual will and social will implies.

Structures for participation are not limited to mechanically aggregating individual preferences. Quite apart from the technical problems of combining preference rankings consistently to determine social choice, we saw in Chapter VI that immediate, unreflective preferences are not necessarily the best guide to policies in the common interest. To realise the objectives of collective self-government, 'participation' should be broadly conceived as an extended process which informs as well as takes decisions, rather than as a political analogue of the market, based on polling individual preferences. Voting and representation are just two elements of such a process. The sort of politics that republican theory suggests is advocated less as a superior mechanism for combining elements to determine social choice, and more as a process of better informing decisions (Goodin, 2001).[6]

Participation as deliberation

This points towards a more participatory deliberative politics, in which decisions are taken on the basis of discussion and reflection, in order to limit domination and to promote autonomy and common goods. The right to vote in regular elections for representatives is only one dimension of participation, but the alternative is not continuous instant direct democracy. Because what is at stake in politics is not just distributing individual goods but also shaping shared goods, bargaining or compromise between interests or preferences taken as fixed is not the most appropriate way to realise these. Political equality may aim at giving citizens an equal chance to influence decisions, rather than an equally weighted vote in a mechanical decision process.

In what follows I show how the problems of numbers, competence and majority tyranny may be addressed by a system of participatory politics in which there is widespread deliberation by citizens who have the opportunity to contribute to policy decisions at many levels.

In recent years the idea of deliberative public reason has received much attention. It springs from the idea that valid political decisions are arrived at in a process of public justification, rather than arbitrary choice, or exercises of power or manipulation. But there are different accounts of deliberation. It can be seen as an ideal or a real process, as intrapersonal mental reflection or as an interpersonal debate. It can be understood as formal reasoning or include broader forms of communication. It can aim to reach right answers, a consensus or working compromises.

The locus of deliberation may also be differently conceived. There are more liberal and more democratic versions of deliberative politics. Some theorists employ the notion of deliberative reason as an ideal criterion for judging laws or policies (that they could have been agreed to through a process of public reason) (Rawls, 1993). Others see it as a model for specific procedures as various as representative politics, constitutional or judicial decisions (Michelman, 1986). Yet others see it as a model for more extensive political participation by citizens. In addition there are different accounts of the legitimate scope of deliberation. For Rawls, for example, in a plural society deliberation between citizens can be conducted only on the basis of reasons that are shared in an overlapping consensus; reasons based in particular private beliefs or comprehensive doctrines are excluded.

There are many issues arising in connection with deliberative politics; here I consider only those which are particularly relevant to republican accounts. Both instrumental and strong republicans favour deliberative politics (though with differing levels of participation), as better realising non-domination and republican political autonomy than a simply extended participatory politics involving, for example, more popular voting on more issues. Republicans are concerned first and foremost to bring citizens to engage with one another.

Thus what is entailed is a process of actual dialogue between citizens, which can take many forms, rather than an ideal or process of monological reflection. This is not just a matter of compromise.

Through this process individuals transcend their narrow interests and fixed preferences. This account of deliberation does not presuppose consensus on questions of the good life. Even those who share common goods, such as the environment, heritage or culture, may perceive, interpret and prioritise them very differently. Deliberative politics requires them to consider other views. Simply allowing different points of view to appear in the discourse may reframe the issues at stake. As well as examining existing views, in this process new perspectives which have not been considered may emerge. It should be noted that the value of deliberation does not depend exclusively on its achieving substantive agreement or consensus, but stems from encouraging people to think in terms of common goods. It also makes for more informed decisions when these have to be taken by people who may disagree, but who must continue to live together. Deliberation may also be superior to ordinary participation in educating and eliciting compliance, if people take part in a decision-making process that they approve of, and have already had to consider the viewpoints of others. Under certain conditions, these are better understood as provisional agreements rather than mere compromises (see also Pettit, 1997a: 190). Even when people disagree, they may still be prepared to resolve disagreements through argument rather than force or compromise where this is inappropriate, as is often the case in environmental questions (Dryzek, 2000).

Justifying deliberation

The status of deliberative decisions in a republican perspective should first be clarified. On one account, democratic decisions are understood to be self-justifying in the absence of any universal principles or criteria against which they may be judged. There the outcomes of democracy, whether based on preferences or some kind of discursive interaction, are respected as the collective expression of the sovereignty of the people (Barber, 1984; Walzer, 1985). Thus, in Walzer's account, political decisions articulate or elucidate already-existing shared understandings between members, rather than principles with claims to universalisability. On this view politics may be, as Habermas puts it critically, a 'hermeneutical self-explication of a shared form of life' (Habermas, 1994: 4). Though with a rather different emphasis, Barber justifies the outcomes of participation in terms of the autonomy of a fair procedure. Even if there are certain internal self-limiting principles, this approach is open to the charge of moral or cultural relativism.

But conceiving deliberation as the source of legitimate decisions does not have to imply a position of radical moral relativism as much as a way of specifying what more widely valid principles require in particular contexts. In the understanding of republican theory advanced here, deliberation involves more than discovering or articulating already existing shared understandings or a 'people's will'. Justice and the common good are regulative ideas that political deliberation should aim at, though what this implies in practice will be different in each case. The republican approach (since Aristotle) has emphasised that good policies call for more context-sensitivity and more active participation by those affected by the decisions than the liberal approach assumes. Deliberation aims to determine the best available solution for issues that arise for people who live mainly in unsought interdependence, but who may yet collectively recognise and build on this. There are better and worse resolutions of problems, more substantively right answers to questions faced by citizens in particular situations (Sunstein, 1988).

A second problem with emphasising participatory deliberation is that it might be thought to be at odds with the principle of 'the empire of laws, and not of men'. To some this principle suggests stronger constraints on all government action in specific cases. But formal procedures cannot predetermine all cases; laws must evolve to deal with different circumstances, and those who are affected by laws should have a say in how they are formed. Political autonomy does not require either a rigid constitutionalism or a process that responds to arbitrary preferences. Republicanism has never been identical to pure procedural democracy. Deliberation itself implies that laws should not be made or changed arbitrarily, on the basis of few voices or without reference to those they affect.

Finally, it may be argued that it is difficult to tell a decision arrived at deliberatively from one determined by an exercise of power or manipulation. The fairness of decisions based on aggregating or negotiating between fixed preferences may be judged by comparing the outcome with the initial range of preferences. But, since deliberation means that positions can be changed for legitimate deliberative reasons (though not from pressure), an outcome different from the initial distribution of positions may still be fair. This makes it much more difficult to distinguish fair from unfair outcomes. This, however, is not a conclusive argument against deliberation but one in favour of extending it, while constraining and countering non-deliberative pressures. Deliberation does not have to be blind to power structures. Since we know that initial preferences themselves may be the result of pressure, reverting to preference negotiation will not be an improvement.

The scope of deliberation

The notion of deliberative rationality has been criticised as demanding and exclusive. Although clearly a fairer basis for decision-making than the use of force or manipulation, the ideal of deliberation has been criticised on the grounds that it does not give all citizens an equal opportunity to affect policies. What does it mean to be reasonable, and what kind of reasons may be advanced in deliberative politics in a plural society? Framing reason according to a narrow conception may disadvantage those who are, for example, less articulate or less educated in formal reasoning. Deliberative procedures may often amplify other inequalities, confirming the dominance of those who are economically powerful in superficially acceptable ways. Second, requiring that deliberation set aside particular religious, moral or cultural beliefs may adversely affect the equality of certain sections of society, whose beliefs are further removed from the mainstream. Furthermore, such a requirement may devalue the contribution which these citizens can make to politics and thus fail to recognise them as equal citizens.

Feminist and other radical critics have pointed to the ways in which the apparently 'neutral' conditions of formally rational argument may in fact exclude or discriminate against women and minorities. Formal procedures of rational speech, such as those adopted in law courts and parliamentary assemblies, may privilege certain cultural styles.

> In conformity with the modern ideal of normative reason, the idea of the public in modern political theory and practice designates a sphere of human existence in which citizens express their rationality and universality, abstracted from their particular situation and needs and opposed to feeling.
> (Young, 1987: 73)

> Appeals to deliberation...have often been fraught with connotations of rationality, reserve, cautiousness, quietude, community, selflessness, and universalism, connotations which in fact probably undermine deliberation's democratic claims...Deliberation is a request for a certain kind of talk, rational, constrained and oriented to a shared problem.
>
> (Sanders, 1997: 348, 370)

On this account, even a deliberative public realm may exclude or marginalise those who do not conform to a particular masculine, rational model. The requirements of public life demand modes of reason or expression, impartiality and a commitment to independence which exclude women and those who are culturally different. There are problems of unequal opportunities to reflect, to speak, to get a hearing, to be understood, and to be considered authoritative, which are hard to identify and difficult to counter. If these criticisms are valid, however, this suggests, not that deliberative politics should be dismissed, but that the ways in which the public realm and deliberation are envisaged and embodied should be modified.

Indeed thinkers in the republican tradition have been sensitive to the ways in which unequal forces and rhetorical power could sway public deliberation. Thus Harrington separated the deliberative and decision-making processes between two assemblies, and Rousseau ruled out interactive deliberation between citizens in determining the general will. But both of these thinkers sought to provide for more independent deliberation, not to rule it out.

These difficulties may partly be overcome by a broader conception of deliberation which allows a wide range of forms of communication and expression, that is not defined in opposition to emotion, and by an expanded and diversified public realm, more friendly to women and minorities.

The second issue raised is the exclusion of particular moral doctrines or cultural values. Some liberals argue either that arguments advanced in political debates must be neutral on questions of the good life, or that they must rely on conceptions that are shared, if only on an overlapping basis, between different groups in a society. Protagonists should not bring their 'comprehensive doctrines' to political debates (Rawls, 1993). Thus, for example, religious reasons for or against the death penalty are ruled out as deliberative reasons, unless shared between all groups in society.[7]

This neutralist approach is grounded not so much on the potential intolerance of individuals as on the inevitability of disagreements between even reasonable citizens in a morally and culturally plural society. Here deliberative politics is an attempt to go beyond mere toleration or compromise to an agreement on public principles of justice on which all can agree as the basis of legitimacy. But as a means of reconciling different moral views fairly, such limitation to public principles cannot be successfully applied. People with different ideas on the value of life and the importance of religion may have as much difficulty in agreeing on public principles of justice to deal with euthanasia, abortion, divorce, religious and sex education in schools, to name just a few examples (Moon, 1993: 59). Comprehensive moral views and publicly shared principles of justice are hard to separate. But it is still often possible for people to engage in deliberation, if moral and cultural values are not regarded as entirely incommensurable.

Moreover, excluding comprehensive doctrines from public deliberation has the effect of privatising values and limiting the possibility of recognition of values to the private sphere. Thus the most deeply held convictions of at least some of the members of society are excluded from the possibility of public recognition. But if values and practices are more than purely subjective, they involve a claim to be realised or recognised as having a wider validity. A neutrality requirement for public reasoning peripheralises an important aspect of human existence – the aspect of values: religious, cultural and moral beliefs based in comprehensive doctrines (Cooke, 1997b: 4).

It also reduces the sense of self-worth which may be derived from contributing to or expressing one's values in public political terms, from being able to influence the character of society and collective life. This diminishes the significance of the public in people's lives, and rules out 'the hope of the kind of richer public life which human interdependence suggests may be possible' (Frazer and Lacey, 1993: 205).

Since deep convictions (or expressions of cultural identity) will not easily go away, and are an important dimension of people's lives, excluding them from the public will not pre-empt conflict, and it alienates some people from the public realm. Requiring people to set aside their comprehensive beliefs in public deliberation may be more difficult for those who are further removed from the mainstream, and render them seriously unequal in practice. Political equality is better realised by allowing all to bring their deepest convictions to political decision-making. As political participation is a way in which citizens gain recognition, all citizens should be able to put forward their beliefs without discrimination. The norms of deliberation should not require people to set aside their most central concerns (Cooke, 1997b: 4).

A more sustainable position acknowledges that political outcomes and public actions express and recognise individual and collective values, and attempts to legitimate them by encouraging all to contribute to their shaping. We shall see in Chapter VIII that, while it may not be possible for all values to be equally publicly endorsed or embodied in political structures, the diversity of participants can be acknowledged, and they can be authorised to express their concerns and values in public deliberation.

Modes and practices of public deliberation

For deliberative politics to be inclusive of all citizens, deliberation must be understood in a broad sense; rather than being strictly formal, it allows for many modes of expression. Thus, in a republican politics of deliberation, all individuals and groups are entitled to make proposals, advance views in their best light, and offer their reasons for these – there are no barriers to the claims and demands that they can make. Any voice may be heard and any claim expressed (Miller, 1995b). These are not taken as sealed bids, so to speak. Every claim can be dismantled and subjected to further scrutiny by others. People are expected to give an account of 'where they are coming from'. They do not have to leave behind their particular experience. This involves reflecting on, instead of bracketing, beliefs based on deep-seated moral convictions. The aim is to develop considered judgements, based on, in Arendt's Kantian term, an 'enlarged mentality', and to define collective aspirations.

The practice of deliberation may often be fairly loosely structured, without narrow institutional procedures or formal requirements for participants. They need to be willing to expose points of view or practices to the light of discussion, to respect others' right to contribute, and to accept that no position is guaranteed acceptance by the mere fact of its being expressed or the strength of conviction with which it is held. This requires reciprocity; people may have to moderate their position if they are to influence others. In itself this encourages people to take more account of the public interest; so this process acts as a *filter*. Even expressions of individual interests have to make a broader appeal, to 'launder' their preferences. As Benhabib puts it, 'the very procedure of articulating a view in public imposes a certain reflexivity on individual preferences and opinions...The process of articulating good reasons in public forces the individual to think of what would count as a good reason for all others involved' (Benhabib, 1996: 71–2).

But they do not always have to meet particular narrow formal standards of reason: reason can be understood quite widely, and accommodate a range of forms of communication. These can include story-telling, greeting and rhetoric, in which people present their experience, acknowledge their listeners and give personal depth to their viewpoints (Young, 1996). (It should be noted, however, that many of these forms of communication also admit degrees of competence, so that those with shortcomings in communication skills may also need complementary measures of support.)

There is another issue of just how much civility deliberation demands of participants. It has been argued that deliberation will privilege the status quo, if only calm and moderate communication is permitted. In many cases, if the structures of decision-making privilege the existing balance of power and exclude or marginalise certain voices, uncivil though non-violent methods may be necessary to get a hearing. Then the thrust of deliberation may need to be extended to more strident measures of demonstration for certain views to gain a hearing at all. The emphasis on deliberation does not mean that all discourse must display a high degree of civility in the sense of politeness or formal language. Deliberation can also accommodate more antagonistic and confrontational forms of politics. The limit on what can be introduced into political debate is determined by the norms of communicative deliberation; it rules out behaviour that undermines the capacity of others to contribute as equals. This privileges political speech and equal access to public debate, but it can justify limiting the mode and content of expression, and so outlawing hate-speech and coercive forms of address.

Politics must take account of moral and cultural diversity, as well as relative levels of advantage. This kind of deliberative politics is better able to deal with diversity than a liberal neutralist approach.

It allows citizens with different ways of expressing themselves and different fundamental beliefs to be accommodated equally within the public realm provided that they are prepared to take account of the views of others. It is true that those who do not value deliberation, who do not want to have any truck with politics at all, or who adhere to traditional notions of authority and inflexibly demand the embodiment of their beliefs, may feel excluded. But for someone with this perspective, to be required to explain the basis of their deeply held beliefs is arguably less counter-intuitive (and marginalising) than to be required to bracket them entirely in the public realm of deliberation.

Sometimes an open discussion of issues and viewpoints can lead to more disagreement in politics. But this may be better than suppressing matters of difference, in ways that are otherwise likely to result in unequal access to the public realm. Conflict has to be recognised as an intrinsic part of politics. There is mixed evidence on how far interaction between people with different views is likely to lead to greater divergence or integration. It seems that in the short run it sometimes leads to greater conflict, but in the longer term, conflict itself may have an integrating force, inducing people to look more closely at (and willy-nilly to better understand) those with whom they have previously had little contact.[8] Learning to deal with conflict is part of being a republican citizen, as different views about the common good as well as sectional interests may cause conflict. Even when people cannot agree, they may gain a stronger motivation to continue working together towards solutions.[9]

But deliberation may also lead to changes in viewpoints on both sides: 'the moral promise of deliberative democracy depends on the political learning that reiterated deliberation makes possible' (Gutmann and Thompson, 1996: 356). People may change their views without thereby betraying their identities. Identities are defined and developed in expression, not definitively defined internally. In this approach to politics, transcending one's initial position is always possible and often essential. It may help to establish or construct common understandings of the common good or public, shared interest.

There is some evidence that major divisions between opposing parties in situations of grave conflict can be narrowed in processes of deliberation. The Belfast Agreement reached in Northern Ireland in 1998 was the outcome of a semi-public process in which radically divided groups, who initially were not prepared to meet in the same room, did progressively, through 'multi-track' processes, come to an agreement. This was accomplished through deliberation at least as much as negotiation, and involved significant changes of position on both sides.

Such diverse kinds of deliberation require more variety of public spaces and institutional structures than either the sort of representative institutions appropriate for reconciling competing interests, or the constitutional tribunals appropriate to jurisprudential reason.

Republican deliberation in multiple publics: pluralising the public

To identify what is in the common good requires the input of many in expression, discussion and action. Interactive deliberation by individuals in a public sphere of action and debate allows the transformation from purely private interests to public concerns. This calls for an expansion of the quasi-Arendtian public realm. In addition to a wide range of modes of deliberation, participation needs an expansion and pluralisation of public spaces. Not only the dominant modes of political deliberation, but existing structures for public political deliberation tend to be exclusive. The exclusionary nature of prevailing political practice was strikingly illustrated in the ruling by the (then female) Speaker of the British House of Commons in 2000 against women MPs breast-feeding their babies in committees as well as in Parliament on the basis of a rule against 'strangers in the House' (Ward and Wintour, 2000)

The prevailing model of contemporary politics is a kind of formalised adversarial interaction in parliamentary and legal deliberation focused immediately on authoritative decision-making processes in a single public realm.

The republican conception of the public is not so closely tied to the central state and its authoritative decision-making. We have seen in Chapter V that the republican emphasis on the 'interest' dimension of the public makes it more diffuse than the liberal control-focused public. The republican public may be seen in plural terms, as it is disengaged from total identification with the legislative and coercive state. It also encompasses the activity of citizens, and the ways in which they resolve (or fail to resolve) the tensions between particular and general interests. Rather than demanding a 'unified public', it thus lends itself more easily to multiple centres. Deliberative politics can operate at two distinct levels. The formal, state public should be paralleled by vigorous informal publics of discussion. In this way decisions and actions are better informed and more reflective of citizens' serious convictions.

This fits in with an increasing emphasis on pluralising what was formerly described as *the* public realm. In fact, there are two distinct kinds of 'realms' of the public. These have sometimes been contrasted as 'strong' and 'weak' publics respectively. First, there are spaces of deliberation oriented directly to policy-making and the authoritative state (Fraser, 1992: 134). These are informed by, and subject to critique by, the deliberation of the second kind of public realm. These are multiple spaces of discourse, which are not necessarily sharply bounded. We speak, for example, of the reading public. They may be more or less formal, and may allow opinions to be exchanged in comparatively open-ended ways. The model in question is an overlapping set of asymmetrical spaces in which opinion is formed. Such spaces already exist to some extent, but they could be greatly extended, and linked into policy-oriented bodies. Thus no single assembly or hierarchy of assemblies is envisaged. Not all public realms come within the ambit of the state; some are principally oppositional or 'counter' publics, as the women's movement was, and the anti-globalisation movement now is.

It may be argued that equality of outcomes in the strong public – or the final results of decision-making – is the bottom line for politics. While addressing this aspect of participation is obviously crucial, reforms in decision-making need to be paralleled by extending equality of voice in discussion of issues in both kinds of public (Goodin, 2001). The importance of deliberation does not depend exclusively on the equal determination of outputs, but also on more equal contribution or inputs.

The value of this dimension of political deliberation is supported by evidence from recent 'Truth and Reconciliation' procedures across the world. These provide an instance of a deliberative procedure in the broadest sense. In many cases they are primarily concerned with providing a forum for those who have been excluded or who have been victims, rather than being directly focused on decisions about punishment or material compensation.

In certain national and international contexts such practices can give public retrospective acknowledgement to experiences of oppression.

Where there are multiple and graduated public realms, a hearing can be progressively obtained for diverse expressions and viewpoints which, in order to be publicly expressed, do not have to conform at once to a single standard of publicity. These kinds of public realm of deliberation can meet the objections to the model of deliberation based on the single authoritative public realm, with a discourse based on a formal conception of public reason, which may privilege the articulate, male, white and highly educated.

Creating public space: public realms or civil society?

If deliberation can take place diffusely through society in multiple opinion-making forums, it may, moreover, without any appeal to legislative institutions, influence people to act in the public good on their own initiative. Some complex social problems, especially relating to the environment, may be best addressed through discourse that inspires voluntary compliance, consciousness raising and decentralised problem-solving (Dryzek, 1990).

The idea of extending responsibility from the institutions of government to citizens is frequently framed in terms of allowing the development of civil society. There are many different accounts of civil society, but certain features recur. 'Civil society' is most commonly used to refer to voluntary relationships and interactions distinct from the state, from churches to trade unions to business federations, from sports clubs to environmental groups. Their political significance lies in the sense of responsibility and relationships of trust that such interactions are held to create: 'the world of family, friends, comrades and colleagues, where people are connected together and made responsible to one another' (Walzer, 1992: 107). The current popularity of the idea of civil society stems from the observation that establishing democratic political institutions and free market economies does not automatically create functioning democratic societies in transitional former communist states, where all political power was previously centralised.

But although there are certain points in common, the republican argument for multiple publics is different in three important respects from the arguments for civil society. Each of these reflects the fact that civil society tends to be envisaged more closely on the model of the market than the forum (Elster, 1997).

First, deliberation and publicity are not normally understood to be central elements of the activities and organisations of civil society. Reflecting its origin in the need for tolerance, the civil society argument does not necessarily prioritise publicity and deliberation as much as create trust or 'social capital'. Civil society is an umbrella term encompassing associations from churches to sports clubs, many of which are hierarchical, non-deliberative and operate out of the public eye. The trust engendered in such organisations may facilitate the broader identifications on which civic virtue is grounded, and the widely reported decline of civil society institutions may well affect the possibility of citizen self-government. But these kinds of association do not necessarily lead people to engage with different others or to consider the wider common good, rather than to move in self-reinforcing circles. Thus it has been noted that the decline of social capital does not seem to be significantly reversed by memberships of strictly protective, optional or temporary groups that involve little personal engagement; and that a distinction needs to be made between 'bridging' and 'bonding' social capital (Putnam, 1995). By contrast, the public spaces necessary for a republican politics are more clearly discursive. They focus on exchanges of opinion and deliberation about common concerns in public between those who are different.

Second, in its most prominent expressions, the civil society argument is premised on a more or less sharp *distinction* between civil society and the state, or the private and the public, understood as the realms of voluntary relationships and coercive authority respectively. Invoking civil society often constitutes a libertarian claim that its constituents are independent and properly free of interference by government, and that aims to bring about the retreat of the state. It thus represents citizenship and civic activity in primarily civil rather than political terms. But we saw that Tocqueville emphasised the stimulus of political institutions and political associations in encouraging civic and social activity. Contemporary evidence too suggests that purely social groups do little to encourage political activism, and that civil activity depends on a frame of political institutions. The retreat of the state does not guarantee the renaissance of civil society. In the republican view, plural public spaces are more continuous with processes of formal decision-making and the state, recognising that these are mutually implicated.

Third, if the institutions of civil society are pictured as multiple, independent and self-regulating, they are also largely *unaccountable* to those whose lives they affect, both within and outside of these groups. Not only is there no inbuilt restraint on inequalities; in fact voluntary associations are likely to amplify disparities of resources. 'For civil society, left to itself, generates radically unequal power relationships, which only state power can challenge' (Walzer, 1992: 104). Such private concentrations of power endanger freedom as much as public institutions. This is what is at stake in the republican distrust of factions and intermediate groups from Machiavelli to Rousseau. The republican concern to expand the say of citizens suggests that organisations in public spheres should be accountable in some way, and that the material inequalities they generate need to be countered.[10]

Publicity, deliberation and accountability, and the connection of informal social interaction with the political decision-making process, are essential elements in the republican argument for expanded public spaces.

Formal spaces and institutions for deliberative participation

What kind of institutions are congruent with republican deliberation? Critics have accused republicans of vagueness in this area too. While it is not possible to specify exactly what institutional requirements the idea of deliberation in multiple public spaces entails, as concrete circumstances affect what is appropriate in each case, a number of guidelines can be offered here for designing participative deliberative institutions.

We saw earlier that freedom as non-domination and participation requires the dispersion of power, traditionally referred to as 'mixed government'. Such checks, often seen as undemocratic, are not unrepublican, since we are not talking about a definitive 'people's will' expressed through a single institution. Counterposing institutions may help to limit the domination of policy by powerful sectional lobbies, who present as great a threat to the common good as intense majorities. Thus the institutions needed to realise freedom also favour the development of deliberative participation.

But instrumental and strong republicans adopt different views as to the kind of institutions entailed. If the principle of non-domination is taken to be the core of republican politics, it suggests that ensuring the *contestability* of all decisions is the most important guideline for designing deliberative institutions. Thus, for Pettit, the main thing is that government should track the common interests of citizens and thus that all institutions should be accountable. Representatives of all interests in society should be chosen by a wide electorate; power should be dispersed between a legislative body with two chambers, each elected on a different basis, and with a strong judiciary maintaining constitutional rights. There should be freedom of information legislation, a system of ombudsmen and other appellate procedures in a wide range of areas. There should be provision for special representation if needed, and the process will be strengthened if there is a range of vigorous social movements (Pettit, 1997a: 193; 1999).

But a distrust of intense majorities leads him to argue that certain areas should be depoliticised, certain decisions allocated to expert tribunals and commissions, and that participation should be limited to contesting, not contributing to decisions (Pettit, 1997a: 194). The people should have access to contest all decisions through a range of consultative bodies and other forums. He extends this to include ex-ante contestation to policies under consideration as well as those already implemented, but rules out more active participation, such as citizen-initiated referendums and veto powers. In summary, on this view the role of people in their own government is one of several editors, rather than 'joint authors' of political decisions (Pettit, 1999: 295).

On this view, republican politics need not entail extensive active participation of citizens, or even the primacy of public debate: 'Democracy is not inherently a collective matter, then; it is not inherently a matter of active control, and it is not inherently the sort of system that confines decision-making to sites that are available to public scrutiny and influence' (Pettit, 2000: 140).

But it is not clear that the power of contestation will be enough to guarantee even non-domination. If political decision-making and the initiating of proposals are confined to a range of elected and unelected officials, this raises all the problems of setting agendas, and manipulating the way issues are posed to promote a particular outcome. This puts the onus on the contester rather than the lawmaker. What has to be confronted is the reality in which some views are not just overlooked, but may be systematically blocked by opposing interests. It is harder (and sometimes too late) to challenge what has already been determined, so the chance for every relevant voice to contribute to initial deliberations needs to be emphasised as well as the power to contest decisions. It must be said that Pettit welcomes informal deliberations in social movements, but to achieve political equality there need to be more active measures to give space for the voices of those who are marginalised. In the light of what we know about adaptive preferences, the voices of those significantly affected will not always emerge to contest already formulated policies, and these voices need to be encouraged to contribute under more participatory conditions. This need not mean that extensive veto powers are required. In an absolute form these are obstructive and undeliberative, and make it impossible to act in situations where some action is essential. While veto power for minorities may sometimes be necessary in extreme situations on major constitutional issues, it may be better to think in terms of weighted or concurrent majorities.

Pettit's focus is more on decision-making than deliberation. It may be true that small bodies are more effective at making decisions than larger ones; but, on the other hand, the more widely informed decisions are, the better they are likely to be. In addition, if more decision-making is set away from public contribution, we have to address more centrally the way in which economic and pre-political inequalities can influence professional or 'non-political' decision-making that is not subject to public scrutiny. Some areas of social life may require less egalitarian debate, or allow more bargaining, but this has to be addressed deliberatively too. Some issues may be constitutionally reserved or depoliticised at certain times, if they have sufficiently serious implications for the autonomy and fundamental interests of citizens.[11] As a general principle the limitation of citizens to quasi-editorial power (if they do not have the resources of editors) may not be adequate to the problem at hand.

If participation is, in addition, inherently valuable in expressing values, gaining efficacy and achieving recognition, we will want to design institutions that encourage more participation, while still guarding against domination. In other words we might aspire to make people 'joint authors' rather than 'joint editors' of their collective lives.

A stronger account of republicanism in which participation is inherently valuable, *and* citizens are thought to offer more to decision-making, supports not only dispersing power among a number of institutions in order to ensure countervailing forces, but also encouraging greater participation at devolved and local levels.

But this alternative does not support democracy through continuous referendums or 'instant direct democracy' in which every decision is subject to majority decision. There are practical difficulties about which citizen-initiatives succeed in reaching the ballot, and how, that would have to be overcome before they could become a central part of republican politics. But it does make publicity and deliberation crucial. Bearing in mind the distinction between deliberation and decision-making, even if the decision on the death penalty is not to be made by referendum, it may be argued that the quality of decision-making and of citizens' views will be improved by a wide-ranging informed public debate.[12]

Not all participation lives up to the ideal of deliberative democracy. But there are ways in which deliberative participation can be promoted. Deliberation may be promoted among people, however different, who have some common world or shared experiences, when they interact with those who are different, and are engaged in deliberation which can affect policy (Sunstein, 2000).

Integrating multiple levels

Deliberative participation among equals requires institutions that elicit the viewpoints and voices of many, and, accordingly, are provided at many levels and in many areas of life. This is an ideal which supports the creation of alternative institutions to expand the range of existing institutions. Government and participation does not have to be exclusively or predominantly at the level of the nation-state. Rather than a single centralised hierarchy, overlapping public realms at a variety of levels are possible. This suggests both more local and more transnational settings for deliberation. The increasing interdependencies of globalisation make it urgent to create more interconnections between states involving deliberative political participation, as exists to some extent, for example, in the European Union. The process of extending deliberative frameworks need not be an all-at-once upheaval; even some piecemeal changes can improve the situation (Barber, 1984). It can include setting up participatory procedures at local levels, in the workplace, in education, among users of health care, and so on, nested into larger hierarchies. Some of these should be less, some more formal or adversarial; some will be primarily consultative (for example, civic forums) and some primarily decision-making. For members of some marginalised groups to have an equal say requires specific measures both to represent those groups in broader deliberative forums, and also to support the expression and articulation of neglected perspectives. This may constitute less a market-place than a 'welfare state of ideas'.

Thus deliberative politics requires more inclusive political institutions at the formal level, with more decentralisation of power to regional, local, neighbourhood and workplace levels within current states. Without idealising the town meetings that still play a role in politics in some New England states, we may argue that small-scale politics provides a base where citizens can initially engage more immediately with issues in areas where they are better informed and have clearer interests. Decision-making in these areas can help to overcome a sense of powerlessness and develop a sense of responsibility. There are still two serious objections to such an extension of decentralised power. First, local politics reflects all the existing distributions of power, including social, economic and gender inequalities, often reinforced by denser social pressure to function consensually. Second, it may encourage the development and hardening of particularist loyalties in 'little republics'. Any devolution of power – even consultative and opinion-forming – needs to deal with these. The first problem may be partly addressed by identifying and encouraging lesser voices to balance out stronger forces – with grants to organise and to articulate minority viewpoints, and support for them in the broader deliberative process, with or without weighted votes.

> Absent the virtues of just generosity and of shared deliberation, local communities are always open to corruption by narrowness, by complacency, by prejudice against outsiders and by a whole range of other deformities, including those that arise from a cult of local community.
> (MacIntyre, 1999: 142)[13]

The problem of parochialism is always present, but multiplying deliberative forums could exacerbate it. Studies of delegates suggest that opinions that have been formed in one deliberative arena are more rigidly defended in the next. To deal with this, it is important to establish connected levels of deliberation, where people become accustomed to having to take into account ever-wider circles of concern.

As there are always other, wider interests at stake, local decision-making needs to be knitted into a larger scale of decision-making. Some of this will necessarily be representative. But we do not have to think of representation as always undermining participation at the cost of self-government (*contra* Arendt and Barber). Strong local government and federal systems can favour participation even without direct democracy. The aim is to expand participation, not to maximise it.

The importance of engaging in deliberation with those who are different suggests that neither the physical neighbourhood, the workplace nor cultural groups should be seen as the absolute base unit of political interaction, even where there are special representation provisions. The need to allow voices to be articulated has to be balanced against the need to avoid ossifying intermediate levels of expression. Promoting interaction with others favours more widely inclusive groups. A number of mechanisms may be considered. These include pooled electorates, where members of different groups are guaranteed representation but must elect some representatives from a group other than their own, so that candidates have to broaden their appeal (Carens, 2000; Van Parijs, 2000).

So we should counter the first problem by support for the weaker or more marginalised, and the second by providing incorporating structures in which citizens become accustomed to taking into account people with opinions that are different from their own.

Common world and public sphere

Publicity is a further dimension of the deliberative process. This is not to say that all stages of all decisions have to be made in completely open forums. It does mean that government activity must aim to be transparent, and that all decisions should be subject at some stage to wide-ranging deliberative scrutiny.

The republican emphasis on publicity means that deliberation gives priority to public debate as a means of deliberation, rather than consulting defined or organised special interests behind-the-

Participation and Deliberation

scenes. (If such consultation gives these interests the ear of government, rather than considering all those who are significantly affected, it is, in a republican perspective, corrupt by definition.) This means including in debate much broader constituencies of concern than has been common in Western democracies, where producers and organised interests – for example, oil companies or farmers – can often play a dominant role in determining energy or food policy respectively.

An essential part of effective deliberative participation is the widespread circulation of information. There needs to be extensive freedom of information at the level of government, and supports for political debate at the more informal public sphere. A quantum leap in the accessibility of information about legislation, policies, and government performance has been brought about by the development of the internet, where governments now provide extensive official information. It is now easy to access documentation previously held in government offices or archives. Similar progress has yet to be made in informing voters on the choices available in political affairs.

The need to expand access to public expression also suggests breaking up news and communications monopolies, supporting public broadcasting and requiring access to political expression through grants for publishing and printing material. Until internet access is as widely distributed as phones or televisions, it should be made available through public institutions such as libraries.

But despite the partial realisation of science-fiction fantasies, modern communications technology, including the internet, does not offer the solution to the provision of information to citizens in the public sphere (Rousseau at least would not be surprised at the level of misinformation on the internet). Nor does it provide an alternative common public world of reference. Broadcasting and news have become so fragmented that they no longer provide a common frame of issues for public debate. This raises a serious difficulty for engaged debate among citizens.

For Arendt, politics was possible between those who were different but shared a common world, providing salient points of reference and a public sphere which allowed indirect personal relations. But the very existence of a common world, and of a common public sphere, is in doubt. We saw in Chapter V that civic virtue may depend on some kind of common experiences; these are also important to ground deliberation. But celebrations, commemorations and public holidays may create a general feeling of belonging without making people any more open to engage with their fellow citizens. The physical architecture and planning of cities to include more genuinely public (as distinct from private and commercial) spaces may encourage more public interaction and sense of ownership of the polity. But more is needed in large nation-states. Here too the kinds of education in interdependence for civic virtue outlined in Chapter V are relevant.

Policy-oriented deliberation

When it comes to more active participation, some participatory processes realise deliberative participation better than others. If citizens are to make a realistic contribution to decisions, these opinions need to be connected with policy formation so that they take account of the larger picture into which these opinions fit, and the real impact of their proposals. What, for example, does a particular proposal to reduce taxation imply for education or health services?

Merely increasing the number of popular referendum votes, or using the large-scale opinion polling widely conducted on behalf of political parties, does not go very far in this direction. Similarly, the use of focus groups, small samples of the electorate, on which governments in the 1990s relied extensively, does little to promote either participation or deliberation. By themselves, more widespread direct referendums (whether citizen-initiated or otherwise) are easily manipulated by intense and financially well-endowed groups, and by the way in which the question or proposition is posed. Referendum processes can be useful only under conditions that elicit more nuanced responses; where, for example, proposals require a wide base of support, spending is limited, and voters are given adequate information. Whereas single choice referendums assume or enforce polarised opinion, multi-option referendums, which offer more than a single choice, and in which citizens rank their preferences, will not only reflect the range of opinion better, but are more likely to elicit significant deliberation (Emerson, 1998; Baker and Sinnott, 2000; Fishkin, 1995; Barber, 1984: 286).

While the practice of citizens voting through internet connections in their homes was until recently a futuristic vision, it now

Participation and Deliberation

seems quite feasible. The question remains whether this is the way forward; even if it were to provide a way of allowing people to defend their individual interests more directly, merely polling citizens in this way would not necessarily elicit informed or reflective voting, encourage the consideration of wider interests, or achieve the expression and recognition which participation can afford. It has both positive and negative dimensions. On the one hand, it provides a public forum in which even a small, dispersed or marginalised minority can develop a voice (though tallies on web counters suggests that they are not always widely heard). On the other hand, the internet may not generate the degree of interaction, virtual or real, that can inform and broaden voters' perspectives. Its anonymity can encourage irresponsible opinions and aggressive speech. But the lack of face-to-face contact may be less problematic than the way in which people can select correspondents similar to themselves to an even greater degree than in everyday life. Thus communication can reinforce the existing views of increasingly polarised groups, rather than expanding their viewpoints. In conjunction with other activities, however, the internet has also been shown to extend and expand interactions. So, for example, a publicly sponsored 'forum' linked to television broadcasts, for example, or on newspaper sites, may be able to achieve more substantial interaction.

In recent years there have been a number of other experimental approaches to consulting citizen opinion in forms of participatory democracy that are better suited to republican politics. These require people to engage with others representing other viewpoints, and are more or less closely tied in with policy-formation. These include deliberative opinion polling and citizens' juries. In these contexts participants are typically encouraged to take more responsible decisions by having to take account of real trade-offs in situations where resources are limited.

Deliberative opinion-polling is designed to overcome the limitations of opinion-polling and focus groups. It canvasses the views of a random sample of up to several hundred citizens on a specific issue. Here, their views are elicited through questionnaires applied both before and after a process of information, discussion and exposure to debate over several days of presentations. Used in Australia in the referendum on setting up a republic in 1999, and in Britain and the

United States on topics as diverse as criminality and electric power pricing, it has been shown that in these processes, participants may significantly modify their initial positions on the basis of added information and exposure to other views (Fishkin, 1995).

Citizens' juries are constituted by smaller, but also randomly selected groups of ordinary people brought together to gain information, examine witnesses and develop opinions over several days in order to contribute to policy-formation. These groups, varying in size from twelve to several hundred, have been used in the United States, Germany and the UK. Again, evidence suggests that people take their responsibilities seriously, often modify their opinions on the issues in question during the deliberative process, and, moreover, are more likely to remain politically active thereafter (Smith and Wales, 2000).

While encouraging informed debate and interaction between widely different perspectives, such practices may be subject to one of the besetting difficulties of juries, that they can be swept along by a dominant viewpoint. To control for this, it may be desirable to run two or more concurrently on the same topic. Up to now, moreover, these processes have been mainly consultative. It may be argued that, if they became more central to decision-making, they would be more subject to manipulative agenda-setting and the selective use of their outcomes. None the less, it is possible to conceive of procedures that require authorities to consider their outcomes, and public checking processes to limit these difficulties, even if they cannot be overcome completely.

The introduction of deliberative participatory structures alone will not guarantee political equality. In contemporary liberal democratic societies, nominal political equality is undermined by inequalities of economic power and social influence. In these structures some voices are either not articulated, not elaborated among those with like perspectives, not publicly expressed, not heard, or simply overridden for non-deliberative reasons. Issues that affect many people do not even reach the agenda, or are persistently blocked or ruled out in the course of processes of debate. A decision that is deliberative in form may in fact be an exercise of superior power. And powerful social groups can define what counts as a deliberative issue or not.

So a greater degree of participation requires a range of conditions to be satisfied: limited material inequality, an informed citizenry, means of communication, spaces in which their views can gain a hearing, and procedures for calling politicians and officials to account apart from the threat of losing the next election. While we may see some improvements in the prospects for some of these areas, the issue of the material conditions of participation is critical. Where are we to start, though? Is this a boot-strapping situation? Since deliberation is so skewed in contemporary society, it may seem that deliberative politics is unlikely to produce the conditions under which deliberative equality would be possible. Even contestatory politics may be too slow and obstructive to achieve the desirable level of economic redistribution (Van Parijs, 1999; Elster, 1998). But while deliberation alone will not transform the inequalities of society, greater publicity, greater awareness and greater deliberation may achieve better results, even under present conditions, than the best schemes of benevolent social engineers, if these lack the support of a substantial civically virtuous population.

Compulsory participation?

A final question arises with respect to the participatory nature of republican politics. If political participation and active civic virtue more generally are important, are there any grounds for making active participation compulsory?

There are conflicting considerations here. First, political participation may be a duty, but we have seen that not all duties are best realised by being enforced. Many dimensions of civic virtue almost by definition cannot be enforced if they are not forthcoming, as it is the voluntary supplement to law. Moreover, we have already seen that it is neither useful nor necessary to expect the same degree of activity from all citizens.

But political participation is not just a particular option: it is the way in which citizens can have a say in shaping the practices that frame our activities. There are several arguments in favour of compulsory voting. At a basic level, the greater the range of participants, the wider the range of interests politicians will need to consider; thus compulsory voting addresses the problem that politicians can be elected by proposing policies which appeal to the classes most likely to vote, even if these are not in the interest of the majority or of the common good (Pettit, 2000: 135). Another argument suggests that if participating in decision-making is an important part of autonomy, requiring someone to vote might just be thought to make them more fully free, as long as it did not try to determine how they should vote. But, of course, in this case, even if autonomy is not infringed, the person may not actually vote autonomously. And if we are to encourage people to take account of the common good, it might be more productive to require them to attend a political debate than to vote. This would still address the educational function of participation, though this may be weakened to the extent that it is entirely detached from a voice in decisions. Second, since political autonomy depends on the joint activity of citizens, it might be argued that the individual has a responsibility to others to participate, because the possibility of self-government depends on the strength of support for the process. If, for example, citizens' juries are to be representative, they must be able to rely on the compliance of the sample chosen by lottery. In much the same way as commentators nowadays suggest that low electoral turnouts diminish (at least to some degree) the legitimacy of the government elected, non-participation undermines others' possibility of political autonomy. Those who do not vote are in part free riders on the benefits of the autonomy-promoting society, as Mill recognised (Mill, 1991).

In practice, however, whether there should be compulsory participation, even at the level of voting for representatives, may depend on whether it will elicit genuine deliberation. In some circumstances – if, for example, it creates strong resentment, or is not deliberative enough – it may be justified but undesirable. But note that this does not imply that compulsory participation is undesirable because it will draw into politics the voices of those least educated or most volatile, a view that overlooks the educational function of more substantial participation.

Compulsory voting is already an accepted feature of a number of liberal democratic states (including Australia), and the requirement of jury service is even more widespread. This is not normally regarded as a serious violation of individual freedom. If republican deliberation is to be taken seriously, it could require people to participate more extensively in deliberative opinion polls or citizens' juries, on the grounds that this would extend citizens' awareness of interdependence, give them a common experience, confront them with the views of citizens who hold different views, and engage them in deliberation with immediate implications for policy.

Thus it might be argued that some degree of participation should be universally required by extending the system of choice by lottery for these bodies, and reducing the grounds for exemption (Barber, 1984: 290).

This justification for compulsory voting is based on the argument that freedom requires decisions about collective goods, and does not have to rely on any stronger assumption that humans have a fundamentally political nature. Without any say in the shaping of social practices and the common goods they embody, the range of autonomy is limited. To require a person to participate in politics promotes a conception of the good life no more specific than having a say in the practices that frame their life. If full-time, permanent and uniform political action were required of all, it could indeed be claimed that requiring participation in political life forecloses on other options. This is not the case with the part-time, periodic or short-term service described here. A person could choose to reject political autonomy – to be a monk in an enclosed order, for example – but it should be recognised that he is passing to others the sustaining of public life, and that political autonomy is not simply an optional extra that individuals can choose to accept or reject.

But republicanism may still be a more appropriate target than socialism for Wilde's facetious complaint that it would take up too many evenings. Modern societies, even more than Montesquieu's or Tocqueville's, revolve around economic activity and private life, areas where people are generally concerned primarily with their own private interests. Is looking for more participation turning back the clock? Even if the conditions can be created, can we ever hope to engage people in political activity? Each citizen is one of millions, and the larger units become, the more complex are the issues and the kinds of decisions that arise. Apart from issues of deliberation, is the idea of widespread participation in any way realistic today? The republican response, again, is that even those private interests are at risk if politics is left to the politicians. There is a crisis of democratic access, of leadership and accountability. Money buys electoral office.[14] It is no longer clear that the representative system alone is adequate to defend the interests of apolitical citizens. And those who wear the shoe know if it fits. Professional politicians and administrators are not alone in having something to contribute to the political process. If new structures allow people to engage with politics, the implicit inefficiency of involving many people in decision-making may be countered by the increased sense of responsibility and civic virtue, and scrutiny of public office-holders, which is lacking or extremely weak in current polities.

Conclusion

No matter how much deliberation there is in multiple forums, decisions still have to be taken on some basis. The important point is that decisions taken after extensive deliberation may be more considered and more acceptable to all. This politics will not always achieve consensus, and yet governments must act and policies which embody certain values and not others will be implemented on contested areas such as pornography, euthanasia, homosexual marriage and abortion. Unlike many material claims, opposing values are frequently not amenable to compromise. Some positions will be endorsed and others will not, but this does not mean that they are not open to deliberation. In a deliberative republic the values embodied in policies cannot be justified in terms of a fixed account of the common good based on nature, a particular culture or even of an overlapping consensus. They have to be defended in deliberation, not taken as self-evidently right either universally or for us in our culture. Deliberatively decided policies are more justifiable in so far as they take into consideration the widest possible range of views, established, constructed and filtered in multiple publics. Those which are implemented can be justified as provisional realisations of common goods, which are the best that can be reached at this point, rather than as simply the will of the whole or the aggregated majority.

So this approach does not assume that full consensus is the final target. Consensus, as critics have pointed out, is not always an index of resolution. Briefly, what are more feasible are provisional formulations of common concerns, tentative embodiments of the common goods of those who deliberate, and more reflective judgements of how to deal with continuing differences, as well as expanded self-understandings. Policies that are not neutral may not be illegitimately oppressive of minorities if these have been the subject of extensive deliberation at different levels, if all voices have had opportunity to receive a hearing, to accommodate the deep concerns of all citizens equally, if certain provisions are made for cases of permanent minorities. Not all deliberation will issue in legislation or coercive state action. But the actions of the state public must be informed and subject to critique in the wider public realm. Contestation is an important part, if not the whole of deliberative republican politics. All outcomes are open to change and evolution through further consideration.

Republican political autonomy is concerned with self-government and realising common goods, not principally by publicly establishing existing shared values but through deliberating among those who share a common world and face a necessarily common future. Republican politics allows the expression and potential recognition of difference. The substance of republican politics is based on interdependence (rather than commonality), is created in deliberation (not pre-politically), emerges in multiple publics to which all can contribute, and is not definitive but open to change.

Yet if politics realises common goods and gives particular recognition to citizens, the political community is necessarily bounded. In the next chapter, I discuss the nature and limits of the political community founded in a deliberative politics of recognition.

CHAPTER VIII

Recognition and Inclusion in a Pluralist World

Introduction

Recognition is a distinctive concern of contemporary politics. As well as being affected by material dimensions of oppression, members of groups such as women, the disabled, gays and lesbians, racial, religious and cultural minorities may suffer from the harms of cultural assimilation, stigmatisation as inferior, or marginalisation from public life.

Issues of identity have gained a new salience in societies of very diverse citizens. The social confirmation of identity is increasingly seen as essential to human flourishing. 'Human subjects can develop an intact self-relation only by virtue of the fact that they see themselves affirmed or recognised according to the value of certain capabilities and rights' (Honneth, 1997: 29). Such personal identity is not expressed purely in individual actions and values, but through social and cultural practices, including legal and political relationships. If legal and political structures and practices that are ostensibly neutral actually reflect the values of a dominant mainstream, they will impinge differently on members of minorities. People may be misrecognised when social norms and institutions overlook their differences, exclude their voices, or marginalise their values from the public political realm. In consequence, we have increasingly seen political struggles not only for just distribution of resources and power, but also for equal recognition. A major dimension of this is providing public legal and institutional equality, but, as the term implies, recognition also requires a deepening of relations of respect between citizens. Where politics provides recognition, citizens may have not only vertical obligations to support just institutions, but also lateral obligations of solidarity with their fellow citizens with whom they form a political community rather than an association of strangers.

What is really at stake in modern claims for recognition, and how do they mesh with the republican emphasis on individual or collective recognition in politics that we saw, for example, in Arendt and Taylor?

This chapter addresses the questions of the intensity and scope of republican political community. Communities are necessarily bounded. Even if it is not moralistic (Chapter V), not coercive (Chapter VI), nor based on a predetermined common good (Chapter VII), a republican politics of recognition between citizens may seem to be excessively exclusive of those outside the polity. Membership of a republican political community implies strong commitments and special obligations to fellow-citizens. Whether this relationship should be identified with nationality, and whether the internal community of citizens depends on external relations of enmity or exclusion, are questions which have to be considered.

Liberal and cultural pluralist approaches to recognition

Because the way in which people are treated in public life affects their very identity, the demand for recognition in contemporary debates on inclusion goes beyond assuring individual members of minorities equal legal and political rights and opportunities. It looks for a more substantial accommodation of many different perspectives and ways of life.

The emergence of these concerns is often described as a turn from a politics of economic distribution to a politics of culture. But it should not be thought of as a turn from justice, so much as a shift of emphasis on what constitutes justice. And, though redistribution and recognition have sometimes been contrasted as principles of justice, in fact they are often interconnected – the drive for recognition may be an essential part of achieving a more just distribution, and a more just distribution may be required to achieve more equal recognition. Recognition both calls for and justifies more equal distribution of resources (Fraser, 1995, 2000; Phillips, 1997; Young, 1997).

Recognition can be defined in more or less substantial terms. Even at the most minimal level it is more than forbearance, when we overlook behaviour or practices we disapprove of, or tolerance, where we consciously allow them but may still disagree with or be indifferent to them. Liberals and others agree that justice requires equal 'respect' for all citizens, but they disagree on what is meant by and required by respect. Neutralist liberals have a thin conception of equal respect as best achieved by a neutral approach by the state to moral and cultural difference, supported by tolerance, non-discrimination and an attitude of civility or respect between strangers. They argue that individuals properly gain positive *recognition* of their personal worth through the love of family members or friends in the *private* or civil realms of society, and of their equal *legal status* as citizens in general laws in the *public* sphere. The public realm should be neutral with respect to potentially divisive cultures, religions and languages.[1]

But as we have seen in the previous chapter, confining difference to the private realm and assuming uniformity in the public realm minimises certain values and practices, and marginalises or oppresses those who hold them. In practice, too, the institutions of the liberal state recognise some cultural or moral values at the expense of others. For example, its marriage laws determine who can marry whom, who is the legal child of whom, and whether or how a marriage may cease to exist. Even if all have the same political and civil liberties, institutions which treat all alike may seriously misrecognise or humiliate those who are different, and thus do not treat citizens equally. Citizens may be oppressed not just by inequality of material resources or power, but by having to live within a template fitted to a dominant culture or lifestyle. The requirement to wear a motorcycle crash helmet affects a Sikh differently from others; meetings of political assemblies late into the night disproportionately disadvantage parents who care for young children. Thus we saw that, for Taylor, those whose culture is disparaged or even overlooked in society are not treated as equal citizens. Likewise for Sandel, a liberal policy of neutral tolerance

> brackets the value of the practices it tolerates. Given its conception of the self, it seeks respect for persons without winning respect for the convictions they hold or the lives they lead. The toleration that results does not cultivate appreciation for the ways of life it permits, only respect for the selves whose lives they are...Respecting persons as

unencumbered selves may afford a kind of social peace, but it is unlikely to realise the higher pluralism of persons and communities who appreciate and affirm the distinctive goods their different lives express.

(Sandel, 1996: 116)

At the very least this may be taken to mean that the range of social practices which are the framework of autonomy should be given weight in arranging political procedures and legal requirements, and that the cultural assumptions of politics should be broadened to avoid such oppression.

But a stronger argument is often advanced: that culture is so important to identity that equality of recognition requires revaluing and supporting specific cultures.

> [T]he democratic process of actualising equal individual rights will also extend to guaranteeing different ethnic groups and their cultural forms of life equal rights to coexistence....From a normative point of view, the integrity of the individual legal person cannot be guaranteed without protecting the intersubjectively shared experiences and life-contexts in which the person has been socialised and has formed his or her identity. The identity of the individual is interwoven with collective identities and can be stabilised only in a cultural network that cannot be appropriated as private property any more than the mother tongue itself can be.
>
> (Habermas, 1994b: 129)[2]

Thus cultural pluralists argue that equality requires more than uniform treatment or non-discrimination, but equal public recognition of the distinct identities of citizens, which may be based in their gender, ethnicity, religion, culture or sexual orientation. This may require gender- and group-differentiated forms of citizenship, with reserved representation, special provisions, rights and exemptions, as well as equal symbolic standing in public institutions.

But it is less easy to discern what exactly is entailed in recognition or what this justifies in practice. First, it has become increasingly clear that, while members of these groups experience some common problems, what is needed to provide recognition differs considerably for women, for the disabled, for gays and lesbians, for minority religions; and for minority races and cultures, for immigrants and indigenous peoples; and, within minority cultures, between language and other markers.

Debates have been particularly heated on the issue of cultural difference, and the idea that the recognition of individuals requires public support for their cultures. Some liberals acknowledge this and argue that liberal democratic states should allow for special cultural rights for minorities, as long as these do not undermine the liberal rights of the individual members of these minorities (Kymlicka, 1995). On this view cultures should be supported because they offer a meaningful range of options for the exercise of individual choice, not because any culture is intrinsically more valuable than any other.

One 'liberal culturalist' approach gives precedence to a 'societal' or 'encompassing' culture; that is, one which 'provides its members with meaningful ways of life across the full range of human activities, including social, educational, religious and economic life, encompassing both public and private spheres' (Kymlicka, 1995: 76). On this basis national minorities have greater claims than other ethnic minorities and the state may give indigenous national minorities more rights than immigrants.

We saw that Taylor adopted a broader view in arguing for the presumption of equal worth among enduring cultures, which justifies measures to promote their preservation for the future even at some expense of individual freedom of language and educational choice. Going further, some theorists of radical multiculturalism argue that we should more positively celebrate difference. What is meant by this may be either that diversity itself should be celebrated, or, more substantially, that the values of all cultures should be granted equal standing and be equally supported by the polity.

The argument goes something like this: identity is dialogical, and is supported by the existence of a culture. So recognition requires recognition of that culture. Equal recognition of minority citizens requires equal recognition of cultures, and this in turn requires sustaining these cultures for their members, promoting and even preserving those cultures for future generations.

The assumption that cultures (or societal cultures) should be preserved, or treated as non-negotiable, is problematic. Cultures themselves are not wholes, like species; they are made of networks of cultural practices. Culture includes aspects, such as language, that are unreflectively absorbed, and other more reflective values about ways of organising family life, reproduction, property and exchanges. There is no definitive account of what is the most central aspect of a culture, or where a culture begins and ends. What is Irish culture, for example? It might be seen as a blend of Gaelic traditions and Roman Catholic religion. But internally disputed is the question which is more fundamental: the Irish language, spoken by a progressively declining minority since the eighteenth century, or the Catholic religion, which has been practised by a predominant majority?[3]

In fact cultures grow and develop, interact, borrow and blend. What was once central to a culture may become less important over time, replaced by other social practices which integrate its members. And a person's identity is not necessarily fixed and wholly determined by a single culture; people negotiate their ways between sub-cultures, more encompassing cultures, and across cultures.

If cultures are not clearly distinguishable wholes but changing ensembles of practices, there are three problems with identifying recognition with guarantees of cultural practices: of negative side effects, of coherence and of desirability.

First, even if it is intended to rectify an imbalance of power, establishing a culture through political requirements of, for example, permanent quotas in office, special institutions or veto powers, can have negative effects. It may pick out the most advantaged members of a group, isolate the group from the wider society, or continue to favour it at the expense of others when it no longer needs such measures. Accordingly the idea of maintaining cultures in this way is problematic. It may ossify certain practices at the expense of others and limit as much as facilitate the autonomy which culture is seen to support. Thus feminists have been wary of the dangers of reification in identity-based measures, and many advocate, for example, more flexible systems of proportional representation to give minorities a voice.

Second, it is simply not possible to respect all cultures equally, because at least some different cultures have opposing and irreconcilable beliefs and practices. Some, moreover, make claims to superior worth over others. It is thus incoherent to speak of celebrating all differences simultaneously, to give equal recognition to all cultures or religious or moral perspectives. It is not clear, for example, how to confirm simultaneously the diverging values of those religious groups who believe that all sexual activity outside heterosexual marriage is wrong, and those who seek the institutional recognition of homosexual marriage.

Third, it may not be normatively desirable to guarantee all cultural practices. Different cultures represent alternative attempts to realise individual and collective goods. It is conceivable that some may realise these better than others even in fairly comparable circumstances. In any case, cultural values or ethos are not radically distinct from, or independent of moral concerns. It is not possible to distinguish radically the moral and the cultural dimensions of life. It is important that people's commitment to their culture is a matter of validity and worth rather than just of difference or distinctiveness:

> If we take a tradition or practice of our culture seriously, then we should treat it not simply as a costume for display or an attribute of our identity, but as a standard which does some normative work in the life of one's community.
>
> (Waldron, 2000a: 242)

So political decisions have to be made about what is and what is not publicly recognised in specific instances. This is to deny that cultural practices and values are more incommensurable or non-negotiable than political viewpoints and moral perspectives. The distinction between individual moral values subject to deliberation and cultural practices which are non-negotiable can be overdrawn.[4] Practices or viewpoints do not have to be taken as sacrosanct because they have cultural roots.

Besides, the equivalent treatment of all religious or cultural beliefs and practices (whether public or private) that is implied in some arguments for the celebration of difference may miss the point of claims for recognition. Putting all on the same footing may diminish or make vacuous the claims of worth implied in culture. This does not mean that we should erect a tribunal to stand in judgement over all cultures, or to allocate rankings of cultures, or to determine which ones fall within and which outside the perimeter of worth. It means that we should not base equal recognition for individuals on the recognition of all cultural practices.

So neither a liberal neutrality of the public nor equal multicultural celebration provides a satisfactory way of thinking about equal recognition.

Recognition and Inclusion

How should a republican state address this? Though we have seen that, from a republican perspective, people need social and cultural practices as a foundation for autonomy, this does not assume that all foster autonomy equally. It may be normatively undesirable to support some cultural practices that involve the domination of members or outsiders. It makes sense to think that there are some cultural practices less favourable to personal and political autonomy, which should be challenged, and others which may for various reasons be tolerated, without being recognised in the sense of giving them equal standing, promoting or preserving them for the future.

Cultural claims, just as moral claims, have to be subject to debate and deliberation. The importance of not misrecognising identity does not mean that all identities must be seen as equally valuable, that cultures must be accepted as indivisible wholes, or that all identities and cultures can and should be equally recognised politically.

None the less there are reasons to take concerns about misrecognition seriously. Developing and expressing identity through the common goods of social and cultural practices is an essential part of living autonomously. Republicans can value culture as the context for personal and political autonomy, and see that treating identities and cultures derogatively affects this autonomy. Even if expressing an identity is not itself the most urgent or important aspect of living, those with a socially stigmatised identity are condemned to a subordinate status, which reduces their chances of effective political interaction. So public recognition or misrecognition is important. Moreover, many specific cultural practices and values have much wider contributions to make to social and political life.

Republican recognition

Republicans have addressed the issue of intersubjective recognition, and have seen political action and citizenship as central to this. We have seen that for Arendt and Taylor, in public political action, citizens are not only treated as legal and political equals but the value of their projects, actions and identities is confirmed by others in the political realm.

The expressive dimension of republican politics thus seems to offer the hope of a richer society than liberalism can offer. The liberal combination of private confirmation and legal respect for all may supply only a partial account of recognition. According to Honneth, who builds on Arendt's distinction between love, respect and solidarity, these are just two of the three levels of the recognition needed to guarantee personal integrity. Personal love and affection in private relations sustains a sense of coherent unique existence and physical well-being, legal respect guarantees the status of independent judgement or moral personality, while political solidarity recognises the individual 'as a person whose capabilities are of constitutive value to a concrete community' (Honneth, 1997: 30).

We saw how this concern for recognition developed out of the discourse of honour. This presented several problems. Honour was fundamentally (as in Cicero and Rousseau) the respect due to those who acted virtuously. But historically honour was understood as essentially unequal, a positional good, its value depending on others not having it; to 'receive an honour' still means to be given a place in a hierarchy. Moreover, the discourse of honour confused status with achievement, as the notion of 'nobility' exemplifies.

Contemporary republicans are concerned to establish systems of more equal honour among participants in a political community, without the social hierarchies of the past (Pettit, 1997b). On the non-domination account citizenship is a publicly recognised social standing that secures people from the arbitrary wills of others, gives them self-respect and equalises their voices. On the political autonomy account citizens gain recognition when public institutions and policies are shaped in ways to which they have contributed, and reflect values they can endorse. In neither case is identity unchangeable or determined solely by cultural affiliation. In a republic, people gain a civic or political identity as politically autonomous citizens who participate in deliberating on the conditions of their common life. Political activity constitutes part of identity.

But this way of thinking of political recognition needs to be distinguished from two alternative possibilities. It might be thought that an emphasis on recognition through political activity and republican citizenship means one of two things.

Political recognition might be thought of as reflecting and reinforcing existing shared values and identity. This kind of thinking can be seen in practice in Ireland after the partition of 1922, when some at least justified the sectarian nature of the resulting states; the first Prime Minister of Northern Ireland characterized it as 'a Protestant state for a Protestant people'; likewise, in the South, the 1937 constitution gave special recognition to the Catholic faith.

Or at the other extreme, it might be thought that political identity supersedes or overrides all other identities. Here a practical example might be found in the French Republic, where citizenship has been interpreted influentially as a universal status that supersedes all others. The republic is unitary, recognises a single official language and a single school curriculum, allows limited local autonomy[5] and rests on a principle of secularity (*laïcité*) which made the public wearing of headscarves by Muslim schoolgirls a major political issue.

These two points about republican recognition and culture need initial clarification.

First, we have seen that contemporary articulation of republican politics does not mean directly establishing the shared values of an existing cultural community, since the values embodied are subject to the filter of deliberation, are politically constituted and contestable. Since the republic does not embody pre-political cultural values, republican recognition should be distinguished from a communitarian establishment of a package of shared values or conception of the good life.

Second, recognising people as citizens does not necessarily mean that *political identity* has to supersede or erode other dimensions of identity. Civic republicanism is sometimes rejected on the ground that it presupposes a view of human nature as most fully realised in political action (Kymlicka, 2002: 294–8). It thus imposes a particular conception of the good life. Even with deliberative resolution of differences, it might be thought that the outcome, or the republican political ethos of society, will necessarily be oppressive. But just as political activity is not the ultimate form of human self-realisation, political identity does not have to be the primary or dominant identity, as distinct from the *framing* identity within which people can become personally and politically autonomous. Being a citizen does not have to mean abandoning other identities or values.

A republican approach to cultural difference neither simply endorses a communitarian embodiment of a single fixed conception of the common good, nor imposes an overriding political identity.

Acknowledging specificity

Going beyond simple tolerance and non-discrimination, there are several dimensions of political recognition often implicitly elided in current claims or theories. These need to be disentangled. I will call these dimensions acknowledgement, authorisation and endorsement (corresponding respectively to the harms of having one's identity and viewpoints overlooked, discounted *a priori*, and relegated to the private).[6]

The first dimension (beyond tolerance and non-discrimination) is that of *acknowledging* specificity, rather than assimilating all citizens to a single model. This is denied when political life fails to take account of significant differences among citizens so that some are disadvantaged in relation to others when all are treated alike. This is as much an epistemic as a normative dimension of recognition: it registers that there is a difference that may affect the equality of some citizens in participating, and taking measures to correct this (without necessarily giving any public endorsement to their viewpoints or values). As we saw in Chapter VII, the common good of citizenship requires that citizens have equal access to participation.

Simply treating those who are not alike in every way as if they were, constitutes a form of misrecognition, or a failure of respect that is the reverse of discrimination, which excludes because of difference. We saw that feminists have long identified the apparently universal norms and practices of public life as forms of such misrecognition. For women, rectifying this needs the acknowledgment that obstacles to their participation in politics are not just private individual problems but public issues for many citizens.[7]

The remedy here calls not for unequal treatment, but for difference-conscious strategies needed to provide equal treatment in the interests of autonomy. These will not all be issues of culture, strictly speaking, as they are also particularly relevant to women and disabled people, for example. What are at stake here are less group rights than group-differentiated individual rights for those who fall into different categories. Precisely what is required is a matter of deliberation in particular cases, but the sorts of policies supported on these grounds have included child-care provisions for parents; access for the disabled; special language rights for minority groups in their interactions with government, education provisions, procedures and funding to increase minority participation in politics; some kinds of special representation; consultation bodies; and exemptions from legal requirements, where these are not strictly universally required – for example, allowing Sikhs to wear turbans rather than helmets on motor bicycles on in building work. [8]

On this dimension, the republican solution is to grant recognition to citizens *in* their identities, rather than *of* their identities. Even this kind of acknowledgement will have an effect on the second dimension, in so far as it entails a symbolic approval likely to affect how people's voices are heard.

Authorising viewpoints

The second dimension of recognition is *authorising* viewpoints. The form of misrecognition in this case may acknowledge difference and allow people to appear in the public realm, but in a limited way, in that they are not granted a serious hearing, or that their voices are systematically not granted anything like comparable authority (as we saw in discussing modes of deliberation in Chapter VII).[9] Certain values are ruled out of serious consideration even when those who hold them can speak in the public realm. By authorising people, you recognise their potential to contribute to the common, overarching public realm, not just to live in their own way separately. As we saw in the last chapter, instead of merely tolerating practices, this means giving public space for citizens to voice their deepest concerns, and giving a serious hearing to claims to influence public debates and public culture. As well as addressing the problem of stigmatisation by others, this dimension of recognition also addresses the problem of adaptive preferences among those who internalise the low esteem with which they are treated in society. Such people may not even conceive of their viewpoint as one which can be put forward for universal consideration. This dimension is more clearly normative than the previous one, since it entails a positive approval of the person and engagement with their concerns or, in Sandel's term, 'respect for the convictions they hold'.

It follows from the deliberative nature of politics that republican recognition of citizens requires taking the voices of others seriously as well as allowing them to speak. 'Being a person is intimately tied up with enjoying a certain status in communion with others, and perhaps the best marker of the required status is that your voice is authorized by those others' (Pettit, 1997b: 52).

The point is not so much to support 'local' expression of particular beliefs for their adherents, as to acknowledge their potentially universal claims in giving them the chance to be publicly expressed. This requires neither continuing special treatment nor actual acceptance of all the viewpoints advanced, but does imply the possibility that these may transform politics:

> Dialogue is not only a means of showing what makes one different, but also of showing that these differences are an important part of what should be regarded as worthy...Cultures may coexist because they are granted respect as tolerance, but it is only through public discussion that other kinds of respect can gain general attention and stimulate solidary responses from other groups.
>
> (Lara, 1998: 158)

In practice, for example, the women's movement and disability advocates have achieved this; they have not just gained greater equality for their members, but have to varying degrees changed the framework of values and practices in political and social life.

> Social movements through their interventions in the public sphere create and generate solidarity through narratives which demand recognition and at the same time aim to redefine the collective understanding of justice and the good life by proposing new visions of institutional transformation.
>
> (Lara, 1998: 1)

Ways of giving previously excluded viewpoints institutional authorisation of this kind may involve various kinds of state-sponsored intervention to subsidise political organisation; guaranteeing representation; or creating specific representative bodies for federal, regional or local self-government. But, unlike some contemporary models of consultation or consociational government (which might meet the requirements of acknowledgment), it is not enough for these to remain insulated from the wider political culture, but they need at some level to be integrated into a wider political forum where a broad spectrum of views encounter one another (Van Parijs, 2000). The other side of this dimension of recognition is that groups cannot claim a right to remain entirely isolated from the rest of society, and to insulate themselves (and their children) entirely from encountering ideas which differ from their fundamental values (Dagger, 1997). This recognises distinct identities without ghettoisation. It suggests that veto power should be seen only as an emergency provision, unlike weighted voting that gives special attention to the central concerns of minorities.

In addition, this dimension of recognition cannot be achieved solely through institutional provisions. It requires civic virtue in citizens who are open to consider and engage with other points of view; and who give parity of esteem by respecting not just individuals, but also the ways in which their cultures embody values, thus showing a deeper appreciation of other ways of life. The state can encourage such openness through educating about interdependence and promoting interaction in public forums, and more specifically through, for example, anti-racism campaigns and equality programmes, which promote perceptions of minorities as equal members, or deconstruct stereotypes or images of them as inferior, or backward.

These voices and viewpoints are subject to judgement and deliberation in the political process, and authorisation does not mean that all practices, viewpoints and values will be given public endorsement. None the less people gain recognition when they are given an open-minded hearing, when their viewpoints are authorised and heard, through institutional provisions and esteem initiatives. Those who have had a say in a fair procedure are more likely to identify with the institutions and other participants in politics. The good of a serious hearing for all may be more attainable than the equal establishment of all cultures.[10]

Endorsing practices

This third dimension of recognition is at the opposite end of the spectrum from liberal neutrality in endorsing or publicly adopting practices and values, as, for example, the Church of England is established as the public religion in England, and French as the official language of France. This may involve constitutional or legislative embodiment, symbolic or material support. Not to be recognised in this sense means that even if you do not suffer disabilities that limit your interactions, and your political voice is heard and respected, yet your way of life is not publicly endorsed by the state. Though historically the process of gaining this kind of recognition

Contemporary Debates

has been an exclusive struggle between competing cultures for predominance, it does not necessarily have to be exclusive, as some communitarian arguments for the endorsement of the shared values of a single community imply. In many cases it may be possible to endorse publicly more than one culture or way of life simultaneously (Parekh, 2000). It is possible, for example, to expand the frame of the public sphere to support more than one religion, to support minority languages, and to provide for the public holidays of different cultural groups. Whereas most liberals see the answer to the inequality caused by the establishment of the Church of England as its disestablishment, an alternative lies in the co-recognition of the other principal faiths in Britain (Modood, 1993).

Extending recognition may even change the definition of the public realm. Thus, for example, instead of giving particular ethnic groups a place in the public realm, a country such as Britain might be defined as a multi-cultural country. It may be argued that in practice any expansion of the scope of recognition changes the public realm more fundamentally. This may come about if new conceptions and practices are introduced; for example, through broadening or diversifying the institution of marriage to include divorce or same-sex marriage. Drawn to its fullest extent, this might extend to a kind of celebration of the idea of diversity and variety as aspects of a society, as Taylor suggests is the case in Canada.

This kind of recognition moves further towards Sandel's 'appreciating the ways of life it permits'. But it does not depend on an *a priori* idea of the equal worth of cultures or the promotion of diversity. On the republican view, it does not follow from arguments for recognition that all cultures should be publicly embodied. Republican deliberative politics gives all an equal chance to influence the public culture, and engages with their underlying concerns without taking them as final, unmodifiable or of equal value.

It is possible to grant equal recognition without endorsing either the values of all, or the values of none, in the public sphere. This contrasts with the misconception that apparently underlies the design of the new common banknotes of the European Union, which feature no particular persons but rather drawings of bridges and windows that are carefully designed not to be identifiable as representing any participating country.

Evaluation and judgement cannot be excluded even in deciding on neutrality of treatment. Because two moral or cultural groups who hold diametrically opposed values cannot both gain this dimension of recognition simultaneously, this form of recognition cannot be regarded as an absolute right of a group. It is a reflection of the ineluctably agonal nature of politics, that in some cases only one value can be embodied in public. Conflict is a reality to be acknowledged.

For republicans, the substantive goods realised in politics embody certain values and not others, so that neutrality is not a real option. But their embodiment is justified in terms other than realising pre-political shared ends, or expressing the will of a dominant group, is provisional and is open to deliberative reconsideration. For republicans this is the best way to approach politics in a plural society, where people have to live with people who are different from them. Republican recognition acknowledges difference, and provides for plural approaches where possible. It takes seriously the claims which members of different groups advance from within their particular perspectives and it needs to provide thorough public justification of any exclusion. But it does not assume that any culture should be definitively embodied in the public realm to the exclusion of others, or that all cultural values will be possible to celebrate simultaneously. In this way it may be possible to confirm the value of a person's way of life in engaging with them, without adopting their policy proposals. Citizens can achieve solidarity through recognition as acknowledgement and authorization more often than endorsement.

The issue is neither promoting difference nor assimilation to a single conception of the good life, but promoting freedom, personal and political, for which some cultural framework is a base. This approach which privileges autonomy may itself clash with some identities. In dealing with a culture or an identity that rejects political autonomy or its preconditions (for example, of gender equality in education) republicanism becomes a fighting creed. But a republican politics, based on the possibility of self-government in particular circumstances, should be sensitive to and respect differences in realising autonomy. In contrast to some liberal and feminist responses to issues from headscarves to arranged marriages, it does not justify imposing received ideas of what gender equality requires, without consulting those involved and considering the complexity of the issues involved.

Republican recognition is achieved by being acknowledged and authorised as a member of a collectively self-governing community.

It does not require living in a society in which one's values are uniquely established in the public sphere. Thus we should understand republican recognition as neither purely individual, as it was for Arendt, nor culturally embedded, as Taylor sometimes tends to suggest.[11]

A republican political community of recognition

So republican politics entails significant equality of recognition among heterogeneous citizens. What, then, is the nature and intensity of the ideal republican community? Can it be strong enough to motivate civic virtue while still allowing room for difference?

The republican polity is a community of those who face a common predicament, common concerns, who are in the same boat; they have not necessarily chosen one another, but have been thrown together historically, and share a wide range of interrelated interdependencies, significantly shaped by their subjection to a common authority. As citizens they have the possibility of collectively shaping their future. This gives rise to lateral relationships and obligations of solidarity between citizens, not just of vertical loyalty to just institutions.

The process of political recognition constitutes a community of solidarity between citizens, who are different but profoundly interdependent. Republican recognition does not depend on the endorsement of a package of shared pre-political values, but on interaction in a common political realm in which those who are different and who hold different views engage with one another. In public life strangers become co-citizens:

> The feelings of friendship and solidarity result precisely from the extension of our moral and political imagination...through the actual confrontation in public life with the point of view of those who are otherwise strangers to us, but who become known to us through their public presence as voices we have to take into account.
> (Benhabib, 1988: 47)

This republican conception of recognition lays considerable weight on the attitudes, relationships and mutual obligations between citizens instead of the liberal contractarian agreement on procedures and institutions, or a pragmatic *modus vivendi*: 'the norms of civility that are required for fostering freedom as non-domination are norms of solidarity with others, not norms of compromise' (Pettit, 1997a: 259).

Models of community

The community of a modern republic may be envisaged in a number of different ways. Political community tends to be understood by analogy to other more everyday relationships. The idea that a republican political community must be homogenising and exclusionary is based on the misapprehension that all relationships fall on either side of a dichotomy between close, face-to-face, homogeneous, emotionally bound communities of those who know one another well, such as families or friends, and distant, diverse, rational or institutionally-mediated associations of strangers (Dietz, 1998). Most relations are not defined by a matrix generated by one or two polarities. Even in families there are different kinds of relationship. Communitarians have tended to take the family, and liberals to take the association of strangers, as the model for the polity. Both analogies are misleading.

Seeking community on family lines elides different kinds of 'recognition': love, respect and solidarity, appropriate in different kinds of relationships. Many community models presuppose intimacy or shared values between members, which indeed cannot be easily extended to large and diverse populations. The analogy of strangers in voluntary association misleads too, because it underestimates the degree of connectedness between fellow-citizens of modern states, where people live in relatively enduring, multiply interdependent relationships.

Rather than having to decide between analogies of stranger or family and friend, the alternative analogy of colleagues may illustrate that it is possible to feel a commitment to people whom one does not know very well, or with whom one does not share a broad range of values.[12] This may help to direct us towards a better understanding of citizenship.

Colleagues

The relations of colleagues are closer than those of strangers, less voluntary than those of friends, and less emotionally charged than those of family. Colleagues find themselves as relative equals in an institution or practice. Yet they are diverse and relatively distant from one another, and may have no close knowledge of, or strong feelings for, one another. They do not generally choose one another, but yet have common concerns rooted in a common predicament. Their commitment is based on this rather than any opposition to another group. This is not a rigidly bound relationship, but can extend to foreign colleagues, and to people in other institutions. In addition it is possible to be a member of multiple sets of colleagues – to be a nurse and a trade unionist, or an economist and a journalist, for example. Thus colleagues are diverse, separate and relatively distant individuals whose involuntary interdependence creates common concerns and the possibility of jointly addressing them.

In so far as such relationships are valuable, they can give rise to *special obligations*, characteristically of consideration, concern and trust. Such obligations are widely recognised in practice so that we may speak of the 'strength of weak ties' (Granovetter, 1973). Moreover, these obligations may be multiple, and are extensible beyond the confines of immediate colleagues on the basis of other interdependencies.[13] (This is not to say that these are the only grounds of obligation; for example, they have to be balanced against other relationships and considerations of need.)

Likewise, citizens are more than strangers to one another but less than family or friends.[14] The republic may be a community of civic solidarity; that is, a relation of citizens marked by equality, diversity and relative distance, instituted involuntarily, but growing through reiterated interaction and practices. This recalls Arendt's conception of the relations of citizens as personal though indirect and public, in contrast to the impersonal or private relations of society.

Salient issues and concerns make them interdependent even when they disagree about how to interpret or deal with them. They may understand the goals of the polity from different angles, and value citizenship for different reasons. Their commitment comes from their mutual vulnerability in the practice of self government, and in its stronger forms from the value they attach to the relationship. 'A sense of sharing a common fate may also be enough to produce significant convergence on the good of citizenship which is part of the republican conception of community' (Mason, 2000: 133). The existence of special obligations is grounded in the good of citizenship among those who are multiply interdependent, and is owed to one another even when government or law has broken down.

On this analogy citizens may be relatively distant and different from one another, have no close emotional engagement, but yet recognise the commitments entailed in a valuable relationship, thicker than the civility between strangers but of a kind different from friends and family (Honohan, 2001a).

This supports the political obligations to co-citizens that are based in largely involuntary interdependencies. We have seen in Chapter V that civic virtue is not best justified in terms of fair play in a cooperative enterprise for mutual advantage, because citizenship is not a strictly reciprocal relationship in which people receive benefits in proportion to their contributions, but a joint relationship that realises the common good of freedom and self-government. This supports a *non-voluntarist* account of civic commitment based on 'associative obligations'. These are 'obligations arising from social relationships in which we usually just find ourselves, or into which we grow gradually...[which] involve no datable act of commitment, and...involve requirements to show a certain loyalty and concern' (Simmons, 1996: 251). Such obligations to family and friends are often recognised. But understanding political obligation in this way has been criticised on normative grounds, not only as being modelled too closely on family relations (a point dealt with above) and as exaggerating the importance to people of the bonds of citizenship, but also as being uncritical of local standards and as relying too heavily on constitutive identities and emotional commitments. I address some of these criticisms in what follows.

But first we should note the sort of commitment that can unite a republican political community of citizens connected by a horizontal bond in a political framework. This commitment is more open-ended than the loyalty to a state that 'patriotism' normally is used to describe today, and closer to the original meaning of putting the common good ahead of particular interests.

Particular commitments or universal standards?

Liberals have in the past assumed that the motivation to observe political obligation can be derived from consent or a sense of the justice of general laws. But in recent years thinkers have acknowledged the power of feelings of loyalty to a particular polity in generating political obligation and civic virtue among citizens. Various attempts have been made to distinguish less oppressive or exclusive forms of commitment than ethnic or cultural national identification have been in practice.

In the context of increasing philosophical interest in the nature and normative justification of nationalism, a kind of 'political patriotism' has been advanced. One approach to this sees citizens as bound by loyalty to *common principles of justice* or *institutions* rather than to common ethnicity, while still anchored in a particular community (Habermas, 1996b: 500). This *constitutional patriotism* is held to be more legitimate and effective, and less volatile and exclusive than ethnic or cultural patriotism. But it may be argued that this is not as satisfactory a resolution of the issue as claimed; for these principles are liable to be too thin to motivate citizens, have to rely on pre-political commitments for support, and so become too substantial to be really inclusive.[15]

Thus another approach proposes that a more substantial form of political patriotism, rooted in a common *political* way of life, can unite citizens. Such a republican patriotism aims to be stronger and more personal than a commitment to liberal principles, laws or institutions. As Viroli puts it, 'between the ideal world of rational moral agents, impartial observers and ideal speakers, and the real world of exclusive and narrow passions, there is space for a possible politics for the republic' (Viroli, 1995: 17).

In Viroli's 'love of country', citizens commit themselves to liberty, and the institutions which have embodied and sustained it in their country's way of life, like Machiavelli's *vivere libero*: 'democratic politics do not need ethno-cultural unity; they need citizens committed to the way of life of the republic' (Viroli, 1995: 176). Thus he argues that such a conception of patriotism is not radically oppressive or exclusive, and can include those who are culturally different within the polity, and others outside it: 'Because it is a love of the particular it is possible, but because it is a love of a particular liberty it is not exclusive; love of the common liberty of one's people easily extends beyond the national boundaries and translates into solidarity' (Viroli, 1995: 12).

But the 'particular way of life' in which liberty has been embodied, of which citizens have been so proud in, for example,

Britain and the United States, has at times been profoundly exclusive of others (and may inherently marginalise). Equally, it may not be possible for all to share a positive view even of a shared history. Thus Viroli's account of republican patriotism places too much emphasis on a specific way of life or history than is compatible with republican equality of recognition.

None the less people who live in societies with histories of division or exclusion may still be able to develop a solidarity based on their common concerns. 'At least some citizens might identify with their institutions even if they did not identify with the historical processes which lead to their emergence, or did not support the historical myths that are told about these processes' (Mason, 2000: 137). This is historically quite common. In Ireland, for example, a sizeable nationalist minority rejected the terms of the Treaty of 1922 with Britain as too limited a step towards independence. This led to a bitter civil war between their forces and those of the new Irish Free State, which they refused to recognise. In time, however, these opponents came to terms with, and eventually came to power in, the state which they had opposed, and worked alongside those who had ordered the execution of relatives, friends and comrades. People may grow together historically, but this does not mean that their political unity has to rest on a positive evaluation of that history. Today in Northern Ireland, if a common polity is possible, it will never be able to rest on a history in which the same events are commonly celebrated by both traditions, Protestant and Catholic. This may be true to a lesser extent of the European Union, where a violent history divides the member countries, even if many common cultural and historical threads, from the Roman Empire to the Enlightenment, are woven through all their histories.

The colleagues model of citizenship provides an alternative account of republican commitment based on common concerns strong enough to unite citizens.

Constitutive identity and emotional commitment

Republican commitment is directed to the common goods shared by people who may potentially be self-governing. Thrown together significantly by their subjection to common institutions and history, citizens' obligations are based on interdependence, rather than on feelings or perceptions of commonality, or agreement on procedures, constitutional arrangements or institutions. Republican commitment to fellow-citizens is indeed motivated by identification with the political community: 'Civility involves not just internalising values, but also identifying with the group whose interests are associated with those values' (Pettit, 1997a: 257). But this identification is grounded in the reflective recognition of interdependence and the good of citizenship. Sharing in the deliberative outcomes of a public realm itself leads to deeper commitments.

Reserving certain obligations to co-members is sometimes defended on the ground that membership is an essential part of an individual's identity. But identities may be positive or negative, and are not passively received but constructed, and something for which people may be expected to take responsibility. In the words of Vaclav Havel: 'identity is above all an accomplishment, a particular work, a particular act. Identity is not something separate from responsibility, but on the contrary its very expression' (Havel, 1998: 46). It is not clear that identity as such gives rise to any obligations to others. Drawing moral lines on the basis of relations constitutive of identity is suspect if those identities are negative or suspect (Caney, 1996).

The fact that any relationship may evince strong feelings of attachment does not make it a good guide to the scope of responsibility.[16] The mere existence of strong feelings is not necessarily a good guide to obligations. Feelings of loyalty or compassion may be appropriate or inappropriate; they are not merely expressive, but reflect perceptions which may or may not be valid.

It may be argued that the value of feelings of attachment lies in the valuable relationships and not in the feelings, or the attachment *per se*. If so, neither feelings of attachment nor a sense of identity can be translated uncritically into moral obligations. 'At best feelings of identification can sometimes explain why people sometimes recognize the obligations they have' (Young, 2000: 157).

On the account of republican citizenship developed here, obligations are based on a reflective perception and taking of responsibility for relations of interdependence, not on an immediate sense of emotional attachment (or 'local standards'). Citizenship is itself an identity based on a valuable relationship developed in interaction, which gives rise to obligations whether or not they are recognised or citizens have such a feeling of identity.

But we should note that this critique of feelings of identity as the basis of obligation is not based on a contrast of universal reason to particular feelings.[17] Solidarity does not have to be seen as either a purely emotional or a purely rational tie. Current studies in a number of disciplines have tended to deconstruct the contrast between reason and the emotions which has been very influential in Western thought (Nussbaum, 1986). Instead of dismissing the role of identity and feelings in moral discourse, we may say that feelings are subject to critical reflection, and identity is something over which we have some control even if we do no choose it freely. Authenticity is not necessarily at odds with autonomy.[18]

The argument here is that republican commitment can be generated among those who participate and interact; that those who recognise their interdependence can accept responsibilities to fellow citizens.

But two kinds of questions still arise. First, do the conditions for such political recognition exist in the modern world? As Taylor suggests, this kind of patriotism may require a high degree of opportunity for citizens' engagement, and may not be able to survive the marginalisation of self-rule.

Second, is it not the case that republics admitting substantial common goods to politics will in practice be at least as particularist, and hence exclusive, as other forms of cultural nationalism? I will discuss this in the following section. First, however I consider the argument that a republic must in practice be rooted in some kind of nationality.

Republican citizenship and nationality

It has been argued that a republic needs to be rooted in a more substantial cultural unity, and that the membership of a republic should correspond to the membership of a nation. This is an important issue which requires detailed consideration.

First we may note that nationalism – the idea that those who share a nationality (however defined) should be self-governing – is distinct from republicanism – the idea that people should be self-governing. For republicans, political autonomy is the goal of self-government. But nationalism specifies the domain of self-government in a way that republicanism does not.

This does not have to be based in any mystical notion of the nation as a higher unity. Thus some have argued that encompassing, or societal, cultures which provide a wide range of options to individuals should be self-determining.[19] While we can acknowledge the importance of culture to individuals, and the need for cultural expression and some level of recognition, we should not extrapolate from the need for individuals to be self-determining to the idea that cultures should be self-determining.

Culture can be taken account of in politics without making a common culture *the* basis of political community. If a full range of cultural options is required for a people to be politically autonomous, it still does not follow that they have necessarily to be constituted as distinct political entities in order to exercise some degree of self-determination (Young, 2000).

The core principle of political nationalism is the notion that the nation is the unit of self-determination. Thus nationalism is in general a form of communitarianism, which roots political community in a perceived commonality of ethnicity, culture or other pre-political base. But there can also be a 'liberal nationality' based on a liberal political culture.

However, some republican theorists have argued that, at least under current conditions, it is both necessary and desirable that a republic should be based in a nation of some kind; that, in effect, the nation is the last, best hope for republican political community (Taylor, 1996; Miller, 1995a; Poole, 1999: 112). These have argued that the degree of unity necessary to support political participation and the material conditions for equal citizenship require an underpinning of nationality, which may be of the liberal kind of nationality in which public culture rather than deep culture or ethnicity defines the nation. (This may be seen as entailing more substantial unity than Habermas's, but less than Viroli's model).

In this section I consider the relationship between republicanism and nationality. I distinguish the republican conception of citizenship from nationality. I contest the claim that a republican community should give a strong priority to a shared even if public culture based on liberal nationality.[20]

The conceptual distinction

We can distinguish the conception of citizenship – membership of the same state – from nationality – membership of a nation – though these are often subsumed under the same term: compatriot. Thus, in practice, emigrants who have naturalised in another country may be co-citizens and co-nationals of two distinct groups of people. In other instances, nationalities may extend beyond a single state; as, for example, there is a long-standing Swedish minority in Finland; or states extend beyond a single nation, as both the Irish in Northern Ireland and the Scots in Scotland are British citizens.

The key feature of nationality is a collective sense of a common identity. Whether based on ethnic descent, linguistic or other cultural grounds, this is often rooted in an 'imagined community', and does not intrinsically require interdependence in practices between co-nationals. Thus the 'ethnic' Germans in the USSR were considered part of the German nation on the grounds of ancestry alone, reaching back in some cases as far as the eighteenth century. Cultural nationality is based on a perceived commonality of pre-political culture or history. Republican citizenship, in contrast, rests not on pre-political commonality, but on the political recognition of multiply reiterated interdependencies, and on interaction within the framework of a state.

The republican conception of citizenship outlined here is closer to that of a liberal nationality, in which citizenship is defined in terms of membership of a shared public culture, rather than a deeper culture or ethnicity. But it is still distinct from it, since republican citizenship rests fundamentally on the possibility of self-government of those who share a common fate rather than on specifically articulated public values.

Thus, in the republican perspective, membership is not defined in terms of culture; there are essentially no antecedent cultural restrictions on membership. This does not mean that it is committed to excluding all cultural values from politics. It may indeed aim to shape the public culture in certain ways, but these values are filtered through the deliberative democratic process. If there are common cultural values in a republic they are not its foundation, but the outcome of political interaction, provisionally embodied and open to change.

> The values that shape the policies of the republic are, ideally, ones that have developed from exchanges between citizens who may have very different cultural backgrounds. They are the product of such exchanges, potentially effecting alterations in the citizens' prior norms, which is a

very different thing from their being the discovered intersection of unchanging ones.

(Gilbert, 2000: 160)

Arguments for nationality as the basis of the republic

But even if we can distinguish republican citizenship from national membership conceptually, it may be argued that, *in practice*, people will recognise the relationships and community of republican citizenship only if it is based on some kind of common culture.

The argument is that in large modern states, in which people cannot personally identify with others, citizens' virtue, or active participation, supporting the common good and accepting the degree of redistribution which republican politics requires, depends on their being able to share certain sentiments and identity, or at least to give priority to a shared public culture. The nation is a necessary base for the republican community: 'Nationality gives people the common identity that makes it possible for them to conceive of shaping their world together' (Miller, 1989: 189).

David Miller argues that a republic needs to be based on a liberal nationality, in which citizens need to share not just loyalty to institutions and principles, but substantial public values:

> [T]he aim is that every citizen should think of himself as sharing a national identity with the others, where...this means belonging to a community that is constituted by shared belief and mutual commitment, that extends over historical time, that has an identifiable homeland and that possesses a distinct public culture that marks it off from its neighbours.
>
> (Miller, 1995a: 188)

This may seem to be approximated in France, for example, where quite a thick public culture, including the French language, a secular state and a centralised national education, has been seen as an essential foundation of the republican structure of equality and freedom.[21]

We saw that Taylor argues on more pragmatic grounds that national self-government is the condition of self-rule and recognition of those who form the nation because 'the nation is the community of modern times' (Taylor, 1993: 43).

Where Miller's argument stems primarily from a concern with motivating action and redistribution, Taylor emphasises also the process of intersubjective recognition in itself. On this basis, both conclude that a certain precedence may be given to the existing more or less public culture of the state, though with some flexibility vis-à-vis minorities and immigrants. For Miller, this may require adherence to a strong public culture or a 'general political ethos', a single official language, and a uniform national curriculum. Though he adopts a republican position that the public culture should be subject to change through a process in which all voices could join, he gives quite significant priority, for example, to the national language, to its history in a national curriculum, and recommends that immigrants and other minorities should accept the institutions and adhere to the political ethos of their new country (Miller, 1995a). In both these views the existing political culture is given a considerable degree of primacy.

The problems of rooting republican citizenship in nationality

It is not clear that it is absolutely necessary or even advisable to tie republican citizenship to national identity in this way.

In the view of many, the nation cannot unproblematically be the unit of self-government in the culturally plural world of today, because nations are both too large for self-government and too small to challenge the power of multinationals and deal with problems of the global environment and security.

But there are more specific reasons why the nation may not be the essential basis for republican political community. In practice a common sense of ethnicity, culture and history is not enough to guarantee political community, or support for redistributive policies. Electoral politics has become polarised in a way that a sense of national identity cannot overcome. A shared British identity did not prevent widespread toleration and support for cuts in welfare spending in Britain under Margaret Thatcher in the 1980s. Similarly, notwithstanding shared ethnicity, there are deep conflicts and resentment between citizens of the old East and West Germany. In practical terms, then, the nation is not indisputably the community of today.

At the 'macro' level of the polity, states are not neatly divisible along national lines. Many states contain more than one putative nation, which are frequently not territorially discrete, so that people typically need to recognise, work with and support people whose values, identity or view of history they do not share. And the prospect that the availability of secession might create more homogeneous states does not seem to be a solution either, as this tends to produce (or make salient) *new* internal differences that give rise to ever more precisely defined nations or national minorities. If recognition is to be granted through modern citizenship, it will have to take account of the inseparability of intermingled cultures in the states of the contemporary world.

At the micro-level of the person, someone may have allegiances to more than one culture or nation. This may be nested: for example, in someone who is both Scots and British; or plural: for an emigrant or someone of mixed parentage. Even in France, where the unity of the nation is a core principle and national unity has been deliberately forged for centuries, Breton, Basque and Catalan cultures persist. Even when people have a common history, they may not view it in the same way, and may interpret shared institutions differently. Nations do not naturally form firm foundations for modern states.

As well as being practically problematic, it is *normatively* unsatisfactory to base political community on a common nationality. Apart from instances in which self-appointed representatives impose their image on the concrete community of the nation (from Hitler to Milosevic), less extreme regimes can also become the focus of blind commitment expressed in the slogan 'My country right or wrong'. Even in its more benign forms, if the focus of *belonging* is to a cultural community it will tend internally to homogenise or marginalise those who do not conform to the national model, and externally to exclude or to limit radically the obligations citizens have to outsiders. (We saw in the case of Taylor the tension in reconciling measures that are understood as required for the political autonomy of the Quebecois and the provisions for immigrants.) To conclude that we should seek to create states of more like-minded citizens threatens to increase the likelihood of oppression, marginalisation and exclusion.

Since we live in a plural world, giving precedence to an existing common public culture will in practice favour some over others and be either oppressive or exclusive. Even if this intended to be in political or civic terms, it smuggles back in the cultural. It is important to be cautious about justifying actions in terms of the public culture. For instance, the elite nature of those selected in Britain in 2001 to sit as 'people's peers' in the House of Lords (the fifteen included seven knights and three university professors) was justified by the chairman of the selection committee on the grounds that it was important to choose people who 'would be comfortable operating in the House of Lords' (Perkins, 2001).

Even a liberal nationality may be seen as too substantial and exclusive (Mason, 2000; Cole, 2000; Gilbert, 2000: 117–19). The nation may appear to be necessary to motivate support for the polity, when opportunities for engagement through political participation are limited. Membership of a nation does substitute a kind of recognition for agency in creating an identification with the state (Poole, 1999: 107). We may admit the power of nationality as an effective myth; this is reinforced when claims expressed in national terms are more likely to gain a hearing than other kinds of claims. But the nation is an inadequate substitute for participation; it does not generate the sense of responsibility in citizens in areas where it matters.

Republican citizenship without nationality?

But are there any reasons to think that a political community can flourish without extensive commonality of culture and agreement on values?

Certainly some degree of basic agreement is a prerequisite for political interaction; even liberal–democracies dominated by the mechanisms of markets and electoral-representative politics need a shared basis of understandings; but we should not exaggerate the extent of uniformity of beliefs and values necessary for a functioning political community. Functioning modern societies are not commonality-based wholes, but loosely coordinated patchworks. Their coherence derives from convergent and common interests, habits and inertia as much as from actively shared values or identity. And over time even conflicts over values appear to have an integrating function (Bader, 2001).

Moreover, redistributive policies which transcend national boundaries have been supported (even with very limited levels of democratic participation and engagement). For example, the expense of the European Union structural funds which gave large transfers to peripheral regions such as Ireland, Spain and Portugal in the 1980s and 1990s were substantially borne by Germany without significant signs of resistance. Since Europe is notoriously marked by diversity of nationality and views of history, the crucial platform that justified these funds was the interdependence, common fate and future of the European countries.[22]

Thus interdependence of fate and future can come to be seen as the basis of political community. 'That sense of sharing a common fate may often be enough to motivate support for policies which aim at the common good without there needing to be a deeper sense of belonging together, which a shared national identity would involve' (Mason, 2000: 134).

The fact that it is hard to find examples of places where citizens do see themselves as bound together without some kind of national commonality may be attributed to the way in which political unity (even with limited participation) has often created national feeling, rather than vice-versa. The nearest thing to a polity which is not based on a nation may be Switzerland, which is ethnically and culturally diverse and bound mainly by notably participatory political institutions and a militia-based system of defence. But Switzerland is quite exceptional in history, location and composition. Many nations are the product of political unity among previously diverse populations. By dint of repeated interaction people may come to have a common history (Gilbert, 2000). States as different as, for example, the USA, France and Cuba may be seen as nations of very diverse people forged through political activity.[23] Indeed it may be argued that all states engage in deliberate *nation-building*. But (as Kymlicka has argued) some kinds of nation-building are more justified than others. Some nations have been created through ethnic cleansing, enforced movement and linguistic oppression. Others are shaped more gradually through institutions such as common education, national media and national symbols. Some combine legitimate and illegitimate means. In any case, the point here is simply that we can see nations as having been created by states, rather than vice-versa (Kymlicka, 2002: 263).

Thus it might be objected that my account of the apparent cultural openness of the republic is illusory, since the republic will always create a particular political culture in using some language and establishing political institutions and practices. We can acknowledge that a republic may create a nation even if these elements are established through deliberative determination and open to subsequent modification. We have seen that republican politics does not claim to be neutral about cultural and moral values; but it may give less precedence to the existing public culture than Miller's liberal nationality. The substance of republican politics is based on interdependence rather than commonality, is created in deliberation, emerges in multiple publics to which all can contribute, and is not definitive but open to change. On the account of republican politics advanced here, there are no *a priori* grounds to think that a state must have a single national language or a uniform national curriculum. This will depend on circumstances, and in any case the public culture itself is subject to political debate and deliberation. This account is more fallibilist, and sees the public culture is more provisional terms.

Second, a non-national republic may be possible if (as is well-documented) many demands for cultural and political autonomy that are couched in the language of nationalism reflect other needs and interests that are currently denied – for fair distribution of resources, freedom of cultural expression, acknowledgement of specificity, authorisation of viewpoints, a degree of public endorsement, or a more active say in the determination of their lives.

If a sense of 'belonging' is to justify political commitments, it should be a matter of engaging in the polity rather than of conforming to existing cultural patterns. Rather than prior commitment being necessary to motivate participation and redistribution, we may argue that participation is necessary for identification. In a republic with plural but overlapping publics, as outlined in the previous chapter, there is more potential for flexibility *vis-à-vis* different cultures and subcultures. These may influence every level of the polity over time.

This will mean stronger connections between different citizens than are envisaged in liberal nationalist states, in so far as there is more public interaction of various forms, through which citizens create further networks of relationships.

Republican solidarity is better understood as a commitment to the people with whom we are interdependent in the polity than in terms of loyalty to a nation, whether ethnically, civically, culturally or liberally defined, to liberal institutions or to principles in a specific historical embodiment.

Against the idea that the nation has to be the focus of community, and that this limits the size of republican polities, in recent years there have been extensive moves towards establishing political institutions and government at levels other than the nation. Local and regional autonomy, transnational organisations and global institutions are all becoming more important in attempts to deal with the limitations of the nation-state. As suggested in the previous chapter, such multiple levels of government can be conceived of on republican lines. A republic which does not depend on pre-existing cultural commonality provides a model for transnational political communities. The continuing development and integration of the European Union could be better modelled in this heterogeneous way, rather than depending on the development of a quasi-national identity and unity among Europeans (Kostakopoulou, 1996). Critics will argue that participation and accountability are precisely what is lacking at these higher levels of government. From a republican perspective the contemporary difference in this respect between national and transnational institutions is one of degree only.

Boundary problems

If self-government is required for the political autonomy of those who are interdependent, we have seen that a variety of interconnecting levels of government can be justified, from local to regional, national and transnational. This may address one aspect of the problem of state boundaries. An apparent advantage of matching the state and the nation is that it gives a criterion for setting boundaries of states, but it does so at the cost of recurrent conflicts. Despite the hegemony of nationalist ideas for more than a hundred years, the fluidity of state borders in that time shows the difficulty in mapping the nation onto the state (Lustick, 1993). Justification of boundaries remains an intractable problem that is increasingly urgent to address.

Liberalism notoriously has not developed any justification for how borders should be drawn. While republicanism – self-government by those who are multiply interdependent – does not provide a clear criterion either, it justifies more porous boundaries and multiple sovereignties. If the arguments advanced here are valid, republics do not have to be radically limited in size and diversity. A republic need no longer be seen as the very small, face-to-face community Aristotle and Rousseau envisaged. Size may be limited by the technological and institutional capacities for mutual self-government and accountability at any level. But these are different from the constraints posed by the nation, or the sovereignty of an organic people. Instead of a single undivided property, sovereignty may be divisible into functions and degrees, practicable at many different levels, which are not necessarily exclusive and which fit better with the overlapping interdependencies of the modern world.

The size, composition and organisation of republics are constrained by the possibilities of self-government, which are determined in turn by the interconnections of fate that arise from geographical proximity, historical interdependencies, common environmental and developmental issues. On the negative side, the limits of a republic may lie in the range of possibility of deliberative dialogue within a society. Not all issues will be resolvable within a single republic: sometimes secession will be the only viable solution. But the boundaries of republics should be considered to be a matter of what is possible on a practical basis, starting from where we are here and now, not as the outcome of an exercise of a universal right of cultures or nations to political self-determination. A republic should be seen as being able to accommodate multiple identities of citizens at multiple levels of government, as in the recent devolution of government in Scotland, still within the British state. This needs a creative approach to institutions, and especially to the issues of accountability and the integration of different levels of government. While the need for involvement and communication suggests developing smaller-scale local levels, increasing interdependence suggests a need for higher-level forums.

This is not an argument for world government. At least at this point, many interdependencies are more regionally clustered. Moreover, the existence of separate republics may be seen as facilitating experiments in collective living. Different states can adopt alternative approaches to different ways of realising the common goods of, for example, welfare, education or health-care provision. While many approaches, and their outcomes, will be specific to particular local situations, some will be more generalisable. Others can learn from their successes and failures and, with due attention to what is strictly contextual, can borrow these practices.

The scope of republican community

In the institution where I work, there is a door marked 'Common room: members only'.

Even if we distinguish republicanism and nationalism, it may still be asked whether a republic is necessarily a mechanism of exclusion. Such relationships of solidarity or community must depend on or result in a radical exclusion of outsiders (Shapiro, 1990: 198). For communitarians and nationalists, patriotism implies a preferential commitment to a very specific community, which gives rise to concern among advocates of global justice and cosmopolitan duties. The problems of global inequality may be exacerbated if recognition as well as freedom, order or material resources are important goods whose distribution is confined within the borders of states.

Even if a commitment to common goods does not require a community that is oppressively homogeneous or determinate of citizens, the question still remains how exclusive will such a community be? Must it depend on the enmity or at least the exclusion of external others? Are obligations of concern and politically constructed rights limited to members?

Citizenship is bounded membership of a specific self-governing political community. Civic virtue entails special obligations to fellow citizens. Thus the boundary of the state is morally salient; the republic is an ethical community with a moral boundary. It represents 'a contour line in the ethical landscape' (Miller, 1995a: 11). Particular relationships with special obligations between citizens create more exclusive ties than liberal cosmopolitans would accept. But I will argue that, like relationships of colleagues, republican relationships and obligations are potentially more permeable and extensible than those between co-nationals sharing a common culture.

Some theorists who invoke republican political ideas have explicitly argued that, in the contemporary absence of a single substantive conception of the good shared by citizens, political community can be cemented only in opposition to a perceived external threat – we become 'friends' or an 'us' only if there is a common foe, a 'them', or a 'constitutive outside' whom we fear (Mouffe, 1992: 235). But we have seen in the example of colleagues that there can be a community based on interdependence within common institutions and a common future, that does not depend essentially on the existence of an outgroup. Groups may be conceptually defined in implicit distinction from one another, and some loyalties may be strengthened in hostility to a common enemy; but it is by no means clear that political unity is so much a function of opposition to an external enemy, as it is formed by a common fate and institutions of authority. On the analogy with colleagues, we may see the ties between citizens as grounded in the recognition of reiterated interdependence, which is more fluid and extensible than Mouffe's model.

Interdependence is a matter of degree, of expanding or overlapping networks, and public realms are multiple and overlapping. A republic is a political community of those who recognise their interdependence and subjection to a common fate and common concerns. It is bounded because this is the only way in which politically guaranteed freedom can be secured in an uncertain world. But it is constituted by those who are multiply interdependent. Republics realise universal values of freedom and participation in self-government. But these always have to be realised in specific contexts in specific ways, and they lead to commitments to particular others. Unlike liberal cosmopolitan citizenship, republican citizenship is not based on the assumption that the division of human beings among states is merely a matter of administrative necessity. Unlike nationalist citizenship, it does not assume that the world can ever approximate units of similar or 'like-minded' people.

Thus it is not as exclusive a community as one based on ethnicity, a single set of shared values or a cultural identity. Resting on interdependence, membership of a republic can be extended more widely than models of political community resting on nationality, even a liberal nationality which may evolve over time. All entail a sharper boundary between those who share a nationality and those who do not.

People become co-citizens literally only by actually becoming members of the same state, or where overarching political institutions are created – as in the European Union. But the extension of citizenship and the creation of such overarching polities is more possible when citizens are defined simply as members of the same polity, living in a common world with common concerns, who have potential for collective action, rather than being preselected by ethnic or cultural identity. If republican politics is not tied to a nation, but can be constructed on local and European or other regional lines, it may also be possible to conceive of some development towards a cosmopolitan citizenship from the bottom up, through the development of increasing webs of relationships or ranges of overlapping economic, environmental and cultural interdependencies, rather than depending on the prior existence of a world-state or based on *a priori* principles of a universal humanity. Republican political commitment grounded in interdependence is more compatible with other claims of interdependence and need than more sharply defined political communities.

Immigration and admission to citizenship

An acid test of the scope of a political community is provided by its provisions for immigration and admission to citizenship. To illustrate the way in which a republican conception of citizenship may be less exclusive than other nationalist accounts, I briefly consider how different approaches deal with the issues of immigration and admission to citizenship. There are clear differences between the provisions implied by nationalism, liberalism and republicanism.

Broadly, liberal theories suggest that applicants for admission should be treated equally, and that limits to entry, if any, can only be justified in terms of their practical inclusion in society. On the other hand, nationalist theory implies that shared ethnicity or culture limits the state's obligations to admit or incorporate applicants, who may be admitted on practical or conditional grounds. It has proved hard to move beyond these two positions.

Thus a state based on ethnic nationality will limit or give preference in admission to citizenship to co-nationals (as in Germany until 2000). Citizenship is primarily a matter of descent (*ius sanguinis*), and naturalisation is extremely difficult. A communitarian position, which rests community on shared values, makes it a matter of choice by the community whom to accept and whom to reject, though those who have been admitted and have become longterm residents should be granted citizenship (Walzer, 1985). A liberal nationality will admit outsiders fairly easily, and will not discriminate on ethnic lines among candidates for admission, but (as in France) will require commitment to the state and competence in the public culture and ensure assimilation through a strong programme of education and socialisation into the existing public culture. It will award citizenship to children born in the state of immigrant parents, when they become adults, since they will have been educated and assimilated into the public culture (Miller, 1995a: 143). On any of these views citizenship is understood as essentially singular, and dual citizenship tends to be regarded as problematic.

On a republican approach, citizenship rests primarily on birth (*ius soli*) and residence in the state as a shorthand for interdependence. Borders are not wholly open, but obligations based on interdependence extend beyond the state, and may give rise to obligations to admit to residence and citizenship. In distinction from the liberal approach, these may be seen as resting in interdependence rather than non-discrimination. Thus they may give some preference to specific interconnections, or recognise the particular strength of certain external claims. On this view dual citizenship is not problematic. There are no wholly consistent examples of republican practice in this respect, but it is approached by some smaller European countries: when, for example, Portugal recognises its African and Brazilian ex-colonial connections in admission; Finland and Ireland in principle grant citizenship on relatively moderate conditions of residence; and Ireland and Portugal recognise dual citizenship (Honohan, 2001b).

From a republican perspective, it is justifiable to require immigrants to learn the language of their adopted country as an essential means of communicating and deliberating with their fellow citizens; but this need not exclude providing education and public services through minority languages as well. Immigrants may also be expected to be prepared to engage with the citizens of their adopted country, and to make some adjustment to its ways in a spirit of give and take. But it is less clear that they should have to adopt 'British norms of acceptance' (or Irish, or American) just because these norms are British, etc., or to swear an oath of loyalty that is not required of citizens by birth.[24] A better criterion might be a declared and evident intention to remain living in the country. Immigrants should make the attempt to adapt to their adopted country, not so much because they are 'last in', but because they need to make their future together with other citizens, rather than just to coexist with them.

Moreover, a republican perspective requires that immigration and citizenship policies be a matter of deliberation, not stipulation, and be applied with the minimum of administrative discretion. The obligations to citizens do not exclude significant obligations to non-citizens. The concern for freedom as non-domination should apply to applicants as well as to citizens. In the words of Abraham Lincoln, 'as I would not be a slave, so I would not be a master'. This means that, for example, procedures for admission to residence and citizenship should be based on statutory criteria rather than administrative orders, and should minimise the discretionary powers of individual officials.

Similarly, the boundedness of the republic should by no means imply a restrictive approach to international aid, especially given the historical interdependence of trade, ex-colonial connections or missionary activities, as well as the increasing economic and environmental interdependence entailed in globalisation.

Conclusion

The recognition and special obligations of citizens, rooted in interdependence in practices rather than commonality, cultural identity or feelings of attachment, are compatible with other relations that arise from interdependence. Economic, cultural and environmental globalisation progressively extends interdependence and, with it, obligations to more distant others on grounds that are at least not radically different from obligations to citizens. These are also more easily extensible than the narrow sense of political obligation as obedience to the authority of a sovereign state.

Rather than being radically exclusive, the relatively substantial relationships and obligations of republican political community are compatible with recognising obligations to more distant people interdependent in other ways. More intense political relations need not justify a weakening of international commitments, and so need not automatically justify extremely restrictive policies on immigration or aid. Rather than having to choose between cosmopolitan and nationally based obligations we should think of people as having responsibilities in irregularly extending and overlapping networks in which citizenship rather than nationality constitutes one of the most important frameworks.

The republican conception of citizenship may be more useful today than either of the two polarised alternatives often offered: the

Recognition and Inclusion

liberal conception, capable of extension, but so thin that it may in practice need to rely on pre-political identities to generate commitment, and the ethnic or cultural nationalist one that elicits commitment at the cost of excluding or oppressing those outside a closed community, real or imagined.

We do not now live in republican communities. The republican ideal calls for significant change in the attitudes and aspirations of citizens, the legal guarantees of non-domination, the levels and kinds of political participation, and the treatment of issues of difference. As well as institutional changes, these would require people to accept certain trade-offs between, for example, individual and common goods, independent range of choice and security of freedom from domination, consumption and self-direction.

But it also suggests that citizens may be able to reclaim power that has been ceded to the state. We saw how political participation was superseded by representation, as the state expanded to include larger numbers. The modern state developed as an impersonal authority separate from its citizens, and enlisted the nation as a means of generating legitimacy and obligation. But the nation-state does not provide a forum for resolving the global issues of environmental risk, economic inequality and intractable political conflict we face today; indeed it often exacerbates them. If this is the case, the time may be ripe for another burst of institutional creativity that would allow people to exercise some joint control within and across the boundaries defined by the nation-state.

Notes

Introduction

1 Rawls refers to the instrumental interpretation of Machiavelli, and particularly to Tocqueville, and rejects what he sees as the Aristotelian and Arendtian comprehensive account of the ultimate value of political life.
2 Brugger's *Republican Theory in Political Thought* also sees republicanism as based on a cluster of ideas, rather than a single idea. His cluster is different from mine, as, in addition to freedom and virtue, he identifies popular sovereignty and an idea of the shape of history as the key themes (Brugger, 1999).

I The Primacy of Virtue

1 Since political communities like the *polis* are not found everywhere, and do not come about automatically, they rely on legislators to set them up. But Aristotle does not focus on what is entailed in setting up a new society as much as suggest directions in which current political systems might be reformed.
2 The emphasis in Aristotle's account of the *polis* is contested, but it may be argued that, given the role of deliberation between citizens, Aristotle has in mind less a general shared conception of the good life than the rational ability to have a conception of the good and to be capable of deliberating jointly with others. See Waldron, 1999; Yack, 1993; and for an opposing view: Mulgan, 1999, 2000.
3 But women are an important part of the partnership in the state, can be educated in virtues to a greater extent than slaves, and have a sphere of their own in the household (even though it is not clear that they rule even there). Women are not excluded from direct political participation in politics on the grounds of unequal physical or military strength, but on the basis of unequal reason.
4 For Cicero, virtuous behaviour is rewarded by the honour paid by other citizens; this outweighs whatever material benefits may have to be sacrificed. This is different from Aristotle's conception, in which virtue is

more important than material benefits, and cannot be expressed in terms of a trade-off.
5 Equally Cicero, unlike Aristotle, does not lay any emphasis on the stabilising presence of a large middle class.
6 Neither distinguishes between the state and society, thinks in terms of a state separate from the citizens who act on behalf of the republic, nor of areas beyond the reach of politics. Even Cicero's *res publica* – the public thing – refers not so much to institutions as to the idea of what is shared in common between the citizens.
7 By contrast, Cicero's *De Republica* was lost until the mid-nineteenth century.

II Freedom in Classical Republicanism

1 There were other roots of popular self-rule within medieval Christendom arising from the experience of communal life in northern Europe. The independence of the towns and city-states gained momentum in the opportunity provided by the contest for political power between Papacy and Emperor from the eleventh century. And democratic expressions also emerged within an ecclesiastical framework, such as the conciliar movement of the late fourteenth and early fifteenth centuries, in which a theory of the sovereignty of the whole church in council, which was, however, influentially contested by the papacy. The notable thinker here was Marsilius of Padua (d. 1340). That a republic was compatible with Christian thinking is shown by the example of Salamonio (1450–1532), who defended a Roman republic against the temporal power of the Pope; and Savonarola (1452–98), a Dominican monk and Aristotelian who supported the Florentine republic of 1494 (Black, 1997; Coleman, 2000b; Skinner, 1978).
2 Machiavelli hints that Christianity could be interpreted in a more dynamic and active sense than the interpretation prevailing among the church leadership of his time.
3 None the less, institutions tend to decay; thus it also requires an exceptional man to act as legislator to renovate a corrupt state.
4 But Machiavelli also argues that authority need not always be bound by law, and points to the benefits that the arbitrary power of the dictators brought to ancient Rome – dealing quickly and decisively with unexpected events. Even this was limited in duration and restricted in the range of powers and limited by the constitution. In contrast, the later power given to the decemvirs was dangerous because it was not limited in terms of powers and duration. 'It is the man who uses violence to spoil things and not to mend them who is blameworthy' (Machiavelli, 1974: 132, 195–7).
5 'The way to make a republic great and for it to acquire an empire is to increase the number of its inhabitants, to make other states its allies, not its subjects, to send out colonies for the security of conquered territory, to fund the spoils of war, to subdue the enemy by raids and battles not by sieges, to enrich the public but keep the citizens poor, and to

attend with the utmost care to military training' (Machiavelli, 1974: 335).
6   Republican ideas were also expressed in these debates by Marchamont Nedham in *The Excellency of a Free State* (1656).
7   In fact he saw the study of ancient authors as itself part of the problem (Hobbes, 1968: 267).
8   The only women given much mention in *Oceana* apart from the 'silly girls' who are described as capable of devising the 'you cut and I'll choose' rule are in brief references to the problem cases of orphans and prostitutes.
9   Also: 'Virtue is not enough for good government but good government is enough for virtue' (Harrington, 1992: 273).
10 The connection between virtue and freedom is closer in Harrington than in Machiavelli: 'the liberty of a man consists in the empire of his reason, the absence whereof would betray him into the bondage of his passions' (Harrington, 1992: 19). People are only virtuous when free, and free when governed by reason.
11 Aspects of republican ideas were exemplified at this time in Molesworth's *Account of Denmark* (1694); Neville's *Plato Redivivus* (1698); Trenchard and Gordon: *Cato's Letters*; and in the work of John Toland, who published Harrington's collected works, Sidney's *Discourses*, and other writings which transmitted republican ideas to their successors in Europe and America.
12 On one interpretation Locke is a republican thinker – since his idea of freedom requires and is compatible with the rule of law – though in his case government is directed to the common good in an aggregative sense of the good of each of the individuals who constitute society (Pettit, 1997a: 40).

III Participation and Inclusion in the Extensive Republic

1   Thus in the modern world 'interest', 'fortune' and 'corruption' develop primarily financial connotations.
2   Montesquieu calls on separation of powers, while recognising the actual overlapping responsibilities in legislation between king and parliament, and in judiciary between judges and parliament. The Cabinet is a part of the executive sitting in Parliament – and there was an even greater degree of overlap in the eighteenth century, when public officials served as MPs.
3   Arguments for the separation of powers were developed in an explicit analogy to the balancing of passions in human psychology (Howe, 1988).
4   Rousseau's state of nature of free and equal individuals is more a historical conjecture than a hypothetical assumption about how contemporary humans would behave if social constraints were removed.
5   All are dependent, masters as much as slaves. For Rousseau no individual can escape dependence through dominating others, as

Notes

Machiavelli suggested in his image of the man of exceptional *virtu*.

6. 'It is only then when the voice of duty has taken the place of physical impulse, and right that of desire, that man who has hitherto thought only of himself finds himself compelled to act on other principles and to consult his reason rather than to study his inclinations' (Rousseau, 1968: 64, 65).
7. Some such role was played in Northern Ireland by the US Senator George Mitchell, who facilitated talks on the constitutional framework in the Belfast Agreement of 1998.
8. Rousseau did, however, have a conception of a public sphere of letters, which was an appropriate forum for deliberation (Kelly, 1998).
9. 'Although the law does not regulate morals, it is legislation which gives rise to morals; when legislation weakens morals degenerate' (Rousseau, 1968: 174).
10. 'It is the bustle of commerce and the crafts, it is the avid thirst for profit, it is effeminacy, and the love of comfort that commute personal service for money' (Rousseau, 1968: 140).
11. Yet if the division of labour is the basis of corruption, a more radical change in society and the economy may be implied.
12. Rousseau describes it as 'a fine and lively feeling which gives to the force of self-love all the beauty of virtue, lends it an energy which without disfiguring it makes it the most heroic of all passions' (Rousseau, 1993: 142).
13. In this context it may be worth remarking that the terror was not a necessary effect of institutionalising virtue. It may be better seen as a consequence of 'the attempt to impose morality when it is alien to both the elite and the ordinary people' (MacIntyre, 1984: 238).
14. 'What looks to twentieth century eyes like broker–state pluralism was, to Publius's contemporaries, subsumed within a familiar scheme of eighteenth-century moral philosophy – namely the principle of countervailing passions' (Howe, 1988: 125).
15. By contrast, the anti-federalists complained that large central government would favour wealth, and that great wealth would distort political equality. In the nineteenth century, issues on the political effects of socio-economic inequality were played out in debates on whether the republic should remain agrarian or develop industrially.

IV Roots of the Republican Revival

1. Kant is sometimes identified as a republican, but his political philosophy is better understood in liberal terms. He took his idea of moral freedom – acting according to a rule you make yourself – from Rousseau. But for him moral freedom was radically separate from any real interests, individual or common, and was a matter of following universal principles of moral reason. In his practical political philosophy he did not envisage citizens, imbued with civic virtue, as participating in their own self-rule. Although a republic could have a monarch, he emphasised that no person should be above the law, or

Notes

  combine legislative and executive functions (and thus, unlike Montesquieu, saw Britain as despotic). He favoured institutions which would channel rather than shape the citizens, declaring that if a republic were correctly constructed it could work for a race of devils (Stedman-Jones, 1994).
2 'The danger of modern liberty is that, absorbed in the enjoyment of our private independence, and in the pursuit of our particular interests, we should surrender our right to share in political power too easily; It is not to happiness alone, it is to self-development that our destiny calls us; and political liberty is the most powerful, the most effective means of self-development that heaven has given us' (Constant, 1988: 326–7). He also argued for institutions to act as the moral educators of citizens (Philp, 2000: 166).
3 The idea of recognition that emerges in Hegel's philosophy of self-consciousness is of particular importance for contemporary republicanism. He emphasised how human identity or self-realisation is dialogically realised in interaction with others. As an admirer of the Greek city-state he sought a modern equivalent in which community and individual freedom might coexist. He saw the importance of politics and gave the state a major role in reintegrating society. But Hegel cannot really be termed a civic republican, as he did not make active political participation a central part of his mature political theory (Patten, 1998).
4 Arendt distinguishes political action from the instrumental approach of a craftsman to work. She sees instrumental (and inherently violent) construction metaphors behind the superhuman founder or legislator in earlier republican and revolutionary theory. For Arendt, states cannot be founded on the model of creating objects.
5 We should note that for Arendt all political actors depend for their self-realisation on the opinion of others. Therefore not all concern with the opinion of others is corrupt. But in a corrupt world it is better to be a 'conscious pariah' than to become a parvenu, someone who tries to ingratiate themselves with the powerful.
6 Feminists have been critical of the way in which she advances a very heroic account of political life, and devalues ordinary family life which has occupied women so extensively. But her argument may be more in line with feminist concerns than initially appears; feminism too has been centrally concerned with creating power through joint action and the importance of public recognition for individual freedom and equality.
7 It should be noted that this distinction is more abstract than the contrast of the liberty of the ancients and the liberty of the moderns described by Constant, and does not map directly on to it. That is more a specifically political distinction between participation in public power and a set of rights protecting privacy.
8 Taylor adopts a complex position in defining liberalism and republicanism as two parts of the one tradition. He advocates republican

autonomy rather than just instrumental republicanism, in so far as political activity is an expression of freedom, and an intrinsic good, though he combines instrumental claims (about preservation of negative liberty) with more substantial claims about the value of public life and common goods (cf. Patten, 1996).

V Common Goods and Public Virtue

1 Quoted in Sandel (1996: 132).
2 Thus Sandel characterises the United States as having evolved a 'procedural republic' where politics is just the reconciliation and protection of individual interests. Such a politics generates apathy, fragmentation and extremism (Sandel, 1996).
3 'The common good I think of as certain general conditions that are in an appropriate sense equally to everyone's advantage' (Rawls, 1971: 246).
4 This category includes what are normally referred to as public goods; these are public in the sense that they often need to be centrally provided and, if they are provided, it is not possible to exclude people from benefiting (for example, street lighting).
5 'Autonomy depends on the persistence of collective goods and therefore the notion of an inherent general conflict between individual freedom and the needs of others is illusory' (Raz, 1986: 250).
6 '[I]n so far as the nation state provides necessary and important public goods, these must not be confused with the type of common good for which communal recognition is required by virtues of acknowledged dependence, and...in so far as the rhetoric of the nation-state presents it as the provider of something that is, indeed, in this stronger sense, a common good, that rhetoric is a purveyor of dangerous fictions' (MacIntyre, 1999: 132–3).
7 'Contrary to what some communitarians propose, a modern democratic community cannot be organised around a single substantive conception of the common good' (Mouffe, 1992: 227).
8 Thus Irish leader Eamon de Valera said in 1921: 'whenever I wanted to know what the Irish people wanted I had only to examine my own heart and it told me straight off what the Irish people wanted' (Lee and O'Tuathaigh, 1982: 17).
9 Republicans do see a greater role for the state in promoting the common good; this is examined in Chapter VI.
10 In many ways, the origin of Cuba's regime is better understood as an example of republican than socialist politics.
11 This dimension could be seen as the equivalent of the traditional virtue of wisdom; the following two as the equivalents of moderation and courage.
12 This may mean that some – those who do what are now low-paid caring jobs, for example – will be paid more, while some will need to accept less.

Notes

13 I borrow the term from James (1992).
14 For this reason, some writers prefer to use the term 'civility', but this term conveys a form of behaviour appropriate to all exchanges between human beings, rather than a more deep-seated orientation to the common good of a particular community; civic virtue better identifies a distinct concept.
15 The idea of a civic religion was considered essential by a wide spectrum of thinkers in early modern Europe, as alternative means of securing loyalty, when a common faith was no longer shared by all citizens.

VI Freedom

1 Thus Patten argues that Skinner's republicanism differs from liberalism mainly in language and emphasis, and in the empirical conditions for freedom he identifies (Patten, 1996).
2 Here I differ from Dagger, who constructs a liberal republicanism on the basis of combining autonomy as a right with a separately grounded republican theory of civic virtue (Dagger, 1997).
3 Human beings are naturally dependent. This makes self-sufficiency an impossible ideal. Freedom can not be the absence of all dependence. There are necessary dependencies, of children upon parents, of the ill on the able-bodied, and many of these are asymmetric. Freedom requires limiting the avoidable dependencies, recognising interdependency and restricting the domination of those who are necessarily dependent (and those who care for them).
4 Although Raz sees freedom in terms of autonomy, he resists this step, seeing politics as too divisive and state power too threatening to give the state a major role in promoting autonomy (Raz, 1986: 3).
5 See also: 'Republican thought...sees political liberty in collective self-determination; while it does not regard political participation as the sole good life for human beings, it attempts to provide outlets for citizen control and local self-determination' (Sunstein, 1988: 1569).
6 Habermas interprets the republican tradition exclusively as the strand from Aristotle to Rousseau in which freedom is identified with citizens' participation in self-legislation, distinct from the personal freedom emphasised by liberals. He sees contemporary republicanism in communitarian terms, as an 'ethical' process of realising or discovering pre-existing common goods, and adopts a critical stance towards its politics. But in fact his own 'discourse theory' shares with the advocates of republican political autonomy an emphasis on (more or less direct) participation in self-government as a part of autonomy. The thinkers I identify as republican see it as constructing, as much as discovering, common goods (Habermas, 1994a).
7 We might think of the point of Yeats's lines addressed to the poor road-mender in pre-Independence Ireland, 'Ireland will get her freedom, and you still break stone', as expressing this possibility of domination as much as the contrast between political and effective freedom, or the Hobbesian irrelevance of forms of government.

Notes

8 Republican freedom may also be understood as collective self-government in a positive sense without focusing on actual active participation by the citizens as individuals. A commitment to a positive conception of freedom may be applied in terms of collective self-government through the institutions of government and courts. Frank Michelman sees a tradition of freedom as self-government in a modern republic in the United States. This does not necessarily require continuous participation by all the citizens, but rather that they should be able to endorse the fundamental laws of their country. The ideal of a self-governing citizenry is expressed in the constitution, and should guide the deliberations of the US Supreme Court. For him positive republican freedom, acting according to reasons that are one's own, is achieved by citizens whose political system is directed towards the common good, which is to be determined dialogically. Because of the plurality of citizens, self-government needs to relate, or mediate between, particular and general, concrete and abstract, similar and different. And it may not be practically possible for the whole citizenry to practise self government. But this should be the model applied by the courts, and in particular the US Supreme Court in making decisions. Rather than applying general law to individuals or protecting radically individual rights, the community's possibility of self-reflective transformation, which takes place in many spheres, is authoritatively expressed in Supreme Court judgements. The model for these judgements is dialogical, based on the capacity of citizens to engage in communicative dialogue, to reflect on original desires and values, and to progressively expand those who are included (Michelman, 1986).

9 Many of the conditions for civic virtue and freedom are the same, because civic virtue itself requires independent judgement and commitment to the common good, though here the emphasis is on the potential for independent self-direction.

10 It should be noted that relative economic equality might still be consistent with deliberative inequality, an issue which will be addressed in Chapters VII and VIII.

11 If this proposal is seen as unrealistic, it should be borne in mind that parental leave, almost inconceivable a generation ago, has become available in a number of countries, and is a live political issue in others.

12 For Raz, the fact that 'tastes and values depend on social forms' is as much a reason to distrust them as to reinforce those social forms (Raz, 1986: 426–7). But Raz differs from republicans here in that he does not derive so strong a role for government. Pettit would express this in terms of tracking their interests. In terms of republican political autonomy it may be said that they are not acting according to purposes they could reflectively endorse.

13 There is a difference between seeing government as tracking the interests of citizens and of allowing them to act according to purposes they could endorse.

14 There are other alternatives with claims to consideration in Northern Ireland: that children should be educated in their own schools, but

Notes

engage in joint extra-curricular projects; or (as has recently been officially proposed) that groups of schools, or 'collegiates', be created, each of which would include schools of all types which would pool resources for many activities and subjects, thereby increasing interaction and understanding.

15 Pettit suggests that there is a possible deontological account of republicanism in which natural rights are seen as rights not to be interfered with on an *arbitrary* basis and thus allow wider scope for state action. He interprets the historical use of rights vocabulary by some republican thinkers as a rhetorical defence of legal guarantees to non-domination (Pettit, 1997: 101).

16 A somewhat different approach emphasises the comparable goods realised in homosexual and heterosexual relations (for example, self-expression), rather than autonomy (Sandel, 1996: 103–8).

17 This approach is more clearly represented in the European Court of Human Rights than in the US Supreme Court, where certain rights, such as freedom of speech, for example, have been taken to be above any balancing interests.

VII Participation and Development

1 Indeed interest and identity interact, and they are both always mediated by self-perception.
2 Compare Barber, 1984, Chapter 10.
3 This kind of participation also may be more or less informed or oriented to wider interests.
4 A striking example that appears to support this view was the 2001 re-election of the Australian government, which commentators partly attributed to the Prime Minister John Howard's much-publicised refusal to admit a ship whose captain had, in a humanitarian effort, picked up scores of drowning Afghan refugees.
5 We should remember that Rousseau himself distinguished the general will from the will of all, and only secondarily understood its interpretation in majoritarian terms.
6 Though see also Dryzek (2000), for whom deliberative politics is a better choice mechanism.
7 These may be limited to constitutional arguments in Rawls, but the perspective has wider application.
8 These issues are addressed by Hirschman (1994), Bader (2001) and Patten (2000).
9 'For those moral conflicts for which there is no deliberative agreement at present, ongoing deliberation can help citizens better understand the moral seriousness of the views they continue to oppose, and better cooperate with their fellow citizens who hold these views' (Gutmann and Thompson, 1996: 43).
10 For an alternative approach which emphasises the shift from central power but through accountability in civil society organisations, see Hirst (1994).

Notes

11 In Northern Ireland it may be argued that it is justified to give Unionists a veto power over the unification of the island of Ireland.
12 Similar effects may be achieved in less controlled environments. For example, in 1986 a referendum which made abortion unconstitutional was passed in Ireland. Several years later a major public discussion followed the judicial hearing of a particularly difficult case involving a young victim of rape. In the course of this discussion public opinion moved significantly in the light of more informed discussion.
13 For MacIntyre, this is the communitarian mistake of attempting to infuse the politics of the state with the values and modes of participation of the local community.
14 It was reported that businessman Michael Bloomberg spent $40 million on his campaign to be elected Mayor of New York in 2001.

VIII Recognition and Inclusion in a Pluralist World

1 Neutrality may be distinguished from benign neglect; neutrality allows the state to favour particular views or values (for example, to establish an official language as a practical necessity) as long as it is not on the grounds of superiority, whereas the principle of benign neglect dictates that no religion or culture should be supported by the state (Kymlicka, 2002: 344).
2 It may also be argued that identity as such is not sacrosanct. Not all identities are valuable, and worthy of support. Moreover, 'stabilising' identity may not be a realistic aim in the light of contemporary critiques of the notion of the self (see, e.g., McAfee, 2000).
3 If being Irish means being Catholic, how Irish was Douglas Hyde, a Protestant pioneer of the Irish language revival, leader of the Gaelic League and the independent country's first President? If it is a matter of language, what about the works of James Joyce, who reworked the Greek legend of Ulysses, written in Hiberno-English and set in Dublin, while he lived in Trieste? Or of Samuel Beckett, who fits neither criterion as he wrote in French?
4 Many misconceptions in debates on multiculturalism stem from modelling the treatment of culture too closely on the model of religion, the context in which issues of tolerance were first systematically addressed historically. But there are significant differences; many aspects of culture are more negotiable than religion. It must be admitted that they are often intertwined in current multicultural debates about education, dress and gender equality.
5 In 2000, M. Chevènement, a leading republican, resigned his French government ministry in protest against the granting of autonomy to Corsica (*pace* Rousseau).
6 This draws in part on Stephen Darwall's distinction between epistemic/appraisal and status/achievement dimensions of respect; while my 'acknowledgement' corresponds to his 'recognition respect', I distinguish between 'authorisation' and 'endorsement' as two separate

Notes

dimensions of his 'appraisal respect'; his terminology is somewhat at odds with the language of current debates (Darwall, 1977).

7 This includes, but is not limited to, institutional misrecognition where applying formally equal procedures leads to systematically unequal outcomes.

8 Even here there may be negative identities that will not be supported; for example, a cultural group for whom racist or sectarian hatred is central to their activities.

9 This was the problem experienced by the prophet Cassandra, who was doomed to speak the truth but not to be believed.

10 For example, some Jews and Muslims in Ireland, when asked about the overwhelmingly Catholic nature of the public culture, reply that they prefer living in a state that acknowledges the significance of religion to living in a secular or neutral state. But secularists too must be allowed to express their position and receive serious consideration.

11 Thus Mouffe: 'The modern form of political community is held together not by a substantive idea of the common good, but by a common bond, a public concern. It is therefore a community without a definite shape or a definite identity' (Mouffe, 1992: 233).

12 Analogical reasoning does not determine any issue conclusively. But here it is used to open up a new line of inquiry on a question where conceptual analysis or constructive theory are not making progress. While citizenship is a legal status, and colleagueship is not, they are both framed by membership of institutions (Barry, 1975; Sunstein, 1993d).

13 This is not to say that all relationships give rise to special obligations, nor that all moral principles spring from relationships; but that valuable relationships give rise to obligations, though these obligations have to be balanced against others and are open to critique. There is an important distinction between relations which are valued and those which are in fact valuable. See Scheffler, 1997.

14 I adopt the term 'solidarity' rather than 'civic friendship' as this can be misleading today. Friendship, understood in the modern sense of voluntary personal relationship values mainly for its own sake, is necessarily limited to a few people, as it too depends on intimate knowledge and emotional bonds. To the extent that it is a voluntary, if gradually established relationship, it is not analogous to citizenship. This notion of civic friendship based on Aristotle's very different account of friendship is more suggestive, but needs adjustment to translate into a world of plural values. A conception of civic friendship modelled on Aristotle's broader account requires distinguishing the civic from other kinds of friendship (Schwarzenbach, 1996).

15 It has been argued that this was the case, for example, in the model of the Federal Republic of Germany which Habermas was addressing (Canovan, 2000). This leads to the more general point that it is not possible to distinguish clearly civic nationalism from cultural nationalism (Brubaker, 1999).

Notes

16 For example, the liberal nationality advanced by Yael Tamir justifies nationality in terms of identity and feelings of attachment (Tamir, 1993).
17 Thus this is a different approach from Tocqueville's contrast of instinctive patriotism and rational patriotism based on long-term self interest.
18 However, Pettit sees identification as an involuntary process (Pettit, 1997a).
19 Raz argues for the presumptive right of cultures to be self-determining on the basis that an encompassing culture (one with a full range of social practices) is the precondition for the options that allow an individual to become autonomous (Raz, 1994).
20 The kind of republicanism identified with the Irish Republican Army, for example, is better understood as an ethno-cultural nationalism, which seeks national self-determination through unification of the island of Ireland, rather than a republicanism in the sense we are examining here. It does, however, have some distant antecedents in the non-sectarian late-eighteenth-century United Irishmen movement, which was part of the expansive republicanism of Madison, Paine and Rousseau. For an interpretation of a civic unionism possible in Northern Ireland, see Porter, 1996.
21 As I have suggested elsewhere, France may be better understood as realising a form of liberal nationality than a republic.
22 This degree of solidarity between members of the EU is present even in a context in which there is considerable resistance to the idea of Europe as a single nation, further integrated and united for defence and military purposes.
23 'Perhaps the greatest achievement was the forging of a common national spirit, something that most other Latin American republics had failed to do. This achievement was the more remarkable in that before the revolution Cuba's sense of national identity was one of the weakest in Latin America' (Williamson, 1992: 457).
24 Such a requirement was proposed by the British Home Secretary, David Blunkett, in 2000.

Bibliography

Ackermann, B. and Alstott, A. (1999) *The Stakeholder Society*, New Haven: Yale University Press.
Allen, A. and Regan, M. (eds) (1998) *Debating Democracy's Discontents*, Oxford: Oxford University Press.
Annas, J. (1995) 'Aristotelian political theory in the Hellenistic period', in A. Laks and M. Schofield (eds) *Justice and Generosity*, Cambridge: Cambridge University Press.
Archard, D. (ed.) (1996) *Philosophy and Pluralism*, Cambridge: Cambridge University Press.
Arendt, H. (1958) *The Human Condition*, Chicago: Chicago University Press.
—— (1968) *On Totalitarianism*, New York: Harcourt Brace Jovanovich.
—— (1977a) *On Revolution*, New York: Penguin.
—— (1977b) *Between Past and Future*, Harmondsworth: Penguin.
—— (1977c) 'Public rights and private interests', in M. Mooney and P. Stuber (eds) *Small Comforts for Hard Times*, New York: Columbia University Press.
—— (1982) *Lectures on Kant's Political Philosophy*, Chicago: Chicago University Press.
—— (1994) *Eichmann in Jerusalem*, New York: Penguin.
Aristotle (1976) *Ethics*, Harmondsworth: Penguin.
—— (1981) *Politics*, Harmondsworth: Penguin.
Audard, C. (1996) 'Political liberalism, secular republicanism: two answers to the challenge of pluralism', in D. Archard (ed.) *Philosophy and Pluralism*, Cambridge: Cambridge University Press.
—— (2000) 'Integration, respect and moral individuality: new views on republican citizenship', presented to conference on Republicanism at Oxford University, mimeo.
Bader, V. (1995) 'Citizenship and exclusion: radical democracy, community, and justice. Or what is wrong with communitarianism?' *Political Theory* 23, 2: 211–46.

Bibliography

—— (1997) 'The cultural conditions of transnational citizenship: on the interpenetration of political and ethnic cultures', *Political Theory* 25, 6: 771–813.

—— (2001) 'Institutions, culture and identity of transnational citizenship: how much integration and communal spirit is needed?', in C. Crouch, K. Eder and D. Tambini (eds) *Citizenship, Markets and the State*, Oxford: Oxford University Press.

Baker, J. and Sinnott, R. (2000) 'Simulating multi-option referendums in Ireland: neutrality and abortion', *Irish Political Studies* 15: 105–26.

Ball, T., Farr, J. and Hanson, R. (1989) *Political Innovation and Conceptual Change*, Cambridge: Cambridge University Press.

Ball, T. and Pocock, J. (1988) *Constitutional Change and the Constitution*, Lawrence: University Press of Kansas.

Barber, B. (1984) *Strong Democracy*, Berkeley and London: University of California Press.

Baron, H. (1938) 'Cicero and the Roman civic spirit in the middle ages and early Renaissance', *Bulletin of the John Rylands Library*, 22, 72–97.

Barry, B. (1975) 'On analogy', *Political Studies* 23, 2/3: 208–24.

—— (2001) *Culture and Equality: An Egalitarian Critique of Multiculturalism*, Cambridge MA: Harvard University Press.

Barry, N. (1995) 'Hume, Smith and Rousseau on freedom', in R. Wokler (ed.) *Rousseau and Liberty*, Manchester: Manchester University Press.

Beiner, R. (1984) 'Action, natality and citizenship: Hannah Arendt's concept of freedom', in Z. Pelczynski and J. Gray (eds) *Conceptions of Liberty in Political Philosophy*, London: Athlone Press.

—— (ed.) (1995) *Theorizing Citizenship*, Albany: State University of New York Press.

Bellamy, R. (1993a) 'Citizenship and rights', in R. Bellamy (ed.) *Themes and Concepts of Politics: An Introduction*, Manchester: Manchester University Press.

—— (ed.) (1993b) *Themes and Concepts of Politics: An Introduction*, Manchester: Manchester University Press.

Benhabib, S. (1988) 'Judgement and the moral foundations of politics in Arendt's thought', *Political Theory* 16, 1: 29–51.

—— (1996) 'Toward a deliberative model of democratic legitimacy', in S. Benhabib (ed.) *Democracy and Difference*, Princeton: Princeton University Press.

Benn, S. and Gaus, G. (1983) 'The public and the private: concepts and action', in S. Benn and G. Gaus (eds) *Public and Private in Social Life*, London: Croom Helm.

Berger, P. (1984) 'On the obsolescence of the concept of honour', in M. Sandel (ed.) *Liberalism and Its Critics*, Oxford: Blackwell.

Berlin, I. (1958) *Two Concepts of Liberty*, Oxford: Oxford University Press.

Bibliography

—— (1982) 'The Originality of Machiavelli', in H. Hardy (ed.) *Against the Current*, Harmondsworth: Penguin.
Black, A. (1997) 'Christianity and Republicanism: from St. Cyprian to Rousseau', *American Political Science Review* 91, 3: 647–56.
Bock, G., Skinner, Q. and Viroli, M. (eds) (1990) *Machiavelli and Republicanism*, Cambridge: Cambridge University Press.
Bohman, J. and Rehg, W. (1997) *Deliberative Democracy: Essays on Reason and Politics*, Cambridge, MA: MIT Press.
Brubaker, R. (1999) 'The manichean myth: rethinking the distinction between "civic" and "ethnic" nationalism', in R. Kriesi, K. Armingeon, H. Siegrist and A. Wimmer (eds) *Nation and National Identity: the European Experience in Perspective*, Chur: Rueegger.
Brugger, B. (1999) *Republican Theory in Political Thought: Virtuous or Virtual?* Basingstoke and New York: Macmillan.
Bubeck, D. (1995) 'A feminist approach to citizenship', IEP working paper 95/1, Florence: European University Institute.
Burtt, S. (1993) 'The politics of virtue today: a critique and a proposal', *American Political Science Review* 87: 360–8.
Calhoun, C. (ed.) (1992) *Habermas and the Public Sphere*, Cambridge, MA: MIT Press.
Callan, E. (1997) *Creating Citizens: Political Education and Liberal Democracy*, Oxford: Oxford University Press.
Caney, S. (1996) 'Individuals, nations and obligations', in S. Caney, D. George and P. Jones (eds) *National Rights, International Obligations*, Oxford: Westview Press.
Caney, S., George, D. and Jones P. (eds) (1996) *National Rights, International Obligations*, Oxford: Westview Press.
Canovan, M. (1992) *Hannah Arendt: a Reinterpretation of her Political Thought*, Cambridge: Cambridge University Press.
—— (2000) 'Patriotism is not enough', in C. McKinnon and I. Hampsher-Monk (eds) *The Demands of Citizenship*, London: Continuum.
Carens, J. (2000) *Culture, Citizenship and Community*, Oxford: Oxford University Press.
Cicero (1927) *Letters* (ed. H. Grose Hodge), London: Loeb Classical Library.
—— (1991) *On Duties*, Cambridge: Cambridge University Press.
Cohen, Jean (1996) 'Democracy, difference and the right of privacy', in S. Benhabib (ed.) *Democracy and Difference*, Princeton: Princeton University Press.
Cohen, Joshua (ed.) (1996) *For Love of Country*, Boston: Beacon Press.
Cole, P. (2000) *Philosophies of Exclusion: Liberal Political Theory and Immigration*, Edinburgh: Edinburgh University Press.

Bibliography

Coleman, J. (2000a) *A History of Political Thought: from Ancient Greece to Early Christianity*, Oxford: Blackwell.

—— (2000b) *A History of Political Thought: the Middle Ages to Renaissance*, Oxford: Blackwell.

Colish, M. (1978) 'Cicero's *De Officiis* and Machiavelli's *Prince*', *Sixteenth Century Journal* 9, 4: 81–93.

Constant, B. (1988 [1806, 1814, 1819]) *Political Writings*, Cambridge: Cambridge University Press.

Cooke, M. (1997a) 'Authenticity and autonomy: Taylor, Habermas and the politics of recognition', *Political Theory* 25, 258–88.

—— (1997b) 'Are ethical conflicts irreconcilable?' *Philosophy and Social Criticism*, 23.

Copp, D., Hampton, J. and Roemer, J. (eds) (1993) *The Idea of Democracy*, Cambridge: Cambridge University Press.

Crouch, C., Eder, K. and Tambini, D. (eds) (2001) *Citizenship, Markets and the State*, Oxford: Oxford University Press.

Dagger, R. (1985) 'Rights, boundaries and the bond of community: a qualified defence of moral parochialism', *American Political Science Review* 79: 436–47.

—— (1997) *Civic Virtues*, Oxford: Oxford University Press.

—— (2000a) 'Membership, fair play, and political obligation', *Political Studies* 48 (1): 104–17.

—— (2000b) 'Republican virtue, personal freedom and the problem of civic service', presented to conference on Republicanism at Oxford University, mimeo.

Dahl, R. (1989) *Democracy and its Critics*, New Haven, CT: Yale University Press.

Darwall, S. (1977) 'Two kinds of respect', *Ethics* 88, 1: 36–49.

Dietz, M. (1991) 'On Arendt', in M. Shanley and C. Pateman (eds) *Feminist Interpretations and Political Theory*, Oxford: Polity Press.

—— (1992) 'Context is all: feminism and theories of citizenship', in C. Mouffe (ed.) *Dimensions of Radical Democracy*, London: Verso.

—— (1998) 'Merely combating the phrases of this world', *Political Theory* 26, 1: 112–39.

Douglass, R., Mara, G. and Richardson, H. (1990) *Liberalism and the Good*, New York: Routledge.

Dryzek, J. (1990) *Discursive Democracy: Politics, Policy and Political Science*, New York: Cambridge University Press.

—— (2000) *Deliberative Democracy and Beyond*, Oxford: Oxford University Press.

Dunne, J. (1997) *Back to the Rough Ground: Practical Reason and the Lure of Technique*, Notre Dame, IN: University of Notre Dame Press.

Dworkin, R. (1986) *Law's Empire*, London: Fontana.

Bibliography

Elster, J. (1997) 'The market and the forum', in J. Bohman and W. Rehg (eds) *Deliberative Democracy: Essays on Reason and Politics*, Cambridge, MA: MIT Press.
—— (ed.) (1998) *Deliberative Democracy*, Cambridge: Cambridge University Press.
Emerson, P. (1998) *Beyond the Tyranny of the Majority*, Belfast: De Borda Institute.
Etzioni, A. (1995a) *The Spirit of Community* (revised edn), London: Harper Collins..
—— (ed.) (1995b) *New Communitarian Thinking*, Charlottesville: University Press of Virginia.
—— (ed.) (1995c) *Rights and the Common Good*, London: St Martin's Press.
Euben, P. (1989) 'Corruption', in T. Ball, J. Farr and R. Hanson (eds) *Political Innovation and Conceptual Change*, Cambridge: Cambridge University Press.
Fink, Z. (1945) *Classical Republicanism*, Evanston: University of Illinois Press.
Fishkin, J. (1991) *Democracy and Deliberation: New Directions for Democratic Reforms*, New Haven, CT: Yale University Press.
—— (1995) *The Voice of the People: Public Opinion and Democracy*, New Haven, CT: Yale University Press.
Fleming J. and McClain L. (1998) 'The right of privacy in Sandel's procedural republic', in A. Allen and M. Regan (eds) *Debating Democracy's Discontent*, Oxford: Oxford University Press.
Fontana, B. (1994) *The Invention of the Modern Republic*, Cambridge: Cambridge University Press.
Fraser, N. (1992) 'Rethinking the public sphere: a contribution to the critique of actually existing democracy', in C. Calhoun (ed.) *Habermas and the Public Sphere*, Cambridge, MA: MIT Press.
—— (1995) 'From redistribution to recognition? Dilemmas of justice in a "post-socialist" age', *New Left Review* 212: 68–93.
—— (2000) 'Rethinking recognition', *New Left Review* (Second series) 3: 107–20.
Frazer, E. (1999) *The Problems of Communitarian Politics*, Oxford: Oxford University Press.
Frazer, E. and Lacey, N. (1993) *The Politics of Community*, Brighton: Harvester Wheatsheaf.
Galston, W. (1988) 'Liberal Virtues', *American Political Science Review* 82, 4: 1277–89.
—— (1991) *Liberal Purposes: Goods, Virtues and Duties in the Liberal State*, Cambridge: Cambridge University Press.
—— (1998) 'Political economy and the politics of virtue', in A. Allen and

Bibliography

M. Regan (eds) *Debating Democracy's Discontent*, Oxford: Oxford University Press.

Gellner, E. (1983) *Nations and Nationalism*, Ithaca: Cornell University Press.

Gilbert, P. (1996) 'National obligations: political, cultural or social', in S. Caney, D. George and P. Jones (eds) *National Rights, International Obligations*, Oxford: Westview Press.

—— (2000) *Peoples, Cultures and Nations in Political Philosophy*, Edinburgh: Edinburgh University Press.

Goldie, M. (1987) 'James Harrington's civic religion', in A. Pagden (ed.) *The Languages of Political Thought in Early Modern Europe*, Cambridge: Cambridge University Press.

Goodin, R. (1988) 'What is so special about our fellow countrymen?' *Ethics* 98, 4: 663–86.

—— (2001) 'Input democracy', presented at the Annual Meetings of the American Political Science Association, San Francisco, CA, mimeo.

Granovetter, M. (1973) 'Strength of weak ties', *American Journal of Sociology* 8: 1360–80.

Grant, R. (1997) *Hypocrisy and Integrity*, Chicago: University of Chicago Press.

Gutmann, A. (1987) *Democratic Education*, Princeton: Princeton University Press.

Gutmann, A. and Thompson, D. (1996) *Democracy and Disagreement*, Cambridge MA: Harvard Belknap Press.

Habermas, J. (1994a) 'Three models of democracy', *Constellations* 1: 1–10. (Also in S. Benhabib (ed.) (1996)*Democracy and Difference*, Princeton, NJ: Princeton University Press.)

—— (1994b) 'Struggles for recognition in the democratic constitutional state', in C. Taylor and A. Gutmann (eds), *Multiculturalism*, Princeton: Princeton University Press.

—— (1995) 'Citizenship and national identity', in R. Beiner (ed.) *Theorizing Citizenship*, Albany: State University of New York Press. (Also as Appendix 2 in J. Habermas, *Between Facts and Norms*, Cambridge: Polity Press.)

—— (1996a) 'Three normative models of democracy', in S. Benhabib (ed.) *Democracy and Difference*, Princeton: Princeton University Press.

—— (1996b) *Between Facts and Norms*, trans. W. Rehg, Cambridge: Polity Press.

Haitsma Mulier, E. (1987) 'The language of seventeenth century republicanism in the United Provinces: Dutch or European?', in A. Pagden (ed.) *The Languages of Political Thought in Early Modern Europe*, Cambridge: Cambridge University Press.

Bibliography

Hamilton, A., Madison, J. and Jay, J. (1999 [1788]) *The Federalist Papers*, New York: Mentor.

Hampsher-Monk, I. (1992) *A History of Modern Political Thought; Major Political Thinkers from Hobbes to Marx*, Oxford: Blackwell.

Harrington, J. (1977) *The Political Works of James Harrington* (ed. J. Pocock), Cambridge: Cambridge University Press.

—— (1992 [1656]) *The Commonwealth of Oceana and A System of Politics*, Cambridge: Cambridge University Press.

Havel, V. (1991) *Open Letters*, London: Faber & Faber.

—— (1998) 'The state of the republic', *New York Review of Books* 45, 4: 42–6.

Hegel, G. (1967 [1807]) *The Phenomenology of Mind*, New York: Harper and Row.

Hirschman, A. (1977) *The Passions and the Interests*, Princeton: Princeton University Press.

Hirschmann, N. (1992) *Rethinking Obligation: A Feminist Method for Political Theory*, Ithaca: Cornell University Press.

—— (1994) 'Social conflicts as pillars of democratic market society', *Political Theory* 22, 2; 203–18.

Hirst, P. (1994) *Associative Democracy*, Cambridge: Polity Press.

Hobbes, T. (1968 [1651]) *Leviathan*, Harmondsworth: Penguin.

Honneth, A. (1995) *The Struggle for Recognition: the Moral Grammar of Social Conflicts*, trans. J. Anderson, Cambridge, MA: MIT Press.

—— (1997) 'Recognition and moral obligation', *Social Research* 64, 1: 16–35.

Honohan, I. (2000) 'Dealing with difference: the republican public–private distinction', in M. Baghramian and A. Ingram (eds) *Pluralism: the Philosophy and Politics of Difference*, London: Routledge.

—— (2001a) 'Friends, strangers or countrymen? Citizens as colleagues', *Political Studies* 49, 1: 51–69.

—— (2001b) 'A civic republican approach to immigration', presented at the Annual Meetings of the American Political Science Association, San Francisco, CA, mimeo.

Hope Mason, J. (1989) 'Individuals in society: Rousseau's republican vision', *History of Political Thought* 10, 1: 89–112.

—— (1995) 'Forced to be free', in R. Wokler (ed.) *Rousseau on Liberty*, Manchester: Manchester University Press.

Horton, J. (1993) *Political Obligation*, Basingstoke: Macmillan.

Howe, D. (1988) 'The language of faculty psychology in the *Federalist Papers*', in T. Ball and J. Pocock (eds) *Constitutional Change and the Constitution*, Lawrence: University Press of Kansas.

Hutcheson, F. (1994) *Philosophical Writings*, London: Dent.

Hutchinson, D. (1986) *The Virtues of Aristotle*, London: Routledge and Kegan Paul.

Ingram, A. (1994) *A Political Theory of Rights*, Oxford: Oxford University Press.
—— (1996) 'Constitutional patriotism', *Philosophy and Social Criticism* 22: 1–18.
Isaac, J. (1988) 'Republicanism vs liberalism?: a reconsideration', *History of Political Thought* 9: 349–77.
James, S. (1992) 'The good-enough citizen: citizenship and independence', in G. Bock and S. James (eds) *Beyond Equality and Difference: Citizenship, Feminist Politics and Female Subjectivity*, London: Routledge.
Jennings, J. (2000) 'Citizenship, republicanism and multiculturalism in contemporary France', *British Journal of Political Science* 30: 575–98.
Jones, C. (1999) 'Patriotism, morality and global justice', in I. Shapiro and L. Brilmayer (eds) *Global Justice*, New York: New York University Press.
Kautz, S. (1995) *Liberalism and Community*, Ithaca: Cornell University Press.
Kelly, C. (1998) 'Rousseau and literary citizenship', presented at the Annual Meetings of the American Political Science Association, Boston, MA, mimeo.
Kittay, E. (1999) *Love's Labor: Essays on Equality, Dependence and Care*, London: Routledge.
Knight, J. and Johnson, J. (1997) 'What sort of equality does deliberative democracy require?', in J. Bohman and W. Rehg (eds) *Deliberative Democracy: Essays on Reason and Politics*, Cambridge, MA: MIT Press.
Kostakopoulou, T. (1996) 'Towards a theory of constructive citizenship in Europe', *The Journal of Political Philosophy* 4, 4: 337–58.
Kymlicka, W. (1990) *Contemporary Political Philosophy: an Introduction*, Oxford: Oxford University Press.
—— (1995) *Multicultural Citizenship*, Oxford: Clarendon Press.
—— (2002) *Contemporary Political Philosophy: an Introduction* (second edn), Oxford: Oxford University Press.
Kymlicka, W. and Norman, W. (1995) 'The return of the citizen: a survey of recent work on citizenship theory', *Ethics* 104: 352–81.
—— (eds) (2000) *Citizenship in Diverse Societies*, Oxford: Oxford University Press.
Laborde, C. (2001) 'The culture(s) of the republic: nationalism and multiculturalism in French republican thought', *Political Theory* 29, 5: 716–35.
Lacey, N. (1992) 'Theory into practice: pornography and the public/private dichotomy', in A. Bottomley and J. Conaghan (eds) *Feminist Theory and Legal Strategy*, Oxford, Blackwell.
Laks, A. and Schofield, M. (eds) (1995) *Justice and Generosity*, Cambridge: Cambridge University Press.

Bibliography

Lara, M. (1998) *Moral Textures: Feminist Narratives in the Public Sphere*, Cambridge: Polity Press.

Lee, J. and O'Tuathaigh, G. (1982) *The Age of de Valera*, Dublin: Ward River Press.

Lever, A. (1998) 'Privacy rights and democracy: a philosophical examination', presented at the Annual Meetings of the American Political Science Association, Boston MA, mimeo.

Locke, J. (1963 [1689]) *Two Treatises on Government*, Cambridge: Cambridge University Press.

Long, A. (1995) 'Cicero's politics in *De Officiis*', in A. Laks and M. Schofield (eds) *Justice and Generosity*, Cambridge: Cambridge University Press.

Lustick, I. (1993) *Unsettled States, Disputed Lands: Britain and Ireland, France and Algeria, Israel and the West Bank–Gaza*, Ithaca: Cornell University Press.

McAfee, N. (2000) *Habermas, Kristeva and Citizenship*, Ithaca: Cornell University Press.

Machiavelli, N. (1974 [1532]) *The Prince* (ed. G. Bull), Harmondsworth: Penguin.

—— (1983 [1531]) *The Discourses* (ed. B. Crick), Harmondsworth: Penguin.

MacIntyre, A. (1984) *After Virtue* (second edn), Notre Dame: University of Notre Dame Press.

—— (1999) *Dependent Rational Animals*, London: Duckworth.

McKinnon, C. and Hampsher-Monk, I. (eds) (2000) *The Demands of Citizenship*, London: Continuum.

Mandeville, Bernard de (1998) *Fable of the Bees and Other Writings*, Indianapolis: Hackett.

Manin, B. (1994) 'Checks, balances and boundaries', in B. Fontana (ed.) *The Invention of the Modern Republic*, Cambridge: Cambridge University Press.

—— (1997) *The Principles of Representative Government*, Cambridge: Cambridge University Press.

Mason, A. (1997) 'Special obligations to compatriots', *Ethics* 107, 3: 427–47.

—— (1999) 'Political community, liberal nationalism and the ethics of assimilation', *Ethics* 109, 2: 261–87.

—— (2000) *Community, Solidarity and Belonging*, Cambridge: Cambridge University Press.

Michelman, F. (1986) 'Foreword: traces of self government', *Harvard Law Review* 100: 4–77.

—— (1988) 'Law's Republic', *Yale Law Journal* 97, 8: 1493–1537.

—— (1989) 'Conceptions of democracy in American constitutional argument: voting rights', *Florida Law Review* 41: 443–90.

Bibliography

—— (1996) 'Democracy and positive liberty', *Boston Review* 21, 5.
Mill, J. S. (1991 [1859, 1861]) *On Liberty and Other Essays*, Oxford: Oxford University Press.
Miller, Dale (2000) 'John Stuart Mill's civic liberalism', *History of Political Thought* 21, 1: 88–113.
Miller, David (1989) *Market, State and Community*, Oxford: Clarendon Press.
—— (1993) 'Deliberative democracy and social choice', *Political Studies* 40, Special Issue 'Prospects for Democracy': 54–67.
—— (1995a) *On Nationality*, Oxford: Oxford University Press.
—— (1995b) 'Citizenship and pluralism', *Political Studies* 42: 432–50.
—— (1999) 'Bounded citizenship', in K. Hutchings and R. Dannreuther (eds) *Cosmopolitan Citizenship*, Basingstoke: Macmillan.
Modood, T. (1993) 'Establishment, multiculturalism and British citizenship', *Political Quarterly* 65, 1.
Montesquieu, C. de Secondat (1900 [1748]) *The Spirit of the Laws*, trans. T. Nugent, London: Colonial Press.
Moon, D. (1993) *Constructing Community*, Princeton: Princeton University Press.
Mouffe, C. (1992) 'Democratic citizenship and the political community', in C. Mouffe (ed.) *Dimensions of Radical Democracy*, London: Verso.
Mouritsen, P. (2001) 'What's the civil in civil society? Robert Putnam's Italian Republicanism', EUI Working Paper SPS 2001/4, Florence: European University Institute.
Mulgan, R. (1999) 'Aristotle, ethical diversity and political argument', *Journal of Political Philosophy* 7: 191–207.
—— (2000) 'Was Aristotle an "Aristotelian Social Democrat"?' *Ethics* 111, 1:79–101.
Mulhall, S. and Swift, A. (1996) *Liberals and Communitarians* (second edn), Oxford: Blackwell.
Nedelsky, J. (1989) 'Reconceiving autonomy', *Yale Journal of Law and Feminism* 1: 7–36.
Nederman, C. (2000) 'Machiavelli and moral character: principality, republic and the psychology of *virtu*', *History of Political Thought* 21, 3: 349–64.
Nussbaum, M. (1986) *The Fragility of Goodness*, Cambridge: Cambridge University Press.
—— (1990) 'Aristotelian Social Democracy', in R. Douglas, G. Mara and H. Richardson (eds) *Liberalism and the Good*, New York: Routledge.
—— (1996) 'Patriotism and cosmopolitanism', in Joshua Cohen (ed.) *For Love of Country*, Boston: Beacon Press.
Oldfield, A. (1990) *Citizenship and Community*, London: Routledge.
O'Neill, O. (1996) *Towards Justice and Virtue*, Cambridge: Cambridge University Press.

Bibliography

Pagden, A. (ed.) (1987) *The Languages of Political Thought in Early Modern Europe*, Cambridge: Cambridge University Press.

Paine, T. (1987) *The Thomas Paine Reader*, Harmondsworth: Penguin.

Pangle, T. (1998) 'The retrieval of public virtue: a critical appreciation of Sandel's democracy's discontent', in A. Allen and M. Regan (eds) *Debating Democracy's Discontent*, Oxford: Oxford University Press.

Parekh, B. (1993) 'A misconceived discourse on political obligation', *Political Studies* 41, 2: 236–51.

—— (1995) 'Oakeshott's theory of civil association', *Ethics* 106, 1: 158–86.

—— (2000) *Rethinking Multiculturalism*, London: Macmillan.

Parfitt, D. (1984) *Reasons and Persons*, Oxford: Clarendon Press.

Pateman, C. (1970) *Participation and Democratic Theory*, Cambridge: Cambridge University Press.

—— (1983) 'Feminist critiques of the public–private dichotomy', in S. Benn and G. Gaus (eds) *Public and Private in Social Life*, London: Croom Helm.

—— (1988) *The Sexual Contract*, Cambridge: Polity Press.

Patten, A. (1996) 'The republican critique of liberalism', *British Journal of Political Science* 26: 25–44.

—— (1998) *Hegel's Idea of Freedom*, Oxford: Oxford University Press.

—— (2000) 'Equality of recognition and the liberal theory of citizenship', in C. McKinnon and I. Hampsher-Monk (eds) *The Demands of Citizenship*, London: Continuum.

Perkins, A. (2001), 'The people's peers: seven knights, a lord's wife and three professors', *The Guardian* (London), April 27.

Pettit, P. (1997a) *Republicanism*, Oxford: Oxford University Press. [(1999) Paperback edition, including new postscript.]

—— (1997b) 'Freedom with honour: a republican ideal', *Social Research* 64, 1: 52–75

—— (1998) 'Reworking republicanism', in A. Allen and M. Regan (eds) *Debating Democracy's Discontents*, Oxford: Oxford Unversity Press.

—— (1999) 'Republican freedom and contestatory democratization', in I. Shapiro and C. Hacker-Cordon (eds) *Democracy's Values*, Cambridge: Cambridge University Press.

—— (2000) 'Democracy, electoral and contestatory', in I. Shapiro and S. Macedo (eds) *Designing Democratic Institutions*, New York: New York University Press.

Phillips, A. (1997) 'From inequality to difference: a severe case of displacement?' *New Left Review* 224: 143–53.

—— (1999) *Which Equalities Matter?* Oxford: Polity Press.

—— (2000) 'Feminism and republicanism: is this a plausible alliance?' *Journal of Political Philosophy* 8, 2: 279–93.

Philp, M. (1989) *Paine*, Oxford: Oxford University Press.

—— (1997) 'Defining political corruption', *Political Studies* (special issue on political corruption) 45, 3: 436–62.
—— (2000) 'Motivating liberal citizenship', in C. McKinnon and I. Hampsher-Monk (eds) *The Demands of Citizenship*, London: Continuum.
Pitkin, H. (1981) 'Justice: on relating private and public', *Political Theory* 9, 3: 327–52.
—— (1984) *Fortune is a Woman: Gender and Politics in the Thought of Niccolo Machiavelli*, Berkeley: University of California Press.
—— (1998) *The Attack of the Blob*, Chicago: Chicago University Press.
Pocock, J. (1971) *Politics, Language and Time*, London: Methuen.
—— (1975) *The Machiavellian Moment*, Princeton: Princeton University Press.
—— (1985) *Virtue, Commerce, and History*, Oxford: Oxford University Press.
Poole, R. (1999) *Nation and Identity*, London: Routledge.
Porter, N. (1996) *Rethinking Unionism*, Belfast: Blackstaff.
Powell. J. (ed.) (1995) *Cicero the Philosopher*, Oxford: Oxford University Press.
Putnam, R. (1993) *Making Democracy Work*, Princeton: Princeton University Press.
—— (1995) 'Bowling alone', *Democracy* 6, 1: 1995.
Rahe, P. (1992) *Republics, Ancient and Modern: Classical Republicanism and the American Revolution*, Chicago: Chicago University Press.
Rawls, J. (1971) *A Theory of Justice*, Oxford: Oxford University Press.
—— (1993) *Political Liberalism*, New York: Columbia University Press.
Raz, J. (1986) *The Morality of Freedom*, Oxford: Clarendon Press.
—— (1989) 'Liberating duties', *Law and Philosophy* 8: 3–21.
—— (1994) *Ethics in the Public Domain*, Oxford: Clarendon Press.
—— (1995) 'Rights and politics', *Indiana Law Journal* 71, 1: 27–44.
Rosenblatt, H. (1997) *Rousseau and Geneva*, Cambridge: Cambridge University Press.
Rousseau, J. J. (1964a) *Oeuvres Complètes*, eds B. Gagnebin and M. Raymond, Paris: Gallimard.
—— (1964b [1750, 1755]) *The First and Second Discourses*, ed. R. Masters, New York: St Martin's Press.
—— (1968 [1762]) *The Social Contract*, Harmondsworth: Penguin.
—— (1974 [1762]) *Émile*, London: Dent.
—— (1993) *The Social Contract* and *The Discourses*, London: Dent
Roy, A. (1999) *The Cost of Living*, London: Harper Collins.
Ruane, J. and Todd, J. (eds) (2000) *After the Good Friday Agreement*, Dublin: University College Dublin Press.
Sacks, J. (1997) *The Politics of Hope*, London: Jonathan Cape.

Bibliography

Sandel, M. (1982) *Liberalism and the Limits of Justice*, Cambridge: Cambridge University Press.
—— (ed.) (1984) *Liberalism and Its Critics*, Oxford: Blackwell.
—— (1995) 'Moral argument and liberal toleration: abortion and homosexuality', in A. Etzioni (ed.) *New Communitarian Thinking*, Charlottesville: University Press of Virginia.
—— (1996) *Democracy's Discontent*, Cambridge, MA: Harvard University Press.
—— (1998) 'Reply to critics', in A. Allen and M. Regan (eds) *Debating Democracy's Discontents*, Oxford: Oxford University Press.
Sanders, L. (1997) 'Against deliberation', *Political Theory* 25, 3: 347–76.
Sapiro, V. (1992) *A Vindication of Political Virtue: The Political Theory of Mary Wollstonecraft*, Chicago: University of Chicago Press.
Scheffler, S. (1997) 'Relationships and responsibilities', *Philosophy and Public Affairs* 26, 3: 189–209.
Schofield, M. (1995) 'Cicero's definition of *Res Publica*', in J. Powell (ed.) *Cicero the Philosopher*, Oxford: Oxford University Press.
Schwarzenbach, S. (1996) 'On civic friendship', *Ethics* 107, 1: 97–128.
Selbourne, D. (1997) *The Principle of Duty*, London: Little Brown.
Sellers, M. (1998) *The Sacred Fire of Liberty*, London: Macmillan.
Shapiro, I. (1990) *Political Criticism*, Berkeley: University of California Press.
Shapiro, I. and Brilmayer L. (eds) (1999) *Global Justice*, New York: New York University Press.
Shapiro, I. and Hacker-Cordon, C. (eds) (1999a) *Democracy's Edges*, Cambridge: Cambridge University Press.
—— (eds) (1999b) *Democracy's Values*, Cambridge: Cambridge University Press.
Shapiro, I. and Macedo, S. (eds) (2000) *Designing Democratic Institutions*, New York: New York University Press.
Sher, R. (1994) 'From troglodytes to Americans: Montesquieu and the Scottish Enlightenment on liberty, virtue, and commerce', in D. Wootton (ed.) *Republicanism, Liberty and Commercial Society*, Stanford: Stanford University Press.
Shklar, J. (1969) *Men and Citizens: A Study of Rousseau's Social Theory*, Cambridge: Cambridge University Press.
—— (1990) 'Montesquieu and the new republicanism', in G. Bock, Q. Skinner and M. Viroli (eds) *Machiavelli and Republicanism*, Cambridge: Cambridge University Press.
Shumer, S. (1979) 'Machiavelli: Republican politics and its corruption', *Political Theory* 7, 1: 5–34.
Sidney, A. (1990 [1698]) *Discourse Concerning Government* (ed. T. G. West), Indianapolis: Liberty Classics.

Siedentop, L. (1979) 'Two liberal traditions', in A. Ryan (ed.) *The Idea of Freedom*, Oxford: Oxford University Press.
Simmons, A. (1996) 'Associative political obligations', *Ethics* 106, 2: 247–73.
Simpson, P. (1998) *A Philosophical Commentary on the Politics of Aristotle*, Chapel Hill: University of North Carolina Press.
Skinner, Q. (1978) *The Foundations of Modern Political Thought*, 2 vols, Cambridge: Cambridge University Press.
—— (1989) 'The State', in T. Ball, R. Farr and R. Hanson (eds) *Political Innovation and Conceptual Change*, Cambridge: Cambridge University Press.
—— (1990) 'The republican idea of political liberty', in G. Bock, Q. Skinner and M. Viroli (eds) *Machiavelli and Republicanism*, Cambridge: Cambridge University Press
—— (1998) *Liberty before Liberalism*, Cambridge: Cambridge University Press.
Smith, A. (1982 [1776]) *Wealth of Nations*, Harmondsworth: Penguin.
—— (2000 [1759]) *Theory of Moral Sentiments*, Amherst, NY: Prometheus Books.
Smith, E. and Spaeth, H. (eds) (1987) *The Constitution of the United States*, New York: Harper and Row.
Smith, G. and Wales, C. (2000) 'Citizens' juries and deliberative democracy', *Political Studies* 48, 1: 51–65.
Spitz, J.-F. (1994) 'The concept of liberty in *A Theory of Justice* and its republican version', *Ratio Juris* 7, 3: 331–47.
—— (1995) *La Liberté Politique*, Paris: Presses Universitaires de France.
Squires, J. (1999) *Gender in Political Theory*, Cambridge: Polity Press.
—— (2000) 'The state in (and of) feminist visions of political citizenship', in C. McKinnon and I. Hampsher-Monk (eds) *The Demands of Citizenship*, London: Continuum.
Stedman-Jones, G. (1994) 'Kant, the French Revolution and the definition of the republic', in B. Fontana (ed.) *The Invention of the Modern Republic*, Cambridge: Cambridge University Press.
Sullivan, W. (1982) *Reconstructing Public Philosophy*, Berkeley: University of California Press.
Sunstein, C. (1985) 'Interest groups in American public law', *Stanford Law Review* 38: 29–87.
—— (1988) 'Beyond the republican revival', *Yale Law Journal* 97: 1539–90.
—— (1990) *After the Rights Revolution*, Cambridge MA: Harvard University Press.
—— (1991) 'Preferences and politics', *Philosophy and Public Affairs* 20, 1: 3–34.

Bibliography

—— (1993a) *The Partial Constitution*, Cambridge, MA: Harvard University Press.
—— (1993b) *Democracy and the Problem of Free Speech*, New York: The Free Press.
—— (1993c) 'Democracy and Shifting Preferences', in D. Copp, J. Hampton and J. Roemer (eds) *The Idea of Democracy*, Cambridge: Cambridge University Press.
—— (1993d) 'On analogical reasoning', *Harvard Law Review* 106, 4: 741–91.
—— (2000) 'The daily we', *Boston Review* 26, 3.
Sunstein, C. and Margalit, E. (2001) 'Solidarity goods', *Journal of Political Philosophy* 9, 2: 129–49.
Tamir, Y. (1993) *Liberal Nationalism*, Princeton: Princeton University Press.
Taylor, C. (1977) *Hegel*, Cambridge: Cambridge University Press.
—— (1985) *Philosophical Papers*, Cambridge: Cambridge University Press.
—— (1989) *Sources of the Self*, Cambridge: Cambridge University Press.
—— (1992) *Multiculturalism and 'The Politics of Recognition'*, Princeton: Princeton University Press.
—— (1993) *Reconciling the Solitudes: Essays in Canadian Federalism and Nationalism* (ed. G. Laforest), Montreal: McGill-Queen's University Press.
—— (1994) 'Charles Taylor replies', in J. Tully (ed.) *Philosophy in an Age of Pluralism*, Cambridge: Cambridge University Press.
—— (1995) *Philosophical Arguments*, Cambridge, MA: Harvard University Press.
—— (1996) 'Why democracy needs patriotism', in Joshua Cohen (ed.) *For Love of Country*, Boston: Beacon Press.
Thucydides (1972) *The Peloponnesian War*, Harmondsworth: Penguin.
Tocqueville, A. de (2000 [1835, 1840]) *Democracy in America*, Indianapolis: Hackett.
Tuck, R. (1990) 'Humanism and political thought', in A. Goodman and A. MacKay (eds) *The Impact of Humanism on Western Europe*, London: Longman.
Tully, J. (ed.) (1994) *Philosophy in an Age of Pluralism*, Cambridge: Cambridge University Press.
—— (2000) 'The challenge of re-imagining citizenship and belonging in multi-cultural and multi-national societies', in C. McKinnon and I. Hampsher-Monk (eds) *The Demands of Citizenship*, London: Continuum.
Van Parijs, P. (1995) *Real Freedom for All*, Oxford: Oxford University Press.
—— (1999) 'Contestatory democracy versus freedom for all', in I. Shapiro and C. Hacker-Cordon (eds) *Democracy's Value*, Cambridge: Cambridge University Press.

Bibliography

—— (2000) 'Power-sharing versus border-crossing in ethnically divided societies', in I. Shapiro and S. Macedo (eds) *Designing Democratic Institutions*, New York: New York University Press.

Viroli, M. (1995) *For Love of Country*, Oxford: Oxford University Press.

—— (1998) *Machiavelli*, Oxford: Oxford University Press.

—— (2000) 'Republican patriotism', in C. McKinnon and I. Hampsher-Monk (eds) *The Demands of Citizenship*, London: Continuum.

Vogel, U. (1981) 'Is citizenship gender-specific?', in U. Vogel and M. Moran (eds) *The Frontiers of Citizenship*, London: Macmillan.

Waldron, J. (1993a) 'Special ties and natural duties', *Philosophy and Public Affairs* 22, 1: 3–30.

—— (1993b) 'Can communal goods be human rights?', in J. Waldron, *Liberal Rights*, Cambridge: Cambridge University Press.

—— (1998) 'Virtue en masse', in A. Allen and M. Regan (eds) *Debating Democracy's Discontents*, Oxford: Oxford University Press.

—— (1999) *The Dignity of Legislation*, Cambridge: Cambridge University Press.

—— (2000a) 'What is cosmopolitan?', *Journal of Political Philosophy* 8, 2: 227–43.

—— (2000b) 'Cultural identity and civic responsibility', in W. Kymlicka and W. Norman (eds) *Citizenship in Diverse Societies*, Oxford: Oxford University Press.

—— (2001a) 'Actually existing cosmopolitanism', seminar paper, European University Institute, Florence.

—— (2001b) 'The logic of cultural accommodation', presented at the Annual Meetings of the American Political Science Association, San Francisco, CA, mimeo.

Walzer, M. (1983) *Radical Principles*, New York: Basic Books.

—— (1985) *Spheres of Justice*, Oxford: Basil Blackwell.

—— (1992) 'The civil society argument', in C. Mouffe (ed.) *Dimensions of Radical Democracy*, London: Verso.

—— (1994) *Thick and Thin: Moral Argument at Home and Abroad*, Notre Dame: University of Notre Dame Press.

Ward, L. and Wintour, P. (2000) 'Speaker extends ban on breastfeeding', *The Guardian* (London) April 7.

White, S. (2000a) 'Rediscovering republican political economy', *Imprints* 4, 3: 213–35.

—— (2000b) 'Should talent be taxed?', in C. McKinnon and I. Hampsher-Monk (eds) *The Demands of Citizenship*, London: Continuum.

—— (2000c) 'Ethics and equality', *Boston Review* 25, 6.

Whyte, J. (1983) 'The permeability of the UK–Irish border', *Administration* 31, 3: 300–15.

Williamson, E. (1992) *The Penguin History of Latin America*, Harmondsworth: Penguin.

Bibliography

Wirszubski, C. (1968) *Libertas as a Political Idea at Rome during the Late Republic and Early Principate*, Cambridge: Cambridge University Press.

Wokler, R. (1995) *Rousseau*, Oxford: Oxford University Press.

—— (ed.) (1995) *Rousseau on Liberty*, Manchester: Manchester University Press.

Wolff, J. (2000) 'Political obligation: a pluralist approach', in M. Baghramian and A. Ingram (eds) *Pluralism: the Philosophy and Politics of Difference*, London: Routledge.

Wollstonecraft, M. (1992 [1792]) *A Vindication of the Rights of Women*, Harmondsworth: Penguin.

—— (1994 [1790, 1792, 1794]) *Political Writings*, Oxford: Oxford University Press.

Wood, N. (1988) *Cicero's Social and Political Thought*, Berkeley: University of California Press.

Wooton, D. (1994a) 'Harrington's *Oceana*: Origins and Aftermath, 1651–1660', in D. Wooton (ed.) *Republicanism, Liberty, and Commercial Society, 1649–1776*, Stanford: Stanford University Press.

—— (1994b) 'Republicanism and the Restoration, 1660–1683', in D. Wooton (ed.) *Republicanism, Liberty, and Commercial Society, 1649–1776*, Stanford: Stanford University Press.

Worden, B. (1994) 'James Harrington and *The Commonwealth of Oceana*, 1656', in D. Wooton (ed.) *Republicanism, Liberty, and Commercial Society, 1649–1776*, Stanford: Stanford University Press.

Yack, B. (1992) *The Longing for Total Revolution*, Berkeley: University of California Press.

—— (1993) *The Problems of a Political Animal*, Berkeley: University of California Press.

Young, I. (1987) 'Impartiality and the civic public', in D. Cornell and S. Benhabib (eds) *Feminism as Critique*, Cambridge: Polity Press.

—— (1990a) *Justice and the Politics of Difference*, Princeton: Princeton University Press.

—— (1990b) 'Polity and group difference', in C. Sunstein (ed.) *Feminism and Political Theory*, Chicago: Chicago University Press.

—— (1996) 'Communication and the other – beyond deliberative democracy', in S. Benhabib (ed.) *Democracy and Difference*, Princeton: Princeton University Press.

—— (1997) 'Unruly categories: a critique of Nancy Fraser's dual systems theory', *New Left Review* 222: 147–60.

—— (2000a) *Inclusion and Democracy*, Oxford: Oxford University Press.

—— (2000b) 'Self-determination and global democracy: a critique of liberal nationalism', in I. Shapiro and S. Macedo (eds) (2000) *Designing Democratic Institutions*, New York: New York University Press.

Index

accountability 5, 18, 22–4, 29, 32, 35–6, 49–51, 64, 66, 68–9, 75–6, 81, 83–4, 88, 90, 92–3, 104, 106–7, 109, 149–50, 155, 162, 172, 178–9, 184, 194–5, 200, 205–6, 216, 224, 235–40, 245–9
Ackerman, B. 201
adaptive preferences 202, 237, 261
agrarian law 38, 60–1, 69–70, 96, 102
Alstott, A. 201
altruism 21, 46, 79, 126–8, 140, 142, 148, 159–60
American revolution 7, 102–3, 110
amour propre see vanity
Annas, J. 39
anti-federalists 104, 109, 293 n15
apathy, political 2, 114–15, 119, 139–141, 149–50, 162, 170–2, 179, 219, 247
Arendt, H. 7, 14, 111, 112, 120–31, 142–4, 152, 155, 156, 163, 164, 167, 168, 181, 188, 191, 207, 210, 217, 228, 231, 240, 241, 252, 237, 258, 266, 268, 290 n1, 294 nn4–6
Aristotle 4, 7, 15–29, 30–2, 35, 38, 39–41, 43, 45, 49, 51, 52, 55, 58, 60, 62, 65, 66, 68, 70, 79, 91, 108, 109, 151, 159, 166, 181, 183, 188, 210, 214, 224, 283, 290 nn1–4, 291 nn5–6
army, standing 76, 79, 108
Athens 7, 15–18, 87, 167
atomism 9, 115, 120, 128, 131–5

Australia 246, 298 n4
autonomy 78, 88–9, 123, 133, 137, 142, 144, 153–4, 178, 180, 186–205, 214–18, 237, 246–7, 253, 255, 257, 258–9, 265, 273–4, 282, 295 n5, 213; and common goods 153–4; role of state in promoting 197–201; *see also* freedom
Bader, V. 279, 298 n8
Baker, J. 242
Barber, B. 8, 10, 181, 217, 223, 238, 240, 242, 247
Baron, H. 43
Barry, B. 300 n12
basic income 200–1, 245
Bellamy, R. 207
Benhabib, S. 229, 266
Benn, S. 158
Berlin, I. 53, 99, 135–7, 181
Black, A. 291 n1
Blunkett, D. 301 n24
boundaries, state 130, 282–4
Bowers vs. Hardwick 211–12
Britain 7, 63, 74–6, 79, 271, 277; constitution 83, 106; House of Commons 64, 231; House of Lords 64, 279; parliament 76, 83, 106
broadcasting: fragmentation of 241; public 198; regulation of 198
Brubaker, R. 300 n15
Brugger, B. 290 n2
Bubeck, D. 177

319

Index

Burke, E. 99, 101
Burtt, S. 163

Callan, E. 174
campaign finance 149, 198, 209, 219, 299 n14
Canada 140, 264
Caney, S. 272
Canovan, M. 300 n15
Carens, J. 240
checks and balances *see* mixed government
Cicero 4, 15, 16, 18, 30–8, 39–41, 43, 45, 50, 52, 53, 54, 55, 62, 172, 181, 183, 258, 290 n4, 291 nn5–7
citizen initiatives 238, 242
citizens, relationship between 142; as colleagues 267–9, 285, 300 n12; as family 130, 267–9; as fraternity 6, 96, 110, 167; as friendship 6, 28–9, 102, 129–30, 266–9, 284–5, 300 n14; moral partnership 32, 38–9, 42, 73; multiple interdependencies of 155; and nationality 273–82; as strangers 266–8; *see also* community: political
citizens' juries 178, 198, 244, 246–7
citizenship 7–8, 11; as activity 6, 8, 15–17, 20, 23–6, 32, 44, 50–2, 66–8, 75–6, 90–1, 115–17, 138, 145, 149, 158–66; admission to 285–8; cosmopolitan 285–6; gendered 148, 166–70; as legal status 30, 36, 67, 101, 103–4, 113, 120, 149, 252–3, 257–8
civic humanism 7, 11, 44, 62, 144
civic virtue 5–8, 10–12, 44, 75, 78–80, 145, 147–9, 157–79, 182, 185, 217, 245, 263, 269–70, 276, 284, 295 n14; in Arendt 126–7; in Aristotle 20–1, 27; in Cicero 33–5; in Harrington 65, 70–1, 292 n10; in Machiavelli 52–57; in Madison 106–7, 109–10; in Mill 117; in Montesquieu 81–2, in Rousseau 87, 94–5, 97–8, 293 n6; in Taylor 140–1; in Tocqueville 115; in Wollstonecraft 99–102; liberal and communitarian accounts 162–4; elements of 160–1; as enlightened self-interest 56, 115; as established disposition 159–60; practice of care and 169–70; promoting 160, 170–8
civil disobedience 126, 162; *see also* obligation, political
civil society 78–80, 116, 127–8, 130, 171, 233–5
civility 80–1, 147, 185, 229–30, 252, 265–6, 269, 296 n14
Cohen, J. 211
Coleman, J. 37, 291 n1
commerce, commercial society 4, 77–80
commonwealth 63–4, 65–7, 72, 76
common good 1–2, 5–12, 73–4, 78–9, 147–58, 166–9, 178–9, 190, 214, 234; in Arendt 124, 126–7; in Aristotle 19–20, 22, 27–9; in Cicero 32, 33–5; in Harrington 64–7, 70–1; in Machiavelli 46–50, 55–6, 62; in Madison 104–5, 106–7; in Montesquieu 82, 115, 117, in Rousseau 90–3, 99; in Taylor 132–5, 139–40, 142; in Wollstonecraft 100–1; alternative conceptions of 76, 151–2, 156–7; citizenship as 7, 155, 165; freedom as 139, 155, 185; of political community 39, 154–8; politically defined 10–11, 58, 157, 205; power as 124; relation to individual good and freedom 55, 154, 159, 164–5, 171, 194–5, 206–8, 209–12; rights as 208; state as promoting 9–11, 135, 142, 158–9, 192–4, 203–5
common world 152, 155, 166, 238, 240–2, 249; in Arendt 121–2, 124, 130
communitarianism 1–2, 8–10, 151–6, 164, 169–70, 175, 191, 203–5, 207, 211–12, 214, 220,

239, 248–9, 258–9, 263–6, 267–9, 271–3; *see also* nationalism
community 10; in Arendt 120, 124, 129–31; in Aristotle 19–20, 28–9; in Cicero 32, 38; in Harrington 73; in Machiavelli 61; in Rousseau 96–8; in Taylor 141–2; in Wollstonecraft 102; as bounded 284–6; and common enmity 130, 284–5; as developing in interaction 130, 157, 281; as extensible 286; and interdependence of fate 142–4, 155–6, 249, 275, 280, 283, 285–6; political 8, 15–17, 266–85; and sense of belonging 27, 140, 142, 156, 166, 172, 177, 242, 276–81; size of 6, 29, 61, 64, 73, 81–4, 104, 108–9, 172, 282; *see also* common world; public space
compassion 54, 97, 128–30
conceptions of the good, shared 2, 8–10, 28–9, 120–1, 129, 156–7, 204–5, 223–4, 247–9, 266
Condorcet, J. 92
conformity 116–18, 128, 131
consociational government 262
Constant, B. 113–14, 116, 294 nn2, 7
contract, social 75–6, 89–93
contractarian thought 6, 9–10, 32, 38, 39, 45–6, 65–6, 75–6, 80–1, 85–93, 105, 112, 108, 165, 266, 269
Cooke, M. 205, 227, 228
corruption 5, 7, 17–18, 62, 78–80, 102–3, 104, 109, 162, 241; in Arendt 127–6; in Aristotle 21–3; in Cicero 32–3; in Harrington 67–8, 70–2; in Machiavelli 45–7; in Madison 104–5, 107; in Rousseau 85–8, 94; in Taylor 141; in Wollstonecraft 99–100; as historical cycle 17–18, 22, 35, 44, 46, 68, 78, 88, 98, 104, 107
Corsica 97, 299 n5
Cromwell, O. 64
Cuba 160, 280, 295 n10, 301 n23

culture, and politics 142–4, 171–2, 252–66, 273–81; public 133, 157, 261–3, 274–81, 287; *see also* nationalism; recognition

Dagger, R. 8, 93, 177, 186, 207, 262–3, 296 n2
Darwall, S. 299 n6
De Valera, E. 295 n8
death penalty 220, 238
deliberation 2, 8, 20, 23–4, 69, 91–2, 106–7, 124, 126–7, 138–40, 157, 161–2, 205, 214–15, 221–45, 275; as public reason 10
democracy, direct 50, 218–21, 238; *see also* participation; representation
dependence 59, 64–5, 67, 69–71, 74, 85–90, 97–8, 100–1, 103, 115, 118, 169–70, 184, 187, 191–2, 198–201, 292 n5, 296 n3
Dietz, M. 169, 267
determinism 58, 62, 65, 96, 128
diversity, moral and cultural 2, 9–11, 149, 154–7, 161–2, 168–9, 174–5, 179, 214–15, 223, 226–30, 238, 241–2, 252–66; in Arendt 120, 124, 129–31; in Aristotle 28–9; in Machiavelli 58, 61; in Harrington 72, 98; in Taylor 140, 142–3
domestic sphere *see* private life
Dryzek, J. 223, 233, 298 n6
Dutch republic 75
duties 5, 149, 161, 164; and rights 160, 206–7, 209; *see also* civic virtue

education 17, 197, 199, 203–4; in Arendt 128–9; in Aristotle 26–7; in Cicero 37; in Harrington 72; in Machiavelli 57; in Madison 107–8, 129; in Mill 117; in Rousseau 95; in Wollstonecraft 102; civic 6, 174–5, 177, 242, 263; by example 21, 56, 117, 126–7, 170–1; and national

Index

curriculum 174–5, 277, 281; religious 175–6, 204, 298 n14; state 176, 204
emotions *see* passions
equality, political 16, 22, 24, 32, 68, 85, 96, 99, 114, 125, 128, 130, 141, 190–2, 196, 197–8, 215, 221–8, 232–3, 237–8, 244–5, 250, 261–6, 293n15
Etzioni, A. 164, 207
European Union 220, 238, 264, 279–80, 285, 301 n22

factions 17, 22–3, 30, 44, 49–50, 68–9, 83–4, 91, 104–5, 108, 235
family *see* private life
federalism 78, 84, 104, 109, 240, 262
Finland 275, 287
Fishkin, J. 242, 244
Florence 44, 45, 48, 51, 56, 63
focus groups 242
fortune 44, 46, 52–3, 292 n1
founder *see* law-giver
France 7, 114, 116; as republic 167, 173, 174–6, 259, 263, 278, 280, 286, 301 n21
Fraser, N. 134, 251
fraternity *see* citizens, relationship between
Frazer, E. 168, 227
free speech 103, 196–7, 208–9, 229
freedom 1–2, 5, 8–9, 2, 31, 39–40, 44, 73, 75–6, 78, 80–1, 112–13, 180–213, 245–7, 254, 257; in Arendt 120, 122–4; in Aristotle 25–6; in Cicero 36–7; in Harrington 66–7; in Machiavelli 57–60; in Madison 103–4, 109–10; in Mill 117–18; in Montesquieu 82–4; in Rousseau 84–93, 97; in Taylor 131–4, 135–40; as common good 139; as compatible with law 5, 26–7, 37, 58, 67, 67, 93, 184, 194; as constraint/ideal 184; and licence 25, 37, 83, 88, 100, 115, 118, 292 n10; natural 75–6, 88; negative 59, 66, 118, 135–7, 144, 181–5, 196, 208; neo-roman 7, 74, 183; as non-domination 7, 59, 66–7, 83, 89, 155, 183–6, 194, 195–6, 288; as non-interference 59, 118–19, 135–7, 181–5, 194–5; as participation in self-rule 1, 5, 16, 25–6, 60, 67, 75–6, 82–3, 89–92, 101, 120, 122–5, 138–9, 156, 187–90, 197–8, 217, 235, 285; positive 101, 111, 135–7, 183; and slavery 15–16, 25, 30, 36–7, 39, 58–9, 62, 88, 183–4; *see also* autonomy; liberty of the ancients/moderns; rights
French Revolution 85, 99, 110, 113–14, 128, 136, 160

Galston, W. 160, 163
Gaus, G. 158
Gellner, E. 175
general will 90–3, 124, 151, 220–1, 235
Geneva 85
Germany 155, 275, 277, 286, 300 n15
Gilbert, P. 275–6, 279, 280
globalisation 4, 6, 155, 199, 219, 232, 238, 277, 282, 284, 288
Goodin, R. 221, 232
Gordon, T. 292 n11
Granovetter, M. 268
Grant, R. 53, 97, 98
Gutmann, A. 174, 230, 298 n9

Habermas, J. 162, 181, 187, 189, 223, 253, 270, 274, 296 n6
Harrington, J. 4, 7, 13, 15, 42, 63–75, 79, 80, 87, 90, 95, 103, 106, 107, 108, 176, 181, 183, 207, 218, 226, 292 nn8–11
hate speech 196, 209, 229
Havel, V. 126, 272
Hegel, G.W.F. 132–3, 294 n3.
Hirschman, A. 3, 79, 298 n8
Hirst, P. 298 n10
history, cyclical view of *see* corruption

Index

Hobbes 55, 63, 65–6, 79, 86, 88, 99, 292 n7
homosexuality 134, 211–12, 256, 298 n16
Honneth, A. 250, 258
Honohan, I. 158, 269, 287
honour 6, 17, 24, 30, 33–5, 54–6, 65–6, 80, 81–2, 86–7, 94–5, 97–8, 100, 107, 111–12, 139, 167, 172–3, 258; *see also* recognition
Horton, J. 165
Howe, D. 107, 292 n3, 293 n14
Hutcheson, F. 79

identity 112, 171–2, 214, 214, 230, 250–9, 263, 265, 271–3, 276–7, 299 n2, 300 n8; in Arendt 120–3; in Taylor 134, 140, 142–4; political 257–9, 272; *see also* culture; nationalism
immigration 109, 142–3, 220, 277, 286–8, 298 n4
India 212
inequality, economic and political autonomy 191–2, 198–201, 235, 244–5; in Arendt 129; in Aristotle 27–8; in Cicero 37–8; in Harrington 64–5, 69–70; in Machiavelli 60–1; in Madison 102, 108; in Rousseau 86–8, 95–6; in Taylor 141; in Wollstonecraft 100
Ingram, A. 207
interdependence 1, 5–6, 8–12, 78–81 148–50, 154–8, 160–1, 165, 169–70, 174, 177, 186–7, 199, 203–4, 210, 242, 246, 266–9, 271–3, 275, 280–8; in Arendt 121; in Aristotle 19–20; in Cicero 31–3; in Harrington 64–5, 73; in Machiavelli 45–7, 60; in Madison 103; in Rousseau 86–9, 97; in Taylor 132–4; in Tocqueville 115; in Wollstonecraft 99
interest groups 8, 119, 127, 227, 241
internet 218, 241–3
intersubjectivity *see* recognition

Ireland 155, 173, 218, 220, 255, 258–9, 271, 301 n20; Northern 155, 204, 230, 259, 271, 275, 298 n14, 299 n11, 301 n20; republicanism in 301 n20
Israel 134
ius sanguinis 286
ius soli 287

James, S. 296 n13
James, W. 177
Jefferson, T. 109, 125
Julius Caesar 30, 41

Kant, I. 293 n1
Kelly, C. 293 n8
Kittay, E. 169
Kostakopoulou, T. 162, 282
Kymlicka, W. 11, 254, 259, 280, 299 n1

Lacey, N. 227
laïcité see secularism
language 134, 142, 153; official 259, 263, 277, 281
Lara, M. 123, 262
law 15–16, 30–1; in Aristotle 26–7; in Cicero 35–7; in Harrington 64, 66–7; in Machiavelli 56–7; in Madison 103–4; in Rousseau 91–3; rule of 35–6, 64, 66–7, 74, 180–1, 183–4, 224; as shaping character 6, 26–7, 37, 56–7, 93–4, 293 n9; *see also* freedom, as compatible with law
law-giver 5, 36, 49, 56, 90, 104, 290 n1
Lever, A. 209, 211
liberal–communitarian debate 2, 9–10
liberalism 1–2, 4–5, 8–12, 76, 80, 85, 98, 99, 111–12, 114–18, 120, 131–4, 139, 144, 148, 150, 151–2, 155, 158, 163, 167, 174, 176, 181–2, 184, 187, 193–5, 205–8, 209–10, 212, 222, 224, 226–9, 252, 254, 266–7, 269, 282, 284,

Index

286–7, 288–9; 293 n1, 296 n1; comprehensive 10; neutralist 8–11, 111–12, 119, 131–3, 139, 225–8, 229, 256, 263–5, 299 n1; perfectionist 11, 132, 205; political 10
libertarianism 1, 131, 135, 141, 196, 199–201, 204, 234
liberty of the ancients/moderns 113–14, 181, 294 n2, 294 n7; *see also* freedom
Lincoln, A. 288
Livy 45
localism 169, 171–2, 239, 262, 299 n13
Locke, J. 4, 7, 63, 75, 76, 99, 102–3, 152, 210, 292 n12
lottery, as means of allocating office 16, 22, 68, 69, 93, 106, 246–7
love, as political bond 53, 82, 96, 125, 128, 130, 164, 258, 267
Lucca 66
Lustick, I. 282
Lycurgus 16, 49

McAfee, K. 299 n2
Machiavelli 4, 7, 113, 15, 42, 44–63, 67, 68, 71, 72, 73–6, 80, 84, 85, 94, 95, 107, 150, 163, 164, 166, 172, 176, 181, 183, 188, 207, 235, 270, 290 n1, 291 nn2–5, 292 n10
MacIntyre, A. 9, 10, 28–9, 160, 169, 203, 239, 293 n13, 295 n6, 299 n13
Madison, J. 4, 14, 15, 77, 78, 102–10, 147, 149, 218, 219
majority rule 39, 92, 125
majority tyranny, danger of 17, 22, 32–3, 49–50, 68–9, 83, 91–2, 105, 115, 117, 119, 219–21, 235–6, 250
Mandeville, B. de 79, 91
Manin, B. 106, 109
market 80, 84, 96, 150, 159, 161, 169, 173, 178, 196, 198–201, 203, 221, 233–4, 239, 279
marriage 3, 27, 100, 118, 204, 252, 256; arranged 265; monogamous 153; same-sex 134, 248, 264, 256
Marsilius of Padua 219 n1
Marx, K. 119
Mason, A. 156, 160, 164–5, 265–9, 271, 279, 280
Michelman, F. 8, 209, 211–12, 222, 297 n8
militia, civic 5–6; in Harrington 72; in Machiavelli 51, 54, 57; in Madison 108; in Mill 117, 176; in Rousseau 94
Mill, J.S. 114, 116–18, 137, 246
Miller, Dale 118
Miller, David 208, 211, 228, 274, 276, 277, 284, 287
Mitchell, G. 293 n7
mixed government 5, 15, 17, 66, 235; in Aristotle 22–3; in Cicero 35–6; in Harrington 68–9; in Machiavelli 49–50; in Madison 106; in Rousseau 92–3; *see also* separation of powers
Modood, T. 264
Molesworth, R. 292 n11
Montesquieu, C. de 77, 81, 82, 83, 84, 87, 90, 96, 103, 105, 106, 107, 247, 292 n2
Moon, D. 227
moral argument and politics 10, 71, 112, 138–40, 157, 203–5, 225–30, 256–7, 261–3, 298 n9
mothering 169–70
Mouffe, C. 151, 284–5, 295 n7, 300 n11
Mulgan, R. 28–9, 290 n2
multi-culturalism 142, 254, 264, 299 n4

nationalism 2, 5, 119, 130, 143, 172, 273–82, 286–7, 289; liberal nationality 275, 276–9, 281
national service *see* service, civic
nation-building 280–1, 289
Nedelsky, J. 187, 195, 211
Nedham, M. 292 n6
Neville, H. 292 n11
non-domination *see* freedom

Index

Norway 173
Nussbaum, M. 273

obligation, political 6, 148, 157–8, 164–6, 178–9, 245–8, 266–7, 268–73, 281, 284, 288; in Arendt 129–30; in Aristotle 26–8, 32; in Cicero 37, 38; in Harrington, 70–1; in Machiavelli 55–6, 61; in Madison 107, 108; in Montesquieu 83; in Rousseau 93–4, 96; in Taylor 140–2; associative 269; and consent 38, 75–6, 108, 165; and fair play 93, 165, 269; and legal obligation 165–6; special 165, 268–9; *see also* civic virtue; community
Oldfield, A. 8
opinion polling 92, 219–21, 242–3; deliberative 243

Paine, T. 99
Palestine 134
Pangle, T. 160
Parekh, B. 162, 164, 165, 166
Parfitt, D. 170
participation in self-government 1, 5–12, 13–14, 16–18, 42–4, 77, 119, 214–49, 281; in Arendt 123–7; in Aristotle 23–5, 39–40; in Cicero 32, 35–6, 39–40; in Harrington 68–9; in Machiavelli 47–52; in Madison 103–5; in Mill 116–17; in Rousseau 98–9; in Taylor 138–40; in Tocqueville 115–16; in Wollstonecraft 101; compulsory 126, 245–8; as contestation 216, 236–7; distinct from direct democracy 238; as editing/authoring 236–7; as instrumental good 11, 156, 216; as intrinsic good 11, 156, 216–17; as ultimate good 11, 120, 123–6, 156; *see also* representation
particularism *see* localism
passions, emotions 21, 24, 26–8, 33, 65–6, 70–1, 79–80, 82, 86–9, 97, 100–2, 103, 105, 119, 219, 271–3, 293 nn13–14; calm vs. aggressive 79
Pateman, C. 10, 148
paternalism 202
patriotism 29, 38, 61, 73, 82, 96–7, 102, 107–8, 129–30, 140–3, 164–6, 171–2, 268–73, 277–81, 284–6, 301 n 17; *see also* education, civic; civic virtue
Patten, A. 182, 296 n1, 294n3, 298 n8
Pericles 17
Pettit, P. 8, 59; civic virtue 155, 171, 172, 173; freedom 183–6, 191–6; inequality 198, 200; participation 215, 216, 219–20, 223, 236–7, 245–6; recognition 258, 261, 266–7, 272, 297 n12, 298 n15, 301 n18
Phillips, A. 167–8, 170, 201, 251
Philp, M.162, 164, 294 n2
Pitkin, H. 8, 53, 56, 58, 59, 60, 63, 158, 168, 188, 189, 217
Plato 17, 18, 29, 30, 33
Pocock, J.G.A. 7, 44, 80
Poland 97
political morality 52–5, 163
Polybius 35, 49
Poole, R. 182, 274, 279
pornography 196, 209, 248
Porter, N. 301 n20
Portugal 280, 287
power 6, 18, 39, 43; in Arendt 124, 188; in Aristotle 22; in Cicero 32–3; in Harrington 66, 70, 75–6, 83–4; in Machiavelli 46, 49–50, 52–3, 57–8, 62; in Madison 106–7; in Mill 117–18; in Rousseau 86, 90, 93; in Tocqueville 114–16; in Wollstonecraft 101; arbitrary 5, 7, 26, 49, 57, 59, 64, 65–7, 75–6, 82–4, 88, 93, 101, 103, 110, 215–16, 219–20, 258; balancing 22–3, 49–50, 93, 104–6, 118, 205, 235; exceptional 36, 57, 58–9, 77,

325

Index

89–90, 291 n4; *see also* mixed government; separation of powers
privacy 93, 103, 119, 122, 181, 206, 210–12; spatial conception of 210–11
private life 17, 33, 55, 97, 113, 100, 115, 148, 167–8, 184, 210, 247, 252, 254, 258, 267–8; in Arendt 120, 121–3, 123, 127–8, 129–30; in Taylor 131, 134, 139
property 3, 6, 16, 191–2, 199–201, 209–10, 255; in Arendt 129; in Aristotle 28, 30; in Cicero 32, 34, 37–8; in Harrington 64–5, 67, 70, 74, 76, 79; in Machiavelli 48, 50, 60, 62; in Rousseau 84, 93, 95–6, 100, 101–2, 103, 108; in Taylor 141
public–private distinction 2; liberal, control-based 2, 10, 76, 118, 119, 158, 182, 184–5, 193–5, 208, 210–12, 226–7, 234, 252–3; republican, interest-based 5–6, 32, 55–6, 62, 67, 73, 78–80, 90–1, 101, 104–5, 107, 117, 121–2, 126–8, 131, 138–9, 158–9, 167–9, 181–2, 192–4, 210–12, 231–2; visibility-based 122–3
public goods 152, 159, 295 n4; *see also* common good
publicity 121–3, 138–9, 158–9, 234–5, 240–2; *see also* recognition
public space 112, 121–6, 138–9, 157, 176, 197, 231–5, 240–2, 261–2
public spirit *see* civic virtue
Publius 103
Putnam, R. 234

Quebec 142, 143, 204, 278

Rawls, J. 9, 10, 11, 152, 222, 226, 290 n1, 295 n3, 298 n7
Raz, J. 11, 153, 154, 156, 165, 186, 203, 205, 208, 210, 295 n5, 296 n4, 297 n12, 301 n19

reason 167, 222, 225–6, 272–3; in Aristotle 20–1, 23–4, 26; in Cicero 34, 38; in Harrington 70–1, 82; in Machiavelli 51, 53, 54; in Madison 106–7; in Rousseau 85–7, 89, 293 n6; in Wollstonecraft 100–2; *see also* deliberation
reciprocity 32, 165, 209, 269
recognition 8, 12, 16, 30, 94–5, 111–13, 152–8, 171–3, 184–5, 196, 204–5, 217–18, 227–8, 231–3, 248–9, 250–89; in Arendt 120–4, 130–1; in Taylor 132–5, 137–9, 141–4; and redistribution 251; *see also* honour
referendums 218, 220, 238, 242, 299 n12; multi-option 242
relativism 224, 269
religion 115, 130, 204, 263–4; in Harrington 71–2; in Machiavelli 57, 58–9; in Madison 108, 295 n15; in Rousseau 95; established 204, 263–4; Christianity 42–3, 47, 52–4, 56, 71–2, 82, 95; civic 6, 175–6, 242, 296 n15; Islam 300 n10; Judaism 120, 128, 300 n10; Protestantism 71–2, 85, 134, 204, 259; Roman Catholicism 134, 255, 259; Sikhism 252, 261; *see also* education; secularism
representation, electoral 114, 119, 144, 206, 215–16, 218–20, 236, 240, 246–7; in Arendt 119–20, 125; in Harrington 69; in Madison 105–6; in Mill 116–17; in Montesquieu 83; in Rousseau 90–1; in Wollstonecraft 101; group 236, 253, 255, 261–2
republicanism: contested 6–9, 11–12; contextual approach 7, 204, 281, 285; instrumental 8–9, 16, 111, 150, 152, 155, 181–5, 214, 222, 236; and liberalism 1, 8, 11, 150, 158–9, 182, 288–9, 296 n6; strong 8–9, 16, 111, 150, 188–90, 214, 217, 219, 222, 236, 238

326

respect 128, 129–30, 176, 250–3, 257–8, 267; *see also* recognition; solidarity
responsibility 126, 129, 131, 142, 170–2, 174, 180, 189, 233, 239, 243, 248, 272, 279
rights 1, 8, 9–10, 24, 25, 32, 36–7, 59, 75–6, 80–1, 85–6, 89, 95–6, 99–101, 103–4, 109, 113–14, 117; in Arendt 120, 131, 132, 137; in Taylor 144; 160, 182, 191, 194–5, 196–7, 206–12, 250, 260–1, 298 nn15, 17; to bear arms 108, 176; economic and social 210; group 260; natural 7, 80–1, 102–3, 210; *see also* free speech; privacy; property
Roman republic 30, 42, 48, 49, 50, 57, 70, 74, 85, 103, 113
Romulus 49
Rousseau 4, 14, 15, 48, 75, 77, 78, 81, 84–99, 100, 101, 102, 104, 110, 112, 113, 116, 121, 123, 124, 126, 128, 130, 151, 163, 166, 167, 173, 181, 186, 188, 189, 200, 207, 220, 226, 235, 241, 258, 283, 292 nn4–5
Roy, A. 157, 212

Sacks, J. 164
Salamonio 291 n1
Sallust 45
Sandel, M, 155, 157; on civic virtue 163, 171; on freedom 172, 189, 192, 208, 211; on participation 217; on recognition 252, 264, 295 n2, 298 n16
Sanders, L. 226
Savonarola 291 n1
Scheffler, S. 165, 300 n13.
Schwarzenbach, S. 300 n14
Scotland 70, 76, 78, 80, 275, 278, 283
Scottish enlightenment 80
secession 278, 283
secularism 72, 176, 204, 300 n10; *laïcité* 176, 259, 276
Selbourne, D. 164

self-government *see* participation in self-government
separation of powers 83, 90, 106, 206, 235, 292 nn2–3; *see also* mixed government
service, civic 169, 176–7; military 176–7; *see also* militia
sexual harassment 154
Shklar, J. 77
Shumer, S. 162
Sidney, A. 7, 75, 292 n11
Simmons, A. 165, 269
Sinnott, R. 242
Skinner, Q. 7, 44, 55, 59, 150, 152, 182, 183, 194, 291 n1, 296 n1
Smith, A. 80, 91, 173
Smith, G. 244
social capital 234
social movements 219, 237, 262
socialism 2, 5, 11, 118, 131, 149, 191, 200, 247
solidarity 128–30, 140, 162, 165–6, 251, 258, 260–73, 279–81, 284, 300 n14
Solon 16, 49
sovereignty 5, 13, 66, 90–2, 123, 283; popular 81, 89–92, 104, 116, 119, 220, 223
Spain 280
Sparta 15–17, 29, 40, 49, 85, 87, 97, 167
Spitz, J.-F. 150, 185
Squires, J. 169
Stedman-Jones. G. 293–4 n1
stoics 18, 31, 35
Sunstein, C. 8, 168, 176, 196–7, 201–2, 203, 208, 224, 238, 296 n5, 300 n12
Switzerland 63, 167, 280

Tamir, Y. 301 n16
Taylor, C. 8, 9, 14, 111–13, 131–44, 152, 153, 166, 166, 251, 252, 254, 257, 264, 266, 273, 274, 276, 277, 278, 294–5 n8; on civic virtue 140–2; on freedom 135–8; on participation 138–9; on recognition 132–5, 138–40

Thompson, D. 230, 298 n9
Tocqueville, A. de 114–16, 234, 247, 290 n1, 301 n17
Toland, J. 292 n11
tolerance 161, 234, 252–3, 257, 262; *see also* respect
totalitarianism 58–9, 93, 98, 111, 119–20, 127–8, 133, 158, 219–20
Trenchard, W. 292 n11
truth and reconciliation processes 232
Tuck, R. 43

United States 7, 271; Congress 106; Constitution 7–8, 10, 175, 202; Declaration of Independence 108; judiciary 8; as model for republics 114; Presidential election 220; prohibition 192; Supreme Court 211, 297 n8, 298 n17; Tocqueville on 115–16

Van Parijs, P. 201, 240, 245, 262
vanity 79–80, 173; as *amour propre* 86–8, 94
Venice 44, 50, 63, 69
veto-power 236–7, 255, 263, 299 n11
Viroli, M. 270, 274
virtues: in Aristotle 20–1; cardinal 33–5, 43, 54, 295 n11; Christian 43–4, 47, 52–3, 71, 92, 164; of commercial society 82, 107; communitarian 164; distinct from legal obligation 160, 164; gendered 34, 52, 97–8, 100–1, 167; as habitual disposition 21, 70–1, 126, 159–60; liberal 163; of prince 52–3; warrior 6, 16–18,
34, 52–3, 72, 80, 163, 166–7; *see also* civic virtue
Vogel, U. 148
voluntary associations *see* civil society
voting in elections 69, 114–17, 119, 134, 149, 161, 170, 215, 220–1; compulsory 117, 126, 245–8; property qualification for 22, 68, 70; weighted 92, 117, 263; *see also* referendums

Waldron, J. 29, 153, 256, 290 n2
Wales, C. 244
Walzer, M. 9, 10, 223, 233, 235, 286
welfare state 199–201, 206, 277
Whigs 75–6
White, S. 201
Whyte, J. 155
Wilde, O. 247
Wirszubski, C. 37
Wolff, J. 164
Wollstonecraft, M. 78, 99–102, 167, 188
women 6, 40, 74; in Aristotle 24, 29; in Cicero 34; in Harrington 69; in Machiavelli 53; in Rousseau 97–8; in Wollstonecraft 99–102; civic virtue and 148, 154, 166–70, 177; freedom for 183, 185, 188, 191, 194, 195–6, 206, 211; participation and 215, 216, 225–6, 229, 231–3; recognition and 250, 252–4, 259, 260–3, 265, 290 n3, 294 n6

Yack, B. 29, 290 n2
Yeats, W.B. 296 n7
Young, I.M. 167, 168, 214, 225, 229, 251, 272, 274